LOSING OUR
LANGUAGE

LOSING OUR
LANGUAGE

How Multicultural Classroom Instruction Is Undermining
Our Children's Ability to Read, Write, and Reason

SANDRA STOTSKY

ENCOUNTER BOOKS
SAN FRANCISCO

Paperback published in 2002 by Encounter Books, an activity of Encounter for Culture and Education, Inc., a nonprofit tax exempt corporation.

Encounter Books website address: www.encounterbooks.com

Manufactured in the United States and printed on acid-free paper.

The paper used in this publication meets the minimum requirements of ANSI/NISO

Z39.48-1992 (R 1997)(Permanence of Paper).

Library of Congress Cataloging-in-Publication Data

Stotsky, Sandra.

　　Losing Our Language : how multiculturalism undermines our children's ability to read, write and reason / Sandra Stotsky.

　　p. cm.

　　Includes bibliographical references and index.

　　ISBN 1-893554-48-1 (alk. paper)

　　1. Reading (Elementary)-Social aspects-United States. 2. Multicultural education-United States. 3. Educational sociology-United States. I Title.

　　LB1573 .S874 1999

　　306.43-dc21

　　98047124

10 9 8 7 6 5 4 3 2 1

Excerpt from Morning Star; Black Sun by Brent Ashabranner.

Excerpt from "Tales of the Bronx" by Jill Pinkwater. Reprinted with the permission of Atheneum Books for Young Readers, an imprint of Simon & Schuster Children's Publishing Division, from Tales of the Bronx by Jill Pinkwater. Copyright © 1991 Jill Pinkwater.

Chapter 6 is a revised and longer version of a chapter entitled "Why Today's Multicultural Basal Readers May Retard, Not Enhance, Growth in Reading," appearing in Readings on Language and Literacy: Essays in Honor of Jeanne S. Chall, Lillian R. Putnam (ed.), Brookline Books, © 1997, Brookline Books.

Excerpt from We Don't Look Like Our Mom and Dad by Harriet Langsam Sobol. Copyright © 1984 by Harriet Langsam Sobol. Used by permission of Coward-McCann, Inc., a division of Penguin-Putnam Inc.

Excerpt from Tonweya and the Eagles by Rosebud Yellow Robe. Reprinted with permission of Dial/Penguin, a division of Penguin-Putnam Inc.

Excerpt from Pacific Crossing, copyright © 1992 by Gary Soto, reprinted with permission of Harcourt Brace & Company.

Excerpt from Apple Is My Sign. Copyright © 1981 by Mary Riskind. Reprinted by permission of Houghton Mifflin Company. All rights reserved.

CONTENTS

PREFACE

Since the 1960s, educational publishers have been making continuous changes in the contents of their basal readers—the textbooks used for teaching children how to read English. Publishers initiated these changes to address several criticisms. One was that the reading selections in these textbooks were not "authentic," an adjective that denoted high-quality children's literature at the time. The burden of this charge was that many reading selections were abridged or altered versions of good literature, or simply created for the purpose of teaching reading skills. This—it was claimed—reduced children's desire to learn how to read. Many of the educators who voiced this criticism were deeply concerned about the low level of academic achievement in minority children. And it was reasonable to consider the quality of their reading materials as one potential influence among many others on their motivation to learn to read.

It clearly was possible to make the case that many of the reading selections that children were asked to read as part of their formal instruction in reading years ago were not of the highest literary quality. That was because publishers were constructing some reading selections and controlling their language, usually to facilitate memorization of the most common words in the English language. But in order to appease a swelling, noisy, and persistent chorus of educational critics opposing the use of basal readers altogether and insisting that children needed to read high-quality literature—and who could argue against that?—publishers began putting nothing but authentic literary selections in their readers. Nevertheless, no research evidence was put forth then or later to support the claim that the "inauthentic" nature of many reading selections reduced children's interest in learning how to read. Nor was there any evidence to suggest that explicit attention to reading skills was detrimental to minority students in particular. To the contrary, the evidence has always suggested that explicit attention to reading skills, especially phonics instruction, was helpful for them and got better results than other approaches.

Another major criticism of the instructional readers was that their reading selections did not adequately portray the ethnic and racial diversity of the United States or the cultures of non-Western people. In addition, the readers were criticized for not providing enough good role models for girls. The instructional readers clearly did not portray the diversity of America's and the rest of the world's population, nor did they offer a broad range of role models for girls. Many of the educators criticizing the unrepresentative nature of their reading selections believed that minority children were also not motivated to learn to read because they were alienated by a body of literature that did not seem to include them. The same argument was not made for girls; on the average, they had always done better than boys in reading and writing.[1] The contents of the readers quickly began to change in order to remedy the civic injustice to minority children and to respond to feminist concerns.

Again, however, no research evidence was presented then or later to link women's choice of career—or the lack of a career—to what they had read in their instructional readers in elementary school. Nor was any research evidence presented then or later to connect the low level of reading ability in minority children to the failure of the instructional readers to show characters and communities that resembled their own families and neighborhoods (as desirable as it was on other grounds for the readers to show their families and neighborhoods as part of the American landscape). What is important to note is that publishers made changes in the readers in response to moral and emotional arguments only. No research studies explored the actual benefits, the possible limitations, and any unintended consequences of these changes. Moreover, publishers continued to make changes regularly, without any basis in documented need or intellectual benefit.

Most of the changes in the contents of the readers have been introduced in the name of multiculturalism, an educational philosophy that has been increasingly promoted in the past two decades in schools of education and by academic consultants to educational publishers. Although at its inception it was not clear exactly how this philosophy might shape the contents of the curriculum, its advocates maintained from the outset that it was the most meaningful guide for correcting social injustices and addressing the academic deficiencies of minority children. They sincerely believed that significant changes in pedagogy and the content of the curriculum could improve these students' self-image, which would in turn improve their academic performance. Indeed, concerns about the low academic performance of black and Hispanic children have, explicitly or implicitly, driven the bulk of the changes in educational policy, program, and pedagogy in our schools since the 1960s—and still do. (Most of the other changes have been driven by feminist concerns, but not because girls did poorly as readers and writers.)

When multiculturalism was first promoted as an educational philosophy, its stress seemed to be on the positive contributions of minority groups in this country and on a balanced portrayal of a variety of cultures around the world. But over the years, multiculturalism acquired an additional meaning. Instead of emphasizing the positive contributions of America's minority groups and a balanced range of social groups from around the world, the version of multiculturalism now promoted in our universities and schools of education seeks to "close young people off into identities already ascribed to them," as Anthony Appiah, a professor in Afro-American Studies at Harvard University, has described this second, "illiberal" version of multiculturalism in a 1997 essay in the *New York Review of Books*.[2] Moreover, as many scholars have noted (and as various chapters in this book will confirm), it now fosters an animus against what are perceived as Western values, particularly the value placed on acquiring knowledge, on analytical thinking, and on academic achievement itself. Its educational goals are now almost completely social and political, not civic and intellectual. Indeed, Shelby Steele, the author of *The Content of Our Character*, argues in his latest work, *A Dream Deferred: The Second Betrayal of Black Freedom in America*, that its thrust today is to stigmatize whites for the sin of racism rather than to help black students succeed academically.[3]

At the same time, according to the assessments conducted every several years by the National Assessment of Educational Progress, the 1990s has seen a decline in the reading scores of black students in all age groups after a period of time in which the gap began to narrow between the scores for black and Hispanic students and the scores for those classified as white. The scores of Hispanic high school students have also declined to the level achieved by their counterparts at the time the NAEP asssessments began to identify them in the 1970s. Worse yet, there are signs that the gap between the reading scores of students classified as white and the reading scores of those classified as black and Hispanic is widening again, in part because the scores of whites show a slight overall pattern of increase but chiefly because the scores of blacks and Hispanics have declined. Despite these signs, there has been no professional or public discussion of a possible connection between these two phenomena—the rise of an illiberal version of multiculturalism in the 1980s and the decline in minority students' reading scores in the 1990s.

This professional "omerta" led to my research for this book. I was puzzled by the absence of professional and public discussion of the changes that have been taking place in the elementary school reading curriculum since race, ethnicity, and gender began to become a main preoccupation of much of the academic world almost three decades ago. Like other members of the reading public, I was aware of the dramatic changes in U.S. history textbooks over these three decades from the many published articles and op-ed essays on the topic. *America Revised,* Frances FitzGerald's examination of old and new U.S. history textbooks, suggested how much had already changed in content and emphasis by the early 1980s.[4] The public outcry over the contents of the original and revised versions of the U.S. history standards in the mid-1990s served to suggest how much more change had taken place since then. The clearest and most striking example of this outcry was the 99-to-1 vote by the U.S. Senate on January 18, 1995, condemning these standards for bias against American history, ideas, and institutions.

Clearly, the instructional readers must have been equally affected by the same academic trends. Their contents and the teaching apparatus surrounding them must of necessity reflect contemporary trends in educational thinking. Otherwise, leading professional educators in the schools would not purchase them for their school systems. Nor would the textbook adoption states—the states that determine what textbooks local schools may consider for purchase—require their use.

Yet the chief issue regularly surfacing in both the professional literature and the media was the battle between those advocating a whole language approach to beginning reading instruction (teaching students to rely on context-based guesswork) and those insisting that the alphabetical nature of the writing system used for English indicated the need for explicit, systematic instruction in phonics, or sound-letter relationships. Why was there no information on the contents of the readers? No one could claim these textbooks were not worth examining. Indeed, they probably play a more fundamental educational role than the history text-books that FitzGerald examined. As the most basic of school textbooks, they are likely to be read by more children than any others except possibly those used in teaching mathematics. They help determine how well children learn to read and write English and how they approach literature. They are especially important for low-income children, who are almost completely dependent on what is provided them in school. And despite the intense hostility of whole language advocates to instructional readers, they are still used for teaching reading in the majority of elementary school classrooms in this country, although to varying extents.

I decided to examine the contents of the leading readers for grades 4 and 6 published in 1993 and 1995 to find out what changes had been made to their contents. Did they still reflect a Dick and Jane world? Did they now portray the America we see around us? Or were their contents driven by the illiberal version of multiculturalism, now prominent in the academy? What I found startled me.

Because of the need to portray a regularly increasing number of social groups around the world, the selections that children are offered in the readers often jump from one culture to another, one historical period to another, and one continent to another in a dizzying sequence. Instead of a realistic picture of their country, children are now given a distorted picture of the demographic realities of American life and American history—one in which the presence of small Asian ethnic groups and a minuscule Native American population is accorded much prominence, while the presence and distinctive cultural influences of the numerous and large European ethnic groups in this country are barely noted. Instead of authentic (or high-quality) children's literature, children are frequently given for literary study—in a stunningly ironic twist—what can best be called pseudo-literature. These are texts that appear exactly the way their authors wrote them; hence, they are "authentic." But they are not of high literary quality, and they often deal—stridently—with the social concerns of adults, not children.

The most startling finding concerned the vocabulary in the readers. At the most basic instructional level, children are deprived of reading materials that expose them to a large, advanced vocabulary in English. Instead of a sequence of reading selections providing an increasing number of rich English words, children are given selections cluttered with words they are rarely likely to see again, proper nouns whose pronunciations require knowledge of another language's sound-letter relationships, and foreign words of no particular relevance to the task of learning English. Sometimes whole selections are offered in another language altogether or in a dialect of English—for example, African American Vernacular English, sometimes called Black English.

I sought to visit classrooms and speak to the teachers using these readers. Although I was able to talk after school hours to teachers who used older or other readers, I was unable to visit classrooms using the series I examined. I called several principals and curriculum coordinators recommended to me by sales representatives, but they either never called back or told me, albeit in somewhat different words, that they did not think their teachers would welcome a researcher in their classroom. Some teachers may welcome a researcher or journalist whose clear purpose is to write sympathetically or enthusiastically about their classroom. But they may well be uncomfortable about allowing observations by a researcher who simply wants to note how they handle the suggestions for developing a "multicultural perspective" that are in their teacher guides—an unclear situation to them.

I do not want to give the impression that the contents of the basal readers tell us all we would want to know about what children read as part of their formal reading instruction and how they are taught. Many series recommend theme books or additional literary works to accompany the use of the basal. I talked with many sales representatives and teachers and found that practices vary enormously from teacher to teacher, from school to school, and from year to year. It is not possible to gather clear information nationally on what teachers use as supplementary reading materials and whether they use them each year and with all their students. Moreover, many teachers skip some of the selections in a reader in order to assign other works from their classroom shelves. Nevertheless, despite these limitations, the contents of the instructional readers and their teacher guides still offer the most reliable and valid information on what children are likely to be reading in formal reading instruction on a nationwide basis and how they are taught this content.

The instructional readers still state that they want children to become successful readers and writers, and they continue to offer many selections that can stimulate children's imagination and satisfy their spirit for adventure. But it is not at all clear how effective they can be in help-ing children learn how to read and write English today and to think ana-lytically. In most readers, the selections reflect a stronger effort to shape children's thinking about themselves, their classmates, their social and political communities, and the social issues of the day in a particular po-litical direction than to develop literary taste, a strong reading vocabulary, and analytical ways of thinking. In addition, the teaching apparatus for many selections is designed to help teachers inculcate what editors and their academic consultants believe are the right attitudes about these so-cial issues. In their zeal to advance their moral mission, the educators and researchers advising the editors of these reading series have created an in-structional tool that in many respects appears to interfere with, rather than foster, children's normal language development, the development of conceptual thought, and analytical ways of thinking—all in the name of broadening all children's cultural horizons, altering the self-image of mi-nority children, and fostering their motivation to read.

Each generation of educators has had its particular social and political goals. The social and political goals of the voices dominating many schools of education and state departments of education today are quite different from those of an earlier generation of educators. The social and political goals of many contemporary educators are also related to intel-lectual goals in a different way. After *Sputnik,* and especially once the War on Poverty began, educators articulated strong academic goals that were designed to achieve what both they and the public deemed were worthy social and political goals: inclusive, informed, and intelligent citizenship. These goals did not interfere with the development of literacy; to the con-trary, they were to be achieved by programs fostering high levels of liter-acy. In contrast, many educators and researchers today, overtly concerned with inculcating such worthy social values as tolerance and mutual re-spect, are seeking to do so through changes in curricular content and ped-agogy that enhance group identity and "redistribute power." They are reshaping the entire curriculum in the process and subordinating intellec-tual goals to the demands of their self-chosen moral mission without any body of evidence to suggest that the pedagogy and curriculum content they are implementing develop the values they claim they seek to foster.

Even if there were evidence that contemporary pedagogy and curricu-lum content do develop tolerance and mutual respect in students, one might expect some professional attention to the intellectual costs of today's social and political goals. That is because there is also no evidence to support the intellectual worth of the pedagogy and curriculum content now being implemented. Indeed, there is almost no research at all on the impact of multicultural education on academic achievement. Nor is it easy to find any expression of interest in professional journals in its effects on academic achievement, never mind a concern about the matter—and this despite the fact that multiculturalism has clearly had a pervasive influence on the contents of the literary selections in the instructional readers, on the kinds of literary selections regarded as both appropriate and desirable for children, and on the pedagogical apparatus accompanying them.

Although many parents are dissatisfied with the academic performance of public schools, with many now seeking such alternatives as charter schools, for example, the public is unaware of exactly what has been taking place in the reading curriculum in the recent past for two reasons. First, educators and educational researchers promoting the most recent changes have not been particularly interested in enlarging general public understanding of the exact nature of the goals they now pursue in the elementary school curriculum or in soliciting informed parental support through open discussion or forums at the local level. Nor have they been willing to discuss criticism of their goals in public in a civil manner. Instead, they tend to be quite hostile to anyone who openly disagrees with what they think is best for all children. Those who complain about the quality of the school curriculum or make academic demands are perceived as educational neanderthals or, worse yet, have the race or sex card thrown at them. That is, attempts are made to discredit their motives. For example, parents and other citizens in the town of Brookline, Massachusetts, who criticized the academic quality of several social studies courses and sought to restore a highly popular and demanding advanced placement European history course that had been eliminated by the high school's social studies department in 1989, as part of a revision to "improve" the curriculum, were accused of being a "bigoted minority" using "brownshirt tactics" and "intellectual terrorism."[5]

Casting aspersions on a critic's motives rather than arguing the merit or logic of their ideas is the preferred mode of defense for many scholars, researchers, and educators today. We can detect this way of thinking even in the subtext of a brochure advertising a reception for alumni sponsored by the Harvard Graduate School of Education in April 1997. Entitled "The Changing Face of Public Education," the brochure called attention to the differences in the "race, ethnicity, income and family type" of students in public schools. The overt concern expressed in the brochure was a growing lack of support for the public schools—a legitimate concern. But by its very focus on the changing face of public education, it insinuated that what is really driving the flight of chiefly white middle-class parents from regular public schools (by means of charter schools, private schools, and home schooling) is not concern about the quality of the curriculum or their academic standards but an unspoken dislike of who attends them.

The public is also unaware of what has been taking place in the reading curriculum in the past decade because concerned researchers and teacher educators have not spoken up, in professional settings or in public, out of fear of having the race or sex card thrown at them. This is a very different situation from the open (and fierce) battle between advocates of phonics or a sight word approach that began in the 1950s and 1960s.

Like many of the early progressives, the advocates of multicultural education bear witness to the profound indifference if not hostility to strong academic goals that has characterized the educational philosophy of most schools of education since their growth in the early decades of this century. But unlike John Dewey, who supported methodologically sound research to help resolve educational issues, the advocates of multicultural education have so far evinced little interest in evaluating the academic impact of their ideas through empirical research and in obtaining evidence to support their beliefs. In a seventy-item bibliography attached to Minnesota's State Board of Education 1997 Proposed Permanent Rules Relating to Educational Diversity—a strengthened version of their 1988 Rules for Multicultural and Gender Fair Curriculum—only one source acknowledges that there is no evidence showing results of multicultural education for either its affective (social) goals or for its academic goals.[6] Geneva Gay, a leader in multicultural education, writes that "research findings that verify the conceptual claims about the effects of multicultural education are rather sparse."[7] She goes on to note:

> Most research and scholarship have been devoted to defining the conceptual parameters of the field, documenting cultural characteristics, and developing

sample curricula and instructional strategies for classroom practice. The fact that multicultural education is a very heavily affective endeavor means that it does not lend itself easily to traditional empirical research methods and paradigms.... Some of the most compelling verifications of the overall benefits of multicultural education are autobiographical and anecdotal stories that leaders in the field share among themselves in their personal interactions.... Consequently, research findings on the effects of multicultural education are still largely preliminary, tentative, and inconclusive.

Not only is Gay admitting that there is no research support at all for the claims of multicultural education, she is also implying that there is unlikely to be any research on its effects on academic achievement because its overriding interest is in shaping children's feelings and attitudes and because she does not think academic research can measure changes in them.

Given the dominating influence of those teacher educators and educational researchers who have been promoting the primacy of social and political goals in the curriculum, there is little one can expect from most of our pedagogical institutions to reverse this anti-intellectual tide. As the major force behind it, they seem to be even more hostile to intellectual goals than they were in earlier decades of this century. For parents and other citizens who want a liberal education for their children, I offer several suggestions in the final chapter for ways to reorient schools away from social and political goals to intellectual and civic goals. But in order to restore the primacy of intellectual and civic goals in the reading curriculum, the public needs to understand exactly what multiculturalism has come to mean in the reading curriculum in the 1990s, how it constitutes an assault on the development of children's language and thinking, and why black and Hispanic children are likely to be among those most damaged by this assault. These are the chief purposes of this book.

ACKNOWLEDGMENTS

I am grateful to many professional colleagues and friends for a critical reading of various chapters of earlier versions of this book. As always, Jeanne Chall put her well-known query, "Where's the evidence?" beside every generalization for which she did not think the evidence was clear— or there. Israel Scheffler generously critiqued the chapters on the progressive movement and pointed me to little-known material on the historical abandonment of teacher preparation by college faculty in the liberal arts and sciences and their unwillingness to grapple with the problems of mass education in a democratic society. James Squire was invaluable as a source of information on the publishing world and for a broad view of the literary and pedagogical issues in the basal readers. James Hoetker and Gilbert Sewall made helpful comments on several chapters, especially the one on today's research efforts on multiculturalism. Susan Arellano, my first editor at Free Press, helped me to clarify my major themes, and Anne Saks Yates, my chief editorial assistant for most of the years I was editor of *Research in the Teaching of English,* gave my manuscript the benefit of the kind of critical reading she gave every manuscript I accepted for the journal before she let me send it off to the typesetters. I am particularly grateful to Philip Rappaport, my editor at Free Press, for the extremely careful and hard-hitting reading he gave my manuscript. Nevertheless, I am completely responsible for how I have responded to all the critiques.

I am indebted to the labor of several research assistants: Ellen Shnidman, Michael Freed, and Carita Gardner. Their insights were invaluable to me as they read through the selections and the teacher guides in the reading series that I examined.

Last but not least, I am grateful to the Harry and Lynde Bradley Foundation for the support it gave me for one year, and to the Boston University School of Education for a two-year appointment as senior research associate, which gave me time to complete this book.

ONE

THE CULTIVATION OF MULTICULTURAL ILLITERACY

Captain had been broken in and trained for an army horse; his first owner was an officer of cavalry going out to the Crimean War. He said he quite enjoyed the training with all the other horses, trotting together, turning together to the right hand or the left, halting at the word of command, or dashing forward at full speed at the sound of the trumpet or signal of the officer.

He was, when young, a dark, dappled, iron gray, and considered very handsome. His master, a young, high-spirited gentleman, was very fond of him, and treated him from the first with the greatest care and kindness.

He told me he thought the life of an army horse was very pleasant; but when it came to being sent abroad over the sea in a great ship he almost changed his mind.

"That part of it," said he, "was dreadful! Of course we could not walk off the land into the ship; so they were obliged to put strong straps under our bodies, and then we were lifted off our legs, in spite of our struggles, and were swung through the air over the water to the deck of the great vessel."

> —From *Black Beauty* by Anna Sewell, in *Classic American Readers, Selections from Famous Writers*, in third- and fourth-grade readers 100 years ago[1]

I decided, after my first voyage, to spend the rest of my days at Bagdad. But it was not long before I tired of a lazy life, and I put to sea a second time, in the company of other merchants. We boarded a good ship and set sail. We traded from island to island, exchanging goods. One day we landed on an island covered with several kinds of fruit trees, but we could see neither man nor animal. We walked in the meadows, along the streams that watered them. While some of our party amused themselves with gathering flowers and fruits, I took my provisions and sat down near a stream between two high trees which made a thick shade. I ate a good meal and afterwards fell asleep. I cannot tell how long I slept, but when I awoke the ship was gone!

—From "Sinbad's Second Voyage," adapted from *Stories from the Arabian Nights,* edited by Samuel Eliot, in the 1953, 1957, and 1962 Houghton Mifflin grade 6 reader

Half a mile beyond Hilltop Baptist church, Queenie turned off the main road onto a wagon trail. It had originally been a sawmill road, but that was a long time ago. Now it was a rutted path. It led through the swampy low ground that Queenie called "the deep woods" and onto the open land of Elgin Corry's farm.

Elgin's family was one of the few in the county to dwell in a brick home. It wasn't big, but it was brick all the same, and snug and clean and cozy-looking. Elgin had built it himself. Besides farming, he hired himself out to local builders when his crops were laid by—whenever jobs were available. A few years back, before times turned so bad, he had bought bricks after a bumper farm crop and had encased his wooden-frame home. The house always reminded Queenie of the story of the three little pigs. It looked to her like one out of a picture book, the way it fitted onto a small rise with shade trees in front and the barnyard in back and cropland off to each side and a pasture in the distance. The whole place had a steadfast look, but most especially the brickhouse, and Queenie imagined that a wolf could huff and puff forever and not blow it down.

—From *Queenie Peavy* by Robert Burch, in the 1979 Harcourt Brace Jovanovich grade 6 reader

Tahcawin had packed the parfleche cases with clothing and food and strapped them to a travois made of two trailing poles with a skin net stretched between them. Another travois lay on the ground ready for the new tipi.

Chano was very happy when Tasinagi suggested the three of them ride up to their favorite hills for the last time.

As the three of them rode along, Tasinagi called Chano's attention to the two large birds circling overhead. They were Waŋbli, the eagle.

Chano knew they were sacred to his people and that they must never be killed.

He looked at the eagle feather in his father's hair, a sign of bravery, and wondered why it was that the Lakotas as well as many other Indians held Waŋbli, the eagle, in such great respect. Someday he would ask his father about this.

—From "Tonweya and the Eagles" by Rosebud Yellow Robe, in the 1996 Houghton Mifflin grade 6 reader

MANY AMERICANS whose memories of public school date back to the 1950s or 1960s indulge in an unfounded nostalgia. They seem to be under the impression that these were halcyon years in public education. To them, the low academic expectations for what children are asked to read today is a recent phenomenon—a couple of decades old at most. Instead, they need to take a close look at what children were expected to read in the primary grades one hundred years ago and compare that with what they themselves were expected to read and with what children are expected to read today. If they did, they would discover that the language base needed for understanding mature academic and literary texts began to erode before midcentury. The decline in the difficulty level of the selections used to teach children how to read has not been a steady one over the course of this century. But there is no mistaking the direction of the movement. What is unclear is how much lower academic expectations can fall without significant breakdowns in thinking and communication at higher levels of education, in the workforce, and in public life.

The passages in the epigraphs help us see some of these changes in academic expectations. In the passage from *Black Beauty*, used in third- and fourth-grade readers one hundred years ago, we find a vocabulary level, complexity of sentence structure, and level of paragraph development that are challenging yet appropriate for nine and ten year olds who have received adequate preparation for school and sufficient primary-grade reading instruction.

The second passage, from an adapted version of "Sinbad's Second Voyage," is in a midcentury reader in one of the best-selling K–6 reading series in the country. As an adaptation, it has an easier vocabulary and less complex sentence structure than the original version. Its vocabulary level and complexity of sentence structure are considerably lower in difficulty than *Black Beauty*, even though the selection appears in a grade 6 reader. To show even more clearly the decline in the reading demands of the instructional readers by midcentury, here is the same passage in an unadapted version from *The Arabian Nights:*

> "After my first voyage, of which I told you yesterday," Sinbad began, "I planned to spend the rest of my days in Bagdad. But I soon grew weary of doing nothing. So I bought goods for a voyage, and gathered together a company of merchants upon whom I could depend.
>
> "From island to island we sailed, trading with great profit. One day we landed on an island fair to see, but apparently uninhabited by man or beast. We wandered about, each at his own pleasure, some here and some there. I ate my noon meal, and lay down in the shade to sleep. But when I awoke, alas, the ship was gone! I ran down to the shore. Her sail was just disappearing over the horizon.
>
> "I was ready to die of grief. I tore my beard, threw dust upon my head, and lay down upon the ground in despair. Why had I not been content to stay at home, with the riches already acquired? Now it was too late."[2]

The differences in language between the adapted and unadapted versions of this tale, as well as between the adapted version and the excerpt from *Black Beauty*, suggest what had happened to the level of elementary reading instruction in over four decades of decline in reading difficulty, from the 1920s to the mid-1960s.[3]

The third passage is from a grade 6 literary reader in one of the leading reading series at the end of the 1970s. By this time, many educators had voiced concerns about the quality of the literature children were reading as part of their basic reading instruction, and many reading series were making an effort to provide a higher quality. The excerpt is from *Queenie*, a fine piece of literature, with a reasonably demanding vocabulary, complex sentence structure, and extensive paragraph development. Although this selection is written with greater complexity in vocabulary and sentence structure than the adapted version of "Sinbad's Second Voyage," it is not much more difficult than the excerpt from *Black Beauty*. To be sure, the paragraphs are longer, requiring a higher level of intellectual effort on the student's part because a longer train of thought must be followed and grasped. But although this excerpt from *Queenie* may be harder than what a grade 3 or 4 student reads today, it is not equal in complexity and difficulty to what a sixth grader would have read in 1900.

The fourth passage, from another leading reading series today, exhibits features that may help to account for the low reading level of many American students today. (I do not claim that this particular selection is representative of all the selections in this reader, because it is not possible to make this claim about any one selection in any reader or about any one literary work of an author, a literary period, or a country; "representation" is a concept from political science that has been misapplied to literary works.) The four paragraphs in the excerpt are scarcely developed, sentence structure is not complex, and the challenging words that should be in a grade 6 reader are almost absent. Were they sacrificed in this story to allow both students and their teacher to devote their intellectual energy to mastering the pronunciation of the many useless proper nouns we see in the excerpt—useless, that is, because they lack the capacity to expand the vocabulary base needed for understanding mature literary and academic English prose? "Tonweya and the Eagles" is in a mid-1990s reader to acquaint students with a particular cultural group and, where teachers are so inclined, to facilitate conversations in the classroom about the group's virtues and the vices of those who have damaged or destroyed its culture. The intellectual cost of passages like these is very high indeed.

Passages like the one from this story, studded with non-English proper nouns, are common to all the leading textbooks and trade books that American children read in elementary school today. Proper nouns like these function not only as a dead-end substitute for authentic vocabulary growth but also as the equivalent of a conversation stopper. I asked an experienced elementary school teacher in a middle-income suburb north of Boston how her third, fourth, and fifth graders respond to the abundance of non-English proper nouns now spilling across the pages of their readers. "It stops them cold," she replied. "Many of them can't go on to read the story."

THE CURRENT CONTEXT

No matter what their grade level, most American students do not read or write very well. Nor do they know much American or world history. Their scores on nationwide assessments of reading, writing, and history knowledge are dismaying. By the time they finish elementary or middle school, their scores on most international tests are equally dismaying, especially since we spend more on public schools than any other country in the world.[4] Students' abysmal ignorance on a subject once covered well in elementary school readers is strikingly obvious in the responses of Massachusetts fifth graders to a question on a recent statewide test in reading asking them to identify and discuss an inventor they would like to meet.[5] Only 55 percent of the students could even come up with the name of an inventor, a concept that had to be interpreted charitably. Students who identified Benjamin Franklin as an inventor tend to think he invented electricity. More than a few students were curious to know how he invented lightning. Only a very few of these ten and eleven year olds understand that Franklin invented the lightning rod, *not* electricity or lightning. On the other hand, and more appalling, the large number of students who chose to discuss Albert Einstein tend to believe that *he* was the one who discovered electricity (probably because they see him as "the smartest person in the world"). Many also believe that Einstein made a holder for the light bulb; did drawings in his book that are similar to inventions we have today, like a car, helicopter, and bicycle; painted the *Mona Lisa;* wrote backward; and invented the plane, the Franklin stove, gravity, the telephone, the phonograph, TV, and even the Morse code.

In an attempt to pinpoint the source of our students' low knowledge base and poor reading ability—the skill on which achievement in writing, history, and almost all other subjects depends—public attention has focused largely on the acrimonious debate between the advocates of whole language (context-based guesswork) and the supporters of systematic phonics instruction. This debate centers on how reading should be taught in the primary grades. But parents and educators have not raised questions about possible connections between students' dismal scores in reading, writing, and history and the changes over the past decade or two in both the kinds of selections teachers now use in reading instruction in the upper elementary grades and the methods they have been advised to use with these selections.

These changes are quite visible in the basal reading series, the chief textbooks used in a majority of the nation's elementary schools to teach children how to read and write English. Although basal readers usually do not constitute the total reading program in any school, their contents and the teaching apparatus they provide do indicate what is taking place in the name of reading instruction in most classrooms. Basal readers that do not reflect contemporary trends in educational thinking jeopardize enormous sales to the textbook adoption states, such as California, Texas, and Oregon, that determine what textbooks local schools may use.

Most of the recent changes in the content of the elementary readers and in the teaching methods outlined in them have been introduced as part of an approach to the curriculum development called multiculturalism. Although it was not clear what changes or additions to the curriculum would be necessary or what teaching methods would be needed to accompany these changes at the time this approach was first articulated in the 1970s, nevertheless, multiculturalism was proposed as the only approach that could broaden the horizons of American schoolchildren and inculcate respect for racial and ethnic minority groups. It was also proposed as the only meaningful way to address the academic deficiencies of minority children, its basic assumption being that changes in their self-image were necessary if changes in their academic performance were to occur. Most teachers, school administrators, school boards, and educational publishers were willing to accept the advice of the scholars and teacher educators who advocated a multicultural approach in their reading programs. Some did so out of desperation for what was promised as a pedagogical magic bullet, others because they truly believed that such changes were necessary for social equality and that group self-esteem was the foundation for academic achievement.

What academic researchers and teacher educators see as the purpose and content of a multicultural education has evolved considerably over the years. Today, it has a clear race-based political agenda, one that is anticivic and anti-Western in its orientation, as examples from the readers in later chapters will corroborate. Telling examples of its anti-Western orientation can be found in the "distortions by omission" in the first version of the National Standards for United States History (a document setting forth what all students should know about U.S. history from their course work in K–12). In a critique of this document, Sheldon Stern, historian at the John F. Kennedy Library and Museum in Boston, noted (1) the failure to include in the standard requiring understanding of the characteristics of West African societies in the era of European contact the knowledge that "African rulers and chieftains had in fact been enslaving and selling other Africans for centuries before the arrival of Europeans"; (2) the failure to note that "beginning centuries before the Western slave trade, millions of Africans were forced northward into slavery by the Muslim Arabs—in numbers possibly comparable to those later taken to the West in the trans-Atlantic slave trade"; and (3) the failure to include in the standard on American Indian life and culture the knowledge of their "warlike and aggressive side" and the fact that "many tribes bought, sold, and owned slaves."[6]

Telling examples can be found in the arithmetic class as well. A New York City parent reported that his fifth-grade son had an assignment, lasting for an entire week, that went as follows: "Historians estimate that when Columbus landed on what is now the island of Hati [sic] there were 250,000 people living there. In two years this number had dropped to 125,000. What fraction of the people who had been living in Hati when Columbus arrived remained? Why do you think the Arawaks died? In 1515 there were only 50,000 Arawaks left alive. In 1550 there were 500. If the same number of people died each year, approximately how many people would have died each year? In 1550 what percentage of the original population was left alive? How do you feel about this?"[7] Note the "feeling" question at the end; it is one of the staple questions in multicultural curricular materials, intended to elicit sympathy for a victim group and hostility to those who are to be perceived as its oppressors.

But at its formal inception in the 1970s, multiculturalism was presented to the public as an educational approach chiefly standing for the inclusion and celebration of America's true diversity. The array of literary selections in the 1979 Harcourt Brace Jovanovich grade 4 literature reader—only one of many possible examples—provides some evidence that this was the case at the end of the 1970s, and that Dick and Jane were now history.[8]

The opening story in this reader is about the relationship between a Navajo girl and her elderly grandmother. The second is about a boy whose move from rural Kentucky to Chicago is eased by an understanding, blind teacher. The third is a humorous tale by Yoshiko Uchida about a Japanese American girl and a rooster who understood Japanese—a story devoid of political overtones. The fourth features a poor rural boy on the last day of school. In the fifth, a genuinely multiethnic group of students learns how to make movies in a school setting featuring a school crossing guard named Mrs. Donadio and a teacher named Mr. Wanneka. The sixth is about a Puerto Rican boy in this country who returns to Puerto Rico to visit family there. The seventh is about a girl named Hannah who visits her grandparents' candy store in the city and enjoys her grandmother's chicken soup—details that, in addition to the author's name, suggest their Jewish identity. These selections are followed by seven folktales or fables: one Vietnamese, one African American, one Russian, one Central European, and three by Aesop. The second half of the reader features animal stories with leading characters that include a Mexican American boy in the Southwest, an Italian American boy in New York City, a girl on a western ranch, a boy recalling a beached whale near Provincetown on Cape Cod, and a black boy catching birds. This reader contains several Laura Ingalls Wilder selections and occasional civic touches as well, such as a mention of the pilgrims and the singing of the "Star-Spangled Banner." The vast majority of the selections in one of the nation's leading readers in 1979 are set in America. They offer genuine diversity in their ethnic content, and no anticivic or anti-Western animus.

Inclusion and diversity are still the goals that the proponents of multiculturalism present to the public at large. Yet schools of education loudly broadcast to their students a definition of diversity that excludes European ethnic groups, a new purpose for a multicultural education, and the reasons why this purpose should guide the shape and content of the curriculum. In the words of a teacher who recently completed a graduate program in education in Georgia, multiculturalism is now understood to mean "the exploration of political and cultural oppression by a dominant force."[9] The last phrase—*dominant force*—is a code word for all white Americans. This new purpose for multicultural education is causing a profound sea change in the content of every subject in the curriculum and in teachers' practices. It has affected all aspects of reading instruction, from the subject matter of the informational material used for teaching reading to the kind of literature regarded as both appropriate and desirable for teachers to use with young children. It has affected most profoundly the very quality of the language that children are given for their instruction in reading. This has happened in part because, as John Honey explains in *Language Is Power: The Story of Standard English and Its Enemies*,[10] many linguists, other scholars, and education professors in both the United States and

Britain see the language that constitutes the basic intellectual tool for academic achievement as that dominant force's chief instrument for cultural imperialism and oppression, and they are ideologically opposed to exposing students to high-quality English prose. I discuss the other reasons that multiculturalism has negatively affected the quality of the language children are given in reading instructional materials in later chapters.

The abundance of non-English proper nouns in "Tonweya and the Eagles" is but one symptom of the deeply negative influence of this new purpose for multicultural education on the language of the readers. We look briefly at several other problems in the passage from this story in the epigraph and in several other passages—all from reading selections that are used today for children's formal instruction in the English language—so that the scope of its influence is a bit clearer. It is by no means just a matter of an improper number of useless proper nouns.

THE LANGUAGE AND ORIENTATION OF
READING INSTRUCTION TODAY

"Tonweya and the Eagles" is in a reading textbook designed for children about eleven or twelve years old, yet in the passage in the epigraph, the most difficult words with respect to their meaning are those that are relevant to the way of life of these Indians: *parfleche* and *travois*. Both are pronounced in a way that differs from the way they would be pronounced according to the usual pronunciation patterns for English words. Because both words are derived from French, the "ch" in *parfleche* is pronounced as "sh," while the "vois" in travois (which would be pronounced as "vwa" in French) is pronounced as "voy" because "vois" is an atypical ending syllable in English and "vwa" is not an easy ending syllable for English speakers to pronounce. The pronunciations of these words, as well as the pronunciation of the many non-English proper nouns in the story, must be practiced first by the teacher and then by the students if they are to be able to discuss the story together in class. The name for the eagle in particular is quite difficult because its pronunciation is very different from what one might at first guess. *Waŋbli* is printed in the story with a phonetic symbol for "n" that is not in the Roman alphabet and, according to the teacher guide, is pronounced as WANG buhl. This attempt at authenticity of written script is pretentious, misleading, and out of place in a reading in-

structional text for English-language learners. The North American Indians never invented any written languages on their own, and the symbol
used for the "n" in the eagle's name was devised by linguists.

As much difficulty as the average native English-speaking sixth grader
might have in discussing this passage without sufficient practice pro-
nouncing its key words, one can only imagine the confusion for, say, Cam-
bodian or Filipino children learning English. If this story were for
leisure-time reading only, the foreign vocabulary would not be important;
good readers have always skipped hard words or difficult proper nouns and
relied on an exciting plot to carry them through in their recreational reading. Children's precious intellectual energy should not be wasted on strug-
gling over the meaning or pronunciation of words that have almost no
utility to them in advancing their reading skills in English, whether they
are native English speakers or learning English as a second language.

To make matters worse, this passage has almost no value in furthering
children's academic language learning. It contains only one reasonably literate English word: *sacred*. This is a word whose meaning, "holy," is
known to almost 70 percent of sixth graders, according to the most comprehensive research we have on vocabulary knowledge in schoolchildren.[11] Indeed, other than *sacred* and the words that relate to the Lakota
way of life, the passage contains no words that could be considered challenging even to fourth graders reading on grade level. This selection was
clearly not chosen for its reading instructional value for sixth graders.

Nor was a selection on Faith Ringgold's art in the 1993 Silver Burdett
Ginn grade 6 reader likely chosen for its intellectual value. The orientation of her political philosophy, as described by the author of this descriptive piece, undoubtedly accounts for its inclusion.[12] The text notes that

> Her painting U.S. *Postage Stamp Commemorating the Advent of Black Power* is
> a response to the unfair advantage that white people have. It exhibits one
> hundred faces: ninety are white, and ten are black. The words *white power* are
> spelled out in large white letters dividing the faces. *Black power* is also spelled
> out, in smaller black letters. . . . It expresses Faith's desire to send a message:
> inequality is wrong and must be stopped.

This selection is a clear example of the attempt throughout the readers I
examined to use reading instruction time in the elementary school for the
purpose of shaping children's feelings in specific ways. It can help develop

feelings of guilt in white children and enables teachers who are so inclined to moralize on American racism. It, too, has relatively short sentences and a simple vocabulary for a grade 6 reader; the only difficult words are in the title of Ringgold's painting.

Let us consider one final example from the 1996 Houghton Mifflin grade 6 reader. This passage, written in a language one might call Japanglish or "Japlish,"[13] is taken from a story by a frequently anthologized writer, Gary Soto.[14] This is the first example of Japanglish I have found so far in the readers. I use it here to provide a succinct illustration of the larger problem of the classroom language stew, discussed at greater length in Chapters 6 and 8, that is being promoted today in professional journals for English language instruction:

> On the *engawa* after dinner, Mr. Ono said to Mitsuo, "Take Lincoln to the dojo. You are not too tired, are you, Lincoln-kun? It is almost eight o'clock."
>
> "No, not at all," Lincoln said as he left the room to get his *gi*. ...
>
> Puzzled at Mitsuo's smile, Lincoln watched him hurry away, *geta* ringing on the stone walk. Lincon shrugged his shoulders as he entered the driveway with a fistful of yen, his monthly dues. On his way down the driveway, Lincoln stopped to *gassho*—salute—to three black belts who were stretching on the lawn, sweat already soaking into the backs of their *gis*.[15]

Again, the only hard words are the non-English words, some of which are italicized in the student text, some of which are not (as shown in the passage). Children also have to figure out their pronunciations if their teacher doesn't provide them; although the "o" in *gassho* is printed with a long mark over it, this long mark does not necessarily tell English readers what the pronunciation of this word is, nor is its pronunciation given at the bottom of the student text page. For children who want to take a stab at it by themselves, it isn't even clear how the word might be divided: Is it "gass ho" or "gas sho"? Far more important, there are no hard English words for even fourth graders on the two text pages from which this passage was taken. Clearly this short story was not chosen for its reading instructional value for sixth graders.

Parents know from their own educational experiences how important vocabulary knowledge is in becoming a good reader and writer. This personal understanding has been regularly confirmed in educational research since the beginning of the century, when research on the reading process and the nature of reading ability began. Children's language development is the engine that drives intellectual growth, and the language of schooling is the engine that drives academic achievement. Thought and language interact at the level of the word. As students acquire the words denoting the concrete information and abstract ideas embedded in the language of the subjects they study, these words become the essential building blocks for conceptual growth, academic achievement, and critical thinking. And until the 1970s, a chief characteristic of a developmental reading program in the elementary school was a substantial increase from year to year in the number of hard English words students were expected to encounter in their reading selections.[16] This was usually the case even though the overall trend from the 1920 through the mid 1960s was to simplify the vocabulary offered at each grade level.

We can find clear testimony to a decline in the total number of hard words offered in the various editions that leading reading series have put out in the past two decades by looking at their glossaries, which generally contain the words that the editors consider hard for that grade level. These are the words they recommend for direct instruction by the teacher before or as students read the selections in which they appear. Before we look at some of these numbers, keep in mind that in the 1970s and early 1980s, many reading series introduced more phonics instruction in their primary-grade readers and improved the quality of their selections in response to the debate on phonics instruction in the 1950s and 1960s and to the stress on basic skills in the late 1970s. Also keep in mind that the reading series differed to some extent in how difficult they were at any one grade level, and there were many more of them on the market than today. These variations among the many reading series on the market enabled school districts and individual schools in the districts to choose a series that they believed would best meet the needs of their students (and to make the distinction between more able and less able students less obvious if the school system or individual school allowed teachers to have readers from several different series in their classrooms to meet the different needs of each reading group).

I use the total number of words beginning with *i* and *v* as a representative sample of the difficult words in a glossary because they tend to be Latinate in origin and are thus more difficult conceptually than the ethnic words used at these grade levels. As we can see in Table 1, the number of words under *i* and *v* in the glossary of the various grade 4 readers I examined shows a considerable drop from the 1970s and 1980s to today. The same phenomenon occurs in grade 6 readers.[17] As we can see in Table 2, the decline in the number of words under *i* and *v* in the glossary of these readers over the past two decades is just as precipitous as the decline in the grade 4 readers. What is more alarming is that the total number of words under *i* and *v* *in the grade 6 readers in the 1990s* is not as large as the total number of words under *i* and *v* *in the grade 4 readers in the 1970s and 1980s*.

The small number of words under *i* and *v* in contemporary grade 6 readers has serious intellectual implications for another reason. Instead of an exponential increase in new vocabulary through the upper elementary grades, that is, from grade 4 to grade 6, the number of words the editors judge as needing instruction in most series in grade 6 in the 1990s is not much larger than the number they judge as needing instruction in grade 4. Not only are children being given fewer hard words in their readers than just one or two decades ago, worse yet, their vocabulary knowledge is not being accelerated over the course of the upper elementary grades as it should. Normally, the more words children learn at any one grade, the more they can be expected to learn in the next grade because their vocabulary knowledge base has itself expanded. Instead, to judge from these

TABLE I

Words Under i *and* v *in Assorted Readers' Glossaries for Grade 4, 1970s–1990s*

READERS	TOTAL NUMBER
1971 Houghton Mifflin	29
1980 Macmillan	32
1981 Scott Foresman	17
1987 Macmillan	38
1993 Houghton Mifflin	9
1993 Macmillan	8
1995 Scott Foresman	15
1995 Harcourt Brace	21

numbers, children are being given about the same number of new and hard words every year. Moreover, at least some of these new and hard English words are not new and hard at the grade level they are taught, according to the vocabulary research done about two decades ago. They may well be new and hard at that grade level today, but chiefly, it would seem, because there has been a contraction in the number of hard English words taught children altogether from kindergarten on. Thus, contemporary reading programs may actually be decelerating children's rate of language learning as they move through the grades. Not only are they introducing a very limited number of new and useful learned English words at each grade, they are also decelerating the rate of growth from year to year.

Interestingly, evidence to support this hypothesis comes from information gathered from recent international reading tests by the Organization for Economic Cooperation and Development (OECD), a respected international statistical agency whose purpose is to gather high-quality, comparable economic and social statistics on its twenty-eight member countries.[18] Using test data from the early 1990s, the OECD found that nine-year-old U.S. students were second only to Finland's nine-year-old

TABLE 2

Words Under i and v in Assorted Readers' Glossaries for Grade 6, 1970s–1990s

READERS	TOTAL NUMBER
1974 Macmillan	59
1976 Houghton Mifflin	53
1980 Macmillan	40
1981 Scott Foresman	25
1987 Macmillan	55
1989 Houghton Mifflin	26
1993 Houghton Mifflin	26
1993 Macmillan	14
1995 Scott Foresman	19
1995 Harcourt Brace	16

students in their reading skills, but on the average showed less "reading progress" by the age of fourteen than students tested in the fifteen other countries participating in the test, coming in sixteenth. In other words, as U.S. students progress through upper elementary and middle school, the less they learn in comparison to their international peers.

THE LANGUAGE OF READING INSTRUCTION YESTERDAY

The instructional readers of the 1970s or 1980s did *not* constitute a golden age so far as the level of vocabulary difficulty in them is concerned. Although some may seem strong in comparison to today's readers and were stronger than many readers published in the 1950s and 1960s, they already reflected the gradual decline in reading difficulty that had been taking place since about the third decade of this century. Jeanne Chall, a prominent reading researcher, and her colleagues showed that reading textbooks became increasingly easier in the years following a study published in 1930 by Arthur Gates, a prominent reading researcher of his day.[19] In his study, Gates urged "more word repetitions and fewer new words" to address the difficulties encountered by a large and growing number of children in the schools, caused in the early decades of the century by both native population growth and immigration.[20] As Chall and her colleagues noted, "The vocabularies of reading textbooks continued to decline through the mid-1960s. With each copyright date, most reading textbooks for each elementary grade became easier as publishers competed with one another and with their own earlier editions for books with ever more limited vocabularies."[21]

However, the Gates study may not be chiefly responsible for the decline in the vocabulary of the readers in the decades after the study appeared. According to James Michener's recollection of his experience working as a schoolbook editor for Macmillan during the 1930s, the real culprit may have been Edward L. Thorndike, the most eminent educational researcher in the beginning decades of the century. Michener writes:

> [I was working for] one of the premier New York publishing companies, Macmillan, where I helped produce textbooks in a variety of subjects for use in schools across the nation. While I was at Macmillan, a radical new disci-

pline began to dominate the writing of schoolbooks. A highly regarded educator and psychologist, Edward Lee Thorndike, compiled a list of words and the frequencies with which they occurred in everyday American life: newspapers, popular books, advertisements, etc. From these basic data, he published a list, sharply restricted, which he said ought to determine whether a specific word should be used in writing for children. If, for example, the word "take" received his approval, use it in schoolbooks. If "discredit" did not appear on his list, don't use it, for to do so would make the books too difficult for children.

We editors worked under the tyranny of that list, and we even boasted in the promotional literature for our textbooks that they conformed to the Thorndike List. In my opinion, however, this was the beginning of the continuing process known as "dumbing down the curriculum." Before Thorndike I had helped publish a series of successful textbooks in which I had used a very wide vocabulary, but when I was restricted by Thorndike, what I had once helped write as a book suitable for students in the sixth grade gradually became a book intended for grades seven through eight. Texts originally for the middle grades began to be certified as being appropriate for high school students, and what used to be a high school text appeared as a college text. The entire educational process was watered down, level by level.[22]

How different today's readers are in comparison to those of the past can be seen in the excerpt from *Black Beauty* for third or fourth graders in 1900. I offer here one more passage from those old readers to show that *Black Beauty* was not atypical.[23] The following passages are from Daniel Defoe's *Robinson Crusoe:*

> So I went to work. I had never handled a tool in my life; and yet in time, by labor and contrivance, I found that I wanted nothing that I could not have made, especially if I had had tools; however, I made abundance of things, even without tools, and some with no more tools than an adze and a hatchet, which perhaps were never made that way before, and that with infinite labor.
>
> For example, if I wanted a board, I had no other way but to cut down a tree, set it before me, and hew it flat on either side with my axe till I had brought it to be as thin as a plank, and then dub it smooth with my adze.
>
> It is true, by this method I could make but one board out of a whole tree; but this I had no remedy for but patience, any more than I had for the time

and labor which it took me to make a plank or board; but my time or labor was little worth, and so it was as well employed one way as another.[24]

The vocabulary and sentence constructions in Robinson Crusoe (and Black Beauty) would be an extraordinary challenge to students in the sixth grade today who have been taught to read with such selections as "Tonweya and the Eagles." Although none of the readers I examined contained excerpts from Robinson Crusoe, I did find an excerpt from Black Beauty in one grade 6 reader, published in 1989 by Open Court, considered the most challenging reading series on the market.[25] But the third and fourth graders at the turn of the century who cut their reading teeth on selections as challenging as the excerpts from Robinson Crusoe and Black Beauty would then have been able to handle the literature they later encountered in their "grammar school readers" in the middle school. Compare the sixth-grade passages in the 1996 Houghton Mifflin reader with the following passage from a story by Edgar Allan Poe appearing in a book published in 1910, intended for seventh graders, only one grade higher:

> It was during one of my lonely journeyings, amid a far distant region of mountain locked within mountain, and sad rivers and melancholy tarns writing or sleeping within all—that I chanced upon a certain rivulet and island. I came upon them suddenly in the leafy June, and threw myself upon the turf, beneath the branches of an unknown odorous shrub, that I might doze as I contemplated the scene. I felt that thus only should I look upon it—such was the character of phantasm which it wore.
>
> On all sides—save to the west, where the sun was about sinking—arose the verdant walls of the forest. The little river, which turned sharply in its course, and was thus immediately lost to sight, seemed to have no exit from its prison, but to be absorbed by the deep green foliage of the trees to the east—while in the opposite quarter (so it appeared to me as I lay at length and glanced upward), there poured down noiselessly and continuously into the valley a rich golden and crimson waterfall from the sunset fountains of the sky.

Literature of this level of difficulty was as common in the middle school readers of the mid-nineteenth century as it was in those in the first two decades of this century. For example, Joseph Addison's "Reflections in Westminster Abbey" is one of the selections offered in McGuffey's

Fourth Reader for Advanced Students, also intended for middle school students. It is worth noting that the *McGuffey Eclectic Readers* had a shelf life of well over half a century in their various editions; this particular reader's last copyright date was 1921. Here is a representative passage from Addison's essay:

> When I am in a serious humor, I very often walk by myself in Westminster Abbey, where the gloominess of the place and the use to which it is applied, with the solemnity of the building and the condition of the people who lie in it, are apt to fill the mind with a kind of melancholy, or rather thoughtfulness, that is not disagreeable. I yesterday passed a whole afternoon in the churchyard, the cloisters, and the church amusing myself with the tombstones and inscriptions which I met with in those several regions of the dead. Most of them recorded nothing else of the buried person, but that he was born upon one day and died upon another. The whole history of his life being comprehended in these two circumstances that are common to all mankind. I could not but look upon those registers of existence, whether of brass or marble, as a kind of satire upon the departed persons, who had left no other memorial of themselves, but that they were born, and that they died.

Passages like these require much more of the reader than a well-developed reading vocabulary. Their rich vocabulary is only part of the challenge. Both Poe's and Addison's prose styles demand the ability to sustain concentration over very long and complex sentences. They require—and reward—considerable reflective thought.[26]

Students who attended grade 7 in the late nineteenth or early twentieth century were a very small minority of the adolescent population. We cannot expect all seventh graders today to be able to read the quality of prose that those students did. But we need to reflect on how low our expectations have sunk in grades 4 to 6. Parents have good cause to wonder when average students today will be able to read the quality of English prose that seventh graders read a century ago if the reading instruction selections are so far below the level of difficulty of yesteryear. The nagging question is how many of them ever will reach that level of reading difficulty altogether if we cannot regain the ground that has been lost in just the past two decades alone.

Despite the central importance of reading instruction in the elementary school curriculum and the central role of basal readers in elementary school reading instruction, the public knows next to nothing about the changes that educational publishers have made in them to respond to the advice of their academic consultants and various pressure groups in the past decade or two. Nor do they know why publishers have made these changes. If anything, the public probably believes, quite erroneously, that the most pressure on educational publishers in the past three decades has come from Christian fundamentalists. But in fact, the most pressure—and the most effective pressure—has come from a variety of other groups, usually at the other end of the political spectrum, as Chapter 7 explains in detail.

Fortunately, the reading selections in today's readers are rarely in hybrid languages like Japanglish or in other languages altogether. But the various problems in the passages reproduced here constitute the barely visible tip of a vast iceberg lurking beneath a deceptively attractive and often enticing surface. The reading textbooks proffered by educational publishers today feature an abundance of dazzling illustrations, often with little actual text on a page. They are also huge and costly.

The most recently formulated goals for a multicultural education have affected elementary school reading programs in many different ways. Later chapters in this book discuss other ways in which illiberal multiculturalism negatively affects the language and content of the selections in the instructional readers. They will explain as well how it leads to the replacement of old ethnic, racial, or gender stereotypes that had almost disappeared by the 1980s with new and profoundly negative stereotypes; to the study of "pseudo-literature," a literature dealing—sometimes stridently—with the social concerns of adults, not children, and often guided by a highly moralistic pedagogy; and to an emphasis on children's feelings and undeveloped intellect rather than on analytical thinking. They will help us see how multicultural education leads, ironically, to multicultural illiteracy—broad intellectual incoherence—rather than to an understanding of any group's culture or history. As dumbfounding examples of the intellectual incoherence that seems to be a result of the influence of today's "isms" on our elementary school curriculum, consider the following Massachusetts fifth graders' responses to the question on inventors. One student whose response began promisingly with "Eli Whitney was the inventor of the Cottin Gin," went on to add: "I think she was black. In social studies we learned a little about her." Another noted that "smart, black inventor Thomas Edison patented many things" and that "many people liked Thomas even though he was black." Before I describe more fully the nature of the anti-intellectual tidal wave now crashing through the reading curriculum in both private and public schools, it is useful to understand how this situation evolved.

TWO

HOW SOCIAL GOALS CAME TO DOMINATE
ACADEMIC GOALS IN THE READING CURRICULUM

What does multicultural education mean to your students? How can they learn about this educational concept and process so that it will become a part of all aspects of their lives?

To help students begin to develop cultural awareness and understanding, they first need to learn who they are—their ethnicity, gender, and social class–and how they are viewed by society. Students need to begin to understand the contributions made by members of their group and other groups to the development of our culturally pluralistic nation. Developing cultural awareness and understanding calls for students to examine not only our national strengths but also our failures: discrimination, prejudice, and differential treatment.

Both students and teachers have participated in relationships of domination, submission, oppression, and privilege which have helped to shape who they are and how they interpret the world. This recognition of students and teachers as historically situated subjects with conflicting gender, race, and class interests is vital to understanding the possibilities and limits of the classroom.

—From the Teacher Editions for Grades 1–6 in the 1993 Silver Burdett Ginn Reading Series

AT THEIR peril do parents and others underestimate the importance of the elementary school reader—its contents as well as its pedagogy. What children are taught to read and how they are taught to read influence not only what they can read in the elementary and secondary school but also what they can read in later years. The statements in the epigraphs reflect the philosophy of those educators now guiding reading instruction in the elementary grades. What parents should ask themselves is whether this is the philosophy they want dominating reading instruction in their children's schools. Do they want their children to learn first what their social class, gender, and ethnicity are and how their society views them, presuming, of course, that their elementary school teachers are skilled enough to know how to help them understand themselves? Or might some parents prefer to have their children taught to see themselves first as American citizens sharing similar understandings about our political principles, political institutions, and the values that sustain them? Even more important, do parents want teachers absorbed with the development of their children's egos, intent on shaping their feelings about themselves and others in specific ways? Or do they want teachers to concentrate on developing their children's minds, helping them acquire the knowledge and analytical skills that enable them to think for themselves and to choose the kind of personal identity they find most meaningful? These are the goals at stake in today's school wars.

The traditional purposes for elementary school readers are to teach children how to read so that they can study mature works of literature at higher grades, learn from textbooks in subject areas, enjoy reading as a voluntary activity, and participate in the economic and civic life of their communities when they grow up. The readers usually feature literary and informational selections that increase systematically in thematic complexity, vocabulary difficulty, and overall difficulty from grade to grade. In the early grades, the emphasis in reading instruction is on teaching students how to use both the relationships between sounds and letters and a word's context to identify the words they know from their own experience—that is, on teaching students how to read. In the middle to upper elementary grades, the emphasis in reading instruction is on the development of a reading vocabulary and on different genres of literary and informational texts—that is, on teaching students how to use reading for learning.

Often by grade 6, but usually by grade 7, most children stop having reading as a subject and instead take "English" or "language arts." They move from a basal reader to a literature anthology or an individualized literature program shaped by their teacher's taste and the school district's curriculum requirements. If there is no individualized literature program for children who read well by grade 3, the instructional readers for grades 4 to 6 serve by default as literature anthologies for them, a situation that gives these textbooks a heavy influence on able children's formal literary education.

In many ways, the literary fare that educators provide reveals as much about the mind-set of the country's educational leadership as do its history books, and perhaps more. The literary works that students read in their formative years as part of their formal curriculum indicate what leading educators want students to learn about their society and others, what they would rather hide about their society and others, and how they want students to relate to the larger society. At a deeper level, the reading fare reveals what educators believe about childhood and about the kind of individuals they want students to become.

The evolution of American education is marked at certain periods by far-reaching changes in the content and pedagogy of reading instruction in the elementary school. These changes are generally related to what educators deem to need greater emphasis at the time: the school's social goals (how students are to behave and relate to others) or its academic goals (the development of a knowledge base and the capacity to think analytically). In this chapter, I outline the evolution of these changes in the past 200 years to show how they have tended to seesaw back and forth between the two sets of goals, depending on the perceived interests and needs of the larger society. We shall see how the forces on the academic side of this educational seesaw have been increasingly less effective and the cycles increasingly compacted, to the point that academic interests have been left almost high and dry by the forces pulling public education and reading instruction in another direction. We shall also see how, despite these shifting concerns, a respect for literary quality in the readers endured through most of these years—until the most recent decades.

THE EMERGENCE OF AN ACADEMIC CURRICULUM
FROM ITS RELIGIOUS ROOTS

In the 1640s, Massachusetts officials acknowledged the importance of literacy by passing a series of laws establishing schools in America. The ability to read and write was seen as vital in maintaining the religious culture based on the scriptures and in preparing children for responsible participation in a self-governing religious and civic community. The *New England Primer,* which appeared in Boston in the late 1680s and continued to be printed until 1830, was the dominant reading text in the colonies. It typically began with the alphabet and syllable families and went on to alphabet rhymes with biblical allusions, the catechism, the Lord's Prayer, the Apostle's Creed, and other materials. From these beginning materials, students were graduated to the Psalter or the Bible.[1]

By the end of the eighteenth century, reading instructional texts began to shed religious selections and by the middle of the nineteenth century contained few overtly religious materials.[2] They continued to stress the notion of personal responsibility and other desirable civic traits through such material as short speeches, historical narratives, and moral lessons. They also featured selections designed to increase children's scientific knowledge. The use of scientific selections reflected educators' attempts to capitalize on the growing interest in scientific information accompanying industrial development. The extraordinary growth of the lyceum movement, conceived in the early decades of the nineteenth century by a Yale graduate with an interest in science and a keen entrepreneurial sense, was but one reflection of the popular interest in new ideas and in the scientific knowledge that was being developed here and in Europe.[3]

The shift from chiefly religious materials to character-forming literary selections, civic and historical material, and informational selections on nature and science was inevitable in a new nation with growing intellectual and practical interests. It was also desirable in a country with an increasingly diverse population. Many educators were concerned about nation building and the creation of a distinctive American identity in a markedly heterogeneous people. Until the American Revolution, civic identity reflected membership in the local community and the colony in which it was located. The cause of nation building could be served in part by reading materials that focused on the history of this country and on the lives of the framers of the Constitution and other national heroes.[4] Nation building could also be served by a uniform pronunciation and spelling system. These were the goals of Noah Webster's spelling book, first published in 1783. In addition to a pronunciation and spelling system, Webster

provided moral selections, American place names, and American historical events in place of religious preaching and English place names and
events. By 1790 his spelling book was the best-selling American reading
text, remaining so for almost a half-century.[5]

Educators as well as others were also concerned with ways to develop
moral character and literary taste in an increasingly secular society. The
new republic was expanding across the continent and being settled chiefly
by Christians of a variety of sects and with varying degrees of religious devotion. The teaching of specific religious doctrines in the common
schools was no longer compatible with the spirit of the Enlightenment, an
influence that had led to the distinction between church and state in the
Constitution for this new republic. Educators also feared students could
become corrupted by the cheaper reading materials becoming available to
an increasingly literate and prosperous public. They wanted to maintain
an emphasis on moral values because they were aware that the American
experiment in self-government depended on shared standards of what was
right or wrong, as well as a willingness to obey the law. At the same time,
they wanted students to read good literary selections.

To a large extent, the spectacular growth in children's fictional literature in the nineteenth century fueled the evolving content of elementary
school readers in the latter part of the century. This was a literature written directly for children, unlike the fairy tales, fables, and legends that
adults had told each other and their children. The development of an
American fictional literature for children actually began about 1820, but
not primarily for enjoyment. The authors of this early children's literature
believed that to train future citizens for a republican form of government
required stories that would "present models of good conduct for imitation
and bad examples to be shunned" and "explain and enforce the highest
principles of moral duty."[6] These writers viewed childhood as a time of
preparation for adult life and not, as authors after the Civil War were to
see it, as a period of innocent joy, free of the responsibilities of adulthood.

The children's literature written in the service of moral training was
not of high quality. It had little humor, imagination, or excitement to re-
lieve its relentless purposefulness. Writing for the middle-class parents
who could afford to buy these books for their children, the authors of this
didactic literature preached obedience to parents, industry, charity, punc-
tuality, and unselfishness. Indeed, before 1860, the most frequent warning

was against selfishness, which was seen as individual striving at the expense of others and the opposite of cooperative social behavior and responsibility. If selfishness or competitive spirit threatened the survival of a decent society, so unselfishness or docility would preserve it. Thus, this early juvenile fiction stressed docility, a term that in the nineteenth century meant choosing to put the wishes of others above one's own. The authors of this fiction—and by extension, the middle-class parents for whom they wrote—believed that morally responsible people were the hope of a republic in which few firm class lines served to maintain order. These authors believed that most social ills were due to lapses in personal morality, not to structural or cultural features of society. They saw their intentions as an answer to the changing social conditions of Jacksonian America. In opposition to the unrestricted freedom of the larger society, they sought to foster in children the internal restraints of conscience that would dampen spontaneity, physical or intellectual daring, adventuresome spirit, and rebellious independence, all of which they repudiated as "restless striving," "willful disobedience," or "selfish ambition."

After the Civil War, as textbooks developed a graded format going from grade 1 to grade 6, children's literature began to diversify in many different directions. But regardless of direction, it was designed to appeal to children. Its authors saw childhood as a special time in a child's life, not as preparation for adulthood. This development took place in England as well as America, and in a few other northern European countries. In part, it reflected the growth of a prosperous middle class and a way of looking at childhood that middle-class parents found appealing and could afford to support. In part, it reflected the interests of talented authors. Great authors began writing great literature for children. To name only a few, Charles and Mary Lamb, Charles Dickens, Rudyard Kipling, Washington Irving, Mark Twain, Louisa May Alcott, Oliver Goldsmith, Robert Louis Stevenson, Mary Mapes Dodge, and Hans Christian Andersen wrote for children, not just for adults or only for adults. Beginning in the nineteenth century and continuing into the twentieth, talented authors began to provide children with a wealth of literature depicting a child's world— a world of fantasy and whimsy, of adventure and courageous deeds.

In 1944, Paul Hazard, a member of the French Academy and a scholar of history and comparative literature, commented at length in *Books, Children, and Men* on the differences he perceived between the European countries of the "North" and those of the "South" in their view of childhood.[7] The "Anglo-Saxons" believed childhood had a right to exist, that "childhood should be understood as a fortunate island where happiness must be protected," "like an independent republic living according to its own laws, like a caste with glorious privileges." On the other hand, the "South," Hazard believed, saw "children as only small candidates for the career of man." Indeed, it took much longer before authors in Latin countries began to write literature for children. As Hazard points out, *Pinocchio*, written in 1880, was the first book for children in Italy written wholly from a child's point of view.

Not only was a genuine literature for children being developed in this country, so, too, were public libraries. An autonomous American institution like the volunteer fire department, the public libraries being established during the latter half of the nineteenth century contained not only books for adults but also this flourishing children's literature. By the end of the century, children were being given a room of their own in public libraries and were being offered books suggesting a very egalitarian approach to gender differences. For example, the children's room that opened in 1890 in Brookline, Massachusetts, featured an extensive collection of nonfiction as well as fiction for boys and girls; in the "Not Fiction" books in the "100 Good Books for Boys and Girls" recommended in its bulletin for December 1894 were *The American Boy's Handy Book*, *The American Girl's Handy Book*, *Historic Boys*, *Historic Girls*, *Spare Hours Made Profitable for Boys and Girls*, *Boys and Girls of the Revolution*, *Boys' Book of Famous Rulers*, *Queens of England*, *Poor Boys Who Became Famous*, and *Lives of Girls Who Became Famous*. "Libraries for children" were an even more remarkable American innovation than the public libraries themselves, in Hazard's judgment, stimulating the development of libraries for children in France and the rest of Europe.

In sum, by the turn of the twentieth century, children were seen as a distinct group of people with needs and interests of their own. The publishers of elementary school readers were unanimous in supporting a choice of selections based on literary quality and their appeal to children themselves. As one historian of reading textbooks put it, "the desire to appeal to the child's imagination became the watchword of textbook compilers."[8] Children also required the best literature that was available. Educators and publishers all stressed "the importance of learning to love what is best to read."[9] The preface to *The Normal Course in Reading, Third Reader*, published by Silver, Burdett and Company in 1896, stated that its "literature is of the choicest. Its subject matter is drawn from topics which attract and engage all children, appealing at once to their intelligence and interest, and giving them something to read about and think about."[10] Another series declared that its selections were the "famous stories that are the rightful heritage of every English-speaking child."[11] Moral values were reflected in these textbooks as much as they were in the *McGuffey Eclectic Readers*. As stated in the preface to Holmes's *Second Reader*, published by University Publishing Company in 1906, its "stories in prose and verse are well adapted to awaken a lively interest in the minds of the pupil, and at the same time to instill principles of truthfulness and honesty, and sentiments of kindness and honor."[12] Character building continued to take place, but within the context of an interesting tale well told—in fables, fairy tales, legends, adventure stories, and biographical selections on the lives of the founders of this country. And the instructional readers developed academic as well as literary skills. They raised questions, encouraged thinking, and invited children to think creatively in response to selections on history, geography, and natural science.

A NEW INTEREST IN SOCIAL GOALS

The cultivation of literary taste, literary knowledge, and the literary imagination fit comfortably with the philosophy of the progressive movement in education, which had just begun to develop about the time these changes were occurring in the literature curriculum. Progressive educators centered their energies on what they believed to be children's natural development. They sought to create a school curriculum built around children's needs and interests, not on adult expectations or on the structure of academic disciplines and the acquisition of subject matter. It is true that they also wanted to free children from what they perceived as the dead weight of the past and to minimize internalization of what they believed to be the flawed values of the larger society. Children were not to grow up and simply reproduce their society. But their belief in education as an instrument for creating a "new social order"—a cooperative, harmonious society of people dedicated to the common good—did not serve as a barrier to the use of reading selections reflecting a view of childhood as a special—and

innocent—period of life. Their philosophy fully supported the goal of exposing children to a high-quality literature—fiction and nonfiction—that
appealed to their spontaneous interests.

The shift around the turn of the twentieth century from the use of
character-building selections for reading instructional purposes to the use
of well-written stories appealing to children's interests came at about the
time that huge new waves of immigrants, most very different in cultural
and religious background from earlier waves of immigrants, were arriving
in America and settling in all its major cities and rural towns. Elementary
education was now compulsory in all states. The children and grandchil-
dren of this generation of immigrants were fortunate: they learned to read
with textbooks whose contents—childhood tales, fantasies, adventure
stories, myths, legends, fairy tales, and fables—offered them a world un-
burdened by the social ills and problems of their times, a world that stimulated their imagination and curiosity. As the decades passed, fiction so
dominated the selection process in the readers that there were increasingly fewer selections on nature and science, with few, if any, voices expressing concern about this development at the time.

Nevertheless, this reading paradise for children—selections that honored the innocence of childhood—did have snakes lurking in it. Although the selections offered by most publishers were in general well
written despite the contrived nature of the language of many stories, especially in the primary grades, and although most selections were chosen
for their potential appeal to children's imagination, sense of curiosity, and
spirit of adventure, the chief problem was not so much their failure to offer
the children of these new immigrants (or black or Indian children) stories
featuring people who reflected their ethnic background or economic circumstances—or the growing omission of science or nature selections—
but the gradual lowering of the difficulty level of the selections (their
readability level), decade after decade. Beginning in the late 1920s and
early 1930s, educators sought to simplify the language and ideas of the selections they chose for each grade level (as we saw in the adapted passage
from "Sinbad's Second Voyage" in the epigraph in Chapter 1 in contrast
to an unadapted version) because of the large number of students having
difficulty learning to read.

At the turn of the century, the level of literacy of the average white
American in the North and Midwest was high; indeed, since before the

American Revolution, the overall level of literacy of white Protestant America was among the highest in the world.[13] One need only consider the forty most common literary works taught in midwestern high schools at the beginning of the twentieth century to appreciate the level at which those who attended high school in the North and Midwest must have been able to read in those years: six Shakespeare plays, *Paradise Lost,* I and II, Milton's minor poems, several works of Sir Walter Scott, Homer's Iliad, Macaulay's *Johnson* and *Milton,* Carlyle's *Burns,* several works by Nathaniel Hawthorne, and other individual works by Oliver Goldsmith, Edmund Burke, George Eliot, Charles Dickens, and James Fenimore Cooper, as well as much other British and American poetry.[14] Although the high school students of 100 years ago formed a small, somewhat select population, this high level of reading was in most respects a reflection of the high intellectual level of the content offered in the elementary school, as Chapter 1 illustrated. It also reflected the advantage of literate homes. In stark contrast to the level of literacy of the average white Protestant American, the members of most ethnic groups migrating to this country around the turn of the century were barely literate. Thus, it would have been surprising if many of their children did not encounter difficulty in coping with the typical elementary school reading program of the day; they did not have the advantage of either literate homes or English-speaking homes.

As publishers of elementary reading textbooks began gradually lowering their difficulty levels to accommodate the increasing range of reading ability in every classroom, especially in major cities, teachers began using within-class instructional groups in an attempt to provide an appropriate instructional pace for children at different reading levels. The practice of dividing students in each grade into sections of "slow, average, and rapid learners" spread rapidly in the mid-1920s as a compromise between the traditional practice of moving large numbers of children "through a year of work at essentially the same pace" and the so-called (and much admired) Winnetka plan of individualized instruction.[15] In addition, many schools began using below-grade-level textbooks for below-average readers. However, they did not use above-grade-level textbooks for above-average readers, further lowering the overall difficulty level of what both low-achieving and high-achieving students were exposed to. This resulted in a situation, as researchers later found, in which reading textbooks published from the

1930s or so to the 1980s tended to be not only too easy for the average student but also much easier than elementary science or social studies textbooks.[16] Moreover, from the 1930s, a sight word approach (or a whole language approach, as it is called today), for which there has never been much evidence, increasingly became the pedagogical approach offered in the readers.[17]

The progressive education movement came under heavy attack in the late 1940s and 1950s. Although many of its adherents at that time subscribed to a plot theory to explain the attacks on their philosophy, their practices, and the public schools, by the early 1950s a "large and articulate public was ready for educational reform of nonprogressive variety," as noted by Lawrence Cremin, the historian of the progressive education movement.[18] Criticism came from the academic community as well as parent groups and the business world.

At a philosophical level, progressive education was attacked for its anti-intellectualism. Indeed, it had been severely criticized almost from its inception for the opposition expressed by many of its advocates to discipline-based learning and to the mastery of subject matter as an educational goal.[19] The clearest object of the critics' attack in the 1950s was the life adjustment movement, an offshoot of progressive education that had emerged in the 1940s. It encompassed the entire school curriculum. Embodying most of its principles and practices, it emphasized communication skills and sought to address, among other things, "the present problems of youth as well as their preparation for future living," their "physical, mental, and emotional health," and "the educational value of responsible work experience in the life of the community."[20]

The almost complete anti-intellectual thrust of progressive education as its critics saw it helped unleash a torrent of articles and books denouncing the tenets of progressive education and the content of teacher training programs in schools of education.[21] The most influential of the critics was Arthur Bestor, a historian who wrote two books in the mid-1950s castigating schools of education for overemphasizing pedagogical method and deemphasizing academic learning. Bestor's criticism of teachers' colleges for their lax academic standards and their lack of emphasis on academic learning in the schools was legitimate. But he did not note in his scathing indictment of "educationists" that some of the blame for this situation could be laid at the door of the scholars in the liberal arts. As Sidney Hook, among others, pointed out, liberal arts scholars years earlier had refused to take seriously the problems of general public education in a democratic society. In Hook's eyes, they were in some respects responsible for the growth of teachers' colleges and the impoverished intellectual climate in them because he believed they had withdrawn themselves from involvement in teacher training and curricular issues, not been cast aside.[22] Regardless of who was most responsible for the anti-intellectual climate in schools of education, there was little doubt that in the public schools themselves, there was a "very real loss of academic centering," as a contemporary historian of education research acknowledged in a 1997 essay.[23]

At the everyday level of reading instruction, the schools were attacked for using the sight word method, a pedagogical method that had now been in place for almost thirty years. This method was based on several principles. One was the notion that "the process of reading should be defined broadly to include as major goals, *right from the start*, not only word recognition, but also comprehension and interpretation, appreciation, and application of what is read to the study of personal and social problems." Another was that "the child should start with 'meaningful reading' of whole words, sentences, and stories as closely geared to his own experiences and interests as possible."[24] The most vocal case against teaching children by a sight word method appeared in Rudolf Flesch's *Why Johnny Can't Read*, which strongly urged a return to a phonics approach.[25] His book hit a raw public nerve and was on best-seller lists for over thirty weeks.

RICOCHET: A BRIEF RETURN TO ACADEMIC GOALS

The shock of *Sputnik* in the mid-1950s galvanized public opinion about the urgency of revising pedagogy and strengthening content in the academic disciplines. It served to give clear direction for public policy. With strong government support, educators engaged intensively with academic scholars for the first time in sixty years to develop more academically rigorous curricula in all subject areas, with special attention to the needs of academically motivated students. The National Defense Education Act, passed during the 1950s and extended during the 1960s, funded teachers to work on curriculum projects in mathematics, science, foreign languages, and later English, reading, and history. This period also saw a rise in concern about Scholastic Aptitude Test (SAT) scores and advanced placement programs in the high school.

However, no serious concerns were expressed about the overall literary quality of the selections in the readers. The social concerns of the progressives had had no negative influence on the kinds of selections children read in school during the first half of the century. In general, from the early 1920s until less than two decades ago, the choice of selections in the readers was guided largely by periodic surveys of children's reading interests, not by adult concerns. And insofar as educational publishers drew on the published children's literature of their time for selections in their readers, the choice of selections was also guided by literary and academic criteria, despite the changes that were made in the language of some selections (especially in the primary grades) to accommodate a more systematic approach to vocabulary development or to eliminate pejorative terms. In other words, although the difficulty level of the selections went down over the decades, overall literary quality (past the primary grades) was reasonably good and children's interests were honored.

Unlike the nineteenth-century readers, which conveyed clearly, understandably, and intentionally the cultural and moral values of a country that was chiefly Protestant and populated primarily by immigrants from northern European countries, the twentieth-century readers from the beginning of the century until the 1960s seemed to provide no "clear image of adult American society and of the child's role in it," according to one historian of reading instructional textbooks.[26] This lack of a clear image may have simply been a result of the effort to appeal to children's natural interests in order to motivate good reading habits, an effort that led publishers to draw freely on a wide range of literary selections. Indeed, researchers who later sought to find in these reading selections ideological sources of influence on later adult behavior usually had their expectations dashed.

One psychologist tried to assess the relationship between national economic growth and images of individual achievement in the stories in second- through fourth-grade school readers in forty countries for two different time periods in the twentieth century. He expected to see more such images in textbooks in developed countries than in underdeveloped ones.[27] To his surprise, for an early period in this century he found no relationship between national economic growth and the number of images of individual achievement in the readers, and for the period 1946–1955, he found a negative relationship. On the other hand, he found a higher stress on achievement in the readers in underdeveloped countries than in those in developed countries, leading him to wonder whether stories in instructional readers were really reflective of the values and interests of "governing groups, classes, or ministry officials." What is puzzling is why he did not raise the more basic question of whether stories in instructional readers influence the behavior and values of young children, at least in any straightforward, discernable way.

The results this psychologist found for the United States were basically confirmed by two other researchers who sampled achievement imagery in more detail in American reading textbooks from 1800 to 1960.[28] They found achievement imagery rising steadily from 1810 to 1890 and then dropping just as rapidly afterward. They also found that moral teaching (implicit or explicit judgments of what was right and what was wrong) dropped steadily from 1810 to 1950, thus inadvertently corroborating the notion that twentieth-century readers were not being used to advance any particular economic ideology or moral dogma.

Another post–World War II researcher was also surprised not to find what she expected when she looked at instructional readers over the whole of American history. Examining first-grade readers from 1600 to 1966 to find out whether they showed boys and girls exhibiting stereotyped behaviors, Sara Zimet found a "diffuse sex role model" present in varying and increasing degrees "from colonial days to the present."[29] In other words, boys and girls were portrayed playing at the same activities. She also found "adult males and females performing similar roles" when they appeared in the readers. From 1600 to 1835, she noted, "the American family was essentially a productive, functional unit." Although the readers presented parents as idealized models of religious and ethical behavior, the readers did not show them participating in "distinctly male or female roles." Further, boys and girls "were treated as adults." From 1835 to 1921, she found children separated from the adult world in a world of their own, and adult characters were almost completely replaced by children and animals. From 1921 to 1966, adults entered the books again, facilitating "their children's wishes, interests, and needs but without distinct interests and needs of their own." According to Zimet, no clearly defined male and female behavior was portrayed for adults or children in the "closely knit nuclear family" of these two periods. Despite the number of trees that have been felled to advance the claim that young girls have been damaged by the stereotypes purportedly present in reading instructional textbooks, Zimet's study clearly suggests that if they have been damaged, the first-grade readers have not been the culprits.

Moreover, they do not seem to have been at fault on another contended issue. As Zimet found from a character count in these first-grade textbooks, textbook authors began to increase the number of female characters in the stories "as formal education was opened to girls (between 1776 and 1835)," a trend that continued, so that "by 1898 and up through 1966, girl characters actually outnumbered boy characters in the texts." Nevertheless, Zimet noted, "a distinct female behavior identity was avoided." While one might logically expect at this point an expression of praise for these authors and publishers, this finding did not lead Zimet to commend them for what she admits this lack of sex role modeling might have reflected: a deliberate spirit of egalitarianism toward the two sexes on the part of authors or educational publishers. Instead, she suggested, it was really part of an attempt to "unify a diverse people under the white Anglo-Saxon middle-class model." Moreover, she speculated, her finding more likely reflected the possibility that textbook authors were engaging in "an unconscious effort to deny the existence of sexuality in children."

By the 1970s, a newer interpretation of the American past was already in vogue in the academic world. A critical stance toward whatever previous American educators or publishers had done was by now almost de rigeur in academic research. One suspects that if Zimet had actually found sex role differences portrayed in the grade 1 readers, textbook publishers would have been hanged as much for showing them as they were for not showing them. In any event, her actual findings must be respected because her study is the only one capturing the portrayal of young boys and girls and their families within the context of the broad sweep of American history.

TO THE OTHER SIDE OF THE COURT AGAIN

The post-*Sputnik* concerns about the intellectual limitations of the curriculum and the needs of the academically motivated student did not have a long shelf life. Less than a decade later, their consciousness and consciences raised by the aftermath of the *Brown v. Board of Education of Topeka, Kansas* decision of the Supreme Court in 1954 and the Voting Rights Act of 1964, Americans became acutely aware of the low level of academic achievement of black and American Indian students. Moreover, the needs of less able students were apparently not being addressed by such conceptual approaches to academic learning as the "new math" or "Man: A Course of Study," the social studies curriculum for the elementary school that had been designed in the post-*Sputnik* years by cognitive psychologist Jerome Bruner. Americans rapidly resolved a long-standing ambivalence about educational efforts aimed at academically able students by turning their attention to the other end of the educational spectrum altogether.

A wave of concern for the "disadvantaged" child swept the country in the 1960s, stimulated to a large extent by President Johnson's War on Poverty. At the center of national attention now were students who were not learning basic academic skills and who were dropping out of school (or receiving meaningless high school diplomas), unable to participate as self-sufficient adults in the mainstream of public life. Beginning in the mid-1960s and on through the 1970s, federal, state, and private funds flowed to various remedial or early education programs designed to address the academic deficiencies of these students. Beginning reading programs were now much more skills oriented than previously. A renewed emphasis on phonics instruction had resulted from the debate on beginning reading methods in the 1950s and from the influence in the late 1960s of Jeanne Chall's *Learning to Read: The Great Debate*, a systematic analysis of the research on beginning reading methodology.

At the same time, English and language arts teachers were beginning to be influenced by the ideas emanating from the Dartmouth Conference in 1966. This conference brought together American and British educators who believed that English teachers had focused excessively on grammar study as a way to teach composition and that the analysis of literary classics and an inflexible regime of formal essay writing did not motivate learning or meet student needs. They articulated a philosophy for English education at all grade levels that placed the student's interests, language experiences, and personal growth at the center of the curriculum. John Dixon's *Growth Through English*, the first book to appear after the Dartmouth Conference, conveyed the thinking of those who had participated in it.[30] The "growth model" Dixon outlined in his book was based on a developmental view of learning that he contrasted to what he saw as prevailing and less appropriate models in language education: a skills model and a heritage model. Participants at the Dartmouth Conference believed that a curriculum acknowledging children's own "encounters with life" would offer them real purposes for learning and motivate them to learn how to use language. For literary study, conferees wanted teachers to reexamine the "canon," take literature "off its pedestal," and make it part of the "living, growing life of every day."

In many ways the student-centered education advocated by the Dartmouth Conference educators was a revitalized formulation of the thinking of the early progressives. But its emphasis was on the use of a variety of informal conversation-based classroom activities for developing language and learning—not only in the English language arts class but across the entire curriculum. This new approach to literacy education, which placed great value on the child's home speech, seemed in the eyes of American educators more humane as well as more appropriate for addressing the educational needs of black and Native American students than did existing pedagogical practices. Thus, although the development of academic skills continued as the focus of instruction in the reading class, the movement away from an academic focus, that is, away from subject matter concerns, was beginning again in the English and language arts class, this time in the form of an emphasis on the process of language learning through informal classroom talk. As the foreword to Dixon's book noted, "post-Dartmouth dialogue among teachers of English" was increasingly concerned with "learning" rather than with "teaching."[31]

In the 1960s, publishers began making substantial changes in the contents of their readers in response to several criticisms. One was that the reading selections in these textbooks were not "authentic" children's literature, but abridged or altered versions of good literature, or that they were simply created for the purpose of teaching comprehension strategies and word meanings, thereby—it was claimed—reducing children's desire to learn how to read. Given the national concern about the low academic achievement of minority children, it was reasonable to *consider* the quality of their reading materials as one potential influence among others on their motivation to learn to read. And many of the selections children were asked to read in those years were not of the highest literary quality, usually because publishers were constructing selections and controlling their language in order to develop a large sight vocabulary or to create de-codable texts. As a result, publishers began increasing the number of au-thentic literary selections in the readers in order to pacify their critics. But no research evidence was put forth, then or later, to support the claim that the "inauthentic" nature of many reading selections reduced children's interest in learning how to read—or that a focus on skills was detrimental to minority students in particular.

Another criticism of the readers was that their selections did not ad-equately portray the ethnic and racial diversity of this country or the cul-tures of non-Western peoples. The readers were further criticized for not providing enough good role models for girls. The readers clearly did not reflect the diversity of the world's population or offer a broad range of role models for girls. Many educational critics believed that minority children were also unmotivated to learn to read because they were alienated by a body of literature that did not seem to include them. (The same argument was not made for girls; on the average they have always done better than boys in reading and writing.) Although the contents of the readers changed rapidly to address the civic needs of minority children and to re-spond to feminist concerns, no evidence was presented then or later link-ing women's status to what they had read in their elementary school readers or connecting the low level of reading ability in minority children to the failure of the readers to show people and communities that resem-bled their own families and neighborhoods.

THE URGENT EDUCATIONAL PROBLEM

Despite the considerable energies and funds invested in remedial reading programs for disadvantaged students, students so labeled did not make enough progress to satisfy their own community leaders or national ex-pectations. Many educators then came to the conclusion that their lan-guage skills were not "deficient," only "different." That insight did not lead to significant academic gains for them, but it did contribute to a new way of viewing them. As anthropologist Charles Valentine remarked in an essay in the *Harvard Educational Review* in 1971, the "initial premise that Afro-Americans are culturally different from other Americans is a proposition that has lately been gaining attention and acceptance among an increasing number of anthropologists and other specialists."[32] To show respect for these putative cultural differences, Valentine proposed a bicultural model of education for Afro-Americans, although he offered few details on its content or on how such a model would lead to improved academic achievement.

By the early 1970s, many educators decided that the key to learning for students who were now being viewed as culturally different from the mainstream was enhanced self-esteem. One should not underestimate the significance that educators attached to this concept. Students were even seen as having a "right" to self-esteem, no matter what they believed, what they said, or how they behaved. Such hyperbolic statements as the following, which appear throughout the teacher guides of one of the current reading series I examined, give a flavor of what elementary school teachers have been told by university educators for well over two decades:[33]

> The right to self-esteem—children have the right to know that they are worthy beings. They have the right to value themselves for whatever they are and whatever they do.

> Self-concept is seen as central, and different instructional strategies are used to achieve success in building positive ones for all students.

> Affirmation and acceptance of individual student's language and cultural heritage in school promotes academic achievement and development of a positive self-concept.

Note the thrust of these three creedal statements, the first by Iris Tiedt, a language arts educator, and the third by Hilda Hernandez, a multicultural educator. Much of the teacher's instructional energies was to be deployed for building positive self-concepts, even though there was no research evidence at the time—and none has ever been forthcoming—to support the notion that a child's self-esteem or sense of self-worth is the key to academic achievement.[34] Thus began the promotion of a variety of practices to build positive self-concepts in minority students, some directed toward their individual self-image and others toward their group identity and group image. To my knowledge, no researcher sought to find out if developing competence in reading was what contributed to their self-esteem.

Although attention was focused on minority students' perception of self and the social group to which educators saw them belonging, not directly on their academic performance, the goal at first was the enhancement of their academic performance. Social goals were not yet ends in themselves, despite some efforts at intergroup education. But once ego development began to be substituted for intellectual development, once psychological goals began to take precedence over academic goals again, the growing obsession with self-concept as the determining component in the learning process could not help but lead to the dominance of nonacademic goals.

STRENGTHENING GROUP ESTEEM: FROM MINORITY LITERATURE TO MULTICULTURAL LITERATURE

Educators seeking to foster the group identity and group esteem of low-achieving students began to introduce new approaches and materials into the curriculum. They began by the early 1970s to use the term *multicultural* rather than the term *minority,* now deemed undesirable because it carried the connotation of low status or inferiority. Minority groups were henceforth to be considered as different cultures in this country, each with its own values, beliefs, and customs, and equal in worth to the "mainstream" culture.

To improve the cultural status of minority groups and heighten their group identity as well, educators sought at first to highlight their positive qualities and note the contributions their members had made to American life. They believed that teaching both minority and nonminority students to understand and appreciate each others' backgrounds would create the grounds for mutual respect. This could be accomplished in part by the use of what was called "multicultural" literature—literary works by or about members of racial or ethnic groups in this country. Educators believed that such a literature could help counter what were perceived to be limiting or demeaning stereotypes in existing educational material or in the media.

Educators also sought to foster group esteem and group identity in minority students by assigning works whose characters used the group's language or language patterns, even if they did not necessarily show the group's positive qualities or contributions to American life. For example, at a professional conference, two English teachers recommended that black students read such authors as Toni Morrison, Alice Walker, Gloria Naylor, and Langston Hughes because these authors provide examples in their novels of the kind of conversational language the students may use.[35] These teachers clearly thought this would have intellectual benefits. They argued that by reading such works as *The Color Purple, Patch of Blue*, and *Kaffir Boy*, black students would be better able and more motivated to read difficult "canonical" works, such as *Pride and Prejudice, Romeo and Juliet*, and *Othello*, and could then discover that "great literature speaks to all people." The literature program they had created in their school was based on the assumption that their students were low achieving and poorly motivated *because* they had been alienated from school. And what was the source of their alienation? In these teachers' eyes, it was their "exposure to only the canon which is viewed as all male, all Western European, and usually dead."

At first, the building of self-esteem of low-achieving minority students seemed to require only the addition to the curriculum of literary works and historical materials about them. Very quickly, however, the scope of the policies and practices designed to promote group identity and group esteem was considerably enlarged. Indeed, the building of egos began to be conceptualized as a massive undertaking, requiring a complete overhaul of the entire curriculum. For example, one educator wrote:

> Token representations of the histories and literatures of culturally different children are inadequate attempts at engaging and inspiring students' participation in the educational process. One piece of literature or one chapter in American history cannot counter the negative perceptions that children of minority subcultures have of themselves or that society has of them. A significant proportion of the curriculum must be dedicated to positive ethnic histories and literatures and the many contributions that all groups have made to American life. Special emphasis should be placed on the predominant minority group of the school. Only when children perceive that they are accepted for who they are—both culturally and individually—can real learning begin.[36]

As this passage suggests, one could not reasonably expect any academic learning to take place for minority students until much of the regular curriculum had been distorted or replaced by what historian Arthur

Schlesinger, Jr., has called "ethnic cheerleading"—the attempt to show only positive aspects of a group's history and literature, not the complete picture.[37] Only then, apparently, could their minds be considered ready to engage in authentic academic tasks.

The pedagogical approaches educators formulated to develop minority students' group identity and group esteem led to a view of our school population and the curriculum that was completely unprecedented in American educational history. Two very different groups of children, needing very different types of education, were now seen as attending the public schools. So-called mainstream students were perceived as needing to read works about other cultures and the nonmainstream groups in this country; they needed to understand how these other groups differed from mainstream culture and to see them as equal in value to their own. So-called nonmainstream students were perceived as needing to see members of their ethnic or racial group in the literature they read, and for many reasons. Seeing characters like themselves in their reading materials would affirm and preserve their social identities, raise their self-esteem, motivate them to learn how to read, facilitate their reading of mainstream works if they learned how to read, and facilitate their participation in public life as members of an accepted social group. In short, for the majority of students in this country, the responsibility of the schools was now to broaden their education by focusing on the history and lives of "the other"—social groups that were not like them—while for "the other" it was to affirm their distinctive characteristics and preserve their group identity even when they participated in the mainstream culture.

STRENGTHENING INDIVIDUAL SELF-ESTEEM

The worth of academic achievement increasingly was denigrated not only by efforts to foster group identity and group esteem, but also by policies and practices that were introduced from the 1970s on to improve individual self-esteem. Some educators seeking to boost the individual self-esteem of low-achieving students began to focus on ways to reduce, if not eliminate, visible differences in academic achievement among students. The self-esteem of lower achievers would rise, they claimed, and they would learn more if visible indexes of differences in academic achievement were minimized, if not eliminated.[38] They also claimed that higher achievers would not learn less than before.

Inspired by these claims, teachers began to eliminate achievement-based groups for reading and math in many elementary schools so that differences in performance were no longer structurally visible within the classroom. One of the acknowledged accomplishments of the early progressives—the use of achievement-based instructional groups to break up whole class instruction—was now perceived as a detriment. In their place, teachers were advised to instruct the class as a whole, exposing low-achieving students to higher-level material than they had heretofore been given and to the thinking of more able peers. Or, teachers were to put lower and higher achievers together in small "cooperative learning" groups, with high achievers responsible to some extent for the performance of the others.[39] In this setting, low-achieving students would also be exposed to the thinking of more able peers. Although there is evidence that under very specific conditions (which include individual accountability) cooperative learning activities can lead to greater academic achievement for students, a careful review of this research turned up only two studies explicitly comparing the achievement of minority students to other students.[40] Although these two studies showed gains for minority students, only one concerned the language arts (and only for a three-month period of time), and white students showed no achievement gains.

In some secondary schools, leveled courses (courses in the same subject with differing levels of difficulty) were eliminated so that differences in achievement between lower and higher achievers were no longer visible at the whole classroom level either. This was especially likely to happen in English and social studies classes.[41] Again, the overt rationale was that low-achieving students would be exposed to higher-level material, more able peers, and hence more demanding questions from the teacher if they were in more heterogeneous groups.

Educational effort went into general policies and practices that reduced the visible value placed on academic knowledge. Some schools eliminated the weighting of a high school course's level of difficulty in calculating grade-point averages as well as class rankings for graduation. The high grade a student received in a less demanding history course, for example, was now equal in value to the high grade another student received in a much more demanding history course.

Schools were urged to place more emphasis on critical thinking skills than on the acquisition of a substantial store of ideas and knowledge with which to think. The arguments for focusing on skills or processes almost always set up as a strawman the teacher who asked for little more than "rote memorization" or the "regurgitation of facts." As one psychologist explained in a typical approach to the topic, teachers were "too much concerned with having students memorize the accepted answers."[42] He saw critical thinking involving "(1) an attitude of being disposed to consider . . . the problems and subjects that come within the range of one's experiences; (2) knowledge of the methods of logical inquiry and reasoning; and (3) skill in applying those methods." He never stated that it also involves a great deal of knowledge about the subject, noting instead that research studies in various disciplines had all pointed to the conclusion that "the content alone of any subject is not likely to develop a generalized ability to reason logically and productively." Although this conclusion might well be unarguable (the exact meaning of this *conclusion* is not quite clear), it does not mean that content knowledge is of little or no relevance to the development of critical thinking. Given the rhetorical shape of arguments like his, it is easy to see why many educators might downgrade the importance of content knowledge in a critical thinking curriculum, rather than place at least an equal emphasis on both process and content.[43]

Although the stated rationale for whole class instruction, heterogeneous classes, and cooperative learning was to give lower achievers exposure to higher-level material than they usually read or to the thinking of more able peers, the overall thrust of almost all of these policies and practices was to increase lower achievers' self-esteem *by altering their perception of their academic status*. None of these policies or practices necessarily required teachers to teach these low achievers more; if anything, their *peers* were intended to serve as the source of stimulation or teaching in place of their teachers. Nor is there evidence (except for certain kinds of cooperative learning activities) that these policies and practices led to academic gains for low-achieving students.[44]

These policies and practices were supplemented by others that in effect raised the status of lower achievers *by lowering academic standards*. This effect was not intended, of course. For the most part, these practices were designed to give all students, not just lower achievers, a heightened feeling of ownership of what they read and wrote. Those advocating these practices believed that a sense of "ownership" or "empowerment" would enhance motivation to learn. Moreover, they felt that enabling students to be "in charge" or "in control" of their own learning was somehow more in keeping with the spirit of the democratic classroom. This appeal to the worth of individual autonomy was often accompanied rhetorically by an appeal to the other side of the democratic coin in an attempt to cover both bases. Being in charge of one's own learning meant being responsible for one's own learning. In the words of the authors of the foreword to Dixon's book, the child was to be "the final arbiter of his own learning—in schools, as he always has been out of school. The open classroom and individualized learning can do no more than mass instruction if teachers continue to deprive their students of that responsibility for their own learning."[45]

Who could disagree in the abstract that students should be responsible for their own learning? No one, however, interpreted this to mean that they should be responsible for doing all the homework their teachers assigned. Rather, the intention was that they (not their teachers) were to be responsible for deciding what they would read or write about. Not surprisingly, practices designed to "empower" students inevitably reduced teachers' demands on what students learned and on ways students could show what they learned. For example, teachers were urged to eliminate teacher-selected materials to the extent possible and allow students to choose what they wanted to read, in secondary as well as elementary schools.[46] They were also encouraged to let students decide for themselves, alone or in peer group discussion, the meaning of what they read on the grounds that their personal response was what mattered and that meaningful learning was based on their own "construction of knowledge."[47] In the writing class, teachers were urged to allow students to choose their own topics and write about what they already knew or really knew best—their personal experiences—in order to facilitate the "writing process," or the way in which real writers develop a piece of writing. In addition, teachers were encouraged to ignore or downplay writing conventions in writing (that is, to allow or even praise "creative" or "inventive," that is, phonetic, spelling) to facilitate the writing process.

Although academic benefits were expected to accrue from a heightened sense of ownership and from the writing and reading process, no body of research evidence yet exists to show that these practices have led to higher levels of academic achievement. An analysis of the NAEP 1984 scores noted that "more attention to the process of reading and writing [was] less clearly related to achievement. . . . Students who reported their teachers emphasized process-oriented approaches . . . wrote no better than those who reported little or no process instruction." The report also noted similar trends for reading instruction where "increased use of such teaching approaches as having students answer their own questions about what they read, take notes, and learn how to find the main idea of a paragraph were inconsistently and sometimes negatively related to reading proficiency."[48]

As an example of how willing some researchers have been to lower academic standards in order to raise the status of low achievers, I call attention to a newly recommended practice that deliberately reduces what is taught in order to improve social relations between more and less able students.[49] Based on their research, two researchers urge teachers to "broaden" the kinds of activities they offer to allow for more "equal status interaction in the heterogeneous classroom." According to these education professors, this sort of broadening "manipulates expectations of others as well as those of the low-status student" in order to produce equal amounts of participation by less-skilled (low-status) students and more-skilled (high-status) students. But as these advocates of equal status interaction candidly confessed, it also reduces the amount of time devoted to classroom activities requiring higher-level academic skills.

Another new practice in the past several decades did aim to improve the academic learning of low-achieving students in heterogeneous classes. But "mastery learning" has been criticized for an excessive emphasis on the teaching and testing of specific skills, allowing little opportunity in the reading or language arts class, according to one observer, for students to read any books at all.[50] It has also been criticized for reducing the learning of more able students. The advocates of mastery learning clearly sought to improve learning for all students, in mathematics and science especially, and the overall results from comparative studies are moderately positive.[51] At the same time, mastery learning has been obliquely criticized for not providing fast learners with "challenging and rewarding opportunities to enrich and extend their learning" and for letting them "bid[e] their time while slower learners complete corrective work." This situation has apparently occurred because mastery learning relies primarily on a group-based and teacher-paced approach to instruction in classrooms, where both instructional time and the curriculum are relatively fixed—the situation in most classrooms. Much probably depends on the range of ability in the classroom.

Even new programs ostensibly designed to increase learning for all students may have serious intellectual flaws. Educators are now strongly advocating interdisciplinary courses on the grounds that they facilitate meaningful connections across disciplines and result in better learning than can be expected from taking individual courses in each discipline. They also have a social rationale. As the authors of the foreword to John Dixon's book noted, "Integrated studies of various kinds" began to be promoted in the post-Dartmouth years, "the argument being that such courses were likely to be 'more relevant to the needs and aspirations of pupils of average and below average ability' than the traditional courses that enshrined the subject disciplines."[52] Nevertheless, interdisciplinary courses, which drastically alter the structure of the academic disciplines, have been criticized—and by eminent educators—on the grounds that they distort or diminish learning in one or both of the disciplines involved.[53]

I do not intend to imply that most educators or researchers in the past three decades have consciously sought to lower academic standards or reduce the academic learning of either the more able or the less able student. I believe most have been sincere in their belief that the self-esteem or group esteem of low-achieving students is the key to their academic achievement.[54] But educators and researchers never pursued their reasoning far enough. Most of the practices they designed to promote a better self- or group image in low-achieving students have tended to distort the structure and nature of the academic curriculum, reduce the value attached to academic knowledge, and diminish the status of academically motivated students. They have tended to do so because the very existence of academically motivated students (especially if they are white), as well as the kinds of programs or practices thought to foster their achievement, were assumed to be the sources of the low self-image of academically unmotivated students. Educators and researchers never sought to ponder why, once academic achievement was reduced in value, low-achieving students would then have had any motivation to respect academic values or seek academic achievement themselves.

ANOTHER TEMPORARY ACADEMIC
BLIP AND THEN RESURGENCE

By the late 1970s, the public became sufficiently concerned about the lack of attention to academic goals to compel the schools to address basic skills again. But this renewed focus on academic goals was just another temporary blip on the social screen of long-term trends in American education. It did have a visible effect on academic achievement, evident in the results of nationwide assessments of reading in the the early 1980s, a subject discussed in more detail in Chapter 9. In retrospect, however, this short-lived academic interlude seems to have served chiefly to mobilize the energies of the advocates of social goals. Social goals aimed at the development of subgroup identity and subgroup esteem had remained firmly in place during this period. Now the entire curriculum became the sought-after prize, but with a new psychological twist.

Beginning in the early 1980s, as immigrant children again increased in numbers in the public schools, social reformers began to shed most of their remaining academic constraints. In the eyes of influential educators, the most effective way to upgrade the status of students whose academic performance in school had barely changed by their designation as members of an alternative culture was not so much to enhance it positively through celebratory readings but to reduce the moral and cultural status of the mainstream. To do so, they began to load the history and literature curriculum with literary works or other kinds of reading that stressed the flaws and failings of the United States, both today and in the past. Although this literature became known facetiously as "victim lit" or "white-guilt lit" for its highlighting of a group's victimization by white Americans, many teachers believed it was useful precisely because it served to elevate a minority group's moral status, build group solidarity, give all students a realistic portrayal of the group's history, and create guilt in white students. The account of Faith Ringgold's art in the grade 6 Silver Burdett Ginn reader, an excerpt from which appears in Chapter 1, is one example of "victim" or "white-guilt" literature in the readers I examined.

Better-known examples of white-guilt lit are such works as Toni

Morrison's *The Bluest Eye* (about a young black girl who is raped by her father), sometimes taught in high school, and Jeanne Wakatsuki Houston and James Houston's *Farewell to Manzanar* (about the Japanese American internment during World War II), frequently taught in middle school. These are works in which whites are presented almost uniformly as despicable, and white society is suggested as collectively and solely responsible for the condition of the nonwhite characters as a consequence of racial differences. When such works have a first-person narrator, as many do, readers are implicitly asked to identify with a character who sees all or almost all whites negatively. There are at least two possible negative results. The first is the readers' feeling that when the nonwhite characters behave badly, it is because they have been brutalized by a white society and, as its victims, cannot be held responsible for their behavior. The second is guilt in those students who have been compelled to classify themselves as whites and thus as members of the group being collectively stereotyped as racist. However, how a heightened sense of victimization and moral superiority can improve a student's motivation to learn has never been made clear. Indeed, there has been a deafening absence of thoughtful discussion in the schools of the possible long-term effects such a literature might produce, especially on white teachers and black and Latino students.[55]

THE ASCENDANCE OF SOCIAL GOALS

In the words of the Silver Burdett Ginn reading series, the curriculum has become a lens for focusing on discrimination, prejudice, and differential treatment in the United States. It has also become a vehicle for extolling the virtues of nonmainstream cultures. Indeed, in a stunning reversal of images from the 1960s to the 1990s, the low-achieving minority child has changed from someone needing access to the intellectual and civic culture of the mainstream to someone who is morally and culturally superior to the mainstream and thus justified in rejecting its intellectual and civic values.

Despite the deep bow that reading educators and researchers have regularly made to academic and literary goals, such goals have almost completely disappeared in their own professional journals in favor of social goals. Many of the social goals now articulated in the teacher guides for the reading series clearly sound appealing in a country troubled by the differences in achievement as well as tensions among its ethnic and racial groups. What reasonable parent would oppose an attempt to improve "human relations among students of different races" and "communication between people of different cultural backgrounds" or to promote the "strength and value of cultural diversity" and "human rights and respect for cultural diversity"? These are common goals that two teacher educators in the University of Wisconsin system found in the eighty-nine articles and thirty-eight books on multicultural education in the major databases less than a decade ago.[56]

Unlike the compatibility that existed between the social goals of early twentieth-century progressivism and the philosophy guiding the pedagogy and choice of selections published in the readers over the course of the first half of the century, the overall thrust of the social goals now spelled out in teacher guides would seem to make it extremely difficult for publishers of elementary school reading series to achieve academic and aesthetic goals. In fact, it is not clear how educational publishers can pursue academic and aesthetic goals at all when, as in the Silver Burdett Ginn series, the selections or recommended pedagogy must first satisfy the following characteristics of multicultural education (this is the order in which they appear, suggesting the priorities of this series' multicultural adviser):

Promotes personal awareness of own multiple group membership, e.g., gender, race, ethnicity, disability

Examines discrimination, prejudice, and differential treatment

Provides knowledge about the history, ideas, and beliefs of the diverse groups contributing to the shaping of American society

Provides examples of the diverse, sometimes conflicting, viewpoints that are a part of our culturally pluralistic nation

Presents material/images that contradict commonly held stereotypes

Recognizes the importance of the development of a positive self-concept

Acknowledges that America's strength and richness is in its human diversity; that there is no one model American

Acknowledges the positive value of social equality and equity

Demonstrates and advocates critical thinking and alternative viewpoints

Encourages discussion of current social issues involving race, gender, ethnicity, class, and disability

Uses life experiences familiar to the students as the basis for personal discussion of social issues

Illustrates the value of active participation in democratic decision making as a means to create positive social change[57]

All of these goals appear under the rubric of "Appreciating Cultures," and are addressed in some way for every reading selection in the material Silver Burdett Ginn supplies in its teacher guides, as part of what is called "Building Background" for the selection before it is read and as part of what is called "Discussing the Selection" after each selection is read. Note that only one characteristic is academic in nature—the third. It alone mentions "knowledge," although it would remain to be seen what constitutes knowledge in this series. And if there is any doubt that social goals have been given priority, the first goal teachers are given when engaging their students in a discussion of a selection they have just read is labeled "Building Self-Esteem."

This reading series is by no means unique in the prominence it accords to social goals. As another example, Scott Foresman provides the transcript of an interview with its chief multicultural consultant in a "Multicultural Handbook" accompanying its reading series. Among the goals she advances for this series' reading selections and the accompanying pedagogy are the following: to help all students "understand something about their own socialization and background"; to "bring societal issues into the classroom, provide a realistic analysis of these issues, and give students the opportunity to reflect and respond to them"; to help students "gain the skills, the knowledge, and the psychological orientation that allows them to recognize that all people are human, all people can contribute, and that differences among people don't mean deficits"; to help students "identify their own values and strive to make them consistent with their actions"; and to work "toward the creation of a just society" by encouraging "students to involve themselves in social action in the classroom and in the community."[58] Only one of the goals articulated by this consultant in this conversation contains even a hint of an academic or aesthetic orientation.

Many of the goals quoted from the Silver Burdett Ginn and Scott

Foresman series would be completely familiar to a member of the now-defunct Progressive Education Association. The philosophy of many of the early progressive educators held, among other things, that students should draw on their life experiences for schoolwork, class time should be used for discussing social issues, the classroom should serve as a site for practicing democracy, and students should engage in community service and collective social activities (although nowhere did John Dewey in his own work suggest that the purpose of the schools was to engage students in politics). Thus, historical antecedents for much of what multicultural educators are doing in the schools today can be found in the thinking and the practices of early progressives. As Cremin observed, the progressive movement in education began "as part and parcel of that broader program of social and political reform called the Progressive Movement" and viewed education "as an adjunct to politics in realizing the promise of American life."[59]

Nevertheless, multiculturalism as it is now being implemented departs radically from the practices of the early progressives in several key ways. These newer trends are not "progressive," despite claims to being "progressive." Nor are they "reform" efforts of a "nonprogressive" kind, to use Cremin's words. Indeed, the charge of anti-intellectualism leveled at the earlier progressives and at the life adjustment movement in particular may be most cogently directed at the late twentieth-century development of multiculturalism.

Today, the contents of reading programs in the schools are undergoing yet another major transformation, not yet complete. The teacher guides for all the series still state that they want children to become successful readers and writers. They still articulate in different ways all the traditional goals of a reading program, such as those spelled out in the 1979 Harcourt Brace Jovanovich reading series: "[1] Word Service/Decoding—To develop competence in identifying printed words; [2] Comprehension—To develop competence in deriving meaning from written language; [3] Language Skills—To develop competence in all aspects of language related to the reading process; [4] Study Skills—To develop competence in using reading as a means of learning, study, and research; and [5] Literary Appreciation—To develop interest and competence in reading literature for pleasure and enrichment." I have no doubt that the publishers are sincere in wanting children to achieve all these goals. And the instructional readers still offer many selections that can stimulate children's imagination and satisfy their spirit for adventure. But in many cases, when the choice of selections seems to be guided by the desire to develop literary taste or academic knowledge, the teacher guide suggests how the selection can be used to achieve social goals that violate both literary goals and academic criteria. In many other cases, the literary selections themselves are problematic. As Anne Scott MacLeod commented in a 1998 essay in the *Horn Book Magazine*, "Didacticism dies hard in children's literature. Today's publishers, authors, and reviewers often approach historical fiction for children as the early nineteenth century did—as an opportunity to deliver messages to the young."[60] Thus, the choice of selections frequently reflects a conscious effort to shape children's feelings about themselves, their classmates, their social and political communities, and the social issues of the day in a specific political direction rather than a desire to develop literary taste or academic knowledge. Moreover, the moral impulses guiding the choice of these selections in the readers seem to entail high academic costs at the level of language learning itself, especially, and ironically, for black and immigrant children.

Few parents seem to be aware of what has been taking place overall in the elementary school reading curriculum, so absorbed have many of them been with the debate about the merits of a whole language or phonics approach in beginning reading instruction. But there is another reason that most parents seem to know so little. Contemporary educators have not been particularly interested in enlarging parental understanding of the exact nature of the curricular goals they now pursue. In many ways, this is not surprising.

Progressive educators in the first half of the twentieth century were for philosophical reasons uninterested in the kind of curriculum most parents may have wanted for their children. Indeed, Richard Hofstadter quotes John Dewey himself in *Democracy and Education* as expressing concern that the curriculum "probably represents the values of adults rather than those of children and youth."[61] Moreover, many progressive educators clearly did not favor a liberal education—an education based, as Hofstadter describes it, on a "primary conviction about the value of the various subject-matter disciplines and on the assumption that the child, through some degree of mastery of academic subjects, would enlarge his mind for the general ends of life and establish his preparation for the professions or business or other desirable occupations."[62] Instead, they seemed to believe, and Hofstadter quotes many of them to this effect, that most students were "incapable by native endowment of entering with some degree of hope into the world of academic competition, mastery of subject matter, and discipline of mind and character." Hence, their focus on social skills, self-expression, self-chosen interests, and democratic living in the classroom and school.

Today's progressive educators have been similarly indifferent to the views and ambitions of the parents of the children they seek to shape or reshape. But unlike the progressives of yesteryear, they seem to have ignored the constraints observed by their philosophical ancestors. Early progressive educators openly communicated the nature of their goals and activities to the public. Their philosophical heirs have not been as open in public in describing the nature of their goals and its specific effects on the curriculum. Nor have they been as willing to discuss criticism of them in public in a civil manner. Instead, they have tended to be quite hostile to parents who have openly disagreed with educators who think they know what is best for the parents' own children.

A particularly venomous antiparent article appeared in the April 1998 issue of *Phi Delta Kappan*, the education journal with the widest circulation in the country.[63] According to Alfie Kohn, the author of "Only for My Kid: How Privileged Parents Undermine School Reform," any liberal parent who criticizes such progressive practices as whole language, portfolio assessments, and "multi-ability reading groups," or the standards put out by the National Council of Teachers of Mathematics, is an ally of the Christian right and selfish to boot. Liberal parents who think their children should have some information in their heads after twelve years of schooling and who want to preserve advanced placement and honors courses in their high schools, a skills-based math curriculum in the elementary grades, the use of worksheets, letter grades rather than progress reports, and such practices as honor rolls and awards assemblies are denounced as "Volvo vigilantes," "anti-child," "without a commitment to the values of the community," and members of an imaginary organization called "Rich Parents Against School Reform." Kohn is angry with these parents not because they want the best for their own children but because he thinks they want the worst for other people's children. They are selfish because they are not willing to "sacrifice their own children" for what "progressive" educators think is best for other children. Kohn also denounces those parents "in some working-class neighborhoods" who have also banded together to restore "graded evaluations." Ironically, the article is a travesty of the spirit of liberal multiculturalism; there isn't one quotation from one of these "Volvo vigilante" parents giving us *their* perspective on these educational issues and on their children's school experiences. Moreover, Kohn never pauses to reflect on why he assumes that black and Latino children are incapable of getting into honors and advanced placement courses or that their parents do not want these advanced courses in their children's schools.

The next several chapters describe the nature of the stealth curriculum that has been created in many of today's readers by the social goals of contemporary educators. Although teachers can teach reading without using an instructional reader, and many today do, the majority of classrooms use readers partially or completely, which teachers often supplement with a variety of individual literary works. An analysis of the contents and pedagogy of the readers in leading reading series therefore provides a good picture of what a majority of children are exposed to in their reading programs today. In the final chapters of this book, I pick up on the ominous note in the final paragraph of the epigraph for this chapter. The hint that no matter what teachers do in their classrooms today, their efforts will necessarily have "limits" as well as "possibilities" is not an idle threat. Prominent educators and researchers have already begun to formulate the outlines of a different set of social goals for the schools that will make the gross distortions of academic and literary goals in many of the current basal readers look academic by comparison.

THREE

THE CULTURAL CONTENTS OF CONTEMPORARY READERS

Appreciating Cultures. Pippi, the main character in this selection, is a determined young girl as well as a strong leader. Pippi's self-confidence helps her find what she is looking for. Brainstorm other female characters from literature who display self-confidence. Have students discuss how these characters contradict commonly held stereotypes about women.

> —From the Teacher Edition for the 1993 Silver Burdett Ginn Grade 4 Reader, before students read an excerpt from *Pippi in the South Seas* by Astrid Lindgren

Appreciating Cultures. Point out that the women as well as the men in this story are shown to be hardworking, resourceful, brave, and self-sufficient. Discuss how this contradicts stereotypes that portray only men as being brave, and women as being helpless, incompetent, and timid.

> —From the Teacher Edition for the 1993 Silver Burdett Ginn Grade 4 Reader, after students read an excerpt from *Little House in the Woods* by Laura Ingalls Wilder

Appreciating Cultures. Encourage students to recall details from the story that suggest Carlota is trying to conform to a standard of "masculine" behavior, such as riding astride rather than sidesaddle and hiding her feelings of pain and fear from her father. Then ask students to discuss how people like Carlota—both female and male—might feel as they try to deny their true selves in order to fit into a culturally determined model for women or men.

> —From the Teacher Edition for the 1993 Silver Burdett Ginn Grade 6 Reader, after students read an excerpt from *Carlota* by Scott O'Dell

F OR MANY years, multicultural educators have leveled the charge of cultural bias or Eurocentrism at the reading materials used in the schools. They have complained that students read only about the culture of Americans of European descent, and almost nothing about Americans of non-European descent. They have also complained that only European cultures have been reflected in the non-American selections used and, correspondingly, that the cultures of non-Western countries have been ignored. It is hard to square these charges with the fact that textbook publishers began to expand the array of Americans and world cultures featured in the elementary school readers in the mid-1960s, a process that has continued unabated ever since. But none of the educators making these charges in the past decade or so has bothered to offer any hard evidence about what actually is included in the leading reading series. The charges have simply been accepted as an accurate description of reality.

Nevertheless, the leading elementary school readers portray a very different reality today. In most series, students learn almost nothing about the authentic ethnic diversity of the United States or about the authentic diversity of cultures around the world. In addition, students learn almost nothing about the religious diversity of this country, or the significance of religious practices in the lives of many Americans. Although there is no across-the-board animus against white male children, their presence is almost nonexistent in some readers. So too are selections showing the extraordinary ethnic assimilation that has already taken place in the United States and that continues to take place. There are three major problems in leading reading instructional textbooks for the elementary grades: demographic dishonesty, cultural dishonesty, and intellectual dishonesty.

This chapter offers evidence for these conclusions and charges, drawn from an examination of what is now being served up to children under the glossy covers of these leading instructional readers—and what is not. In it, I describe the subtle ways in which the cultural contents of reading textbooks manipulate children's sense of the country and the world in which they are growing up. We begin first, however, with a brief overview of the cultural contents of earlier readers in the twentieth century up to the 1980s because it is necessary to have some understanding of what children were reading in their reading textbooks yesterday in order to appreciate the changes in the reading textbooks published in the mid-1990s.

CULTURAL CONTENTS OF THE READERS FROM 1900 TO 1970

To give a wide-ranging but cogent overview of the major trends in the instructional readers from 1900 to 1970, I draw on a dissertation completed at the University of Idaho in 1980.[1] This unpublished study seems to be unknown in the field of reading, possibly because its author was in civic education, not reading education (although that would not excuse its complete neglect by reading researchers).[2] Yet, it provides the most comprehensive and systematic information we have on the trends in the civic and cultural contents of the readers for the first two-thirds of this century. Charlotte Iiams, a social studies educator, was interested in finding out what views about American citizenship were reflected in basal readers for grades 1 to 6 over the course of the century. She rightly suspected that the "decline of pride in the American nation" apparent in public life by 1970 would best be revealed in textbooks used for reading instruction. The content of the readers might be more informative than the content of history or civics textbooks, Iiams reasoned, because instructional readers are under no professional obligation to be impartial in their approach to social or political issues. (In fact, history textbooks have been criticized in recent years for their bias on many social or political issues.[3]) Unlike history or civics textbooks, they are not expected to present social issues directly and give students a range of views on them. Because they are used for the development of reading skills rather than for the learning of subject matter, Iiams noted, they can be far more one-sided or biased in the points of view they present through their choice of content. This is an important point for parents and other citizens to keep in mind when looking at the contents of readers.

In order to characterize the extent to which civic attitudes were conveyed in the reading textbooks, Iiams used a scale that progressed from "no mention of nation" to "neutral" to "patriotic" to "nationalistic" and to "chauvinistic." The following kinds of selections served as her index to civic attitudes:

1. *Stories about soldier heroes, Revolutionary and Civil War battles, the causes of war, and war-related civilian experiences.*

2. *Stories about the lives of national heroes such as George Washington,*

Abraham Lincoln, Benjamin Franklin, and Paul Revere (and in the South, Robert E. Lee). These stories often focused on their childhood, their interaction with children as adults, and their kind acts to animals.

3. *Stories from American history such as those about Columbus, the pilgrims (or in the South the Virginia settlements), Lewis and Clark and Sacajawea, the Pony Express, and Daniel Boone.*

4. *Selections about national symbols and songs, such as verses about the flag, patriotic hymns, stories about the writing of the "Star Spangled Banner," the Liberty Bell, and the signing of the Declaration of Independence; orations delivered at dedication ceremonies and inscriptions from monuments; Fourth of July orations; and information about Memorial Day and Armistice Day.*

5. *Stories about public servants such as police, firefighters, mayors, and the Coast Guard, or about the mechanics of government, such as how an immigrant becomes a citizen or the necessity of paying taxes.*

6. *Use of the word* patriot *itself or its derivatives, whether in introductions to stories or in headings for groups of stories.*

She also looked at indications of social class, the treatment of the American Indians and black Americans, the portrayal of religious diversity, the number of stories about immigrants and people in other countries, the first acknowledgments of the existence of a multiracial society in this country, attitudes toward the poor and charity, and the number of stories about lame or sick children and children who would die at an early age. As all this suggests, Iiams truly covered the waterfront with her survey of cultural content, enabling us at the end of this chapter to gain a deeper understanding of contemporary America when we compare what she found with what is in today's readers.

What did Iiams find? In the first two decades of the twentieth century, she judged overall content as ranging from patriotic to nationalistic in the intermediate-grade readers but from little to no patriotic content in the primary readers. She also found that books published for use in the South were more nationalistic than most books intended for northern children.

These patterns continued to some extent during the period between the wars (1920–1940). By the 1950s and 1960s, most textbooks ranged from neutral to barely patriotic in thrust in both the primary and intermediate grades. This evolution could be seen in the gradually diminishing presence of war-related stories designed to give children a common history and common political ideals.

Before World War I, events that led to war, battles, and war-related civilian experiences were frequent topics. Stories about the Revolutionary and Civil Wars were plentiful, as were stories about national heroes and symbols, patriotic hymns, tales about famous events in American history, Fourth of July orations, and information on Memorial Day.

After World War I, the causes of wars were no longer a topic, and in most readers the wars had become, to use Iiams's word, bloodless. Armistice Day became a subject for stories, but Memorial Day was mentioned less frequently, and Fourth of July orations disappeared forever. Soldier heroes were often replaced by inventor heroes and civilian leaders, "whether on territorial frontiers, fighting fires, or producing new products," and civic cohesion was stimulated not by military events but by stories emphasizing the need for children to engage in courageous conduct or personal sacrifice. Introductions to stories about courage urged children to find ways to be of social service to their country. In addition to the inventors and civilian leaders, the policeman and the fireman made their debut in the post–World War I readers, usually in primary-grade readers, and they were always helpful. Occasionally story children had contact with a friendly mayor or helpful Coast Guard.

After World War II, the use of war-related stories to inculcate a national sense of citizenship almost disappeared. The readers completely avoided war stories showing the physical suffering resulting from war. In the few war-related stories that did appear, the enemy was never named, unless the story was about the Revolutionary War. Right conduct in personal life had won the day. In contrast to the McGuffey readers of the nineteenth century, where child characters who were "thoughtless or cruel or disobedient suffered swift, improbable, and dreadful consequences," the children who populated mid-twentieth-century readers almost always engaged in right conduct, thus never needing punishment as a way to learn their lesson, and they were almost always rewarded for their unselfish conduct in order to supply the happy ending the stories seemed to require. National heroes and inventors continued to appear, but they were now joined by dedicated athletes. On the other hand, Memorial Day and Armistice Day were no longer mentioned, and the word *patriot* and its derivatives continued to decline, except for a brief period right after the war. The kind policeman and fireman continued to make their appearance in the readers but never in urban areas. Rarely did a story hint at the mechanics of government by showing people voting, or paying taxes, or becoming a citizen, or by suggesting why citizens needed to pay taxes.

Iiams's comments on matters of class are also of interest. She found no one rich in the America of the readers throughout the seventy years. Most families were ordinary people living in small towns, as did most Americans until after World War II. "Some working poor" appeared as minor characters before World War II and gratefully accepted the charity that was offered them in the name of civic duty by those more fortunate than they were. After World War II everyone was middle class. Citizens of foreign lands now tended to resemble the earlier American poor, and were always grateful for what Americans gave them.

The trends Iiams detected throughout these seventy years illumine the gradual evolution of broad cultural attitudes on our ethnic pluralism as well. Before 1917, Iiams found the readers "unconcerned with contemporary cultures other than mainstream America and the American Indian."[4] Religious diversity was mentioned exactly twice. Interestingly, the Indian stories tended to be sympathetic, often expressing admiration for the skills Indians possessed. The most sympathetic accounts "sought to develop a concern for the enormity of the adjustment that must be made by the Indian and to condemn the injustices perpetrated against that race."[5] On the other hand, black Americans were mentioned only in a few, pre–Civil War stories, were called servants rather than slaves, and were never shown in illustrations. People in other countries or remote lands were seldom mentioned, but when they were it was because of a fascination with what constituted exotica then—Turks, Eskimos, or the politeness of the Japanese and charming Oriental manners.

Between the wars, she found what she interpreted as patronizing stories of people in other countries and American minority groups. Black Americans appeared as slaves or servants, easily frightened, superstitious, and good humored. Indians appeared more often than in earlier years as savage obstacles for settlers, and stories of harsh Eskimo life were more frequent. A few stories told about immigrants to America, and their problems and contributions. Other countries were mentioned more frequently than earlier in the century, but the emphasis was still on the quaint and exotic.

Black Americans did not appear at all in the readers of the immediate post–World War II period. On the other hand, there were stories about Indians, some portraying them as heroes in pioneer days, others pointing to their problems adjusting to the majority society. Immigrant stories increased in frequency and in the variety of national origins. But in stories that were not about one of these immigrant groups, the characters seemed to be all of northern European ancestry. She also found more stories about foreign lands, including those in which Africans appeared in their native villages.

Racial integration in American society did not appear in the readers she examined until 1965. Now pictures of groups of children became multiracial. Sometimes new stories were written, sometimes old ones were revised, in order to feature blacks in the most favorable role. Black Americans began to appear as professionals in both biographies and incidental roles in stories about children. Sometimes prejudice was dealt with, but not always sensitively, in her judgment.

Iiams was right to conclude that what was in the readers in the beginning decades of this century helps us better understand many contemporary social and political issues. Some of these stories clearly suggest the pervasiveness of unconscious racial prejudice at the time. They also help us appreciate the many changes for the better that have taken place since then, for example, the change in attitudes toward charity and the way in which poverty is now handled. In the early part of the century, poor children had no choice but to be grateful to their classmates or other parents for individual charity because no other mechanisms existed for alleviating poverty. Today, Iiams suggested, a story about charitable gifts from students to a poor classmate or his or her parents might be considered an insult.

Perhaps the most striking change she found was in the frequency of stories about lame or sick children, or children who would die at an early age. The early readers contained vast numbers of such stories; they hardly appear after World War II. Such a difference reflects the advances made in medicine and sanitation in this country. And, as Iiams pointed out, it stimulates thinking about the kinds of changes one might find in a society when fear of early death for one's children is eliminated.

CULTURAL CONTENTS OF THE READERS
IN THE 1970S AND EARLY 1980S

After 1970, to judge again from the only fairly comprehensive study that has been done,[6] dramatic changes took place in the civic and cultural content of the readers, reflecting new views on a variety of social and political issues. The author of the study, a psychologist, was interested in finding out whether there were references to religion and whether traditional family values were presented. Explicitly concerned about the portrayal of conservative positions, Paul Vitz examined the grade 3 and grade 6 readers in eleven leading basal readers published between 1978 and 1984, looking at a total of 670 stories and articles (but not plays, poems, or other reading materials). His findings serve to extend the trends Iiams found in her survey of readers from 1900 to 1970.

Vitz found scant representation of religion, noting that "while Catholicism, Judaism, and the black church—that is, 'minority religions'—receive occasional minor representation, Protestantism is omitted completely." Corroborating Iiams's results, he found "for all practical purposes the concept of patriotism . . . absent from these books." For example, only 5 of the 670 stories he examined had any patriotic theme, and not one dealt with such figures in American history as Daniel Boone, Paul Revere, Patrick Henry, or Nathan Hale. He found a lack of support for business—no stories about Henry Ford, Andrew Carnegie, or any recent examples of this Horatio Alger type. Nor did he find a single story in which "an immigrant to this country finds happiness and success in business or in a profession." Even the life of American workers went unmentioned; there were no stories about labor or labor unions.

Vitz was struck by a feminist emphasis in these readers that he saw as overdone, ahistorical, and hostile to romance, marriage, and motherhood. Only five stories presented any form of romantic love. On the other hand, he found many stories featuring a role reversal for the heroine, such as a dragon-slaying princess. Nonfictional stories of female successes were frequent and all in traditional male activities, such as the stories about the women fliers Amelia Earhart and Harriet Quimby. He found only one story on the Wright Brothers (one page long) and nothing on Charles Lindbergh or other male aviation pioneers. Fictional stories showing competition, especially physical competition between girls and boys, almost always had the girl winning. Other fictional stories contained "women soldiers, judges, and merchants at times and places where there were none." Describing the situation metaphorically, Vitz found stories about "Wonder Woman and the Wimp" common, and stories portraying traditional sex roles almost entirely excluded.

Vitz's comments on the historical inaccuracies he found in the readers are echoed by Anne Scott MacLeod in her 1998 essay in the *Horn Book Magazine*, the leading journal on children's literature in the country.[7] Commenting on historical fiction written for children in the past two to three decades, she notes that many "evade the common realities of the societies they write about. In the case of novels about girls or women, authors want to give their heroines freer choices than their cultures would in fact have offered."

It is instructive to contrast Vitz's perspective on what he found in readers published from 1978 to 1984 with that of three educational researchers at universities in Texas who examined four leading reading series published in 1978 for sex role bias.[8] Comparing their results to several other surveys of sex role bias in series published earlier in the 1970s, the Texas researchers found a huge drop in the number of stories focusing on males in the 1978 series. In their article, they compliment publishers for just about managing by 1978 to replace the large number of stories about males in earlier basal readers with "stories describing subjects whose sex was not defined." They also laud publishers for their efforts to equalize representation of the sexes in selections with characters whose sex was defined. (Interestingly, in a companion article, one of these Texas researchers and a teacher colleague complain how few selections were in the categories of "famous events" and "historical perspectives of regions and states."[9] They seem to have missed an obvious connection. The large number of selections about males in the earlier readers that had been "replaced" were most likely about well-known historic events and perspectives.) In other words, their results mesh with Vitz's results; it is their interpretation of these results that differs.

Although they were looking largely at the same phenomenon, the differences in purpose between the Vitz study and the Texas-based research clearly illustrate how educational research can be used to advance academic or social goals. Vitz was concerned about historical knowledge, historical accuracy, and the imbalance in the values he saw reflected in the readers he looked at. On the other hand, so far as we can tell, the Texas researchers were interested only in equality of representation. At least they do not comment on a distortion of history and a contradiction of reality as the price for achieving equality of representation.

There have been no other large-scale, systematic studies of cultural and civic content in basal readers besides Iiams's and Vitz's work in the past forty years. In one sense, it is surprising that there have been no others and that the two that have been done were not by researchers in the field of reading or English. An observer might be puzzled about why there have been so many studies of the contents of American reading textbooks from the seventeenth to the mid-twentieth centuries but so few studies of the contents in reading textbooks in the latter half of the twentieth century, given the stridency with which contemporary moralists decry the bias they claim exists in the curriculum. In another sense, it is perhaps not surprising that there have been no surveys of cultural content since World War II by researchers in the field of reading, or that both the Iiams and Vitz studies have never, to my knowledge, been referred to, never mind commented on, in any professional journal in the field of reading or English. (Iiams's dissertation abstract is in *Dissertation Abstracts International*; Vitz's research was published in book form as well as summarized in at least two journal articles.) This neglect has clearly benefited educational publishers, consultants, and researchers reluctant to let the public know about the most recent changes in these basic textbooks or to discuss them in public. It has allowed editors and their academic advisers to turn contemporary readers into an expression of their social catechism without popular discussion, never mind consensus on what they have done.

THE CULTURAL CONTENTS OF CONTEMPORARY READERS

In order to draw well-supported conclusions about the contents of today's readers, I examined all the instructional readers for grades 4 and 6 in the reading series published by D. C. Heath (1993), Harcourt Brace (1995), Houghton Mifflin (1993), Macmillan/McGraw-Hill (1993),[10] Scott Foresman (1995), and Silver Burdett Ginn (1993). I chose to look at only the grade 4 and grade 6 readers (and their teacher guides) in these series because the contents of two readers per series give a good picture of what is in a whole series. Although different editors may be responsible for different grade levels in a series, nevertheless a publisher aims for consistency in the pedagogical approach it recommends across readers and in the philosophy underlying the choice of selections in each reader. I chose to look at upper elementary grade readers to get a good sense of the kind of literature a publisher thinks is appropriate for children before they graduate to a literature anthology in grade 7.

I offer no statistics on the color or gender of the authors of the selections in these series. It is true that many educators seem to think these are the most important features of a literary selection.[11] Initially, I attempted to gather information on the authors' backgrounds, but I soon discovered that an author's ethnicity does not necessarily correlate with the cultural content of the author's work. The version of a folktale that is published may be the work of someone of an altogether different ancestry, as is the case, for example, with a Jewish folktale retold by Julius Lester, a black American. Or an author from one country or culture may write stories set in another country, as does Rudyard Kipling. Further, many works, poems especially, have no easily discernible cultural content, even when the author is an "ethnic." Then there are unresolvable issues. Sometimes the ethnicity of one of the author's grandparents is identified, but not that of the others. How should the author be classified? Rather, why *should* the author be classified by only one grandparent's race or ethnicity? Moreover, of what importance is the particular ethnicity of an author if this person deals with another ethnic group altogether? I decided that the cultural elements in a selection were chiefly what mattered, not the author's genealogy.

Distribution of Literary Selections

Because of all the changes in the instructional readers in the past decade or two, I constructed a chart showing the distribution of the selections in the readers across genres to see if there were differences among the series in the proportions of the various types of selections they offered. Adapting traditional literary classification schemes, I grouped selections into one of five categories:

1. *Historical and realistic fiction*

2. *Fantasy, mysteries, humor, and science fiction*

3. *Tall tales, fables, and legends—pieces that (except for those by Aesop) are generally anonymous*

4. *Poems and songs*

5. *Essays, narrative nonfiction, informational selections from newspapers or social studies or science textbooks, biographies, and autobiographies*

Although the specific genre of every selection is spelled out in the contents for each reader (e.g., poem, realistic fiction, historical fiction, fantasy, biography, or autobiography), the numbers in these five groups offer a clearer picture of what is in the readers than would numbers for every single genre represented in them.[12] These categories show three basic kinds of imaginative prose, as well as poetry and, presumably, acccurate information about the real world.

Tables 3 and 4 show the distribution for the five categories for grades 4 and 6 and the total number of reading selections in each reader.[13] The readers clearly differ in the amount of imaginative literature they offer in contrast to the number of information-oriented selections and poems. At both grade levels, Houghton Mifflin and Macmillan have a much smaller number of imaginative pieces than the other three.[14] To some extent, the smaller number of imaginative pieces in these two series is compensated for by the length of those they do offer, but not entirely. They still give much less page space to fantasy and science fiction than do the other series. On the other hand, they give greater prominence to social studies and science selections. This is a response to reading researchers and educators who have recommended more informational selections, especially from social studies and science textbooks, in order to provide reading instruction for more than literary genres.

Distribution of American Cultural Content

More interesting differences emerge in American cultural content.[15] But before I discuss them, a brief description of the categories I used is in order here so that it is clear how I went about assessing the charge of cultural bias, or "Eurocentrism." I began by sorting selections into three categories: American, foreign, and general cultural content. The last category accounted for selections I judged to have no easily distinguishable national content, chiefly poems or informational articles on science or nature.[16] Under American cultural content, I distinguished chiefly nonethnic cultural content from chiefly ethnic cultural content. I considered selections with no identifiable ethnic touches or major ethnic characters as portraying the American mainstream, a term used by a wide variety of academic commentators on American culture as well as by such prominent multicultural educators as James Banks to refer to a "white Anglo-Saxon Protestant culture."[17] If a selection focused on an American ethnic group[18] or one or more of its chief characters could be identified through illustrations or the text as belonging to a racial or ethnic group outside this white Anglo-Saxon Protestant culture, I placed it in the ethnic category. Within this subcategory, I distinguished between selections about ethnic groups or characters in affirmative action categories (African Americans, Asian Americans, Native Americans, and Hispanic Ameri-

TABLE 3

Distribution of Reading Selections in the Grade 4 Readers

SERIES	HISTORICAL OR REALISTIC FICTION	SCIENCE FICTION/ FANTASY/ HUMOR	FOLKTALE/ FABLE/ TALL TALE/ LEGEND	INFORMATION/ BIOGRAPHY/ ESSAY	POEMS	TOTAL NUMBER IN STUDENT TEXT
D. C. Heath (1993)	12	7	13	14	6	52 (590 pp.)
Harcourt Brace (1995)	7	11	6	8	12	44 (623 pp.)
Houghton Mifflin (1993)	5	6	3	14	13	41 (530 pp.)
Macmillan (1993)	7	2	5	10	18	42 (596 pp.)
Scott Foresman (1995)	15	6	14	17	15	67 (859 pp.)
Silver Burdett Ginn (1993)	11	10	4	11	11	47 (544 pp.)

cans) and selections about ethnic groups or characters not usually in an affirmative action category (such as the Amish, Greek Americans, or Italian Americans, even though this last group does constitute an affirmative action category in New York). The groups that are not in affirmative action categories are European ethnic groups and are sometimes referred to as "white ethnics."[19] Under foreign content, I distinguished between selections that originate or portray life in countries from which the groups in the affirmative action categories or their kin came (all non-European countries) and selections that originate or portray life in countries from which European ethnic groups or the ancestors of mainstream Americans came or which the latter also settled (e.g., Australia and Canada), today or years ago.

All of these categories and subcategories were needed for determining cultural bias. When a literature program is castigated as "Eurocentric," the epithet generally refers to selections by or about those in the mainstream and their kin in other parts of the world (as in British, Canadian, or Australian literature), today or many years ago—and to selections emanating from countries that those of European ancestry might see as their place of

TABLE 4

Distribution of Reading Selections in the Grade 6 Readers

SERIES	HISTORICAL OR REALISTIC FICTION	SCIENCE FICTION/ FANTASY/ HUMOR	FOLKTALE/ FABLE/ TALL TALE/ LEGEND	INFORMATION/ BIOGRAPHY/ ESSAY	POEMS	TOTAL NUMBER IN STUDENT TEXT
D. C. Heath (1993)	13	9	11	22	6	61 (587 pp.)
Harcourt Brace (1995)	15	6	0	11	12	44 (653 pp.)
Houghton Mifflin (1993)	9	1	6	12	18	46 (539 pp.)
Macmillan (1993)	13	2	1	8	22	46 (592 pp.)
Scott Foresman (1995)	13	8	3	26	13	63 (846 pp.)
Silver Burdett Ginn (1993)	14	6	6	12	12	50 (576 pp.)

origin (e.g., France, Germany, Italy). Hence, I have labeled the category for these selections "European" and the category for all the other cultural selections "non-European." Interestingly, the charge of Eurocentrism rarely, if ever, refers to selections about the acculturating experiences of these European ethnic groups in this country, for one very good reason: the typical classroom literature program has rarely included literature about these immigrant groups and their tensions and conflicts with the dominant culture—or, as the case is just as likely to be, with each other or other racial groups in this country.

Tables 5 and 6 shows the number of selections in each category as a percentage of the total number of selections. Somewhat surprisingly, the category with the highest percentages tends to be general content; indeed, the selections in this category range from about one-fifth to almost one-half of all selections in a reader. Houghton Mifflin and Macmillan have the highest percentages in this category in their grade 4 readers and two of the three highest percentages in their grade 6 readers, a reflection of the high number of poems and informational selections in these series. It is possible that having a large number of selections in this one category helps publishers cope with one of the dilemmas they now face. The larger

TABLE 5

Distribution of Content in the Reading Selections for Grade 4 as Percentages of the Total Number of Selections

GRADE 4 READER	AMERICAN	CONTENT		FOREIGN	CONTENT	GENERAL CONTENT	TOTAL NUMBER
	MAINSTREAM	ETHNIC		EUROPEAN	NON-EUROPEAN		
		NAA	AA				
D.C. Heath	42	2	17	11	2	25	N =52
Harcourt Brace	27	0	16	7	16	34	N =44
Houghton Mifflin	15	0	22	5	12	46	N =41
Macmillan	14	0	19	0	19	48	N =42
Scott Foresman	37	1	21	3	16	21	N =67
Silver Burdett Ginn	32	9	13	9	6	32	N =47

Note: NAA = Selections not about persons or an ethnic group in an affirmative action category. AA = Selections about persons or an ethnic group in an affirmative action category.

the number of selections with no readily identifiable cultural content, the smaller the number that convey any cultural content at all—and the fewer arguments about what that cultural content should be. Nevertheless, it is not possible or desirable to eliminate selections with cultural content altogether in the instructional readers, even if one's priorities are simply good writing and accurate information. There have to be stories in them. So what is at stake is the cultural content of those selections comprising one-half to four-fifths of the contents of the instructional readers.

What impressions might the selections with cultural content make as a whole on elementary school students? How strong a sense of our ethnic and racial diversity might students get from reading through an entire reader? The answer is: quite strong. As Figures 1 and 2 show, all series devote a generous number of selections to America's ethnic groups in their grades 4 and 6 readers. In grade 4, the number of selections with chiefly ethnic content or a focus on ethnic characters as a proportion of the total number with American content is one-third or a little over in D. C. Heath (31 percent), Harcourt Brace (37 percent), Scott Foresman (38 percent), and Silver Burdett Ginn (40 percent), and well over half in Macmillan (57 percent) and Houghton Mifflin (60 percent). In grade 6,

TABLE 6

Distribution of Content in the Reading Selections for Grade 6 as Percentages of the Total Number of Selections

GRADE 6 READER	AMERICAN	CONTENT		FOREIGN	CONTENT	GENERAL CONTENT	TOTAL NUMBER
	MAINSTREAM	ETHNIC NAA	AA	EUROPEAN	NON-EUROPEAN		
D.C. Heath	28	3	13	18	10	28	N =61
Harcourt Brace	23	0	27	14	2	34	N =44
Houghton Mifflin	17	0	30	0	13	39	N =46
Macmillan	9	2	22	7	17	43	N =46
Scott Foresman	27	0	31	11	8	22	N =63
Silver Burdett Ginn	14	0	18	16	12	40	N =50

Note: NAA = selections not about persons or an ethnic group in an affirmative action category. AA = selections about persons or an ethnic group in an affirmative action category.

FIGURE 1:

Ethnic Content as a Percentage of Total American Content in the Grade 4 Readers

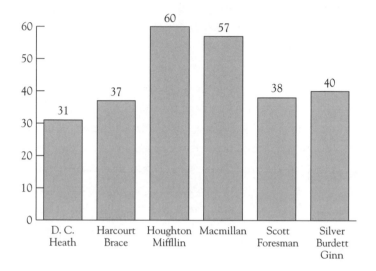

FIGURE 2:

Ethnic Content as a Percentage of Total American Content in the Grade 6 Readers

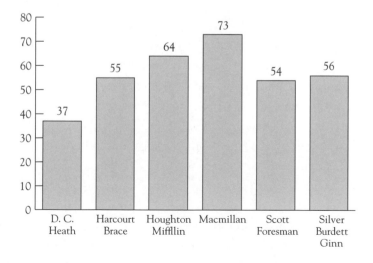

the proportions range from 37 percent in D. C. Heath, 54 percent in Scott Foresman, 55 percent in Harcourt Brace, and 56 percent in Silver Burdett Ginn, to 64 percent in Houghton Mifflin and 73 percent in Macmillan.

This generous view of American ethnicity now given to the elementary school child, however, is extremely skewed. Almost all the selections about ethnic groups or characters are about people in the affirmative action categories.[20] The few selections in grade 4 that are not in these categories are about the Amish, a Greek American family in the Great Depression, a contemporary Polish American family, an unspecified European immigrant family, and two groups of American Jewish families—a very limited view of the ethnic diversity of this country's inhabitants. An even more limited view is provided in the grade 6 readers. The few selections at this grade level are about undifferentiated European immigrants who came through Ellis Island, an Eastern European immigrant (probably Slavic) who became the inventor of robots, and an American Jewish family. Few elementary school students are likely to know that this ethnic profile bears no relationship to the ancestral or contemporary realities of our current population. I am not suggesting that fidelity to this country's ethnic profile should be a criterion for selecting stories for a reader. But if it were, it has been overwhelmingly violated in all the series.[21] According to the 1990 U.S. Census, descendants of five European ethnic groups alone (Germans, Irish, French, Italians, and Poles) constitute over 50 percent of the total population.

As Figures 3 and 4 show, the number of selections reflecting the cultures of non-European countries as a proportion of the total number of selections reflecting foreign countries also deviates considerably from the ancestral reality of our current population, over 70 percent of which is of European origin, excluding people classified as of Hispanic origin, some of whom are also of European origin. This number is much more than half in the Harcourt Brace, Houghton Mifflin, Macmillan, and Scott Foresman grade 4 readers; indeed, their percentages range from 60 percent to 100 percent. Their non-American selections tend to be set in China, Japan, Africa, Mexico, and other Central or South American countries. Only the D. C. Heath and Silver Burdett Ginn grade 4 readers have a larger number of selections about European countries (or countries settled by the British) as a proportion of the total number about foreign lands. Their non-American selections are set in such countries as England, Sweden,

FIGURE 5:

Ethnic American Content and Non-European Content as a Percentage of Total Cultural Content in the Grade 4 Readers

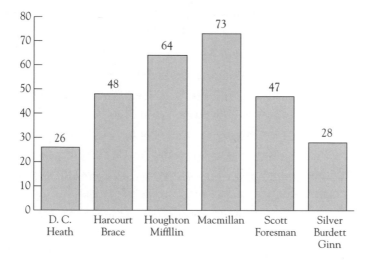

Note: *Ethnic American content in this figure refers only to affirmative action groups.*

FIGURE 6:

Ethnic American Content and Non-European Content as a Percentage of Total Cultural Content in the Grade 6 Readers

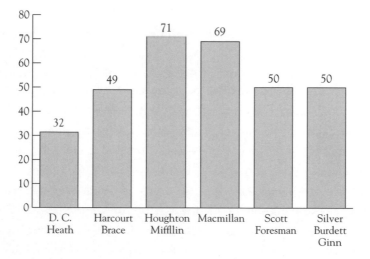

Note: *Ethnic American content in this figure refers only to affirmative action groups.*

Australia, and Finland. In four grade 6 readers—Houghton Mifflin, Macmillan, Scott Foresman, and Silver Burdett Ginn—the number of selections reflecting the culture of non-European countries as a proportion of the total number of selections about, or coming from, foreign lands also diverges considerably from the ancestral backgrounds of the majority of the inhabitants of this country. Indeed, in two—Houghton Mifflin and Macmillan—the proportions are 100 percent and 73 percent, respectively.

An even more telling representation of these two sets of deviations from demographic realities can be seen in Figures 5 and 6, which combine the number of selections about groups or people in the affirmative action categories with the number of selections about non-European people or countries as a proportion of the total number of selections with meaningful cultural content. In grade 4, the proportions are 26 percent for D. C. Heath, 28 percent for Silver Burdett Ginn, 47 percent for Scott Foresman, 48 percent for Harcourt Brace, 64 percent for Houghton Mifflin, and 73 percent for Macmillan. In grade 6, the proportions are 32 percent for D. C. Heath, 49 percent for Harcourt Brace, 50 percent for Silver Burdett Ginn, 50 percent for Scott Foresman, 69 percent for Macmillan, and 71 percent for Houghton Mifflin. In two series, therefore, students may well see America as a country with a chiefly non-European heritage, populated mostly by people from non-European countries. In two others, the proportions are about half and half. These are all highly skewed profiles of this country's current demographic realities and cultural history.

Ethnic Integration

In the course of reading through all the readers, my attention was caught by an occasional selection showing ethnic integration or cultural assimilation as a natural, if not prominent, feature of American community life. I call this category "Ethnic Integration" because it includes selections whose cast of characters have a variety of genuinely diverse ethnic names (e.g., Italian, Armenian, German, and Spanish), whose illustrations suggest children or adults of various races interacting together, or whose characters are portrayed as nonwhite but whose theme is nonethnic (e.g., the loneliness of an elderly person, or a father and son fishing together in a clearly American setting). These selections contrast markedly with those that focus only on a particular ethnic group, deal with themes relating only to the

FIGURE 5:

Ethnic American Content and Non-European Content as a Percentage of Total Cultural Content in the Grade 4 Readers

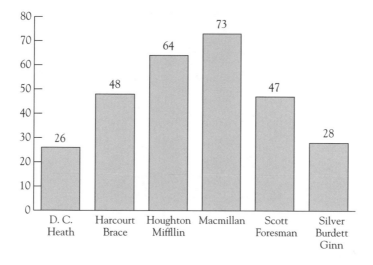

Note: *Ethnic American content in this figure refers only to affirmative action groups.*

FIGURE 6:

Ethnic American Content and Non-European Content as a Percentage of Total Cultural Content in the Grade 6 Readers

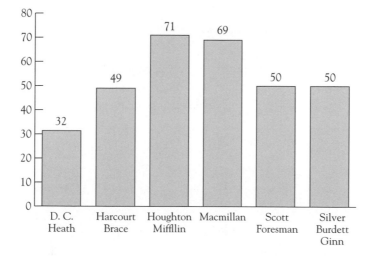

Note: *Ethnic American content in this figure refers only to affirmative action groups.*

group's life or history, and show the group having little, if any, social inter-action with other groups or the broader society at large.

There are a variety of ways in which ethnic integration is conveyed as a feature of American life. In some selections, it is dealt with explic-itly as a feature of American life. One example is a story in Harcourt Brace's grade 4 reader about a Japanese boy who comes to an American school and joins the baseball team. The story deals with the jealousy of the American boy whose position on the team is now in jeopardy be-cause of the Japanese boy's playing ability, ending up with the implica-tion that the competitive spirit is best directed against the other team than against those on one's own team even if at first they seemed like outsiders. Another example, in Scott Foresman's grade 4 reader, is a story about an American family of European descent with two adopted Korean children.

More subtle are stories in which ethnicity is never brought out ex-plicitly as an element of the story. These stories imply that people can dif-fer in race or ethnic background from Americans of European descent but can be otherwise undistinguishable as Americans. For example, D. C. Heath's grade 4 reader offers a biography of Wesley Paul, a young boy who wants to become a marathon runner. Nothing in the story suggests that his ethnic background played any role in his ambitions or achievements. We infer from the photographs accompanying the story that he may be a Korean American youngster, but we read the story for what it says about Wesley Paul as an individual, not as a representative of any group. This reader features another story like this worth mentioning: a true story about two winners of the Young American Medal for Bravery. That the two boys who rescued an elderly woman from her burning home in Vir-ginia Beach are black (as suggested by the illustrations) is never men-tioned; their ethnicity is irrelevant. It is their characters that readers are to respect. The Harcourt Brace grade 6 reader also features a selection telling about the deeds of bravery performed by children of different racial backgrounds without mentioning details in the text that identify their ethnic backgrounds.

Even when ethnicity has relevance in a story, whether or not tex-tual details reveal it, it can be dealt with matter of factly or unobtru-sively in an integrated setting. When dealt with in this way, students can learn a great deal about some of the realities of American history and community life despite the barrage of messages they pick up from other materials and the media insinuating that immigrants and black Americans have encountered, and continue to encounter, nothing but hostility in American public life. In Harcourt Brace's grade 4 reader, one story focuses on the competition for class president in a fourth grade with children of different backgrounds. What is at issue are leadership qualities, not ethnic considerations, although the ethnicity of the Puerto Rican boy who is one of the contenders is made quite clear by the details the author gives about his family life. In Harcourt Brace's grade 6 reader, a racially mixed neighborhood in Harlem, with black and white children playing together despite the lack of communication between the sets of parents, serves as the setting for a young black boy and his friends who are trying to teach a dog to talk. A different setting for the ethnic and civic integration that took place historically in this country appears in a selection in Silver Burdett Ginn's grade 4 reader about a young boy in a Greek immigrant family growing up during the depression in upstate New York. The names of characters and places suggest the multiethnic nature of the community, but ethnicity does not drive the plot of the story. Neither does it drive the plot in a play in the D. C. Heath grade 6 reader about a multiracial group of children trying to come up with ideas to make money.

The excerpt from *Bicycle Rider* in Silver Burdett Ginn's grade 4 reader is perhaps the best example of this phenomenon because it conveys a reality of earlier American community life that is very difficult to find in the readers. The story is a true one of young Marshall Taylor, a boy from a poor black family in a small Indiana town in the last decade of the nineteenth century, who grew up to be the first black participant in national bicycle races in this country and a world champion bicyclist. Nothing in the story itself reveals that the family is black. We learn that he is black only from the illustrations and the epilogue. In the selection, people interact in this small midwestern town without any hint that racial differences matter or that there are cultural differences between white and black families of moderate means. A decent civic community is portrayed.

In some cases, ethnic integration is suggested by the illustrations accompanying a selection whose central characters (if there are any) are not ethnic or chiefly ethnic. In a D. C. Heath grade 4 story about book report day in a typical American classroom, the teacher happens to be black. In a story about one of Encyclopedia Brown's escapades, in Houghton Mifflin's grade 4 reader, the only adult character, a dentist, is illustrated as black. In Silver Burdett Ginn's grade 4 reader, in a story about a white boy and his pet, the pet store owner is portrayed as black. Also in that reader, photographs accompanying an informational selection about plants and flowers show a multiracial assortment of children. Although this way of showing ethnic integration is often scoffed at by those who believe it is little more than painting by number (making faces different colors) and glosses over ethnic or cultural differences, it is appropriate as long as it is not the only way it is shown in the selections. It is an authentic feature of American society and accurately portrays contemporary American society.

Sometimes ethnic integration appears in the names of characters or business establishments in the context of cultural assimilation. Some of the best examples occur in Silver Burdett Ginn's grade 4 reader. One selection, about a Thanksgiving Day gathering in the home of a Polish American family (identified as such in the student text), conveys the multiethnic America any city dweller would recognize as a reality. It refers to a professor named Mazzacchi, a Spanish grocery store, a German market, an Indian spice store, and Murphy's Butcher Shop. Another is the novella entitled *Two Piano Tuners*, whose major characters and their circle of friends have names and a focus of interest—classical music—that suggest they are Jewish. But there are no identifiable ethnic customs or foods, and the setting is clearly American. A story with clearer ethnic touches in both the Macmillan and Harcourt Brace grade 6 readers shows a seventh-grade French language class that seems to consist only of Mexican American students.

Unfortunately, selections that suggest ethnic integration and cultural assimilation as a part of life in our civic communities are small in number (and not always great literature). At first, this may seem surprising in the light of the fact that a large majority of all the selections in the readers were written in recent decades, not before World War II when most northern cities were characterized by separate ethnic neighborhoods and segregation existed in the many areas of community life. But the paucity of selections showing ethnic integration and cultural assimilation must be judged as a reflection of editorial policy—or the advice of a publisher's academic consultants. And there are fewer such selections in the grade 6 readers than in the grade 4 readers, not a good sign.

Gender Portrayal

A strong feminist perspective comes through directly in just a few selections, particularly in those about females who have been pathbreakers in their field, such as the story about Nellie Bly, the journalist, in Silver Burdett Ginn's grade 4 reader. The editors' introduction in the student text reads as follows: "One hundred years ago, if you were a girl, nobody even thought of asking you what you wanted to be when you grew up. Women were expected to stay at home. When Elizabeth Cochrane decided in 1885 that she was going to be a reporter, she knew she would have to fight for herself as well as for all the people whose stories she wanted to tell" (p. 369).

A strong feminist perspective can also be picked up in dialogue clearly influenced by our own times. One example appears in Silver Burdett Ginn's grade 6 reader in an otherwise moving piece of historical fiction about a special family quilt, handed down for generations, that has been used to comfort and heal family members when they were sick. When the sick boy in a dream encounters the ancestor who made the quilt, she tells him that she once wished she could draw pictures, go to London, and study to be an artist, but couldn't do so because "a girl doesn't do those things."

A strong feminist perspective is often reflected in the material in the teacher edition, as suggested by the quotations in the epigraph for this chapter. Here it is objectionable—not because the stories themselves contain problematic material, but because these Appreciating Cultures suggestions turn politically innocent pieces of fine literature that have been popular for many decades into fodder for discussions of women as victims of society today.

For the most part, however, a feminist perspective is reflected more subtly—and more appropriately—in the major characters in the selections and in what they do. Girls are scuba divers or are lost in the wilderness and survive by their wits or with the help of Indians. The only problematic selections are the numerous feminist fairy tales. They are neither subtle nor clever.

Although it is fortunately not across the board, the animus against white males is quite visible in a few readers. For example, in Houghton Mifflin's readers for grades 4 and 6, there are no more than one or two selections with white American boys as major characters. In the grade 6 reader, a white male does not appear until the seventh selection, a story about a young boy who learns he must be more sensitive to his father's feelings about him and who sobs deeply at the point in the story when he develops this insight. The author's message is clear: white males need to develop more sensitivity to others. The editors' message is also clear: boys should be seen crying so that the stereotype of the female as the one who cries is broken. (Although these messages may not be objectionable or inappropriate in themselves, it raises questions when there are no stories in which females exhibit these behaviors or in which males appear strong and determined. Indeed, I cannot recall one story in these readers in which a female cries.) Macmillan has a grand total of one story with a white male as a leading character in its grade 4 reader. Harcourt Brace has a few more in its grade 4 reader, although the first one does not appear until page 170, a long way into the reader.

The grossly diminished presence of white males is apparent in other ways. Of the eighty or so people singled out for attention in Harcourt Brace's grade 4 teacher guide in a regular one-page feature entitled "multicultural connections," my research assistants and I could determine only five white American males: Henry Ford, Walter Reed, Alexander Calder, Babe Ruth, and Simon Flexner. Many of those mentioned, whether American or not, must be as obscure to the teacher as they were to me— for example, Michael Werikhe (Kenya), leader of a crusade to save the black rhinoceros; and Emperor Shung-Nung (China). The few selected for attention in a similar feature in the student text itself suggests even more clearly the narrowness of the editors' understanding of this country's diversity. Of the eight people brought directly to students' attention, four are black Americans (Jackie Joyner-Kersee, Augusta Baker, Martin Luther King, Jr., and Rosa Parks) and one is Japanese American (Kristi Yamaguchi). Many Americans of Spanish-speaking background may be surprised and concerned to learn that Fidel Castro (rather than, say, Henry Cisneros or Cesar Chavez) is one of the two representatives of Spanish-speaking males (the other is Dr. Eduardo Matos Moctezuma of Mexico). The eighth is a disabled person (Jim Abbott).

In general, white males seem to have greater opportunity for inclusion in a reader if an author teams them up with a girl in a story or if the reader features mystery stories or science fiction. White males no longer have a future in stories about the settling of the West. In fact, many students may well end up thinking that the West was settled chiefly by females, most often accompanied by their parents. Four readers feature excerpts from Laura Ingalls Wilder's works, and several other stories about the settling of the West feature females as the central character. A white boy is the central figure in only one story about the West: a tale about a dogsled race in Wyoming that the boy wins because of a magnanimous gesture by an elderly Shoshone Indian.

Religion in America in the 1990s

For many years, the role of religious beliefs in American history was all but banned as a focus of attention in history textbooks. However, major events and movements with religious dimensions are now covered more thoroughly than they were ten or thirty years ago in all leading history textbooks, although more adequately in some than in others.[22] For that reason, I was interested in looking at how religious beliefs might be portrayed in the selections in these readers, if featured in them at all.

It is manifestly clear to any serious observer of the American scene that although contemporary America is a far more secular society than the America of 100 or 200 years ago, religious beliefs continue to play a significant role in the personal lives of most Americans as well as in public affairs. It is a frequently noted phenomenon, substantiated by cross-cultural survey data on church attendance and support, that more Americans practice their professed faiths than do the inhabitants of any other modern industrialized democracy in the world.[23] Moreover, about 87 percent of Americans identify themselves as Christians, although there is probably more religious diversity in this country than in any other country in the world. Religion remains a vital element in American culture, regardless of race, ethnicity, or gender. Indeed, surveys of volunteerism show that Americans still give more of their volunteer time to activities connected to their religious communities than to any other volunteer activity.

One therefore has to be struck by how little contemporary readers show the America that any impartial observer can see. My research assistants and I went through all the selections in the grade 4 and grade 6 readers, noting anything that suggested a spiritual dimension to the characters' lives, for example, when a selection mentioned a religious festival, a religious ritual or ceremony, the Bible, attending church, the existence of a church, parochial school, catechism class, Sunday school, saying grace before a meal, crossing oneself, praying, or a minister, priest, nun, rabbi, or other cleric. These indexes of religious significance were not completely absent across readers and appeared more frequently in some series than in others. But for the most part, any child reading the selections in any one reader would be unlikely to sense the enormous influence of religious belief in private and public life in this country.

Several inaccurate impressions may emerge from these readers regarding the presence of a spiritual life in early and contemporary American life. The readers imply that a spiritual dimension to communal life exists chiefly among the Indians and, to some extent, among the Mexican Americans. Occasionally a selection about a black community portrays its spiritual life, but not as often as for the others. Students are likely to see symbols of Catholicism in the selections about Mexicans or Mexican Americans because writers from this group naturally include mention of the religious symbols, authorities, and ceremonies that were prominent in their own childhoods. Students will not see the Catholic faith observed by members of other ethnic groups in the United States that are Catholic because, with one exception, there are no selections about identifiable members of these groups in the readers.

The readers also imply that the Indians have been the most deeply spiritual people in the world, and with a spirituality that borders on superstition. This image is so pervasive that it is ironic at a time when educators express concern about the creation of stereotypes, especially those with a negative cast. It would not be surprising if the many selections about the Central, South, and North American Indians in these readers tend to foster a stereotype of Indians as a basically nonintellectual people, relying not on thinking but on their instincts, on appeasing the ancient spirits that roam the earth, on animal gods, and on traditional learnings. The unintended implication is that they are incapable of fitting into modern society, and several selections in these readers do show Indian children or adults who feel uncomfortable in the modern world around them. The image of the entrepreneurial Indian in the casino business emanating from the media today must pose a jarring contrast to the image conveyed in the readers.

Perhaps most surprising of all, the readers imply that Protestant religiosity is an almost completely historical phenomenon. Except for the selection on the Amish in one reader, there is not even a hint in these readers that an extremely large number of Americans profess to be devout observers of the religion of the majority of Americans. The Bible is suggested as a living source of guidance in just a few stories, all of which take place many years ago. Characters never interact with other characters who might be viewed as evangelicals or fundamentalists. Nor do the communal activities of white Protestants appear in the background of any story. Since they do appear in books, stories in children's magazines, reading textbooks, and other publications designed to serve the educational needs of Christian day schools (and many home schoolers), it is clear that the editors or series' authors have avoided them like the plague. That such a large number of Americans are totally ignored in the context of an avowed attempt to portray contemporary America's diversity is striking testimony to the narrowness of the vision brought to the education of young Americans by those who have claimed an intention to broaden it.

Most of the references to religious practices or beliefs are in two grade 4 readers. In the Scott Foresman grade 4 reader, students can read about Laura Ingalls Wilder's family going to church, a Christmas celebration among Mexican Americans, a family with a child with cerebral palsy going to church at Christmastime, a black community that participates actively in its church and sings the gospels, a boy who prays, and a boy who crosses himself. In several stories that take place beyond U.S. borders, students can also read about Indian groups who believe in rain spirits or a god of peace and the Muslim beliefs of the bedouins.

In the Silver Burdett Ginn grade 4 reader, students can read about a black family that says grace before meals, the celebration of Hanukah by Orthodox Jews in Brooklyn, a boy who goes to Sunday school and lives in a house with a Christmas wreath on it, a Puerto Rican American family with a picture of the Virgin Mary on the wall, an informational selection about the origins of words that notes some which come from the Bible, a

Wilder excerpt showing children praying before bedtime, and a poem set in the Southwest that seems to be a spiritual celebration of nature, in addition to a story about a Finnish family celebrating Christmas and decorating a Christmas tree.

In the other grade 4 readers, there are no more than one or two stories in each that hint at the religious dimension of the lives of their characters, suggesting by contrast with the other two readers some editorial or authorial sensitivity to the subject and the crucial role of the editor or authors in the choice of selections. There are references to religious values, symbols, ceremonies, and authorities in a few stories in each of the grade 6 readers, but many fewer than in grade 4.

It is not clear why there are so few references to the religious practices and beliefs of contemporary Americans in the readers. Are editors afraid that their series will be charged with violating the separation of church and state? Surely elementary school teachers who are expected to deal with sex education should also be capable of explaining religious symbols and practices when they appear in a story without seeming to proselytze. When the stress is on understanding the culture of various social groups, it seems misleading to provide students with selections that omit a highly significant element in the culture of most groups in this country, especially that of black Americans and newer immigrant groups.

A COMPARISON OF CONTEMPORARY READERS WITH THE EARLIER READERS

How do the results of my survey compare with what Iiams and Vitz found in their surveys of earlier readers? When we look at the content of these six grade 4 and 6 readers from the perspective of the questions that Charlotte Iiams and Paul Vitz explored, we need to keep in mind that Vitz looked at grade 3 and grade 6 readers in eleven series published in the early 1980s, and Iiams randomly surveyed the contents of a smaller number of readers in different decades over the course of the century. With respect to overt civic content, there is very little reflecting Iiams's six indexes to civic attitudes in these readers. In today's readers, selections about national symbols and songs are almost nonexistent at these two grade levels. In the grade 4 readers, the only national American holiday that manages to get some attention is Thanksgiving—in three selections.[24] I found only one mention of the Fourth of July—in a story about a former steel mill town that appears in both the Macmillan and Harcourt Brace grade 4 reader.

Among the 1993 and 1995 grade 6 readers I examined, we can go from famine to feast. Harcourt Brace has almost nothing to encourage positive civic sensibilities; indeed, it seems to go out of its way in this grade to create negative ones. A Rod Serling play portrays average, small-town Americans as people who are so filled with hate, prejudice, and suspicions of others that they end up destroying each other. This reader also includes a few selections that raise the issue of racism in relation to blacks, as well as two selections on the Vietnamese that are somewhat negative to Americans. In the one that talks about the cultural adjustments the Vietnamese have to make here, the author (and the editors) fail to take advantage of the opportunity to draw students' attention to the presence and importance of our civic culture, as if they no longer see basic differences between our culture and the cultures of most of the immigrants coming here today. Houghton Mifflin's sole contribution to the development of civic sensibilities at this grade level is a story about the internment of West Coast Japanese Americans during World War II.

The scale is slightly tipped the other way in two other readers. The Macmillan reader offers an ode to Martin Luther King, Jr., and the Scott Foresman reader, in a startling display of patriotic sentiment, includes John Greenleaf Whittier's "Barbara Frietchie," although the label of "classic poem" given it by the editors in the table of contents may hint to some students that it is by a dead white male and thus old-fashioned or of little relevance today. Thus, one cannot help but be impressed by D. C. Heath's effort in grade 6. Among other selections, D. C. Heath includes two pieces on the Statue of Liberty and Ellis Island; the folk song and legend "Sweet Betsy of Pike"; stories about Lewis and Clark's expedition and Sacajawea; and stories about a successful Mexican American entrepreneur, an Eastern European–born inventor of robots, and a female lighthouse keeper in mid-nineteenth-century Maine. Silver Burdett Ginn's reader is neutral at this grade level, with no pieces with anti-American bias or patriotic thrust.

What is in grades 4 and 6, however, is not a completely accurate indication of civic content in the readers. The content of the grade 5 readers needs to be taken into account because it is the grade in which students traditionally study American history. Most of the readers do offer selections to accompany this emphasis in the social studies class. Vitz's survey inadvertently resulted in a much more jaundiced view of the content of reading series in the late 1970s and early 1980s than it would have had he also noted the content of the grade 5 readers.

In the grade 5 readers in the series I examined, editorial sensitivity to the need to develop students' sense of membership in their national civic community is evident, although the depth of this sensitivity varies considerably. Houghton Mifflin offers a single informational selection on immigrants to this country. Scott Foresman also offers a selection on an immigrant to America, but also features a photobiography of Abraham Lincoln, the only appearance he makes in all six series in these three grades. Macmillan includes an excerpt from Walt Whitman's "Song of the Open Road" and a fictionalized biography of Benjamin Franklin with a mouse as the narrator. Harcourt Brace provides two-page photo-essays on the American Revolution and "Women in Washington," a view of historical pathbreakers, in addition to a number of pieces with historical settings and allusions, from pre-Revolutionary America and the days of the underground railroad to a Paul Bunyan tale and a poem on Johnny Appleseed by Rosemary and Stephen Vincent Benét. With civic content in its grade 6 reader, D. C. Heath uses its grade 5 reader for several selections with historical settings ranging from pre-Revolutionary America to the settling of the West. Silver Burdett Ginn pulls out all the stops at this grade level; it features Walt Whitman's "I Hear America Singing," an article on today's immigrants, and, in a unit entitled "Land of the Free," articles on the White House and the Liberty Bell, an excerpt from a biography of Benjamin Banneker on designing Washington, D.C., an essay on "What Is an American," Katherine Lee Bates's "America the Beautiful," and the Thanksgiving play excerpt from Nicholasa Mohr's *Felita*. Silver Burdett Ginn deserves commendations for the breadth and depth of the civic content in its grade 5 reader.

The limited amount of civic content in these readers overall is matched by the profile of significant Americans deemed worthy of attention through biographical selections. To be complete on this question, I include the subjects of the biographical selections in the grade 5 readers as well as in the readers for grades 4 and 6. The names that would be familiar to many adults today are Marian Anderson, Benjamin Banneker, Jackie Robinson, Bill Cosby, Matthew Henson (the codiscoverer of the

North Pole), George Washington Carver, Roberto Clemente, Sacajawea, Amelia Earhart, Rachel Carson, Nellie Bly, Martin Luther King, Jr., astronaut Sally Ride, Bonnie St. John (a young woman with one leg who became an Olympic ski medalist), Elizabeth Blackwell, Helen Keller, Abraham Lincoln, Benjamin Franklin, James Audubon, and Walt Disney. There are also stories on Hans Moravec, an inventor of robots; the cartoonist Jim Davis; Laurence Yep, a contemporary author whose work is featured in all series; Jacob Lawrence, the first successful black painter in this country; and Faith Ringgold, a contemporary black artist and writer. Of all these people, Robinson, Clemente, Ride, and Ringgold are the only Americans featured twice across series in these grades.

What is striking about this list of people is the narrowness of its portrayal of America's ethnic diversity. Not one well-known American from a European ethnic group is included (Lincoln, Keller, Blackwell, Franklin, Carson, Ride, and Disney are all from the Anglo-Saxon Protestant mainstream). Even more startling is the impoverished sense of American achievement in science and technology conveyed by the list despite American pre-eminence today and historically in these areas—only one inventor (Moravec), but no Thomas Edison, Alexander Graham Bell, Elias Howe, John Hayes Hammond, James Watson, Albert Sabin, or Jonas Salk, for example. George Washington Carver as a scientist bears a heavy representative burden here. Nor are there any significant entrepreneurs such as Henry Ford, George Eastman, S. B. Fuller, or George Westinghouse, or even contemporary ones such as Bill Gates or An Wang. And with the exception of Abraham Lincoln, all the presidents are gone, from George Washington, Thomas Jefferson, and James Madison to the two Roosevelts and John F. Kennedy.

This is not to say that young students will learn nothing more about American history than what is conveyed by these biographical sketches or the civic content elaborated on above. (Although they are studying some American history in their social studies classes, it is not clear that they are learning much there, according to the 1994 NAEP assessment of U.S. history.)[25] In some series, a fair amount of American history can be gleaned from some of the pieces of realistic or historical fiction, or from a few of the informational articles. Of the almost two dozen selections in the grade 4 readers that seemed to provide some historical information, over a dozen are about the settling of the West, all set in the latter half of the 1800s or around the turn of the century, almost always accompanied by selections about the Indian tribes in the West—usually implying their victimization by the settlers. That seems to have become an almost de rigueur pairing: no stories about the settling of the West unless accompanied by stories about Indians, preferably victimized Indians. To sum up, it seems that the trends Iiams and Vitz detected have continued, if not accelerated.

———————

There are three major academic problems apparent in today's readers. The first is cultural dishonesty. The number of selections with cultural content about what is called the American mainstream is not high in five of the six series and seems to be at the point of disappearing in two of them. Children clearly need to learn how to read nonfiction, textbook excerpts, and poetry, but it is not at all clear why these genres could not contain more cultural content than they now do about mainstream history, our political process, and significant leaders. There seems to be a relationship between the increase in selections about ethnic groups in the affirmative action categories and non-European peoples, and the increase in general content. The net effect is the disappearing of an American culture as a whole, as we see in the percentages in the first column in Tables 5 and 6, especially in the grade 6 readers.

The second problem is intellectual dishonesty. Stories about the great achievements in American science, technology, and political life in the past 200 years are missing—and they are missing, it seems, simply because a story about them would call attention to a white male. The attention accorded to the achievements of such women as Sally Ride, Nellie Bly, and Amelia Earhart (in American space exploration, journalism, and international flight, respectively) is dishonest when the men who made the original breakthroughs in these fields are completely ignored. Children should be able to read stories about both males and females of distinction. It is highly contradictory for a country that eagerly seeks to develop greater interest in science and mathematics in its youngsters to withhold from them stories about those who were responsible for its most important scientific and technological achievements. When a story about Amelia Earhart is accompanied by a poem about the Wright Brothers (a touch that reflects some creative thinking by the D. C. Heath editors to address the neglect of the real pioneers in the history of American aviation), something is backward even though the poem is by such gifted writers as Rosemary and Stephen Vincent Benét. Students should be reading a story about the Wright Brothers (and Charles Lindbergh) first.

That American students are not learning about famous American inventors, discoverers, or scientists, female or male, in their reading or social studies classes is suggested by the results of a small study I conducted with data from a statewide assessment of fifth-grade students in Massachusetts in November 1997.[26] In response to an open-ended question about the inventor they might like to meet if they could go back in time, only 55 percent could even name an inventor, scientist, or discoverer, and most of these students provided highly inaccurate information about the person they identified. Among the most discouraging findings of this study was the almost total absence of any females in the list of names students came up with. The sole female in the almost 800 responses I read was Ruth Wakefield, the "inventor" of "chocolate chip cookies." Elementary school students are likely to be learning little about presidents, too. Sol Stern, a New York City parent, reports asking his third-grade son whether he had ever been taught about George Washington. His son looked at him and asked: "George Washington Carver?"[27]

The third problem is demographic dishonesty. The real diversity of the United States has been almost completely suppressed in five of the six series. The almost total exclusion of stories touching in some way on the historical or continuing presence of America's European ethnic groups does not speak well for the integrity of an educational philosophy claiming that students should be taught respect for the cultural heritages of all Americans. It may well be that most members of European ethnic groups have assimilated into the American mainstream (as have many members of Asian and Latin American immigrant groups), but historical selections about European ethnic groups are as valid as historical selections about non-European ethnic groups in this country. One might also raise eyebrows about the series' failure to show the ethnic diversity among black Americans themselves today. They are not a monolithic group. Although there may not yet be good fictional literature by Ethiopian Americans or Haitian Americans, surely there must be well written articles on them. And why not something on Colin Powell, at the least?

What students see in the selections, one must remember, is a function of what selections editors or series' authors choose to include in the readers. If these instructional readers were designed to help children grasp this country's diversity along its most meaningful dimensions, then the readers are a sociological failure. Indeed, they portray a mythical country bearing as little resemblance to reality as the readers of fifty years ago were perceived to bear.

We do not know the extent to which children have had their understanding of this country's diversity warped not only by skewed reading programs but also by skewed history textbooks. But it would not be surprising if most children now believe that white Americans comprise a cultural monolith. They may well think that black Americans do too. As I discuss more fully in later chapters, many educational researchers and faculty at schools of education are now doing their best, despite the daily realities of the cities and suburbs they live and work in, to convince each other, their students, and the teachers, parents, and school-age children they may work with that culture is a phenomenon that maps isomorphically onto skin color and inheres in it.

The other danger in presenting American pluralism in oversimplified and incomplete ways is, as sociologist Nathan Glazer, comments, "hypostatization" of identities and cultures. As he notes in a book on immigrant America, "We fall into the danger, by presenting a conception of separate and different groups fixed through time as distinct elements in our society, of making our future one which conforms to our teaching, of arresting the processes of change and adaptation that have created a common society."[28] The traditional openness and fluidity of American society are in serious danger of disappearing as a motivating force in children's lives—not because this openness and fluidity no longer exist but because textbook editors and authors are imposing a spurious and artificial ethnic or racial grid onto the images children are forming of themselves and others.

Glazer is not the only one to worry about the possible loss of authentic choice and self-determination in the United States. In his review of Glazer's latest book, Anthony Appiah offers a perspective similar to Glazer's, as I discuss in Chapter 1.[29] He points out that the "primary demand of multiculturalism—to teach children mutual tolerance and respect—does not mean, as many contemporary advocates of multiculturalism assume, that the curriculum must be radically changed by the addition of a large number of new subjects." To open "young people to the variety of social identities in the world," he asserts, does not mean that one also has to force them "to live within separate spheres defined by the common culture of their race, religion, or ethnicity." Yet it is another irony that a deeply appealing faith in limitless horizons is being subverted not by reality but by the narrow views of those who profess to seek equity and justice for poor minority children.

FOUR

THE CORRUPTION OF CHILDREN'S LITERATURE AND LITERARY STUDY

Appreciating Cultures. During the middle to late 1800s, the United States government encouraged immigration by offering free land in the West to anyone who would settle on it and build a homestead. Between 400,000 and 600,000 families were given land on which to build farms and homes. Thousands of Native Americans had their land taken from them by the government and were forced to leave their homes. Have students discuss books they have read or films they have seen about Native Americans and white settlers. Ask them how the Native Americans' position is represented.

—From Silver Burdett Ginn's Teacher Edition for Grade 4, p. 274, *before* "Pettranella" is read.

Appreciating Cultures. Tell students to imagine how homesteaders and Native Americans must have felt during the settling of the frontier. Discuss how they would feel if the government suddenly told them they had to leave so that people from other parts of the country and the world could move in. What are some problems that would develop? Have students find out what happened to the Native Americans when they were forced out.

—From Silver Burdett Ginn's Teacher Edition for Grade 4, p. 280, *after* "Pettranella" is read.

IF YOU tried to guess what "Pettranella" is about, based on what the Silver Burdett Ginn teacher guide suggests telling students for "building background" for the story and for discussion afterward, you might well think that it was about a conflict between some Native Americans and some homesteaders. You would be quite wrong. There isn't a single encounter between a Native American and the family in the story, nor are Native Americans ever mentioned. "Pettranella" is about a family that left Europe by ship, landed in Canada, and then traveled overland to settle in Wisconsin, leaving a beloved grandmother behind in the old country. Pettranella is the young daughter who finds a way to keep a promise she made to her grandmother involving a gift of seeds.[1]

The function of these regular pre- and postselection pedagogical suggestions in the Silver Burdett Ginn teacher guides, called Appreciating Cultures, is to identify a historical and cultural context for a selection *and* the political issue or policy that will enable teachers through class discussions and related activities to cultivate the particular feelings that multiculturalists want students to acquire toward the issue or policy and toward American society. The Appreciating Cultures sections shown at the start of this chapter have the potential to do this well with respect to the homesteading policy and the pioneers who settled the West. By placing this immigrant story solely in the context of the government's homesteading policy and the fate of the Native Americans, they can elicit negative feelings toward the European-descended population of this country (as the ones who benefited from this policy) as well as the homesteading policy. They can also stimulate negative feelings toward the characters in the story, reduce students' identification with them, and diminish sympathy for its politically innocent theme (the wildflowers that spring up every year from a gift of seeds are a lovely way to remind the family of an older, loved family member left forever in the family's move to a faraway new land). They may even be able to foster a hostile attitude to all pioneer stories, no matter how appealing their characters or themes may be.

These sections serve anti-intellectual as well as antiliterary and anti-civic purposes. For "Pettranella," not only does the postselection section want students to focus on imagining their own and other people's feelings, it also gives them a slanted and incomplete historical and cultural context for the piece. Students are not given, here or in the selection itself, any details on the language, customs, and beliefs of these European immigrants in order to help students appreciate the immigrants' culture. Nor are they told why this family left Europe, what conditions caused them (and many others like them) to leave their homeland, what gave them courage to travel halfway across the world to an unknown country to live, and what alternatives they had. This information is as legitimate and as significant a part of the background to the piece as is the U.S. government's homesteading policy. Without this information, students cannot discuss sensibly what other courses of action may have been possible for those nineteenth-century European (and Asian) immigrants who left their homelands for the New World in order to create a better life for themselves or simply to survive. In addition, the context given for "Pettranella" disassociates it from its genre: other immigrant stories to America. What the average reading teacher may not realize is that in the name of cultivating "social awareness" and a sensitivity to others, she has been co-opted into using literary study not to develop literary appreciation or analytical thinking but to shape her students' feelings about our society and certain social issues in a particular way.

———————

Several decades ago, a group calling themselves whole language educators sought to eliminate the use of basal readers on the grounds that they were driven by skills teaching. They saw no virtue in beginning reading materials that were constructed of either common but irregularly pronounced words (such as *said, pretty,* or *mother*)[2] or phonetically spelled words (such as *man, keep,* or *hold*), in the first case, to help children develop an initial sight vocabulary, in the second, to help them learn the regular relationships between sounds and letters. This emphasis on skills, they asserted, resulted in unmotivating literature for children to read. Without any research evidence, they claimed that the use of constructed, adapted, or abridged selections in older basal readers was one reason that many children had not learned to read or to love reading years ago. To survive this attack, educational publishers began using only "authentic" literature in their basals, and reduced the amount of skills instruction in their teacher guides. Eventually publishers began putting some skills teaching back into their teacher guides in response to teacher demand and student need. But whole language educators never let up on their claims for the benefits of authentic literature.

At its inception in the 1970s, the multicultural movement was independent of the whole language movement, but as it evolved and gained momentum, it allied itself philosophically to the whole language movement's insistence on authenticity because this concept covered the kinds of reading selections that multicultural educators wanted in the curriculum. They too wanted authentic works in the readers—by and about members of the social groups that they felt had not been portrayed (or portrayed adequately or positively) in reading textbooks.

Publishers of the basal reading series learned their catechism well. They now make sure they highlight the use of authentic literature and the benefits supposedly gained from its use. For example, Scott Foresman proclaims that "children learn best when reading authentic literature" as the first of its six guiding principles.[3] In its statement of program philosophy, Houghton Mifflin trumpets that "prioritized strategies and skills, important to the reading process, are best learned through authentic literature."[4]

Alas, words can easily be unhitched from their original semantic moorings over time. One might well think that the adjective *authentic* is synonymous with *the highest quality*, but it is not. Most reading selections today probably do appear exactly as their authors composed them, making them unquestionably authentic. But many are not examples of literature except in the generic sense that any kind of text, no matter what its quality, constitutes literature of a sort. These selections are what I call "pseudo-literature." Some are benign in their rhetorical thrust even if they have little literary or intellectual merit. Others embody the anticivic and anti-intellectual spirit of many education professors today. It is not just the presence of pseudo-literature in children's readers that is problematic; it is also the pedagogy accompanying them. This pedagogy is especially problematic because it has rapidly spread like a malignant cancer from the diseased tissue of pseudo-literature to the healthy tissue of authentic children's literature. This pedagogy constitutes a radical departure from accepted and acceptable criteria for literary study for children. It makes literature for children a stimulus for either sociological analyses of their society or political activism. And it has encouraged as one of their responses to literature an identification with the feelings of groups deemed to be victimized and an implicit antagonism to those who are to be perceived as their victimizers, as the material in the epigraph illustrates.

PSEUDO-LITERATURE AND ITS USES

Pseudo-literature serves several purposes for multicultural educators today. It can feature members of particular groups of people who might not otherwise be portrayed in the "right" number of selections (or at all) if genuine literature had to be used. It can highlight those social communities or natural environments that children are to see as the victims of a prejudiced and exploitative white society and simultaneously create the correct stereotypes of this society. It can plant the seeds of contemporary social dogma in children's minds in offhand, unobtrusive, casual ways. Genuine children's literature cannot easily be used for these purposes. The following selections illustrate these various functions of pseudo-literature. They appear in Scott Foresman's readers, but I do not intend to imply that this publisher is the only one to use pseudo-literature.

Its first and third use can be seen in a selection in its grade 4 reader describing a family with two adopted Korean sons.[5] The first four paragraphs reproduced here open the selection, the fourth appears about midway, and the last paragraph closes the selection.

The Levins are a family. Eric and Joshua Levin are brothers. Their dog is named Melby.

Eric plays the cello, and Joshua loves to play Frisbee. Both boys are adopted, and both are Korean by birth.

The Levins adopted them when they were very young. Eric, who is ten years old, was only a few months old when he became part of the Levin family. Joshua was two and a half years old and is eleven now. Eric doesn't remember anything before he came to America, but Joshua has a few memories of his Korean foster family. Eric and Joshua are brothers through adoption. Each boy has a different biological mother, but in the Levin household they are brothers.

The boys feel special about being Korean and a little different from their friends. They think about Korea and wonder what it's like. Their parents bought them a book that has pictures of Korea in it, and the boys enjoy looking through it. They continue to keep the clothing they wore when they came to America in special boxes, and they like to take out the tiny clothes and look at them. . . .

The Levins like to do things together. On weekends they go walking in the woods. They also like to cook together. They have learned how to make some Korean dishes. One of their favorites is *bul-go-gee*, a sliced marinated steak. They serve it with rice and *kim chee*, a pickled cabbage dish that is a staple of the Korean diet. The boys enjoy shopping at the Korean market, and they help with the cutting and slicing that is involved in the preparation of the meal. The best part, of course, is when the work is over and the family sits down to dinner. . . .

The Levins are not a typical family. No one in the family is biologically related to any of the others. Nevertheless they are a family because they choose to be one. Like other families, they live together and play together. Most important, they share work and share love.

Offering no dramatic tension, no examples of unusual achievement, no complex characters, and few complex sentences, the selection was likely chosen because it shows Asian Americans and has a clear piece of social dogma to impart to children—this one on what defines a family. As suggested in the closing paragraph, all that is necessary for a group of unrelated people to be considered a family is the fact that they have chosen to live together.

The selection also illustrates the author's belief that students acquire a significant understanding of another culture when they learn about its daily cuisine and see the names of its common foods in its own language. The teacher guide uses the paragraph on Korean foods to promote the idea that the food we choose to eat should reflect our cultural "heritage."[6] Under the caption of a Teachable Moment on "cultural differences," the guide points out:

Students may not know why the boys make and eat Korean foods. Help them understand that even though the boys are American, they are Korean too and need to understand their background and heritage. Eating Korean foods reminds them of their homeland. Invite students to imagine what it would be like to move from their neighborhoods to a country where people speak a different language, eat different foods, dress differently, and have different customs. What would they miss about their old way of life?

This Teachable Moment illustrates two problems with the thinking of contemporary multicultural educators. The first is the implication that we are, culturally speaking, what we choose to eat, although it is not at all clear how eating Korean foods can remind these two boys of a homeland they cannot remember because of their age when coming to America—a homeland in which they were too young to have eaten that food before they left it. The second is the implication that parents described or illustrated as white Americans do not have a heritage to offer their children. Why is the Levins' heritage not as important for these Korean boys as their own? Moreover, the selection never suggests that in addition to being Americans, the parents might have another heritage worth imparting to their adopted children. To put it in the way in which this story seems to define heritage, why aren't bagels given equal time with kim chee?

Nonetheless, it is hard to believe that fourth graders are interested in the menus of daily life around the world or in their preparation. Yet multicultural educators must think so; this reader provides an even larger vocabulary for foreign foods in another example of pseudo-literature in it. In "Yagua Days," about the most exciting thing its Puerto Rican characters (and their animals) do is eat. And they eat quite a variety of foods in the course of this short story. Of the thirty-six words and phrases in the Spanish Word List at the end of the selection, twelve are items of food. Such a vocabulary will not nourish literacy in either Spanish or English.

A prime example of the second purpose for pseudo-literature is an inflammatory selection entitled "They Will Tear Up the Earth" in the grade 6 reader. The selection is a chapter from a book entitled *Morning Star, Black Sun: The Northern Cheyenne Indians and America's Energy Crisis*, by Brent Ashabranner, which describes the course of events in a conflict between the Cheyenne and large mining companies that took place in the context of the quest for a domestic source of energy in the 1970s. Students are told that this is nonfiction, yet it is not a piece of nonfiction in any straightforward sense of the term, although it is based on the author's visits to the Cheyenne, on records and other written documents, and on interviews with key figures in the episode. It is a semifictionalized piece of journalism for young readers, and a piece of advocacy journalism at that. The following paragraphs give the flavor of the piece:

> The Cheyenne in the room listened quietly. Knowing Ted Risingsun, they knew he had something else on his mind. "But then," Ted continued, "I got to thinking about where I would go when I finished all that dancing. I doubt if I could come back here. We've already leased or given permits to lease over half of our land. . . . I've heard that to build those gasification plants and run them and take out the coal for them there will be ten white people working and living on this reservation for every Cheyenne here. If that happens, I don't think there will be a Cheyenne tribe anymore.

"Now most of us are poor. I don't have to tell anyone in this room about that. But we have these hills and grass and trees and streams, and if we don't give them away, no one can take them away from us. We've got our tribe's whole history and culture right here. So maybe we're not so poor. But even if we are, I think I would rather be poor in my own country, with my own people, with our own way of life than be rich in a torn-up land where I am outnumbered ten to one by strangers." . . .

The Cheyenne Tribal Council did not answer Consol the next day or any time soon, but the company did not withdraw the offer. It was an offer that sent shock waves through the Tribal Council and into every Cheyenne home. For the first time the Indians of this small and isolated tribe began to understand what leasing their land to a big coal company would lead to. It was not only the stripping bare of a large part of their land to rip out the coal, though that was bad enough. But the companies didn't want the coal unless they could build generating or gasification plants of the "mine mouth," as company officials expressed it. Then would come the miners, plant builders, plant operators, and their families, and the Cheyenne would become a minority group on their own reservation.

The Consol offer had done another thing. It had shown the Cheyenne how poorly they had fared financially under the guidance of the Bureau of Indian Affairs.[7]

The chief problems with this selection center on how it is used. Not only is it passed off as a simple piece of nonfiction, it is not treated in the way in which a piece of sensational journalism should be dealt with in a reading instructional textbook—as the object of critical reading. Students are not asked to explore the author's rhetorical intentions for the piece, or to consider whether all the facts are given in this account of a struggle involving the government, the coal companies, and the Indians. Because the selection is presented as a piece of nonfiction in a basal reader, the political issues it deals with bypass the sort of analysis that should take place in a social studies class. Although some people might argue that the Indians deserve our sympathy and that there is nothing wrong with a selection about them that is little more than an open-and-shut case of villains and victims, that does not justify the pedagogy at work here. Advocacy journalism is being used to help students internalize several simplistic political stances: an uncomplicated sympathetic stance toward the Indians *and* a negative stance toward all the forces depicted as damaging to them.

The rhetorical goal of this selection is to cultivate children's hostility toward the U.S. government, big business, white Americans,[8] and developers. The postselection question in the student text and the response criteria suggested to teachers in the teacher guide make clear that developers are one target. In the student text, under a caption entitled "Thinking About It," students are asked to discuss the following question:

> "We want to change your community. We want to improve your way of living," say some people called developers. What will you need to find out before you agree or disagree to let them do what they have in mind?

In the teacher guide, teachers are urged to judge their students' responses according to the following criteria:

> Do students weigh the positive and negative aspects of the offer? Do students understand that the authors had to research their subjects? Do students identify factors that would need to be addressed before letting developers change a community?

What more could the editors have done to handle this piece more responsibly? Students and teachers should have been informed that, as Ashabranner noted in later chapters in his book, the Cheyenne won their case completely over the next decade with the help of Secretary of the Interior Rogers Morton and the Environmental Protection Agency at crucial points. The selection should have had an epilogue telling students how the Cheyenne used the political processes and institutions to their advantage, suggesting the complexities of the larger problem the Cheyenne face in becoming economically self-sufficient and leaving students with a feeling that justice was served this time. Instead, the selection ends on a militant note: "It was time once more for the Cheyenne to fight." In effect, the editors have given students a dishonest reading experience.

A third example, also in the Scott Foresman grade 6 reader, shows how the author of a piece of pseudo-literature can use the mouths of babes to convey a politically correct idea—in this case, the notion that knowing only one language, English, is a dishonorable state of being. It also shows what an author may do to make a piece of pseudo-literature extremely attractive to editors seeking to meet diversity quotas for the characters presented in their selections. Here are the opening paragraphs of the selection:[9]

> There is no place on earth like the Bronx. It's part of New York City, and I live there. My name is Loretta Bernstein. I live on Burnridge Avenue between the two 112s—112th Street and 112th Avenue.
>
> I am ten years old. I am a short, skinny, Jewish, African American kid. My ancestors came from Ethiopia and were all black and Jewish too. We are called Falashas and are descended from the Queen of Sheba.
>
> It's easy to tell who I am in a crowd because I wear big, round, red-framed eyeglasses all of the time and my official forest-ranger hat most of the time.

Contrary to what one might expect, the story deals with friendships among a group of children in the Bronx with different backgrounds and contains absolutely nothing about Loretta's Ethiopian or Jewish heritage or how she got her name, not one an Ethiopian Jew is likely to have. Nor does the teacher guide explain to the teacher who the Falashas are, how they came to this country, or the fact that most of the Falasha community in Ethiopia was rescued by the Israelis and airlifted to Israel a number of years ago. Indeed, the only background knowledge the guide provides is on the five boroughs in New York City and on the New York Botanical Garden, which is mentioned in the story.

Because the guide provides no cultural or historical information on the Ethiopian Jews (nor suggests that students do research on the topic) and the story offers almost nothing in the way of plot or character development, one is compelled to conclude that the selection was included not only for Loretta's stereotype-smashing genealogy but even more for the phrase "monolingual lout," which one of her Spanish-speaking friends uses to denigrate another friend. Here are the paragraphs describing the conversation of these children (p. E97):

> Julio also speaks Spanish—mostly to his grandmother. He says that considering the neighborhood we live in, there is no excuse for all of us not to know at least one language besides English. He even thinks Suzie Q should learn Gaelic.
>
> The first time he told her that, Julio had to explain to Suzie Q that Gaelic is the ancient language of Ireland, the place Suzie Q's ancestors came from.

Suzie Q was sitting on Julio's stomach as he spoke because she thought he had said "eat garlic," not "speak Gaelic." Suzie Q took it as an insult and threw Julio to the ground as punishment.

"Your rabbit's foot didn't protect you from Suzie Q," I said after Julio had brushed himself off.

"Suzie Q is not a bad guy," he said. "She is simply a monolingual lout of my acquaintance." Then a clean, unwrinkled Julio smiled at Suzie Q and sauntered off. An embarrassed Suzie Q ignored his remark.

That night I looked up *monolingual* and *lout* in the dictionary. I kept my findings to myself. I like Julio.

The epithet of "monolingual lout" here is only one of a few hints scattered throughout several reading series that there is something wrong with people who speak only one language—English—an implication that is never made about people who speak only Spanish or Chinese.

The anti-intellectual thrust of contemporary multiculturalism comes through clearly in the related social studies activity provided by the editors. Rather than gather solid information from reference works, the editors suggest that students investigate the language of a bilingual student in their class and gather information from that student about that student's people and country.

A PEDAGOGY OF EXPLOITATION: ABUSING THE STUDY OF GENUINE CHILDREN'S LITERATURE

In many schools of education, educators are encouraging teachers to use literature for the benefit of the social studies in order to foster connections between language arts and the social studies. They believe children's literature can enhance historical understanding and civic literacy.[10] The effort to do so, which can be carried out without abusing the literary work, often takes two different exploitative forms in some teacher guides. In one, the teacher guides suggest the social issues that children are to discuss based on what they are reading. Even the most whimsical literary selection may be used as a springboard for examining what the editors or their consultants perceive as the social issue embedded in it and for engaging in classroom activities related to it. Clearly there is no way to know how many teachers actually use these suggestions in their classrooms, and, it should be made clear, all the teacher guides also provide many appropriate, non-politicized questions and activities to explore and extend students' understanding of a selection. But it is reasonable to assume that many teachers will heed the consistent message coming to them from many, if not most, schools of education and from their guides about the importance of cultivating a "multicultural perspective" and use some of their students' learning time for the multicultural questions and activities now recommended for the elementary school classroom. But analytical thinking cannot be developed by questions, information, and activities designed to elicit an expression of young students' feelings, uninformed opinions, and limited personal experiences on complex social issues.

The Silver Burdett Ginn teacher editions provide a number of examples of this sort in its Appreciating Cultures subsection, which appears in a boilerplate section called Discussing the Selection, following two other subsections: the first one labeled Reader's Response ("Building Self-Esteem: Use the Reader's Response question to explore students' oral or written affective responses to the selection"), the second labeled Returning to the Reading Purpose ("Return to the reading purpose established at the beginning of the selection. Ask students if their reading goals were achieved").[11] Again I use one reading series for these examples but do not intend to imply that it alone exploits literature for nonliterary purposes. Appreciating Cultures offers this suggestion after grade 4 students read an excerpt from George Selden's *The Cricket in Times Square*, an innocent fantasy about animals and insects:

> Because of advanced medicine, people live longer today than they ever did in the past. There are many elderly people, however, who live in poverty with no one to care for them. Many were unable to save enough money during their working years to provide a good quality of life after they retired. Discuss what students can do to help these people find food and shelter, and provide for their basic necessities.

After a selection from *Mary Poppins*, Appreciating Cultures offers the following suggestion for grade 4 children to discuss:

> In the United States, with more women entering the work force and a greater number of single parent households, there is an increasing need for child care

centers. Have students discuss this issue and what can be done so that parents can earn a living and still know that their children are being well taken care of. Have students draw up a list of suggestions for dealing with this problem.

Such issue-oriented suggestions appear after most of the serious selections too. Grade 6 children are asked to "brainstorm ways in which our society might help" poor Mexican American migrant children "have the same opportunities available to children in other socio-economic classes" after they read "The Circuit," a fine short story about a Mexican American migrant child.[12] After they read a Japanese folk tale in which a young boy listens respectfully to what his grandfather tells him, Appreciating Cultures suggests that grade 4 children first "brainstorm how our culture treats older people" and then "list ways that the quality of life for older people might be improved." After they read a story about visitors from space, Appreciating Cultures suggests that grade 4 children "investigate the number of immigrants permitted in the United States over the past decade" and then debate "whether or not immigration laws favor certain ethnic groups." After they read I. B. Singer's "The Parakeet Named Dreidel," Appreciating Cultures suggests that grade 4 children discuss "how the Christian celebration of Christmas in the United States is emphasized on television, in advertising, and through store and street decorations. . . other religious holidays or celebrations that are observed, such as Kwanza, Hanukkah, or the winter solstice . . . and ways the celebration of winter religious holidays might be handled in a more balanced way by the media." It is possible, of course, that many of these politically correct suggestions were written with tongue in cheek by the editors in order to cope with the advice of politically correct consultants *and* to rationalize the offering of some wonderful but politically incorrect pieces of children's literature like *Mary Poppins*. It is difficult to believe that editors who respect children's literature see fantasies like *The Cricket in Times Square* and *Mary Poppins* as appropriate vehicles for stimulating the social consciousness of nine-year-old children about the problems of the elderly poor or child care in single-parent households. Only humorless moral didacts could. But in any case, Appreciating Cultures has little if anything to do with the appreciation of any culture.

In the other form this exploitative effort takes, the teacher is encouraged to engage children in a variety of forms of social activism as the final activity for a selection. For example, to follow up a celebratory poem about the Southwest, Appreciating Cultures suggests that grade 4 children write letters or "support an environmental group." To follow up a story set in Norway during World War II dealing with the way in which a group of children assisted the resistance movement, the editors on a page titled Cultural Connections suggest that grade 6 children brainstorm ideas for community projects to carry out on their own. To follow up a Japanese tall tale, "Three Strong Women," Cultural Connections suggests that grade 6 children write a speech honoring a social activist.

Both ways of using literature for nonliterary purposes in the Silver Burdett Ginn readers help teachers arrive at a stage in the development of multicultural understanding that Carl Grant, the series' consultant who constructed this concept, labeled Affirmation and Advocacy. According to Grant, a teacher who has achieved this level of development (1) demonstrates and advocates critical thinking and alternative viewpoints, (2) encourages discussion of current social issues involving race, gender, ethnicity, class, and disability, (3) uses life experiences familiar to the students as the basis for personal discussion of social issues, and (4) illustrates the value of active participation in democratic decision making as a means to create positive change.[13] What the Silver Burdett Ginn teacher editions do not indicate is how teachers demonstrating any of these characteristics necessarily advance the intellectual growth of their students. Nevertheless, the political goals for the social activism encouraged in almost all the readers are spelled out clearly for teachers here. As one of the Cultural Connections pages indicates, teachers must help their students develop the "social action skills" that will enable them to "call attention to or eliminate unfairness in school communities and society." In particular, as a quotation on this page from the writing of James Banks makes explicit, teachers must give students who are members of "oppressed ethnic groups" practice in "social action strategies which teach them how to get power without violence and further exclusion." To accomplish this goal, Banks wants teachers to provide "excluded ethnic groups" with "experience in obtaining and exercising power . . . within a curriculum that is designed to help liberate" them.[14]

How teachers are to do this and what these children are to be liberated from in the elementary school are anybody's guess. All that such exhortations may liberate them from are the demands of literacy learning itself. But it doesn't take much guesswork to figure out what constitutes unfairness in school communities and society. The postselection questions in the student text or the postselection informational material in the teacher guides usually make that clear. For example, one Appreciating Cultures section suggests that grade 6 children find out what Native American tribes are trying to do about their unfair situations today after reading a story about an Indian trickster. After an Asian folktale about a princess and an admiral, another suggests that grade 6 students discuss differing expectations for male and female leaders. After a selection on two Native American artists, yet another suggests that grade 6 children learn how Native American children were deprived of learning about their own heritage. One can feel only sympathy for editors who sensed the irony in the phrase "Appreciating Cultures" when they created material for this section to comply with their consultants' advice.

The section labeled "Choices for Turning Back to Literature: Multicultural Perspectives" in the Macmillan teacher guides is of the same ilk. The title of this regular feature has its own special touch of irony. The feature does not deepen students' aesthetic response to a literary work, rather, it tends to show teachers how to use literary selections to advance political consciousness raising or ethnic affirmation, or both. The following multicultural perspective appears after students read a story about a young Seminole girl:

History's Influence

Share with students information about historical events that have shaped and altered Native American cultures. For example, the Everglades were not the original home of the Seminoles. In the early 1800s, the U.S. government forced most of the Seminoles to move from their lands in northern Florida to what is now Oklahoma. Those who refused to move—Billie's ancestors—escaped capture by fleeing southward into the swampy Everglades. Their ability to adapt to such a difficult environment is evidence of their strength and courage.

Begin a discussion about the effect history has on the present. Ask students to suggest ways the story would be different if told from another time in history—if Billie had lived a hundred years ago, or if she lived a hundred years from now. Ask:

- Why do you think Billie doubts the legends of her tribe?
- Why do you think understanding Seminole history is important for her?

Finally, ask students to discuss the aspects of their own cultures or heritages that have affected their lives.

Although the historical background of almost any selection on the American Indians can reveal unfairness to them, it should be noted that neither the tale about an Indian trickster in the Silver Burdett Ginn reader nor the selection about the Seminole Indian girl in the Macmillan reader involves historical events or political cruelty. The first showcases oral storytelling; the second is an adventure story. But teachers are to use them, for purposes of a multicultural education, to highlight the Native Americans as victims and, implicitly, to generate antagonism to American society.

Macmillan also uses authors' biographical sketches to hint at societal unfairness and victimization. For example, its grade 6 reader provides the following sketch of Gary Soto.[15]

> Gary Soto's success as a writer may have surprised some people—perhaps even him. Recalling his childhood in a poor Mexican-American family, Soto says, "I don't think I had any literary aspirations when I was a kid. . . . We didn't have books, and no one encouraged us to read."
>
> Later, as a college student, Soto discovered a collection of poems and thought, "This is terrific; I'd like to do something like this." He felt that writing would be a way to communicate the problems and emotions of people like the Chicanos he knew.

Note that Soto is described as coming from a poor family, but he is not quoted as saying that his family did not encourage him to read. Unnamed people failed to encourage him. This lack of specificity conveniently allows students to wonder whether bigoted teachers who assumed Mexican Americans were incapable of broad reading were responsible for his lack of literary aspirations as a child. It is a pity that the sketch does not tell us how he was nonetheless stimulated and able to go to college later on.

Macmillan also uses authors' biographical sketches to suggest the kind of social action that children should favor. The sketch of James Ramsey Ullman in its grade 6 reader tells students that he participated in the Freedom March in Montgomery, Alabama. A sketch of Mildred Pitts Walter tells students that she undertook a "peace walk" in the Soviet Union. Why this walk was held in the Soviet Union and for what purpose is not, however, made clear. The examples of social activism mentioned in authors' biographical sketches have a consistent political tilt. I have found no authors commended for participating in tax revolts, if indeed any did. Nor do authors seem to be volunteering in such organizations as the Boy or Girl Scouts, coaching Little League, raising money for their public libraries, tutoring in the schools, or doing service work in hospitals. They may well have done these things, but these are not the activities offered as models of social activism for students. Apparently, they are not viewed as activities that serve to liberate anyone.

A PEDAGOGY OF MANIPULATION: GROUNDING LITERARY UNDERSTANDING IN FEELINGS

Silver Burdett Ginn's description of the stage reflecting advanced development of multicultural understanding makes it clear that teachers are to use their students' personal experiences as the basis for discussing social issues. Throughout all the reading series, students are encouraged to ground their understanding of what they read in their own personal feelings or experiences or, if this is not possible or desirable, then in the imagined feelings or lives of others. For example, in preparing students to read a survival story about an Inuit family living near the Arctic Circle, the teacher guide for Houghton Mifflin's grade 6 reader suggests that "students think of experiences they have had in which their strength and endurance were tested to the limit."[16] This suggestion may sound innocuous enough here, but consider how this strategy is used elsewhere in this reader.

Before they read a story about a Japanese American girl and her family during World War II, a Journal Page in a student workbook encourages students to write answers to the following questions: "How do you feel about the fact that the United States required Japanese American people to leave their homes and live together in camps? Do you think this could happen again? Why or why not?"[17] Later, to help students "analyze" the issues of bigotry and prejudice, a Journal Page contains a writing assignment labeled Discussing Prejudice that asks students: "What do you think is the cause of prejudice? How do you think prejudice can be overcome? . . . If you wish, write about any personal experience with prejudice you may have had."[18] Note that the first question in the first group of questions is a "feeling" question. It clearly intends children to feel ashamed of their government and their country. That is, no normal child could answer, "Good!" In the second set of questions, students are to dredge their personal experiences for only negative examples to write about. Never have I found teachers in any teacher guide directed to ask students to recall examples of interethnic or interracial goodwill if an experience-based example is to be discussed. One wonders why students cannot be asked to come up with both negative and positive examples in the name of even-handedness. And despite the pretense that analysis is involved, it is not possible for students to analyze the issues of bigotry and prejudice after reading the story because they have been given no adequate information on them. All they can do is give their uninformed opinions, which is what they are encouraged to do by the phrase: "What do you think?" For this story, teachers could have been directed to ask their students to do research to find out whether prejudice against Japanese Americans has diminished or disappeared and why. Better yet, teachers could have been given some factual information on the rates of intermarriage today between Japanese Americans and white Americans and on the current academic and economic achievement of Japanese Americans, and urged to invite their students to discuss what these facts might imply about the history of prejudice toward Japanese Americans in this country.

Selections on American Indians are almost always used to create guilt in students. The way in which the Macmillan readers foster the guilt that students are supposed to feel about the treatment of the Indians in this country is no different from the way Silver Burdett Ginn takes care of this task. In each case, a selection about a Native American tribe is used as a springboard to ask students how these groups felt about what had happened to them. But this does not mean that a selection actually has to feature Indians, as I noted at the beginning of this chapter with respect to "Pettranella."

Sometimes the "feeling" questions are less malevolent than downright silly. Only one answer is possible to, "How do you think it would feel to have graphite in your eyes or whirling around your legs?" or, "How do you think it would feel to be in a 'whirling world of smoke'?" both in the Macmillan grade 4 teacher guide for use with an autobiography about growing up in an old steel mill town.[19] The teacher guide does provide other kinds of questions to explore or extend students' comprehension of the selection, but the "feeling" questions may well be used and are clearly useless from an educational perspective.

In other cases, the strategy of eliciting students' sympathy for the dire situations in which others find themselves lets editors convey to teachers a politically correct understanding of the social problem illuminated by the selection. Teachers can then convey this understanding to their students. This strategy is exemplified in "The Scribe," a highly tendentious piece of pseudo-literature by Kristin Hunter about a young black boy who sets up a free business service for people who cannot read or write in his blighted neighborhood. Before the story is read, Houghton Mifflin's grade 6 guide asks teachers to put a Latin motto on the chalkboard and to ask students "how they feel about being required to respond to a written statement they cannot read with understanding." Teachers are then urged to "emphasize that illiteracy is usually the result of lack of opportunity rather than lack of intelligence or effort," in the abstract a good message.[20]

The "feeling" question here is designed to encourage students' empathy with the elderly black people in the story. In the story, the boy's mother explains, "In the old days, nobody cared whether our people got an education. They were only interested in getting the crops in." The mother goes on to say, "Sometimes I think they *still* don't care. If we hadn't gotten you into that good school, you might not be able to read so well either. A lot of boys and girls your age can't, you know." The implicit message to both black and nonblack children, and one that the teacher is undoubtedly expected to support, is that some black children do not read very well (perhaps in that very teacher's own class)—and not because of limited effort on their part but because their schools and teachers are deficient, a situation for which uncaring whites are solely responsible. The children thus cannot be held responsible for their poor performance.

This piece of pseudo-literature exudes an antiwhite animus. For example, the policeman who tells the boy he cannot conduct his business without a license is described as "tall, heavy, and blue-eyed." The story continues as follows:

> In our neighborhood, when they see a cop, people scatter. That was why the back of my neck was burning.

"What are you trying to do here, sonny?" the cop asks.

"Help people out," I tell him calmly, though my knees are knocking together under the table.

"Well, you know," he says, "Mr. Quick and Mr. Dollar have been in business a long time on this corner. They are very respected men in this neighborhood. Are you trying to run them out of business?"

"I'm not charging anybody," I pointed out.

"That," the cop says, "is exactly what they don't like. Mr. Quick says he is glad to have some help with the letter-writing. Mr. Dollar says it's only a nuisance to them anyway and takes up too much time. But if you don't charge for your services, it's unfair competition."

Well, why not? I thought. After all, I could use a little profit.

"All right," I tell him. "I'll charge a quarter."

"Then it is my duty to warn you," the cop says, "that it's against the law to conduct a business without a license. The first time you accept a fee, I'll close you up and run you off this corner."

He really had me there. What did I know about licenses? I'm only thirteen, after all. Suddenly I didn't feel like the big black businessman anymore. I felt like a little kid who wanted to holler for his mother. But she was at work, and so was Daddy.

"I'll leave," I said, and did, with all the cool I could muster. But inside I was burning up, and not from the sun. . . .

I was so mad I didn't know what to do with myself that afternoon. . . .

Finally I went to the park and threw stones at the swans in the lake. I was careful not to hit them, but they made good targets because they were so fat and white. Then after a while the sun got lower. I kind of cooled off and came to my senses. They were just big, dumb, beautiful birds, and not my enemies. I threw them some crumbs from my sandwich and went home.

At no point does the teaching apparatus suggest that students explicitly discuss the symbolism in the last paragraph, the author's intentions for this episode, or even who the boy's enemies might be. Never does the teaching apparatus suggest that students discuss the racism attributed to all of white society by the author. Instead, it is implicitly left as a fact of life that all students are to understand, accept without question, and retain at an emotional level.

Worse yet, the story conveys in an extremely subtle way a touch of anti-Semitism that many students may also respond to and accept. The two men who cash checks and offer other services for a fee in this black neighborhood, and who are seen by the young black boy as preying on the elderly people in the neighborhood, are referred to as Mr. Quick and Mr. Dollar. The mother's innocent explanation of the origin of "scribes" sets the stage for an inference that is never disconfirmed explicitly by the illustrations for the story or by the text, even though there are clear clues about the race of all the other characters. The mother explains that there "was a time in history when nobody could read or write except a special class of people." They were known as "scribes," she goes on, and it was "their job to write down the laws given by the rabbis and the judges. Jesus criticized the scribes because they were so proud of themselves. But he needed them to write down his teachings." One wonders how many black youngsters now listening to the rhetoric of Louis Farrakhan and his disciples will be readily disposed to see Mr. Quick and Mr. Dollar as the "bloodsucker" descendants of those early scribes. Such is the stuff of children's literature these days.

ORIGINS OF A PEDAGOGY EMPHASIZING
THE STUDENT'S PERSONAL LIFE

The origins of a pedagogical emphasis on students' personal experiences and feelings as the basis for learning can be traced to the 1966 Dartmouth Conference, but it has been more strongly promoted by those advocating a way of teaching literature called "reader response," even though its originator, Louise Rosenblatt, did not suggest asking students to read their lives into what they read or necessarily to give an affective response to literature. Instead, she sought to legitimate the idea that a reader's own initial response to a literary work, whether affective or analytic, was to be valued. To her, it reflected a transaction between the text and what a reader brought to it from personal experience.[21] The current interpretation of this pedagogical philosophy—asking students to relate their lives to what they read—can be seen in every professional journal in the English language arts, in other publications on the teaching of literature, and in many states' English language arts standards documents. This interpretation is also used for evaluating the pedagogical apparatus in reading series and literature anthologies. For example, the monograph put out by the California Literature Project to help teachers implement California's 1988 English-Language Arts Framework for K–12 indicated in its evaluations of reading series whether they suggest that the teacher help students relate their purposes for reading to their personal experience or provide ways for students to relate more personally with the works.[22]

To some extent, the rationale for this effort sounds reasonable enough. Why not have students make connections between what they read and their personal lives or imagined feelings based on their personal lives? Perhaps it could improve comprehension of the literary experience. Perhaps it could enhance student motivation to read. There are a number of problems with this philosophy, however. One is that it may lead to abuses, as suggested by the advice on how to help students appreciate "Pettranella." This story about immigration has nothing to do directly with the Native Americans, yet students are asked to imagine how the Indians must have felt during the settling of the frontier, not the more relevant "feeling" question (if one is thought necessary) of how it might have felt to leave one's native country to move elsewhere or how it might have felt to come to America.

A second is that it is not necessarily desirable for teachers to urge students to read their lives into the literature they are reading and to ground their understanding of a literary work in their personal experience (or in their imagined personal experience). Such a practice may interfere with the development of an adequate interpretation of a literary work; many literary works have the capacity to enlarge or contradict what students know from personal experience.[23] It is also possible that over time, such a practice may encourage self-centeredness and a limited perspective, and diminish the capacity of literary works to stimulate the imagination.

Third, the view that it is desirable for students to relate their personal lives to what they read may affect the kinds of selections that editors or consultants choose to include. One wonders, for example, if this view is what accounts for the presence of "Last Summer with Maizon" in Macmillan's grade 6 reader.[24] In this story, a girl has to write an essay about how she spent her summer and, in front of the class, reads that her father had died and her best friend moved away. After class, the teacher speaks to her, saying that she was sorry to hear about her father's passing away and then assigns another essay. This one, the teacher says, is about "all of your feelings about your father's death. It doesn't matter what you write, a poem, an essay. . . . Just so long as it expresses how you felt this summer. Is that understood?" When the girl answers yes, the teacher says, "Good, then I'll see you bright and early with something wonderful to read to the class." Hopefully, most teachers will find this story insensitive and appalling.

Fourth, the view that it is desirable for students to be able to relate their personal lives to what they read may affect the kinds of selections that editors or consultants choose to exclude. The superb fantasies that have long been among the best children's literature in the English-speaking world do not readily lend themselves to this kind of grounding because it is a grounding that in fact violates what fantasy is all about. Nor do the great children's fantasies typically or explicitly deal with social issues. One wonders whether this "limitation" of fantasy helps account for its diminished presence in some reading series.

Finally, no body of research evidence from studies on reader response even suggests that this is a useful strategy for improving comprehension and motivation. Indeed, there is no reason that an affective response is to be preferred to an analytic response or why teachers should not simply encourage students to make whatever kind of response they prefer. Encouraging a view of the world through the lens of one's life experiences is not necessarily stimulating or illuminating for young students.

WHY WAS DEVOTION TO LITERARY QUALITY AND LITERARY STUDY ABANDONED SO RAPIDLY?

One is compelled to ask how an almost 180-degree change in literary standards and in the purposes for literary study could occur, given the value that educators have long placed on the teaching of literature for developing literary taste and knowledge. The legitimate effort to broaden the cultural contents of what children were exposed to did not inherently carry with it the implication that these new selections would be of lower quality (or of no literary quality at all) in comparison to the selections they displaced. Nor did this effort imply that these new selections should be used to address social issues and promote social activism, especially in the absence of adequate historical information. Ironically, although many educators sincerely think that a focus on social issues is tantamount to cultural broadening, it actually seems to have led to a more limited view of other peoples, especially when the effort to increase social awareness or sensitivity to others results in the portrayal of nonwhite groups of people as little more than victims of oppression and implies that they have only positive values (for example, that all Native Americans were peace loving). These new selections almost consistently withhold from students the negative features of the cultures of these nonwhite groups (for example, the warlike nature of many Indian groups and the existence of human sacrifice and slavery in many). Inclusivity, and the legitimate effort to increase sensitivity to others, would not have led to lower standards if a concern for literary quality at increasing levels of text difficulty had consistently trumped criteria emanating from ideological agendas.

How could so many elementary school teachers become convinced so easily by advocates at universities or in state departments of education of the desirability, never mind legitimacy, of the new forms of literature or the new uses for literary study? Most elementary school teachers are not ideologues. Clearly many may have felt, and may still feel, intimidated by the intellectual authority of university educators and the legal authority of staff members at state departments of education. They may also have become reluctant to voice criticism of anything to do with matters of race, ethnicity, or gender. But there are probably many more who truly believe that they are teaching nothing but quality literature and that using literary study as the point of departure for discussing social issues without adequate historical information on these issues is not an abuse of both literary study and the educational process.

Changing Literary Standards

Tendentious journalism and other forms of pseudo-literature may have come to be accepted as good literature by many teachers because many of the newer selections in the readers are featured as the recipients of literary awards—often in the social studies. One striking feature of a table of contents in contemporary readers is the number of selections described as award winners. Understandably, editors want to publish award winners or are encouraged to do so by authors and consultants. Such awards undoubtedly help to reassure everyone, especially teachers, that these selections are of the highest literary quality. This is not to say that all the selections that have received an award are of problematic quality, especially those receiving awards before the 1970s. But one cannot help but suspect that nonliterary criteria were uppermost in the minds of those judging *Yagua Days* (Notable Social Studies Trade Book and Reading Rainbow Selection); *No Star Nights,* the autobiography about growing up in the polluted environment caused by the steel mills (Notable Children's Trade Book in the Field of Social Studies, ALA Notable Children's Book, International Reading Association Children's Book Award); *Teammates*, a story about Jackie Robinson (Notable Social Studies Trade Book); *The Scribe* (the book that includes this story received the Christopher Award and the Spring Book Festival Award, and it was a finalist for the National Book Award); "They Will Tear Up the Earth" (the book from which it was taken won the Carter G. Woodson Book Award and was an ALA Notable Children's Book); and a grade 6 selection on artist and writer Faith Ringgold that is brimming over with hostility to white society (the book from which it was taken won an ALA award). In the face of all these awards, elementary school teachers may well be seduced into thinking that these stories are examples of good children's literature.

Wholeness as Synonymous with Authenticity as Synonymous with Literary Quality

Part of the answer may also lie in the apparent acceptance by elementary school teachers of the notion that the wholeness of a literary selection establishes its authenticity and thus its literary merit. Their apparent acceptance of this notion is to some extent understandable because wholeness did coincide with merit at the time the cry for authentic literature was raised several decades ago. At that time, basal readers were severely criticized by whole language advocates for containing too many selections that were adapted or abridged, were snippets of larger works, or were composed to control vocabulary difficulty and to facilitate the teaching of a sight vocabulary or phonetically regular words. These critics also claimed that students spent more time on learning skills (memorization of a sight word vocabulary, phonics, or strategies for reading comprehension) than in reading and enjoying the selections. These critics wanted the situation reversed. They wanted children to read whole, undoctored pieces of quality literature, respond to a literary work as a literary work, and only then engage in skills work if the content of the work happened to lend itself to a skills lesson (e.g., the meaning of the prefixes in the prefixed words in the selection).

Teachers were urged to switch to the use of regular story books, if possible, and abandon the use of readers altogether. For that matter, teachers still are being urged to do so because many of them, like the twenty-eight-year old kindergarten teacher quoted in a January 1994 *New York Times* article, seem to believe that Dick and Jane—the white middle-class suburban children symbolically dominating all midcentury primary grade basal readers—still lurk behind the covers of reading textbooks and have apparently not been told that Dick and Jane departed for another world decades ago.[25]

A switch to whole works of literature was not easy for teachers to make. Nevertheless, any traces of a skills-driven pedagogy as well as any use of inauthentic literature became the bêtes noires of reading instruction. To survive, publishers redesigned the readers to include only authentic selections, showing teachers how to approach them as pieces of literature and providing work on skills as an option and in the context of the selections themselves. After all, who could disagree in principle that a whole literary work was better for children to read than a less than whole work? *Wholeness* meant "just as the author wrote it," and, at the time, the use of unadapted and unabridged works meant the use of quality literature.

An Expanded Concept of Literature

Wholeness undoubtedly loomed even larger in importance in teachers' thinking as other forms of literature began to be introduced into the basal readers. Because of a growing belief by social studies and language arts educators in the value of having students learn how to read primary documents, publishers began to draw on such sources as personal essays, diary entries, autobiographies, and family chronicles for reading selections. Such genres were particularly useful for portraying groups that had not yet produced much quality fiction or poetry, and they were clearly authentic, although the literary standards that applied to fiction or poetry did not necessarily apply to them.

Thus, it is not surprising that the claim that their selections represent literary quality has disappeared in some of the promotional material in publishers' textbooks. For example, in the Guiding Principles for Scott Foresman's 1995 readers, the first principle says only that "children learn best when reading authentic literature." There's nothing about quality literature here. Nor does the publisher claim they are all whole. Like other publishers, it uses excerpts from longer works—usually whole chapters—in order to find enough suitable material. That some of the authentic literature in the readers may be neither whole works of literature nor of high literary quality is a contemporary development. But it is possible that many elementary school teachers continue to construe the use of "authentic" in its original sense and believe that if selections are described as authentic, or as unadapted and unabridged, they are therefore of high quality, especially if they receive awards.

However, the possible reasons that elementary school teachers may have willingly altered their standards for good children's literature do not account for why teachers have come to accept the new uses for literary study—if they really have. Here part of the answer may lie in the dominance of issue- or problem-oriented approaches in the social studies and the influence of the universities in their treatment of works of literature as social documentaries. Because some teachers are always looking for new approaches to what they do, the use of literature for focusing on social issues may have seemed appealing to them. It did not eliminate the initial personal response to literature that university educators were insisting on, but it did give teachers something more to do with the literary work (other than focusing chiefly on students' spontaneous responses to it) since the animus against teaching reading skills extended even to the teaching of the formal elements of literature—something they might have done years ago. Both teachers and publishers had been given a clear message from authoritative educational sources that helping students to understand why literature is literature is also no longer an appropriate focus for teaching. An analytic approach to a literary work inevitably draws on teacher knowledge and on traditional categories of knowledge, something to be avoided at all costs at a time when children are supposed to construct their own social knowledge.

The injunction against teaching the elements of literature can be seen in the comments in the 1988 monograph by the California State Department of Education explaining why a particular K–8 reading series was not being recommended. Although the series was commended for being literature based, it was beyond the pale because of its focus "on skills and formal elements of literature rather than on issues and ideas."[26] Indeed, as suggested by a more recent monograph, *Selecting Core Literature*, put out by the Los Angeles County Office of Education, the purpose for literary study is now no different from the purpose for the social studies—and in some ways goes far beyond what one would expect social studies materials to do. As stated in this monograph, the purpose of literary study is to "offer exposure to issues that the reader may confront in life."[27] Consider the philosophy embedded in the following paragraph, which appears in a section labeled "The Thinking, Meaning-Centered Curriculum and How It Encourages Controversy":

> In language arts, a broad-based literature program allows students to encounter new and different ideas that challenge their thinking. When literature became the content, questions of who selects the material, what will be read, and how writing will flow from the reading of literature arose. At the heart of those concerns is that students are exposed to a variety of ideas—some of which may differ from the ideas they have been exposed to in the past. And frequently, the ideas will challenge them to think, reflect, and question in a thoughtful, constructive manner. Also, students are asked to express their own ideas and thoughts about a story. This offers them an opportunity to synthesize the information and draw some personal significance or meaning from it. For students to think critically, creatively, and rationally, and to ultimately become able citizens, they must experience real content that offers numerous opportunities to explore multiple perspectives, understand what motivates people, and how our society evolved to what it is today. And in so doing, controversy should be skillfully and safely mediated by educators in a thoughtful manner as a model for what we expect of students. This guided approach is seen as an alternative to unnecessarily sheltering or censoring children from reasonable opportunities to confront controversy and dissent.[28]

After a steady exposure to such a philosophy, how many elementary school teachers would even suspect that children's literature might have other—and better—purposes than helping students to confront controversy and dissent?

———————

The hidden price that students pay for the presence of pseudo-literature is high. In some series, children have been completely deprived of some of the best writers of children's literature in the world (and not just the English-speaking world)—for example, Hans Christian Andersen, David

McCord, Edward Lear, Rudyard Kipling, Kenneth Grahame, the Benéts, Robert Louis Stevenson, E. Nesbit, P. L. Travers, Mary Norton, and Lewis Carroll. Works created to appeal to a child's imagination and sense of adventure have been replaced by selections such as "They Will Tear Up the Earth" that demonize white society, highlight the groups to be seen as its victims, and fuel their emotions, not their minds.

The good news is that there are still some genuine pieces of children's literature left in the elementary school readers (although more in some series than in others)—pieces intended to delight the imagination or inspire a sense of wonder about the world, not to achieve the social and political agendas of grim-faced social-activists-turned-educators. The bad news is that some fine pieces of children's literature from the past are being excluded from the elementary school curriculum on the grounds of authenticity itself. If they contain any words or phrases now considered offensive to a minority group, as one editor told me about one of the Pippi Longstocking stories, they are henceforth banished from the curriculum. Offending words cannot simply be removed because that would mean tampering with the authenticity of the work. Apparently it is considered professionally more ethical to censor a work than to edit it—or to have children read it in its authentic form and discuss the offensive words as an authentic activity in becoming a literate and responsible citizen.

Students pay an even higher price for the pedagogy accompanying much of the literature they read. The way in which participatory activities are suggested in the readers does not tend to promote informed participation in public life. Instead, they promote mindless social activism. Rarely is it recommended that children do some research on the topics they are asked to brainstorm or write letters on. And when it is suggested as a possibility, they are not asked to investigate the various points of view on the social issue or to come to an understanding of the complexities that may be embedded in the topic or to their own point of view on it. The judgment about what stance they are to assume regarding the issue or topic has been made for them (as in these Appreciating Cultures sections), leaving no doubt about what perspective they bring to their "research." As these examples demonstrate, children are not asked to find out about the social and political problems that Indian tribes face or why people want to migrate to the United States.

Such approaches to and uses of literary study do not encourage or develop disciplined inquiry and critical thinking. Indeed, they undermine the habits of the mind that the schools are supposed to develop. Instead of rational and reflective thinking, they encourage spontaneous thinking based on feelings—and on feelings that are often deliberately aroused and oriented in a particular direction by the nature of the selection or the thrust of the teacher-led discussion. In essence, such suggestions abuse the purposes for reading instruction. And students without parents who can offer appropriate intellectual guidance are those penalized the most by the emphasis on mindless social activism.

Attention must be called to two striking hypocrisies in the increasing use of reading selections as vehicles for discussing contemporary social issues or as stimulants for particular forms of social activism. One is that this abuse of literary study is subject to the same kind of criticism leveled at the readers several decades ago. The literary purists of yesteryear railed against the skills-driven reading curriculum, insisting that literature needed to be read chiefly for its own sake if all students were to learn how to read and enjoy reading. They did not want literary selections chosen for ulterior purposes—then, because they facilitated a particular sequence for skills instruction. Today, we see a reading curriculum increasingly dominated by social goals and social issues. The thrust of contemporary social studies is corrupting literary study altogether, marginalizing both authentic children's literature and authentic purposes for studying children's literature. But where are the voices protesting the issues-driven reading curriculum?

The second hypocrisy is that children have never been particularly interested in reading about social issues. The many surveys of children's voluntary reading interests over the past century, beginning in the early 1920s, have consistent results. As one of the most recent ones noted, done in the late 1970s, children continue to establish the same literary categories set down by professionals in the field years ago (e.g., humor, riddles and jokes, adventure, animals, magic and fantasy), and do not choose books from an issues approach.[29] It is unlikely that children have suddenly changed since that study.

There is no reason to believe that an issues-oriented reading curriculum will teach students how to read and enjoy reading. Indeed, one might more readily make the case that an issues-oriented curriculum would be less effective than a skills-driven curriculum in achieving these goals. Compelling students to read preachy or boring pseudo-literature and to follow up delightful fantasies with a sociological analysis of contemporary life is more likely to create boredom, resentment, or even cynicism than joy in reading. Are students likely to become more enthusiastic readers after reading "They Will Tear Up the Earth" or "The Scribe" in Scott Foresman's grade 6 reader or after reading *The Little Prince* and *The Voyage of Odysseus*, selections from *The Borrowers*, *The Hobbit*, *The Wind in the Willows*, *The Phantom Tollbooth*, and *A Wrinkle in Time*, as well as stories about Robin Hood and Maid Marian and St. George and the Dragon, all of which were in the 1987 edition of Macmillan's grade 6 reader? This question is susceptible of an empirical answer. Yet an issues-oriented curriculum seems to have been accepted with equanimity by many educators in our schools of education.

FIVE

THE NEW MORALISM AND ITS CIVIC AND ACADEMIC COSTS

I N 1978, Frances FitzGerald wrote a widely acclaimed series of articles in the *New Yorker* magazine examining U.S. history textbooks in the twentieth century.[1] In her conclusion, FitzGerald urged textbook writers not to show a "lack of respect for history." Her pleas were directed to writers on both sides of the political divide. She deplored a view of American history that "sanitized" relations among social groups—that minimized, if not ignored, conflicts among ethnic, racial, and other social groups in this country. She was also critical of the "incessant moralism" and "manipulativeness" of education reform movements. Today, over twenty years later, it is difficult to find the handiwork of professional sanitary crews in the school curriculum; tensions and clashes among various social groups are threaded throughout the English language arts curriculum as well as the social studies curriculum. Almost all contemporary reading instructional textbooks call attention through their content to our contemporary and past social problems. Although some do so to raise children's consciousness about them or to present their complexities, the moralism and manipulation that FitzGerald warned against have become dominant qualities in many of them. And it is not only the children who are being preached at or whose thinking is being shaped in a certain direction. Their teachers are often the target because many know almost as little history as their students today, or don't know the "right spin" on an issue.

Although the two tend to go together in the readers, moralizing is not the same as manipulating. When an author or the editorial material in a teacher guide *moralizes*, it means using a reading selection to cultivate a specific moral perspective on a social issue or social group; in particular, students are meant to see specific social groups as the victims of prejudice or neglect and to identify and sympathize with them. Authors or editors become *manipulative* when their materials contain a second purpose: to make children think that the source of all social problems lies in the very nature of our society and its dominant values. The major goal of these efforts is not to develop children's analytical or critical thinking but to influence their feelings and attitudes. In the readers, the attempt to shape or alter children's feelings and attitudes is sometimes embedded in the selections themselves, the authors having chosen to use their own work, implicitly or explicitly, for these purposes. When the selections are authentic works of the literary imagination or straightforward pieces of information, the political or social message may be embedded in related material in the teacher guide. Sometimes the attempt to influence student feelings and attitudes can appear in both the selection and the material in the teacher guide. And sometimes the attempt is extremely subtle, consisting chiefly in the kind of selections with which a particular selection has been grouped—manipulation through association.

The instructional readers I examined attempt to shape or reshape children's attitudes or feelings on chiefly four problems: the treatment of disabled people, white racism, the fate of the American Indians, and the protection of endangered species and other aspects of the environment. Selections on the disabled are now associated with multicultural education because the disabled tend to be presented as victims of prejudice or neglect. Selections on the environment are also associated with multicultural education because the environment is viewed as a victim of exploitation or neglect, albeit a silent victim.

Editors or their academic advisers have become ingenious in choosing selections or providing material in the teacher guide that convey an unflattering portrait of American society in their efforts to cultivate the "right perspective" on these four problems. Their efforts raise two issues—one professional, the other academic. The professional issue is the use of the readers to influence children to feel negatively about their society through a subtle manipulation of their reading materials or other learning activities.[2] The academic issue is less obvious. Many editors or their consultants have become so taken by the apparent freedom with which they can use the readers to shape children's feelings that the results of their efforts now prevent fulfillment of their primary responsibility: to help teachers develop children's intellects. The pedagogy now in many instructional readers is bad not only because it is unprofessional but because it interferes with children's acquisition of academic knowledge as well as their capacity for analytical thinking. In the preceding chapter, I noted the high literary costs of the new pedagogy. This chapter shows its higher civic and academic costs.

EXPLOITING THE DISABLED TO AROUSE ANTICIVIC FEELINGS

To illuminate the anticivic and anti-intellectual potential of many selections in current reading textbooks, we need look only at the thrust of several of the selections about disabled children and adults in them. A century ago, death and disease were regular visitors to almost every home, afflicting rich or poor, young or old alike. The stories about crippled or dying children that Charlotte Iiams found so prevalent in readers at the beginning of this century showed how unfortunate children coped with their physical or mental limitations, and how they often surmounted them. These stories were meant to build children's personal character. Today many, but not all, of the stories about the disabled in the readers are there to sensitize children to disabled people's needs, feelings, and frustrations and to teach them to respect the disabled. Although this is good stuff for Sunday school, it rarely makes for good literature. These stories usually imply that the problems faced by the disabled in our society result less from their physical or mental limitations than from defects in other people's or our society's character, thus inflaming a disabled child's sense of victimhood.

One illustrative morality tale—in Houghton Mifflin's grade 4 reader—is about an adult with Down's syndrome.[3] The teacher guide makes sure that teachers do not miss the point of this piece of pseudo-literature. When the youngest child in the family with which Uncle Joe is staying makes friends with him, teachers are to have students discuss why. As is common practice in teacher guides, the editors provide a "possible response." In this case, the possible response tells teachers in no uncertain terms what sociological generalization they are to convey to children in case no student gives the right possible response: "At five and a half, Amy has developed fewer prejudices against people in general, retarded people in particular, and is more able to recognize Uncle Joe's kind nature."[4] And when students complete the story, teachers are to ask students "why they think [the family is no longer disturbed by Uncle Joe's sloppy appearance and manner]." The possible response? That family members "love Uncle Joe and are able to see beyond their own selfish concerns. They have also come to value Uncle Joe's feelings."[5] The guide suggests that teachers have their students "work in small groups to suggest ways in which class members, family members, and individuals can encourage and support people with Down's syndrome or other intellectual challenges."[6] This story was highly recommended by the Council on Interracial Books for Children, as the editors inform both teacher and student.[7]

What are the problems with all of this? First, students are being given a tendentious story; it implies that the essential problems facing the mentally retarded are the prejudices, selfishness, and lack of sensitivity to their feelings in others, even their own family members. Second, students are to infer that any concern about the appearance and manners of a mentally retarded adult is not legitimate but a sign of selfishness. Those most bothered by Uncle Joe's appearance and manners—the older children in this white middle-class family—are depicted as ill mannered and narcissistic. The message is that one must accept people for what they are by nature and not attempt to help them achieve social norms, as if all Down's syndrome adults can't help but be sloppy slobs—not actually the case in real life. Third, the story is used to encourage social activism in fourth graders on behalf of a group that they are now to consider oppressed. Finally, the story and the guide present a jaundiced, if not paranoid, way of looking at child development. What is being suggested through the possible response to the question about why only young Amy is capable of making friends with Uncle Joe is the notion that adult society is filled with prejudices and that children naturally develop these prejudices as they grow up. This serves to justify the concentrated efforts teachers must make through the curriculum to undo all these presumed prejudices and inculcate right thinking and right behavior, even if it means displacing academic goals.

The prize for the most anticivic selection on the disabled in the readers goes to the Scott Foresman grade 6 reader for an essay on the deaf. To make sure the intended messages are grasped clearly by both teachers and students, the editors follow up a tendentious story about a ten-year-old deaf boy whose parents are also deaf with an essay in which the author of the story spells out her reasons for writing it. The plot of this story, set in 1899, revolves around the desire of the family who are "part of a hearing community" to send their son to a school for the deaf and, later, his satisfying experiences at this school. The guide urges teachers to stress "the differences between being born into a community and adapting or learning to fit into a community or culture."[8] Indeed, the editors suggest that those who do not hear belong to a different community and have a different group identity. To illustrate the loaded nature of the story, here is a passage from the story soon after the boy arrives at the school and has made a friend:

"Where your home?"

"From near M-u-n-c-y, P-a. Where yours?"

Landis shook the letter P. "Philadelphia. Here."

"Good for you. Easy go home," Harry answered.

"Maybe. Like school better. Home, only-one deaf. Small fun."

"Your mother, father talking?"

"Yes."

Harry was surprised. "Both?" Sitting at the school dinner table he usually knew which children came from hearing families, especially the younger ones. Their hands were stilted, harder to understand. He liked this boy's signs. They were large and friendly. "Brother, sister deaf?" Harry asked.

"No brother, sister."

"Who teach-you sign-language?"

"Visiting preacher. Name E-r-v-i-n. During small."

"I know preacher! I know, I know! Can hear? Yes. That same man who tell mother, father about deaf school." Harry was elated that they might know the same person. "Before, teacher here. Now preach-around, around P-a farms. Bring news from all ears closed." He extended the sign for "all" to show how large the scope of Mr. Ervin's travels was.

"Yes, yes," Landis nodded, "same man."

"Beautiful signs," Harry said. "My father not like hearing, but welcome E-r-v-i-n. I think because preacher sign good. Look same deaf."

"E-r-v-i-n mother, father deaf."

"Not-know before." Harry's hands stopped. No wonder Preacher Ervin signed so comfortably. "How you deaf?" he asked Landis.

"Sick. S-c-a-r-l-e-t f-e-v-e-r. Three years-old. Lose hearing. You?"

"Born deaf. Mother, father, all deaf."

"Easy for you."

Harry did not understand.

"You not lonely," Landis explained. "My mother, father not like signing.

First want me talk. Read-lips." Landis's face broke into a perfect imitation of the big, chewing mouths the hearing people who worked about the school used to make the children understand.[9]

In her explanatory essay, the author, Mary Riskind, tells children that she wrote her story because she wanted them to understand that "deaf people have the same needs and the same aspirations that hearing children have." At the beginning of her six-page exhortation, Riskind explains that although she can hear, she thinks of herself as a deaf person, as someone who is very much like children who are "first-generation Americans." She also notes that both her parents were profoundly deaf and always used sign language to communicate to each other and to their three hearing children. The parents led a completely normal life, occupationally and socially. They were part of a smaller community of similarly deaf people with whom they associated for social purposes, but they fully participated in the community at large, with their children acting as their interpreters and speakers. Even their church sponsored a signing minister who visited them once a month. Nevertheless, Riskind remembers that the deaf until recently "were almost an invisible minority" who were sometimes "discouraged from signing and encouraged to become as much like the hearing as possible in order to get along in a hearing world." We all have "our hearing prejudices," she implies. Just as we have opened up opportunities for women, she argues, we need to do so for the deaf.[10]

The point of the essay is quite clear: the deaf have been victimized by the prejudices of the larger society. Students should appreciate the significance of sign language as their "cultural" heritage and realize that the deaf have problems not because they cannot hear but because the hearing want them to become as much like the hearing as possible. Yet at no point does the guide suggest that children discuss whether the deaf might want to become as much like the hearing as possible. Nor are they asked to ponder whether in fact signing was discouraged because of prejudice against differences or because of good intentions by the educators of the day? Moreover, Riskind's personal history fails to support the charges she makes in her explanatory essay. So from whence comes this charge of prejudice against the deaf? Is it no longer possible to present a chiefly positive picture of a subgroup's experience—that of her parents and their friends, for example—even if it was true?

Riskind's essay illuminates several problems inherent in the growing practice in today's readers of accompanying literary selections with not just a short biography of the author but a short essay by the author spelling out exactly why he or she wrote the piece and what interpretation was intended. First, this practice may well serve to inhibit the exercise of the literary imagination. It also contradicts one version of the Reader Response pedagogy that has been advocated for years whereby students are to "construct" their own meaning of the literature they read. If students are told why an author wrote a piece of fiction and the interpretation they are to make, what is the point of reading the selection? In effect, they are being denied a literary experience. They should have been given the information in an expository selection. Finally, this practice allows both the explanatory essay and the work of fiction to escape critical reading. For expository or persuasive pieces of writing, in which authors typically articulate their purposes and lay out the details to support them, it has been standard practice to ask students to analyze the author's logic and supporting details to determine if the argument is logically presented and adequately supported. One cannot do this with an author's explanatory essay in the elementary school. How can a teacher or student question what the author herself says is why she wrote the work and what she intended it to mean? Nor is it reasonable to ask young students to determine if the author has in fact written a story that adequately conveys her intended interpretation. In this way, a fictional piece of propaganda can also evade critical scrutiny.

Some selections moralize on their own. The author of one of two stories on the mentally retarded in D. C. Heath's grade 4 reader promotes her subtext without editorial assistance and without supplying her own explication de texte.[11] She describes young Leo as "slow in reading, slow in numbers, slow in understanding nearly everything that passed before him in a classroom." Nevertheless, Leo thought "he would never get over it" after he had been separated from the rest of his classmates in the fourth grade "and placed in a room with other children who were as slow as he." To understand why this author was going after special education programs—programs devised by well-intentioned educators to provide the specialized help mentally retarded children need—one needs to know that mainstreaming, or the "inclusion" of even severely disabled children in the regular classroom, is now advocated by today's moral didacts. Although they claim that is how the children will best learn and how nondisabled children will best learn to respect those with disabilities, the research on whether the disabled benefit academically and socially from being mainstreamed has produced inconclusive results; much depends on the particular disability. Nor is it clear that the effects of inclusion on the regular classroom are necessarily positive.

Usually one or two selections on disabled people appear in almost all the readers. The disabilities range from blindness and deafness to mental retardation and cerebral palsy. Although most of the authors do not moralize in their own work, and some are genuine literary selections, it is telling to find no articles on the founding of Gallaudet College or the achievements of its deaf graduates, for example. There are no articles on the discovery of the polio vaccines. Or on Franklin D. Roosevelt's accomplishments despite the effects of polio. Or on the invention of the self-driven motorized wheelchair. Or on the work of Louis Braille (although there is a fine story on guide dogs in Harcourt Brace's grade 4 reader). Or on the public health measures in the first half of this century that dramatically reduced the death or disfigurement of children by smallpox.

The blinkered nature of the thinking behind the choice of many of these selections in the readers becomes clearer when one finds only one selection in all twelve readers—in Silver Burdett Ginn's grade 6 reader—about the story of Helen Keller and her extraordinary teacher, Annie Sullivan. Here is a story that should be in every reading series, if only as a model to inspire prospective teachers. It is also a story that can inspire great respect for a disabled person. Helen Keller was in fact accorded great respect and honor for her character and achievements by the entire world, and she never saw herself as a victim of prejudice. She never used sign language or spoke in dialect despite being profoundly deaf. Nor would she have ever said, as did Riskind in her essay, that "she was proud to be deaf," even though Keller was deaf and Riskind was not. Is Helen Keller's story disappearing because it cannot be used to indict the world in which she grew up?

USING WHITE RACISM TO AROUSE ANTICIVIC FEELINGS

Racism is presented in the readers as a defect in only white people. There is not a hint in the readers that prejudice can flow in the opposite direction or between ethnic groups themselves. Selections dealing with racism tend to highlight the victimization of blacks, American Indians, and Hispanics. Asians are presented as victims only in selections about the experience of Japanese Americans before or during World War II—in Houghton Mifflin's and Scott Foresman's grade 6 readers. Otherwise, Asians are not endowed with the moral status of victim.

Selections are not anticivic because they discuss racial prejudice. What makes a piece of fiction or a particular version of someone's biography anticivic is the highlighting of a person's or group's victimization and a blanket indictment of whites or the larger society. For example, although Faith Ringgold is a multitalented and successful artist, the selection on her in the Scott Foresman grade 4 reader highlights her status as victim (e.g., "It was hard enough being an African American woman artist . . .").[12] The selection on her in the Silver Burdett Ginn grade 6 reader, an excerpt from which appears in Chapter 1, clearly indicts all whites for the victimization of blacks. So, too, does Mildred Pitts Walter's *Have a Happy . . .* in the Houghton Mifflin grade 4 reader, as suggested by the following excerpt dealing with the response of the central character, a young boy, to his father's experiences looking for a decent job:

> "I'm getting tired of going on these little penny-paying jobs thinking they're going to turn into something and it's always the same—nothing."
>
> There was silence. Chris didn't remember ever hearing such bitterness in his daddy's voice. He kept his eyes on his plate as Daddy went on. "I feel like giving up and never going out there again."
>
> "Now certainly is not the time to think of giving up," Mama said.
>
> "You think I'm not even trying. I know you think I'm no longer the man of this house with you taking care of us," Daddy said angrily.
>
> "How can you say that?" She tried to take the edge off of his anger. "That's not what I think at all, Bruce. I still think there is something out there for you."
>
> "I'm glad you think so. There may be jobs, but not for me. I file an application and I'm told I'm overqualified. If I get to an interview, one look at me and I'm just not what they're looking for."
>
> *One look at me* rang in Chris's mind. This is happening because we're Black.

The teacher guide picked this theme up with this advice to teachers: "Ask students what it means to be discriminated against (to be treated worse than another person for an unfair reason). Then encourage students to talk about how discrimination can affect not only a person's feelings, but also his or her day-to-day survival."[13] Note first the focus here on students' imagined feelings. Note also that nothing positive is suggested for discussion. One wonders why the guide did not suggest that teachers also have students discuss whether the situation might be different for many black Americans today and whether students can point to positive interactions among races today.

Although prejudice or neglect is a significant part of the black experience in this country, it is possible for an author to bring it into a story about a successful black American without turning the story into a moral scolding of all of white America. For example, the story of black inventor and entrepreneur Elijah McCoy in the Harcourt Brace grade 6 reader is an interesting and informative piece that does not end up as a moral lesson about American society, even though the text is not at all shy in describing attitudes toward blacks in mid-nineteenth-century America. The focus is on McCoy's distinctive accomplishments over the course of his life, not how he as a victim overcame victimization.[14] The selection on Jacob Lawrence in Scott Foresman's grade 4 reader is similar in tone and substance. Prejudice is mentioned, but it is not central to the selection.

It is even possible to offer selections about talented blacks without ever mentioning their race. The story of Pele, the "King of Soccer," in the Silver Burdett Ginn grade 4 reader never once mentions his race, although the illustrations make it clear. Similarly, the selection on Bill Cosby in the D. C. Heath grade 4 reader focuses on individual perseverance, his unique talents, and the value of education.

It is thus ironic to find a two-page feature in Harcourt Brace's grade 6 reader, designed to help students make connections between the selection on McCoy and other readings, that violates Cosby's philosophy even as it brings in his name. Stressing how Cosby broke racial barriers when he became a television star, the text points out that television is "only one of many careers that were once closed to Blacks and others" and urges students to do research on "entertainment, sports, or other professional careers that once excluded African Americans, Latinos, or others," to find out "when these barriers were broken and by whom." This example is a clear reflection of the anti-intellectualism of today's multiculturalists. Instead of using this opportunity to invite students to do research on other important inventors of the nineteenth century, black and nonblack—to keep McCoy in the category of inventor—or to to do research on other successful nineteenth-century entrepreneurs, black and nonblack—to keep McCoy in the category of entrepreneur—students are directed to focus on the existence and overcoming of racial or other barriers in the entertainment and sports world. It comes as no surprise that the editors also choose to include Rod Serling's television script "The Monsters Are Due on Maple Street" in this reader. For this selection, the editors do not have to moralize; the narrator at the end of this short drama about extraterrestrial visitors to a stereotypical small town in America does it for them with the following words:

> The tools of conquest do not necessarily come with bombs and explosions and fallout. There are weapons that are simply thoughts, attitudes, prejudices—to be found only in the minds of men. For the record, prejudices can kill and suspicion can destroy.[15]

The moralism on racism in the readers is problematic in several ways, whether it is implicit or explicit in the selection or urged by the editors. Such selections can make white children feel ashamed of their country and of being white, especially when selections that might contribute to positive feelings about other aspects of their country's history have been almost completely excluded. Several decades ago, a story like Jackie Robinson's (in the Scott Foresman and Houghton Mifflin grade 4 readers) or Roberto Clemente's (in the Houghton Mifflin grade 4 reader) was more likely to be used to foster civic pride in the progress the United States was making toward racial justice. Today they are used to portray almost all whites as racists and to imply that America is a profoundly flawed country not worthy of respect—and this despite the fact that there is far less racism in this country today than ever before and that groups that have suffered from official or informal prejudice in the past have achieved a greater degree of equality here than in any other country.

A more serious problem is the possible effect on young nonwhite children of stories highlighting the victimization of nonwhites. Unless such stories are placed in a broad historical context—the larger story about the advances made by blacks and others since World War II and the growing integration of ethnic groups into all aspects of public life in America—they can easily stimulate hostility to American society (and ul-

timately to its political principles, institutions, and values) in young readers. Discussions of racism in relation to historical events take place more
appropriately in the history class where the efforts, or lack of efforts, of
Americans to address racism can be placed in their historical context.
When such selections are discussed in the literature class, they are not
likely to be historicized—or historicized with all the relevant facts—because fourth or sixth graders are unlikely to be studying their historical
contexts in their social studies class at precisely that time. Nor are such selections necessarily discussed with adequate or accurate background material, to judge by the material in the teacher guides. The selections on the
internment of Japanese Americans in World War II are a case in point.

Scott Foresman's grade 6 reader features several tales by Yoshiko
Uchida, a talented Japanese American writer who was interned with her
family during World War II. Before students read the story, the editors advise teachers to "activate prior knowledge" (a phrase meaning, "Ask students to recall what they may already know about the topic" or, as is more
likely the case, "Give students the historical context for the selection") by
explaining

> that the United States' relationship with Japan was not always friendly. Dur-
> ing World War II, the United States was at war with Japan. Tell students that
> the story they are about to read is about Japanese Americans during World
> War II who were imprisoned because of their Japanese ancestry. Tell students
> that this is an example of racial prejudice. Ask students to think of possible
> reasons why the United States chose to imprison Japanese Americans and
> discuss how this policy might have made Japanese Americans feel.[16]

There is not a word about Pearl Harbor or any indication of the scope of
U.S. government policy, which affected only Japanese Americans living
on the West Coast in America, not in Hawaii or on the East Coast. The
thinness of this background information for the events leading to the internment policy is surprising. On what basis can students think of possible
reasons for the imprisonment? Why weren't they given all the reasons for
this policy? How can intellectual growth result from a discussion of how
this policy might have made Japanese Americans feel? Is a range of answers even possible? Could anyone have felt good? What can students
gain from discussing what they imagine are someone else's feelings? They
have been given no informational material to analyze. Students are dis-

cussing only their uninformed speculations about other people's reasons
for doing things or their feelings.

The teacher guide for Houghton Mifflin's grade 6 reader does better
with respect to background knowledge; it provides a page full of solid information on the U.S. entry into World War II as an introduction to
Uchida's story, "The Bracelet." After mentioning Japan's earlier invasion
of China and other countries, as well as the attack on Pearl Harbor, the
editors ask teachers to explain to students that

> during the war the United States government took drastic steps—steps not
> permitted by the United States Constitution—to prevent possible coopera-
> tion between Americans of Japanese ancestry and the enemy. Under order
> from the military, Japanese Americans, even though they were American cit-
> izens and showed no evidence of disloyalty, were forced to leave their homes
> and live in concentration camps.[17]

Although the text is incorrect on the citizenship issue (many Japanese Americans were not citizens because our laws had not allowed them to
become citizens), and the camps are more appropriately called internment
camps to distinguish them substantively and ethically from Nazi concentration camps and Soviet gulags, Houghton Mifflin clearly attempts to
treat teachers and students as intelligent people. However, these editors
could not resist the impulse (or perhaps the advice of an academic consultant) to push student thinking in a particular direction. In a later note,
they advise teachers:

> Remind students that the United States was also at war with Italy and Ger-
> many. People of Italian and German descent, however, were not forced to
> leave their homes. Ask students to speculate as to why only people of Japan-
> ese ancestry were treated in this manner.[18]

Student speculation here, it seems, is to be based on thin air—and incorrect facts. Relevant information about the anti-German hysteria in
World War I would clearly complicate the simplistic charge of racial prejudice the editors are seeking to elicit. Even more damaging would be information on the (relatively small) number of German and Italian
nationals in America who were also interned during World War II.

The editors tip their hand when they recommend related stories for
students to read. They suggest that students might be "interested in another story about a young girl affected by the events of World War II, this

one a Japanese girl who lived in Hiroshima, Japan." *The Story of Sadako and the Thousand Paper Cranes* "tells the true story of a young girl who died from the effects of the first atomic bombing."[19] There is not a word about Sook Nyul Choi's works for the same age level about a young Korean girl and the effects of Japanese aggression on the Koreans. No matter where the Japanese lived or what they did, it seems, students are to conclude that they were the primary victims of the war in the Pacific.

An obsession with white racism may have influenced the amount of academic information children are given on other topics as well. As one example, for the story about Marian Anderson in the Houghton Mifflin grade 4 reader, the teacher guide notes that her achievements paved the way for other black American singers at the Metropolitan Opera. But it does not say who these singers are, such as Leontyne Price, Kathleen Battle, or Jessye Norman. One can only wonder why the editors did not leap at a chance to give students some authentic cultural information, although it may be missing simply because of hasty editing. Still, an opportunity for intellectual enrichment had clearly been missed. One can also wonder why the children were not offered stories about Price, Battle, and Norman instead of Anderson. Their stories might be far more motivating to black youngsters today than Anderson's story because they are all currently active as singers and symbolize what is possible today. It is hard to discount the nagging thought that someone felt that if the readers focused on their successful careers, black and white children might well conclude that blacks do not necessarily have to combat prejudice in order to be successful. Unfortunately, a regular diet of selections about black Americans who had to overcome prejudice to succeed encourages the notion that if a black person does not get ahead, it is because of prejudice.

I am not suggesting that selections that touch on slavery or racism or allow the teacher to raise the issue are inappropriate in a grade 4 or 6 reader. There are fine literary selections appropriate for elementary schoolchildren that do so, such as Sharon Bell Mathis's *The Hundred Penny Jar* in the Silver Burdett Ginn grade 6 reader. Mathis's work deals with human beings who were affected by racism, but she does not impose contemporary perspectives on the characters' dialogue or on the narration of events in the past. Children will be able to infer that slavery, the Civil War, and Reconstruction affected far more than the characters in Bell's novel. Literature can function as a source for sociological generalizations without a teacher's prodding.

An obsession about white racism also seems to inhibit significant information about other countries as well. For example, the informational material given teachers in the grade 6 Macmillan guide after students read *The Cay*, a novel set in the West Indies, pointedly omits the fact that the British were the first to abolish slavery in the nineteenth century:

> African slaves were the plantation owner's solution to their labor problem. Spain began bringing slaves from West Africa to the islands in the sixteenth century. Other European countries followed suit. By the late seventeenth century, there were more enslaved blacks than free Europeans on the islands.
>
> Throughout their inhuman existence, the slaves clung to their African heritage, keeping alive their language and beliefs. Some escaped to remote areas of the island where they intermarried with island natives, creating a unique blend of African and native beliefs. Slavery was abolished by the nineteenth century.

Note that the sentence on the abolition of slavery by the nineteenth century is the only one in the passive voice, with no indication of agency. Note also that the statement is not completely accurate. Although the British abolished slavery and the transatlantic slave trade in the nineteenth century, the East African slave trade was not abolished until after the middle of the twentieth century.

Racism in this country is apparently considered in most series an appropriate topic for discussion in the elementary school. However, to judge from their notable absence, the editors and their academic advisers appear to feel that it is rude to include selections that mention racism and other social problems in other countries (unless it is another Western country, as in a Dickensian selection about the exploitation of young boys as chimney sweeps in England in the Scott Foresman grade 6 reader). As a result, students learn about the Africa or Asia that appears in its folktales, not the Africa or Asia in its current fiction or in the news. Students read nothing about the caste system in India, the ethnic genocides taking place in Africa, or the ongoing destruction of major forms of animal life and their habitats also taking place there. Such exquisite sensitivity results in vast gaps in children's cultural knowledge.

It is ironic that the war-related civilian experiences that Charlotte liams noted as disappearing after World War II have returned as a topic. Now, the civilians portrayed as being hurt have been victimized by America, not the enemy. Students read in Houghton Mifflin's grade 6 reader about the suffering of the Japanese Americans who were interned in America during World War II, but find nothing about the suffering of the Koreans during and after World War II. When a piece of nonfiction about victims does appear and America is clearly not the oppressor, as in a selection about the Vietnamese boat people (in the Macmillan grade 6 reader), nothing in the piece itself or the teacher guide suggests from whom they are fleeing. Nor is there any mention of the oppression suffered by the Chinese in an article about a Chinese artist who visits the United States, or of the human sacrifices practiced by the Aztecs in a tale about their devotion to peace (both in the Scott Foresman grade 4 reader).

One example of an attempt to avoid discussion of negative aspects of another culture in the Scott Foresman grade 6 reader is an article about an outdoor game played by the ancient Mayans (somewhat similar to basketball). The author notes that in some games, "the losing players would have their heads cut off as a form of ritual sacrifice to the gods."[20] Elsewhere, the author notes that people would bet "precious stones, slaves, houses, and land."[21] In the twenty-five pages of teaching apparatus for this five-and-one-half page article, the editors never once suggest that students engage in a discussion of the role of slavery or the significance of beheading as a religious sacrifice to explore the culture of the Mayans. Instead, students are to be invited, among other things, to discuss the equipment worn by the Mayan players, to think about why the size of their ball courts differed, to draw pictures of the ball field, to explain the stone rings at the tops of the walls, and to compare the game with modern sports. For a "culture" question, they are to consider what "future generations will conclude about our culture from seeing our sports stadiums."[22] Only at the bottom of one editorial page do the editors acknowledge that students may be interested in some politically incorrect details. In suggesting how students might go about writing up a summary of the article, the editors warn teachers to "help students avoid overemphasis on individual kinds of equipment or jewelry, punishment suffered by losers, or other colorful but minor details."[23]

The Macmillan editors managed to avoid the problem altogether by using a selection on the Mayans in grade 6 that stresses their writing system. The background information they provide in the teacher guide studiously omits any mention of human sacrifice as part of the game of Pokta-Pok or as part of "the proper ceremonies" performed by the Mayans when they sought to get the "right weather," as in the following passage:

> The Maya realized that, as mere humans, they could not control forces of nature, like wind and rain, which affected their crops and, therefore, their livelihood. By viewing these forces of nature as gods, the Maya could assure themselves that if they performed the proper ceremonies, they could expect favorable weather.[24]

EXPLOITING THE FATE OF THE AMERICAN INDIANS TO AROUSE ANTICIVIC FEELINGS

The readers abound with selections on the Inuits and the American Indians, with a few on Indian groups in Central and South America as well. Because no writer can be unaware of the tragedy that befell the Native Americans in the Western Hemisphere, it is not easy for even talented writers to avoid the implication of moralizing when telling stories about the Indians. What an author inspired by a literary muse tries to do is keep the moralizing in check, as does Scott O'Dell in his well-known *Island of the Blue Dolphins*, excerpted in the Harcourt Brace grade 6 reader. But many authors of the selections on the Indians in these readers make sure that students learn how badly Americans dealt with the Indians, through comments by adult characters in a piece of fiction or made directly by the narrator of an informational selection.

We find the fictional device in the Silver Burdett Ginn grade 6 reader about a Ute boy who goes to Colorado to search for a father he never knew. The story notes that Cloyd remembers "his grandmother's parting words as he left for Colorado. She told him . . . their band of Weminuche Utes hadn't always lived at White Mesa. . . . Colorado . . . had been their home until gold was discovered there and the white men wanted them out of the way." In an informational selection on the Sioux in the Houghton Mifflin grade 4 reader, the narrator speaks directly. The ending notes that in the "decade following the building of the railroad, professional hunters killed millions of buffalo for their hides, which could be sold for a high price" and that by the "late 1800s, the Sioux and the other Plains Indians had lost the buffalo—and their way of life."[25]

Some authors and editors romanticize the Indians as a deeply spiritual people living in harmony with their surroundings and avoid commenting on the warlike nature of many tribes. For example, the Scott Foresman editors provide teachers with some brief background information on the Cheyenne, one of the most warlike tribes in the West, that is positively ecstatic about their spiritual and nature-loving qualities:

> In the Sioux (Lakota) language there is a phrase that sums up the world view of many American Indians in regard to the environment and all creation. This phrase is mitakuye oyasin—"we are all related." Mitakuye oyasin is invoked as a prayer before one eats a meal, as one enters the purification lodge, and after one smokes the sacred pipe in a ceremony.
>
> By saying this prayer, we remind ourselves that there is an interrelationship among all the things that God has created. We remember that all two-legged, four-legged, and winged creatures; all finned ones, crawling ones, and rooted ones living on mother earth are sacred, equal, and interdependent.
>
> In every American Indian society, the earth is thought of as a mother. Chief Luther Standing Bear talks about this idea in his 1933 book *Land of the Spotted Eagle* (University of Nebraska Press): "[The Lakota] loved the earth and all things of the Earth, the attachment growing with age. The old people came literally to love the soil and they sat or reclined on the ground with a feeling of being close to a mothering power. It was good for the skin to touch the earth and the old people liked to remove their moccasins and walk with bare feet on the sacred earth. . . . The soil was soothing, strengthening, cleansing and healing."[26]

This information accompanies one of the most emotion-arousing selections on the Indians in all twelve readers I examined. (For an excerpt from the story, see Chapter 4.)

The Houghton Mifflin selection on the Sioux, another warlike group in the West, also claims to focus on their culture, but at no point are their warring activities ever brought out, in either the text or the notes in the teacher guide. A Plains Indian tale by a contemporary writer in the Harcourt Brace Grade 4 reader about a wolf's guiding a lost brother and sister home to their family conveys a picture of a peaceful people caring about animals and their environment; it notes only that there are not too many wolves left because they have mostly been hunted or driven away. In its own offering on the Sioux, the editors of the Scott Foresman grade 6 reader apparently felt obliged to call attention in the teacher guide to Chief Luther Standing Bear's three references to the "war-path" and suggest that students do library research "to find out more about various aspects of historical Sioux life."[27] The editors were clearly caught between a rock and a hard place with this piece, because their explicit purpose for including it was to "emphasize the sense of community, the respect for the elderly, and the importance of religion that characterized the Sioux," despite the fact that "popular culture has often portrayed historical Native Americans as warlike." The editors no doubt wanted the piece because it was authentic—it was written by an Indian.

In other selections aimed at attitude formation in students, Americans are more than greedy or land-hungry settlers who physically displaced or destroyed many Native Indian communities. They are portrayed as attempting to destroy their customs and languages. In an informational selection about two contemporary Pueblo artists in the Silver Burdett Grade 6 reader, the narrator makes no bones about what she thinks has happened to their traditions:

> Like many Native American children who lived on reservations, Pablita and Patrick went to mission schools. . . . They lived at the mission schools and rarely saw their families. They were not allowed to speak their own languages or to take part in activities related to their people's past, because the schools wanted them to give up their traditional ways. Both Pablita and Patrick, however, kept their love for their people's ways in their hearts.[28]

The mission schools are shown as deliberately destructive of Indian culture in a piece of fiction in the Macmillan grade 6 reader as well. The major character, a girl, is a good student living on a Navajo reservation who learns about a school for "minority students—blacks, Hispanics, American Indians—who showed unusual academic ability." She applies and is accepted but is worried about having to give up her bilingualism— "In literature class they talked about books and writers that she had never heard of." She becomes depressed at school, but thanks to a teacher's encouragement, she perseveres. It is instructive that in neither story is formal education seen as a value for Indian children. No one points out that one goes to school in all cultures precisely to learn about books and writers one has not yet heard about or read.

The implication of most of these selections is how uncaring of the environment Americans are, how little sense of community we have, and how lacking we are in a meaningful spiritual life. Indeed, in the grade 6 Macmillan reader, a story that focuses directly on a contemporary Seminole girl's exploration of the relationship between her people's folklore and the modern world suggests an instinctive spirituality in Indians as well as a natural feeling for the environment.

The D. C. Heath editors are the only group of editors that show how the American Indians can be presented sympathetically but without moralizing and without romanticizing them. In the grade 4 reader, the editors skillfully arrange a group of selections to convey a more realistic image of the American Indian. Following an excerpt from a Laura Ingalls Wilder story and an excerpt about the hard life of pioneer children from Russell Friedman's *Children of the Wild West*, the editors offer a short selection about the Indians of the Great Plains, noting that "long before white settlers began to cross the prairie, the Great Plains was home to American Indians [who] lived in close touch with their environment."[29] The positive attributes of the Indians are alluded to only in the last sentence of the piece: "The Indians lived as part of a community, sharing the land with its other inhabitants."[30] But although this ending seems to imply that these Indians are a peace-loving group, this selection is immediately followed by a legend about a young Indian boy who guides a buffalo stampede in such a way that it tramples to death the warriors from a neighboring enemy tribe coming to wipe out his own people. The piece does not detract from the more basic message that the Great Plains had been the home of all these Indian groups, but it does make it clear, without directly saying so, that many Indians also had to fear each other in their struggle to survive, long before the Europeans arrived on the scene.

In the grade 6 reader, the D. C. Heath editors offer a group of completely nonmoralizing historical selections, all of which present the Indians positively but realistically. These include selections about Sacajawea and Lewis and Clark's travels, and a story set in 1849 about a brave young white girl who gets separated from her pioneer family, learns how to fend for herself in the wilderness, and is then helped by a group of Indians to get back to her people. There are no contemporary stories like those about the Seminole girl or the Ute boy, no informational selections implying how peaceful they all were, and no retrospective accounts by contemporary Indians like those of the Pueblo artists that contain various digs at Americans.

The tragic encounter between the American Indians and the European explorers and settlers clearly warrants study in the social studies class. However, the abundance of selections on the American Indians (and the Inuit) in these reading series does not stem from their influence on our literary culture. As the Macmillan teacher guide notes when commenting on the oral tradition of the Navajo and other Indian tribes: "Native American tribes had no written language."[31] Native Americans are also few in number today, and very few students in classes across this country are Indians. One can only surmise that the number and kind of selections on the Indians now in the readers are simply one more expression of the moralizing impulse so characteristic of many in the academic world. It is not that the selections about the Indians are necessarily untruthful. It is that only positive aspects of their lives are shown. Students' attitudes are being shaped to see Indians only in positive terms and whites only in negative terms. They are also being shaped to judge the European presence on this continent— indeed, the very existence of this country—as illegitimate, and its fundamental political values destructive. In the words of one California parent commenting on the problems he found in his children's elementary school, "Dammit, I get so mad when my kid comes home saying . . . that the country would be a better place if the Europeans never came to America."[32]

EXPLOITING ENVIRONMENTAL CONCERNS TO AROUSE ANTICIVIC FEELINGS

Children are more likely to gain useful knowledge on environmental issues in the selections offered on this topic than in those offered on the disabled, white racism, or the fate of the American Indians. For example, in Houghton Mifflin's grade 5 reader, the editors introduce a story about a polar bear cub in the Atlanta Zoo with a page full of information about how polar bears have been hunted, how many were once living, the laws that have been passed to protect them, and the dangers their habitats now face from people searching for oil and minerals beneath the Arctic ice.

The Silver Burdett Ginn grade 4 reader is exemplary; it does no moralizing. Free from either overt or hidden messages, it offers well-written selections on plants, flowers, and animals. Its editors apparently decided to allow students to draw their own conclusions about the need to protect animals.

But the editors of the Macmillan grade 4 reader seem to have overindulged their penchant for moralizing. It has over a half-dozen morality tales on the environment, nature, or animals alone. These sermons occur in the selection itself or in the teacher guide or in both, and in fictional as well as informational selections. In fact, by cleverly weaving in poems by American Indians before or after several informational selections on nature, Macmillan manages to turn a good part of the whole grade 4 reader into a lesson on the environment. It begins its moralizing with a selection on a "lost lake," followed by the author's comments on the littering problem he encountered years later in returning to the area. The environmental theme is picked up again in a story about the Bronx Zoo and its role in species preservation; it not only exhibits animals, it even helps "to preserve animals that are losing their homes in nature."[33] After a little boost to Hispanic self-esteem with a short two-page selection on Felipe Archuleta, "one of the first woodcarvers in New Mexico to create realistic-looking and life-size wooden animals,"[34] there appear a group of informational selections on birds, bees, bears, worms, fish, geese, and other living creatures, followed by a poem by a "Native American of the Yakima Nation." In a later unit devoted to environmental issues, preceded by a short poem on the need to be careful about the earth and ascribed to yet another anonymous Native American, we find a selection dealing with acid rain, pollution, government efforts, and recycling, containing the admonition to students under "What Can You Do?" to, among other things, "refuse to buy things that are excessively packaged." This is followed by a selection on whales, a fantasy about a boy's dream about the litter of the future (also in Harcourt Brace's grade 4 reader), a plea for trees, and a selection on Rachel Carson. Topping it all off is a selection about a former steel mill town (also in Harcourt Brace's grade 4 reader), with illustrations and text vividly depicting the soot and the grime that covered everything in the town before the steel mills finally closed down and the stars could be seen again. This reader is clearly an example of overkill.

To see how an informational piece evolves into propaganda, it is instructive to look at a story about the bald eagle in D. C. Heath's grade 4 reader. At first the message is subtle: "Scientists want to find out as much as they can, so that they can save this beautiful but endangered bird from extinction."[35] The article goes on to present reasons for its extinction: DDT, the decline of old-growth forests, and the cutting of lumber. Then insinuation begins. The "forests that eagles require have been cut down for lumber or replaced by towns and vacation homes." At this point we begin to infer that we are a greedy and shortsighted people to build homes that have displaced the eagle. Finally, the article makes an unsubtle appeal to children's emotions by mentioning the cruelty of leg-hold traps. At this point, the article has become a piece of propaganda designed to arouse feelings and alter attitudes.

Propaganda comes in imaginative pieces as well. In Harcourt Brace's grade 4 reader, the author of a story about a man who begins to chop down a kapok tree in the Amazonian rain forest does not even bother to give it a plot. As the man takes a nap, a variety of animals, insects, and other jungle creatures take turns whispering pleas and warnings in his ear. "Senhor, this tree . . . is my home, where generations of my ancestors have lived. Do not chop it down." "Senhor, . . . the forest will become a desert." "Senhor, a ruined rain forest means ruined lives." "Senhor, do you know what trees produce?"[36] At the end of the selection, the editors ask in the student text: "What do you think Lynne Cherry (the author) wants you to learn about rain forests?" As if there could be any doubt! As a temporary sop to the lumber industry, another question asks: "Do you think it is always wrong to cut down trees?" But later in this reader, the lumber industry is taken care of for good. In a story about a child's dream, his uncle catches a fish and then removes the fly from its mouth, letting it swim away. Responding to the child's question, he says: "I like to leave the river the way I found it. It's like cutting trees, Mark. You keep cutting trees and soon you're going to have bald mountains."[37] Harcourt Brace's protective attitude toward each and every tree is matched by Scott Foresman's concern for pandas. A story on China's precious pandas in its grade 4 reader makes the point how "precious, or valuable, every panda was."[38]

The bottom of the slippery slope for an unchecked penchant for manipulating children into social activism can be seen in a Houghton Mifflin grade 4 informational selection on rivers. As part of its coverage of rivers in America, it not unreasonably discusses their pollution from factory runoff and illegal dumping by cities. But the article concludes with, "Find out what you can do to help keep rivers in your area clean," not "What can you do to keep rivers in your area clean?" The Scott Foresman editors are especially helpful to activist teachers with respect to a Puerto Rican folktale about the Tainu Indians. Although the folktale itself does not moralize, the teacher guide talks about saving rain forests and gives the address of the Rain Forest Action Network.

Students are likely being preached at on environmental issues in more than their reading classes and possibly developing a negative reaction to the whole subject out of sheer annoyance. Nevertheless, there may well be a steep increase over the next decade in selections about nature or the environment. Most children like stories about animals because they are familiar to most children. Issues like hunting, overbuilding, cutting down forests, polluting our rivers, and littering are easy for young children to understand, although the complexities of economic policies to address these concerns are beyond them.

Although children stand to gain more academically useful knowledge from the selections on the environment than from those on the other social issues dealt with in the reading series, nevertheless, the effort to shape children's feelings does influence the quality and kind of information provided on environmental issues. Again, information one might legitimately expect is not given. For example, a selection in the Harcourt Brace grade 6 reader mentions violations of the international agreement not to hunt whales, but it does not indicate what countries are sending commercial ships near the Alaskan coastline and violating the agreement.[39]

Of greater significance are some major pieces of information that should have appeared in these readers if the authors and editors had approached environmental concerns with a stronger academic perspective. Rachel Carson is the only well-known American singled out in the total group of selections on the environment in these readers. Although she clearly warrants mention, one suspects her story was valued by the Macmillan editors as much for its demonization of the pesticide industry as for her accomplishments as a woman on an environmental issue. Curiously, there is nothing in any of the Macmillan readers on John Muir, Gifford Pinchot, Theodore Roosevelt, Frederick Law Olmsted, or other early pioneers in the national environmental movement. Given the abundance of environmental selections in the Macmillan readers alone, it would have been quite reasonable to have included selections on their achievements. Students should learn that America was the first country to establish national public parks and playgrounds and to preserve huge areas of wilderness. Americans also produced the first body of literature on the subject. Students should learn about the achievements of scientists and engineers in combatting environmental problems, such as the development of emission controls for automobiles. Today's children will learn none of this in their readers.

————————

In conclusion, the new moralism in the readers and teacher guides is deeply problematic on several counts. When teachers read in teacher guides that social goals are more important than academic goals, many may be indifferent to whether they are giving their students unbalanced or inaccurate information on historical events. When teachers infer from teacher guides that the most valuable response their students can make to their reading materials, whether expository or literary, is an emotional one, many may not spend their time trying to elicit a more demanding kind of response—an analytical one. And when teachers are led by their teacher guides to believe that the source of all social problems lies in the very nature of our society and in its dominant values, many may end up inadvertently fostering an antipathy to the very political principles and institutions that have enabled our society to address these social problems.

It is not possible to determine to what extent teachers are inadvertently promoting anti-intellectual and anticivic goals. No systematic nationwide research is possible. We do know, however, that the number of post-secondary students who require remedial course work in reading is extremely high; one of the commentators in a 1998 report on the costs and consequences of remediation in higher education notes that "one third of the nation's freshmen entering public higher education are now under remediation."[40] And, as Chapter 9 discusses, scores on the 1994 NAEP assessment of U.S. history were shockingly low at all age levels tested, while scores on NAEP assessments in reading have been declining in the last decade, especially those of minority students, after a period of rising scores in the late 1970s and early 1980s.

SIX

SPANGLISH, SWAHILI, AND DIALECT: INNOVATIVE WAYS TO DEPRIVE CHILDREN OF LITERATE ENGLISH

In the wee hours of the morning, the family made a circle around Grandma Ida, Beth, and Chris. Grandma Ida gave the *tamshi la tutao-nana*: "In this new year let us continue to practice *umoja, kujichagulia, ujima, ujamaa, nia, kuumba,* and *imani.* Let us strive to do something that will last as long as the earth turns and water flows."

"Now," Uncle Ronald said, "let's leave this house with the word *harambee*. In Swahili that means pulling together."

"*Harambee!*" they all shouted. They repeated it seven times, with Chris's voice the loudest of them all.

—From *Have a Happy* . . . by Mildred Pitts Walter in the 1993 Houghton Mifflin grade 4 reader[1]

TRY READING the passage in the epigraph. How easy is it for you as an adult to pronounce the Swahili words in a passage that appears at the end of this novel? Probably not very easy. Even if you had spent some time practicing their pronunciations over the course of reading the story, you might still hestitate over such words as *tutaonana, kujichagulia, ujamaa,* and *kuumba* because their spelling patterns diverge from typical English ones. There is a more important question, however. How likely are you to see any of these Swahili words again in outside independent reading? The answer? Not very likely. They are not words that contribute to the vocabulary needed by the typical middle or secondary school student in an English-speaking country.

One can only speculate why such a story is offered as fourth-grade reading material since the teacher guide provides no justification for including it for instructional purposes. Is it there to teach nonblack children to respect other languages? To enhance the self-esteem of black children on the grounds that this may have been the language of their ancestors in Africa? (In fact, most of their ancestors came from the western part of Africa and spoke other languages.) Or to pique black children's interest in learning Swahili as a second language? Whatever the reason, students and their teachers will spend valuable time learning the meaning of words with no real utility for English speakers, readers, and writers.

THE PRESENCE OF NON-ENGLISH VOCABULARY AND NON-ENGLISH TEXTS

Although basal readers are supposed to teach children how to read and write the English language, non-English words, phrases, and sentences can be found throughout the readers. In addition, selections are sometimes offered in both an English translation and the language in which they were originally written (almost always Spanish). Yet as far as I can determine, the teacher guides do not spell out how such selections and the use of non-English vocabulary could develop children's ability to read English. Such selections were probably chosen for the sake of social goals: to facilitate group identification and group esteem.

There are two general problems with the use of non-English words in reading selections: not only are their meanings for the most part useless to children trying to become literate readers and users of English, their pronunciations can be difficult to acquire or at cross-purposes with English pronunciation patterns. Thus, for different reasons they may confuse both the children in the class who do not speak the language the words come from as well as those who do.

A Useless Non-English Vocabulary

One could easily justify the teaching of some commonly used Latin or French words or phrases in grade 6, but no internationally used words from these languages appear. Most of the non-English words that appear in the readers are specific to various American ethnic groups or non-American cultural groups and are not commonly used in English. Many are part of the vocabulary of everyday life. For example, a story set in

Argentina, in Harcourt Brace's grade 4 reader, contains the following words: *estancia* ("ranch"), *gaucho, siesta, zamba* (a dance), *asado* (a slow-cooking meat), *mate* (a house), *pampas* ("grasslands"), *nandu* (an ostrich-like bird), and *carbonada* ("stew"). Although elementary school students are likely to encounter *siesta* and *gaucho* elsewhere, they are unlikely to see the other words in either their literary or academic reading, at least for many years. Macmillan's glossaries for grades 4, 5, and 6 contain the Inuit words for "snowy owl" and "It's coming"; the Spanish words for "the check," "that one," "a kind of greeting," and "potato"; the French word for "boat"; the Yankton Sioux word for "otter"; the word for an Italian cheese

SWAHILI GLOSSARY

Swahili vowels are pronounced as follows:
    a = like the *a* in car
    e = like the *a* in play
    i = like the *ee* in fee
    o = like the *oe* in toe
    u = like the *oo* in moo
    The consonants are pronounced the same as they are in the English language. The g in *gele* is hard, like the g in go. The accent is almost always on the next-to-last syllable in the words used here.

harambee (ha-ram-be), a call to unity and collective struggle, pulling together.
karamu (ka-ra-mu), feast.
kwanza (kwan-za), first.
Kwanzaa (kwan-za), an African-American holiday celebration that begins on December 26 and ends January 1. Founded in 1966 by Dr. Maulana Karenga, the holiday is a time of ingathering of African-Americans to celebrate their history.
nguzo (n-gu-zo), principles.
saba (sa-ba), seven.
tambiko (tam-bi-ko), pouring drink for ancestors — a libation.
tamshi la tambiko (tam-shi la tam-bi-ko), statement made when pouring drink for ancestors.
tamshi la tutaonana (tam-shi la tu-ta-o-na-na), statement of farewell.

From *Have a Happy . . .* by Mildred Pitts Walter in the 1993 Houghton Mifflin grade 4 reader.

("mozzarella"); and the Seminole term for the Florida Everglades. Are words like these worth learning as core words in a developmental reading program for the English language?

Some of the non-English words are highly abstract nouns, as one can see in the Swahili glossary shown here that Houghton Mifflin provides in its grade 4 student text before students begin their reading of Mildred Pitts Walter's *Have a Happy.* . . .

SEVEN PRINCIPLES OF KWANZAA

imani (i-ma-ni), faith.
kujichagulia (ku-ji-cha-gu-lia), self-determination.
kuumba (ku-um-ba), creativity.
nia (ni-a), purpose.
ujamaa (u-ja-ma), cooperative economics.
ujima (u-ji-ma), collective work and responsibility.
umoja (u-mo-ja), unity.

RITUAL SYMBOLS OF KWANZAA

bendera (ben-de-ra), flag.
kikombe (ki-kom-be), a cup.
kikombe cha umoja (ki-kom-be cha u-mo-ja), unity cup.
kinara (ki-na-ra), candle holder.
mazao (ma-za-o), crops.
mkeka (m-ke-ka), mat.
mishumaa (mi-shu-ma-a), candles.
mishumaa saba (mi-shu-ma-a sa-ba), seven candles.
vibunzi (vi-bun-zi), ears of corn.
zawadi (za-wa-di), gift or gifts.

SWAHILI GREETINGS

Habari gani (ha-ba-ri ga-ni), What's the news?
Kwanzaa yenu iwe heri (kwan-za ye-nu i-we he-ri), Happy Kwanzaa.

CLOTHING

buba (bu-ba), elegant robe or gown.
busuti (bu-su-ti), a robe with a scarf at the waist.
dashiki (da-shi-ki), a loosely fitting shirt for boys and men; a loosely fitting blouse for girls or women.
gele (ge-le), a head wrap.
kanzu (kan-zu), a robe for men.

From Walter, *Have a Happy* . . . .

Indeed, one wonders how well average fourth graders can understand the English meanings of *self-determination* and *cooperative economics* even though the author tries to illustrate the meaning of all these concepts in the novel and the editors advise teachers to point this out to students as they read it. In order to understand and discuss this novel, students are expected to learn the meanings and pronunciations of thirty-three words or phrases in Swahili.[2] Wouldn't it be better for all children, including African American children, to spend their time learning thirty-three literate English words instead? Moreover, as Thomas Sowell has pointed out, Swahili was the language of Arab slave traders in East Africa. It is not clear why African American children, or other children, should identify Swahili with African Americans.

Undoubtedly, most of these non-English words are critically important for the group that uses them, but most are useless for developing the ability to read mature works of literature or academic texts in English. The energy most children have to expend to learn literate English words is great enough, without their being burdened to learn the meanings of non-English words with no real significance for their development as readers of English. They constitute a distraction from the hard work at hand, which is for students to become familiar with the meanings of as many literate English words as they can.

I am in no way suggesting that foreign vocabulary should not appear or be taught in these readers. They can be, in grade 6 especially, but in general they should be those words (or abbreviations) that appear in more difficult English prose, such as *pro bono* or *carte blanche* (or A.D. and R.S.V.P.), usually of Latin or French origin. They should also be identified on the page in the student text as foreign vocabulary—and italicized and footnoted.

The Treatment of Non-English Vocabulary

One might reasonably expect that a textbook designed to teach students how to read English would indicate the meaning, origin, and pronunciation of all the non-English words in its selections at the bottom of the student pages on which they appear. The only exceptions might be those few words whose meanings can easily be guessed from context or those words or phrases that are paraphrased immediately in English in the text, with an indication in the teacher guide of the language the word comes from if it is not clear from the rest of the text. In many readers, the standard practice is to italicize and footnote the foreign language word, but not all books observe in these practices. Table 7 captures the bewildering variety of ways in which non-English vocabulary appears in these series.

A particularly troublesome practice appearing in several readers is the attempt to pass off foreign words as English. Chapter 1 shows one example of this phenomenon: the excerpt from a story written in Japanglish. More frequently this phenomenon occurs with Spanish words. For example, the Spanish words in the story set in Argentina in the Harcourt Brace grade 4 reader are italicized the first time they appear in the text, but not afterward. And the editors have deliberately not provided their translations and pronunciations on the pages in the student text, it seems, in order to build the self-esteem of any Spanish-speaking students who may be in the

TABLE 7

Number of Selections Featuring Non-English Words in the Readers for Grades 4 and 6

	D. C. HEATH		HARCOURT BRACE		HOUGHTON MIFFLIN		MACMILLAN		SCOTT FORESMAN		SILVER BURDETT GINN	
GRADE LEVEL	4	6	4	6	4	6	4	6	4	6	4	6
Whole original text appears next to its English translation						1	2		2			1
Non-English words not italicized, footnoted, or paraphrased on the page							1		3			
Non-English words italicized or in quotations, but not paraphrased on the page	3					1	2				1	1
Non-English words italicized and/or footnoted, paraphrased or translated on the page				3	1	3			4	3	3	6

class. The teacher guide asks teachers to "have Spanish-speaking students work as peer tutors with other students to help them discover the meanings of the Spanish words in the selection. They may also be able to help with the pronunciation of Spanish words and names." The guide eventually gives the teacher the definition and pronunciation of all these words in a postselection activity, but not before or while students read the story.

The failure of a student text to provide a translation or paraphrase for non-English words on the page on which they appear is a much more serious problem than the failure to provide their pronunciation. Nevertheless, the lack of a pronunciation guide for a non-English word on the page on which it first appears in the student text has serious consequences in discussion-oriented elementary school classrooms. Many of these words are proper nouns whose pronunciations must be learned if students are to discuss characters and settings. Yet children will encounter words from many languages—Arabic, Swahili, Portuguese, as well as Spanish—without a clue to their pronunciation on the page where they appear. For example, the Scott Foresman grade 4 student text does not give students the pronunciations of either *Praia do Forte, Bedouin, sheik, Hamed, macaw, Yucaju, Tenochtitlan, Itzcoatl, Tezozomac, Papago, I'itoi* (a "Great Spirit" of the Papago Indians), or *kiva* (a ceremonial chamber). Moreover, although the teacher guide does tell teachers how to pronounce most of them, many of these non-English proper nouns will probably require considerable oral practice, by the teacher as well as by the students, to judge by the amount of time I spent practicing their pronunciations. One wonders why the Scott Foresman editors did not begin to sense that many of their reading lessons were turning into pronunciation lessons for both teachers and students. A grade 4 teacher I visited in a working-class suburb south of Boston commented on the time she had had to spend practicing the pronunciations of the Hawaiian words in a story about Hawaii before her students read it.

Original Texts and Their English Translations

Six original texts are paired with their English translation in these readers: two poems, a play, an autobiographical piece, a story, and a selection by a "hearing-impaired" Inuit written in both English and an unnamed script that is stylized as Inuit (and is, presumably, the script the Inuit use). After looking through all the editorial material in the teacher guides, I still could not determine what meaningful educational purposes are served by using space in an instructional reader for selections that are in languages other than English. If there are meaningful purposes for this practice, the editors of these readers have not provided them. What the editors do suggest as reasons for this use of text space make no sense, for example, to develop the "skill" of connect[ing] "Spanish to English" or of "listen[ing] for words that sound something like English words"[3] or to have grade 4 students "compare the rhythm and rhyme in both the English and Spanish verses."[4] Mercifully, the Silver Burdett Ginn editors do not ask students to do anything with the original Spanish version of the six-line poem it provides with an English translation in its grade 6 reader. Mysteriously, in the one case where it was possible to give children genuine cross-cultural information—the Inuit narrative in Macmillan's grade 4 reader—there is not a single word in the student or teacher text about the history, purpose, and authorship of the unusual written alphabet the Inuit may use.

Do reading textbook editors or their educational consultants believe that children are culturally enriched simply by seeing what an unknown language looks like in print or by listening to an audiocassette of a language they cannot comprehend? If they truly believe that there are benefits to be obtained from listening to a language one does not understand, teachers might ask their students to listen at home to a non-English language channel on their television sets or radios.

CULTURAL AND INTELLECTUAL INCOHERENCE

A second major problem arises in readers containing a large amount of ethnic American and non-American content: their cultural and historical scatter. Students frequently move from one social group to another, with the setting sometimes shifting from one continent to another and from one historical period to another. For example, a themed unit in Macmillan's grade 4 reader entitled "Remember When . . ." features a story about an African American child's great-grandparents, a Maidu Indian tale, an autobiographical story of life in a former West Virginia steel mill town, and an excerpt from a social studies book about the Inuit people. A themed unit entitled "Leave It to Me" in its grade 6 reader contains a fairy tale parody that takes place in an imaginary kingdom, a biographical sketch of a Vietnamese boy's grandmother, an excerpt from an adventure novel that takes place in the Swiss Alps, and an African folktale. A themed unit in Harcourt Brace's grade 4 reader on "Dreamers," or characters determined to achieve their goals, features a fantasy in time and a fantasy about a river in this country, an African folktale, a contemporary piece of realistic fiction set in this country about the baseball-playing ability of a young boy from Japan, and an autobiographical piece set in Argentina.

How this cultural and historical scatter, more pronounced in some readers than in others, ultimately affects children's world knowledge and general comprehension can only be surmised. And the situation is even more problematic because these children may be experiencing a somewhat similar phenomenon in their social studies curriculum, whether it is a problem-oriented one or a sequence of units on various cultural groups in different continents over differing historical eras. It is unlikely that hopping from one cultural group to another and often from one century or continent to another can give children a stable understanding of any cultural group or its history, even when editors of a reader make an effort to locate these groups and their place names in a historical time frame or geographical setting. In its grade 4 reader, Harcourt Brace provides excellent maps of the world to accompany a story about the rain forest, as well as an informative time line of events and map of Massachusetts for a story about the pollution and eventual clean-up of the Nashua River. But this is not a uniform practice across series or even within the Harcourt Brace readers. No map of South America or Argentina is provided to accompany the story set in Argentina; teachers are asked to supply one for their class.

The cultural incoherence in the readers is an almost unavoidable characteristic of the groupings for the literary selections. Informational selections can be much easier to group coherently than literary selections. For example, by using a large number of informational selections on topics in the social studies and science, the Houghton Mifflin readers offer coherent groupings that allow students to develop a fuller understanding of each topic. A unit on ancient Egypt in the grade 6 reader contains three selections showing the purposes and characteristics of history writing, followed by another unit on exploring the oceans, with four selections showing the purposes and characteristics of science writing, each selection in each unit revealing somewhat different purposes and characteristics. From these two units, students can build an increasingly refined understanding of each topic and the different ways in which ideas are articulated and organized in historical and scientific writing. None of the other series groups its informational selections together in a way that allows for a focused development, however brief, of knowledge about a particular informational topic.

In addition to the historical and cultural scatter, the selections in most groupings do not have literary or intellectual connections to each other or to the unit's organizing topic or theme that allow for a progressively deepening understanding of the topic or theme. For example, one unit in the Scott Foresman grade 4 reader centers on the family: students first read three selections, which allow them "to discover what makes a family a family, and what makes each family unique"; then two selections that "explore how families pass along their heritage and customs from one generation to the next"; then two selections written by children who have written about family members ("genre study"); and, to end the unit, five selections by one author about her childhood memories ("author study"). A promising beginning with respect to the first five selections peters out with respect to the last seven selections.

Finally, the editors' choices from a vast pool of available selections often seem to be motivated by more than just the organizing concepts, leading to further problems. For example, two groups of selections illustrating the concepts of courage and survival in two different readers both have an unarticulated feminist twist. In D. C. Heath's grade 6 reader, a unit organized under the title "Meeting the Challenge" groups a biography of a twelve-year-old New Jersey girl who helped to break open Little League for girls, a Chinese fairy tale about a widow whose youngest son must exhibit great courage in the face of many ordeals in order to rescue her brocade from the fairies, and a piece of realistic fiction about a twelve-year-old girl who uses her intelligence to survive a winter by herself in the Montana wilderness in 1849 before she is rescued by a group of Indians. In Houghton Mifflin's grade 6 reader, a unit organized under the title "The Spirit of Survival" groups an adventure story about a contemporary girl who sets out to find the wild boar living in the woods near her home, a piece of fiction set in the South in 1855 about an "African American girl who leads a group of teenagers out of slavery" to freedom, a true story about a teenage girl who with her father survives a plane crash at sea, and a short novel about a young Inuit sister and brother who face incredible challenges in bringing a killed caribou back to their starving family. With respect to the development of the unit's topic, the Houghton Mifflin teacher guide notes that these selections "reveal how an author presents characters through internal and external conflicts in adventures." It is possible that students will learn from either group of selections that a person's character can be shown through the conflicts he or she faces, that courage comes in different forms, and that young people from a variety of cultural groups and historical periods are quite capable of meeting challenges to survival. These are useful generalizations for students. But neither cluster provides a cumulative learning experience, with each selection building in a meaningful way on the previous one. And the total exclusion of white boys from the ranks of courageous young people by the editors' choice of selections in both these clusters may implicitly qualify these generalizations in children's minds.

One may doubt whether children will be able to gain significant insights into concepts like survival and courage when the topics are not illuminated with any systematic breadth or depth and editors seem to be guided more by ideological than intellectual considerations. That is why I was struck by the intellectual elegance of the conceptual organization of the selections in the readers published in 1995 by Open Court, a series with a deliberate balance between mainstream American and British writers and other writers (ethnic American and non-American). As the series itself indicates, it maintains a "commitment to classic literature." The ways in which selections are related to each other and to their organizing concepts in what the series aptly calls "learning units" suggest what can be accomplished when editors are not rigidly bound by social or political considerations in their choices.

The selections in a unit entitled "Surviving" in its grade 4 reader are linked to each other and the unit concept (as spelled out on page 12 of the teacher guide). A biographical account of Matthew Henson's expedition with Robert Peary to the North Pole shows how "one can survive in a harsh climate through the direct teachings of those familiar with the environment." A piece of fiction about a young boy's efforts to remember the teachings of an Apache farmhand in order to survive a plane crash in the Arizona desert shows how "one can survive in a harsh climate by recalling previous survival techniques learned either directly or indirectly." An excerpt from *Island of the Blue Dolphins* about an abandoned young Indian girl's efforts to survive on an island in the Pacific shows how "resourcefulness and courage can enable one to deal with extreme danger." A tall tale shows how ingenuity and a positive attitude "can turn a bad situation into a good situation." A poem by David McCord about a grasshopper shows that perseverance is necessary "in surviving a prolonged hardship." An excerpt from a story by Pearl Buck about the attitudes of Japanese villagers who survive the destruction of family, friends, and homes by a giant tidal wave shows how "time can help one heal emotionally when faced with disaster or extreme hardship." A poem by A. A. Milne suggests the value of a little solitude for coping with "everyday difficulties." An autobiographical piece by a survivor of the Holocaust shows how "poetry and music can help one express fears and hopes during a trying time." An excerpt from Anne Frank's diary shows how "writing is one way to express inner fears, helping one cope with a difficult situation." Finally, an informational article on music and slavery, together with two black spirituals, show how "music and dance can help one momentarily forget hardships and still hope for better times."

This unit contains a variety of selections sequenced in a way to enable students progressively to deepen their insights into the nature of the resources human beings draw on to survive hardships or disasters. The unit encourages not the superficial generalization that all kinds of people can meet challenges to survival but an insight into the different resources that human beings in different places and times have drawn on to survive. The unit encourages the development of an intellectual and emotional depth that is not possible when the range of selections offered is restricted for social or political purposes. Moreover, although the selections in the 1995 Open Court unit deal with the lives of many different groups of people in a variety of places, not all the stories are about children, and there is no gender or racial bias. Nor is there any attempt to downplay racism as one of life's challenges (or to give it an anti-Western tinge).

One more example from this grade 4 reader shows how students can be provided with an intellectually coherent experience and an opportunity for genuine intellectual growth at the same time they are exposed to the lives of a variety of human beings, in this country and elsewhere, and to authentic inclusiveness. A grade 4 learning unit entitled "Technology," whose conceptual structure is spelled out in the teacher edition, begins with an informational article on the wonders of the pyramids to show that "before the use of animals, human labor was slow and backbreaking." The next pieces are historical fiction about the Great Wall of China, showing a "monumental achievement of ancient technology built with human labor," and a folktale about ancient China, showing that the "horse was used in farm labor, warfare, transportation, and recreation." Then there is an informational article about "the workhorse" to show that the horse "has provided many services to humans over the ages: on the farm, in the factory, in mines and quarries, in hunting and herding, on ranches, and even in the building of railroads." This is followed by "The Wonderful Machine," from a Laura Ingalls Wilder book showing that in the late 1800s "new technology began to replace the use of horses for farm labor." Next is another piece of historical fiction, "Thrashin' Time," showing that as machines began replacing the horse on farms, people's attitudes ranged from optimism to reluctance. There is then an excerpt from *Black Beauty*, showing that for centuries "the horse played a crucial role in delivering messages." This excerpt is followed by an informational article, showing that the role of horses as messengers "changed over the ages, from being the key player in the first postal system to being completely displaced by the telegraph." Children are then given a biographical account of George Stephenson, an inventor of locomotives and an engineer who laid out railroads, showing that many inventors "had a critical role in the replacement of the horse by machines." The unit concludes with a poem about progress suggesting that "technological progress also has its drawbacks" and a piece of historical fiction from Alice Dalgliesh's *America Travels*, showing that "modern technological advances, such as the invention of the car, have changed the way we live and work."

This unit is an extraordinary pedagogical achievement. In addition to the clear links each selection has to other selections and the unit concept, it shows how chronological organization of selections spanning different cultures and vastly different historical eras can give students a powerful insight into a profoundly important social development. Literary selections can be taught as literary selections, but an analysis of the unit as a whole, after students have completed it, can help them achieve an understanding of a significant extraliterary concept—the benefits of technological advances to the human condition.[5]

THE NATURE AND SCOPE OF THE ENGLISH VOCABULARY

Perhaps the most troublesome feature of many selections in these readers is the nature of the reading vocabulary in them. In grades 4 through 6, a major goal of an instructional reader is to build up children's ability to read and then use literate English words (those words at or above a seventh-grade reading level). Because of the expansion of its original lexicon by the borrowing of foreign words, the adding of new meanings to existing words, and the coining of altogether new words, English may have the most extensive vocabulary of any written language in the world. There are, in fact, one-quarter of a million main entries in *Webster's Third New International Dictionary*. Any lessening of opportunities to learn the staggering vocabulary of the English language has far more serious consequences for children trying to learn to read and write English than it would have for children trying to learn other written languages. It is therefore with great dismay that one must regard the scope and nature of the vocabulary being developed in many readers.

Dialect and Slang

One striking feature in many readers today is the number of selections featuring non-standard English. Table 8 shows the numbers across readers. Following are some examples of the black dialect or slang that students encounter:

> "That ungrateful boy," Mama grumbled, "never says thank you, but always demandin' somethin'. Seems that's all I do, take Jerome Johnson somewheres. Now he want a tricycle at eleven years. Lordy, what's comin' next?" . . . "What they say, Mary?" ("Ride the Red Cycle," Scott Foresman grade 4)

> "What kind of talk you talking, Rabbit? . . . you have to come botheration me about pull me out my bed." ("Bo Rabbit Smart for True," Scott Foresman grade 4)

> "Can't nobody put shackles on Brother Wind, chile. He be special. He be free." ("Mirandy and Brother Wind," Macmillan grade 4)

> "Didn't say nothing to nobody but one another. Just up and decided to do it." ("The Lucky Stone," Macmillan grade 4)

> "I was scared quiet; she was scared loud." ("Memories of Family," Scott Foresman grade 4)

> "She sweetest, goodest safe." ("A Wolf and Little Daughter," D. C. Heath grade 4)

> "Wouldn't nobody believe it." ("Louella's Song," Houghton Mifflin grade 4)

> "Shore, Shore, Fannie's fetchin' more. We gotta dance. . . . Member, 'fore mornin' we goin' to be." ("Slaves No More," Houghton Mifflin grade 6)

> "I know you not scared of boys." ("Sister," Houghton Mifflin grade 6)

"What in the world you want it for?" ("Memories," D. C. Heath grade 6)

"The ones flyin were black and shinin sticks, wheelin above the head of the Overseer." ("The People Could Fly," Scott Foresman grade 6)

Timothy explained, "D'nawth is alles d'bleak beach on any islan'," but he couldn't say why. (*The Cay*, Macmillan grade 6)

In these examples of black dialect, final letters are omitted in some participles such as *demandin'*, *somethin'*, and *comin'*, but not in all; the apostrophe indicating a missing letter is omitted in one selection but not in others; the final "s" is omitted in some but not all of the third-person singular verbs; and the uninflected form of the verb *to be* is used in some examples but omitted altogether in others. We also find double negatives as well as other differences from standard English. Even if one could justify exposing students to black dialect in reading instructional material, there is likely to be more confusion than understanding about what constitutes black dialect and how to write it. Moreover, not only is there no one form of black dialect, there is in fact no one correct way to transcribe it. The editors of only two series—Harcourt Brace and Silver Burdett Ginn—had the good sense not to include any stories with black dialect or slang.

Dialect is not restricted to selections featuring African American or West Indian characters. It appears in a selection about small-town America—for example, "He ain't a mite better'n you or me and he needs takin' down a peg or two" ("Lentil," Scott Foresman grade 4). Slang or street talk is featured in a story in Houghton Mifflin's grade 6 reader: "The Scribe" contains such phrases as "digging the action," "hearing him first-name," and "all the cool I could muster." Dialect also appears in a selection show-

TABLE 8

Number of Selections Featuring Dialect or Slang in the Grades 4 and 6 Readers

	D. C. HEATH	HARCOURT BRACE	HOUGHTON MIFFLIN	MACMILLAN	SCOTT FORESMAN	SILVER BURDETT GINN
GRADE LEVEL	4 6	4 6	4 6	4 6	4 6	4 6
Dialect or slang	1 1		1 3	2 1	4 2	1

ing the dialogue of deaf children (see the excerpt from "Apple Is My Sign" in Chapter 5).

Stories in dialect are highly questionable for the purposes of reading instruction in the early elementary grades, regardless of the race or ethnicity of the child. An African American teacher in a Boston suburb told me she would never use stories in dialect for reading instruction with her students, no matter what color. It is a misconception of the goals of reading instruction to teach children how to read using people's oral speech written down when their speech deviates from standard written English. Dialect in literature is appropriate only for stories studied as literature. Moreover, such selections may imply to many children that most blacks speak in dialect, which certainly is not the case. They contribute little to the development of a reading vocabulary if the dialogue in which dialect is used occupies most of the text space for the story.

Equally as important, there is not a whit of published and peer-reviewed research evidence to suggest that the presence of dialect in an instructional reader increases "cross-cultural" communication, tolerance of dialect speakers by nondialect speakers, or either reading ability or self-esteem in black children. If anything, it is likely to exert a negative influence on the development of language and writing skills in the very children who most need exposure to well-written English, as the results of scores in a number of Los Angeles schools teaching Ebonics seem to suggest.[6]

A Cultural Smorgasbord of Proper Nouns

Yet another group of words in these readers requires extra learning time but also bears little or no relationship to literacy in English. Most of these words are names of individuals, gods, goddesses, spirits, places, kings, queens, and other rulers in the various non-Western cultures featured in the selections. The more cultures a reader features, the more languages the proper nouns will come from and the more varied will they and their pronunciations be. For example, in the glossary for Macmillan's grade 6 reader, *Mai, Maizon, Paulo Mendez,* and *Mongo* are four of the eighteen words under *m; Quito Sueno* is one of three words under *q;* and *Eliscue, Eronni,* and *Emeke* are three of the seventeen words under *e.* By the time children finish six years of elementary school in a highly multiethnic and cross-cultural reading program, they may have acquired an immense fund of proper nouns that are almost totally useless for comprehending mature literary and academic texts in English in the secondary school. Whether they can pronounce even half of them is anybody's guess.

A Relative Paucity of Literate Words

The glossary at the end of an instructional reader contains only those words used in the selections "whose meanings, pronunciations, and/or usage are unfamiliar or difficult," as one group of editors put it.[7] These are the new words highlighted for direct instruction by the teacher before or as students read a selection. The differences among the glossaries of the grades 4 and 6 readers in the number and the difficulty level of the words in them are startling and informative. And they may be related to the differences in the amount of ethnic content in a reader.

Tables 9, 10, and 11 show all the words under i and v (except proper nouns) in the glossaries of the readers for grades 4, 5, and 6 in the six series. I chose to study the words beginning with these two letters because in the upper elementary grades and above, they tend to be literate English words, usually derived from Latin. Beside each word, I noted the grade level assigned the word by two vocabulary researchers, Edgar Dale and Joseph O'Rourke.[8] In the 1960s and 1970s, they tested over 44,000 words and phrases to determine the lowest grade level (4, 6, 8, 10, 12, 13, or 16) at which a word could be said to be known in print by most of the students at that grade level in a representative national sample. For example, a word found to be known by a majority of students only at grade 8 and above could not be assumed to be known by a majority of students below grade 8. It would have to be considered a candidate for direct instruction if it appeared in a reading selection for students with a reading level below grade 8.

Note the variations among the readers for each grade level in the number of words that the editors believe have unfamiliar or difficult meanings. However, keep in mind that the numbers in themselves are not quite as meaningful as they seem if editors place in the glossary many relatively known words at that grade level that they believe are still difficult enough to warrant pedagogical attention. What really matters is the number of hard words per grade—that is, the number of words that are still not known at that grade according to a measure of word difficulty. Tables 12, 13, and 14 summarize the information in Tables 9, 10, and 11 showing the total number of words under i and v in the glossaries in these twelve readers at

TABLE 9

Words Under i and v in the Glossaries of the Grade 4 Readers and Assigned Grade Levels

D. C. HEATH (1993)	HARCOURT BRACE (1995)	HOUGHTON MIFFLIN (1993)	MACMILLAN (1993)	SCOTT FORESMAN (1995)	SILVER BURDETT GINN (1993)
imaginative 8	idiosyncrasy 13	idle 6	ignite 6	indicate 6	identical 6
immense 8	immediately 6	impatiently 6	immortal 8	inspire 8	illustrate 4
impact 8	immersion	impossible 4	incinerate 10	inky 12	imagination 4
indifferent 12	heater 12	infield 4	ingot 13	inseparable 6	immigrate 6
inhabitant 8	impatient 4	inform 6	intimidate 10	image 6	impertinent 10
intentionally 6	inning 6	inning 6	investigate 6	indignant 12	impress 6
intercom 6	innocent 4	instructions 6		imperfect 6	inaccurate 6
interview 6	instinct 8	introduction 4	vigil 12	impress 6	indignant 12
	instructor 4	investigate 6	vigilante	improve 4	infectious 6
veer 13	insulated 10		group 12	infection 4	initial 6
version 6	intensity 8			illuminate 8	innocent 4
veterinarian 6	intention 6				insane 4
vigil 12	international 8			verse 4	inspiration 6
vision 4	interrupt 6			virus 8	integrate 8
vulnerable 12	interview 6			veterinarian 6	intention 6
				violin 4	introduce 4
	vacation 4				invent 4
	vain 10				investment 6
	veterinarian 6				
	vigorously 8				vegetation 8
	violinist 4				venture 8
	volcano 4				verse 4
	volunteer 4				victor 6
					vigil 12

Note: Grade levels assigned by Edgar Dale and Joseph O'Rourke, *The Living Word Vocabulary* (Elgin, Ill.: Dome Press, 1976).

each assigned grade level in Dale and O'Rourke's research on word difficulty, as well as the total number that is higher than the grade level of the reader itself. As these three tables show, the reader with the most hard words beginning with these letters at each grade level has about twice as many hard words as the reader with the fewest in each grade. This finding suggests the wide variations in students' exposure to a literate vocabulary, depending on the reader used for their reading instruction.

TABLE 10

Words Under i and v in the Glossaries of the Grade 5 Readers and Assigned Grade Levels

D. C. HEATH (1989)	HARCOURT BRACE (1995)	HOUGHTON MIFFLIN (1993)	MACMILLAN (1993)	SCOTT FORESMAN (1993)	SILVER BURDETT GINN (1993)
immaterial 8	identical 6	immensity 8	immortal 8	idle 6	idiomatic 12
impair 13	ignorant 8	immigrant 6	impetus 12	illustration 6	illegal 4
imperceptible 16	illuminate 8	improvement 4	incongruous 13	illustrator 4	illiterate 10
indicator 10	improvise 13	incinerator 6	intimacy 10	imagination 4	illness 6
indignant 12	incriminating 8	incubator 6	insistent 8	innovation 16	illustration 6
inevitable 8	indicate 6	influence 6	valiant 10	invent 4	immigrant 6
inflict 9	indignant 12	instinctively 12	vandalize 6	invention 4	identical 6
ingredient 8	influential 10	inspiration 6	vantage 12	incubator 6	imprint 8
insignificant 8	inherit 6	insulin 10	vestige 16	immigrant 6	improvisation 13
insurmountable 12	initiative 10	intact 12	vigil 12	inflation 8	independence 4
interpreter 8	insufficient 8	intend 6	vital 8	inhalation 6	inefficient 8
intromittent —	intimidate 10	invention 4		inhale 6	infectious 6
iridescent 16	inventiveness 6	inventor 4		interrupt 6	infinite 8
	irresistibly 6			investment 6	ingenious 6
vale 12	irritation 6	vague 8		imprint 8	inscription 8
venomous 8		verge 12		intersect 8	insert 6
viewer 10	vague 8	vital 8		intersection 6	insignificant 8
vindictive 13	veranda 10	volcano 4		ingredient 8	interior 6
visualize 8	vertical 8	vow 6		invade 8	interruption 6
	vigorously 8	vulnerable 12		vow 6	invalid 8
	violently 6			venture 8	invaluable 12
	visualize 8			vertical 8	inventor 4
	volt 6				investment 6
					invitation 4
					vast 6
					venture 8
					verdict 6
					vessel 6
					vestige 15
					vibrate 6
					vie 16
					viewpoint 8
					vigil 12
					villain 6
					violator 6
					violence 6
					volunteer 4
					voyage 4

Note: Grade levels assigned by Dale and O'Rourke, *The Living Word Vocabulary*.

TABLE 11

Words Under i and v in the Glossaries of the Grade 6 Readers and Assigned Grade Levels

D. C. HEATH (1993)		HARCOURT BRACE (1995)		HOUGHTON MIFFLIN (1993)		MACMILLAN (1993)		SCOTT FORESMAN (1995)		SILVER BURDETT GINN (1993)	
immigrant	6	illuminate	8	ignorant	8	ill at ease	—	immigration	6	illusion	8
immobilize	10	imperious	15	ignore	6	illegitimate	8	incarcerate	16	imitate	6
impassive	13	implication	10	illusion	8	imperious	15	intern	10	immortal	8
impoverished	12	impression	6	imitate	6	inculcate	16	internment	12	impressionist	12
impressionable	10	improbable	8	immense	8	improvised	12	immerse	13	incredibly	6
improvise	13	incident	6	immunization	8	indulge	12	immaculate	12	infantry	6
incognito	13	incisive	16	impulsive	8	inferno	12	immune system	8	influence	6
ineligible	8	inconsequential	13	indestructible	8	ingenious	6	independence	4	ingenuity	10
ingenious	6	incriminate	8	indignation	12	intercept	8	inflammation	8	inhabitant	8
inhibit	16	indignantly	12	infect	6	ironic	10	infuriate	6	inherit	6
inkling	10	informal	8	inlay	8					inlet	4
intensity	8	inheritance	8	instinct	8	valiant	10	vault	4	inquiry	8
intercede	13	intact	12	instinctively	12	veer	13	vaporize	4	inspect	4
interest	8			intact	12	venison	6	version	6	inspiration	6
interlock	19	vantage	12	interpret	8	verbal	8	vindictive	13	instinct	8
		virtually	13	involuntarily	8			voyage	4	instinctive	12
vain	10	vulnerable	12					voyager	4	intention	6
valiant	10			vague	8			vulnerable	12	intricate	10
venture	8			vein	6			vague	8	invasion	4
vermin	13			veteran	6			verify	8	irresolute	13
vexation	12			vigor	8					vain	10
vie	16			virtuous	10					vanish	4
viper	10									verbatim	12
										vertical	8
										vibration	6
										vineyard	4
										volcano	4
										vulnerability	12

Note: Grade levels assigned by Dale and O'Rourke, *The Living Word Vocabulary*.

TABLE 12

Total Number of Words Under i and v in the Grade 4 Glossaries at Each Assigned Grade Level

ASSIGNED GRADE LEVEL	D. C. HEATH (1993)	HARCOURT BRACE (1995)	HOUGHTON MIFFLIN (1993)	MACMILLAN (1993)	SCOTT FORESMAN (1995)	SILVER BURDETT GINN (1993)
4	1	7	3	—	4	7
6	5	7	5	2	6	10
8	4	3	1	1	3	3
10	—	2	—	2	—	1
12 +	4	2	—	3	2	2
Total	14	21	9	8	15	23
Over 4	13	14	6	8	11	16

Note: Grade levels assigned by Dale and O'Rourke, *The Living Word Vocabulary*.

TABLE 13

Total Number of Words Under i and v in the Grade 5 Glossaries at Each Assigned Grade Level

ASSIGNED GRADE LEVEL	D. C. HEATH (1989)	HARCOURT BRACE (1995)	HOUGHTON MIFFLIN (1993)	MACMILLAN (1993)	SCOTT FORESMAN (1993)	SILVER BURDETT GINN (1993)
4	—	—	5	—	4	6
6	—	8	6	1	10	17
8	8	8	3	3	7	8
10	2	4	1	2	—	1
12+	8	2	4	5	1	6
Total	18	22	19	11	22	38
Over 5	18	22	14	11	18	32
Over 6	18	14	8	10	8	15

Note: Grade levels assigned by Dale and O'Rourke, *The Living Word Vocabulary*.

TABLE 14

Total Number of Words Under i and v in the Grade 6 Glossaries at Each Assigned Grade Level

ASSIGNED GRADE LEVEL	D. C. HEATH (1993)	HARCOURT BRACE (1995)	HOUGHTON MIFFLIN (1993)	MACMILLAN (1993)	SCOTT FORESMAN (1995)	SILVER BURDETT GINN (1993)
4	—	—	—	—	5	5
6	2	2	5	2	3	8
8	4	5	12	3	4	6
10	7	1	1	2	1	3
12+	9	8	3	7	6	6
Total	22	16	21	14	19	28
Over 6	20	14	16	12	11	15

Note: Grade levels assigned by Dale and O'Rourke, *The Living Word Vocabulary.*

These tables also show how the number of words in a glossary can mislead; a large number does not necessarily mean that the reader has more hard words than a reader with a short glossary. For example, the Harcourt Brace grade 5 reader has twenty-two words in its glossary beginning with *i* and *v*, while D. C. Heath has only eighteen; *but* all eighteen in the D. C. Heath reader are over grade 6 in word difficulty, while only fourteen in Harcourt Brace are. Nor does a short glossary necessarily mean that the reader has few hard words. The D. C. Heath grade 4 reader has just fourteen words beginning with *i* and *v* in its glossary compared to twenty-one for Harcourt Brace, fifteen for Scott Foresman, and twenty-three for Silver Burdett Ginn; *but* thirteen of these fourteen words are over grade 4 in level of difficulty.

Is Cultural Content the Source of Influence on Vocabulary Load?

The question that leaps out from these tables is why some series seem to have fewer hard words than others. One factor may be the variation in cultural content across series. The series with fewer selections about ethnic America and non-Western cultures almost consistently have larger numbers of literate words than the series with the most selections about ethnic America and non-Western cultures.

Are differences in vocabulary load a reflection of differences in cultural content? To explore this question, I constructed a table for all the words under *i* and *v* in the Open Court readers for grades 4, 5, and 6 published in 1989. Recall that this is a series with an explicit commitment to classic literature. I used the 1989 series for this comparison in order to be fair; the number of pages in these readers was closer to the number in the other series than was the number in the lengthier student texts in Open Court's 1995 readers (in the 1995 series there are 638 pages in the grade 4 text, 734 pages in the grade 5 text, and 761 pages in the grade 6 text). The contrast between Open Court and most of the other reading series is revealing. To judge by the number of words in Table 15, Open Court has a larger number of literate words in its readers for grades 4 and 6 than in all the other series, and it has close to the number of words in grade 5 that Silver Burdett Ginn has. Table 16 shows that Open Court also has more hard words in grades 4 and 6 than the other grades 4 and 6 readers. Only in grade 5 does D. C. Heath equal Open Court in the number of hard words over grade 6.

Open Court is widely regarded as a hard series because it contains more difficult selections than the other reading series.[9] Although the exact reasons that its selections are more difficult are not clear, it is possible that the language used by Open Court's array of classic authors contributes to the difference (particularly since it also contains some of the same ethnic authors and ethnic selections I found in the other series). Some of the authors in its grade 4 reader who are not present in the other grade 4 readers are Pearl Buck, William Blake, Henry Wadsworth Longfellow, Lewis Carroll, L. Frank Baum, Emily Dickinson, Walter de la Mare, Ogden Nash, and Rudyard Kipling; it also contains several biblical selections. The authors in its grade 6 reader who are not present in the other grade 6 readers include Philippa Pearce, Willa Cather, May Swenson, e.e. cummings, Mary Norton, Ernest Lawrence Thayer, Anna Sewell, J. R. R. Tolkien, E. Nesbit, Antoine de Saint-Exupéry, Mark Twain, and Alfred, Lord Tennyson.[10] In addition, Open Court's grade 5 reader features works by Edgar Allan Poe and Hans Christian Andersen, writers who are totally absent from all the other series. The animus against "dead white male" authors may also be a contributing factor. I am *not* implying that ethnic authors do not use, or are not capable of using, the same vocabulary. The real question is whether editors are favoring certain kinds of selections by ethnic authors, or selections by certain ethnic authors, so that students end up reading works filled with dialogue containing

TABLE 15

*Words Under i and v in Open Court's Glossaries for Grades 4, 5, and 6
and Assigned Grade Levels*

OPEN COURT (1989) GRADE 4 (447 pp.)				OPEN COURT (1989) GRADE 5 (446 pp.)				OPEN COURT (1989) GRADE 6 (445 pp.)			
idiosyncrasy	13	idly	6	iguana	12	immortal	8	ichthyosaur	12	immense	8
ill-naturedly	8	illusion	8	impertinent	10	implore	13	illumination	8	impulse	8
image	4	impatient	4	impose	8	impress	6	implement	8	indent	6
impressed	6	impression	6	impudent	10	inferno	12	incident	6	induction	10
indifferently	12	incubator	6	indefinitely	8	inlet	6	indisputable	8	inquiringly	8
indaba	—	indignantly	12	inhabitant	4	inherit	12	indulgently	16	inscription	8
innocent	4	innocently	4	insistence	12	insistent	8	inquisitive	6	insignificant	8
inoculate	12	inspect	4	insufficient	8	intent	6	insert	6	insolent	10
inspire	8	instinct	8	intent	12	intention	6	insolence	10	insure	6
integrity	10	intently	10	interlaced	8	in vain	6	instinctive	12	intermit-	
interest	6	interpret	8	investigation	6	involved	6	intently	10	tently	12
intervail	—			involuntarily	10	irony	10	intimately	10	in tow	6
								intrepid	16	isolated	8
various	6	veer	13	vague	8	vast	6	invariably	12	intelligibly	8
vent	4	venture	8	version	6	vicinity	6	illuminate	8		
veranda	10	verbal	8	vital	8	vivid	6				
vibrate	6	vision	4					vogue	12	valiant	10
volunteer	4							vague	8	vantage	12
								valor	8	vendor	12
								variation	8	vermillion	12
								vengeance	8	vigorously	8
								vexed	16	virtually	13
								villa	10	visage	12
								virtuous	10		

Note: Grade levels assigned by Dale and O'Rourke, *The Living Word Vocabulary*.

TABLE 16

Total Number of Words Under i and v in the Open Court Glossaries for Grades 4, 5, and 6 at Each Assigned Grade Level

ASSIGNED GRADE LEVEL	OPEN COURT (1989) GRADE 4	OPEN COURT (1989) GRADE 5	OPEN COURT (1989) GRADE 6
Grade 4	8	1	—
Grade 6	8	11	5
Grade 8	6	9	16
Grade 10	3	4	9
Grade 12 and above	7	5	13
Total	32	30	43
	Over 4 = 24	Over 5 = 29 Over 6 = 18	Over 6 =28

Note: Grade levels assigned by Dale and O'Rourke, *The Living Word Vocabulary*.

few literate words, works narrated in a first-person voice rather than by a third person, and works without the detailed character descriptions and mood-setting passages common in nineteenth-century literature. I am not making a literary judgment by this observation, only an observation on vocabulary load.

The differences revealed by the tables in this chapter appear to be generalizable across the total literate vocabulary for each reader. Table 17 shows the total glossary count for readers in grades 4, 5, and 6 for the 1993 editions of the Houghton Mifflin and Macmillan series, the 1993 edition of Silver Burdett Ginn, the 1995 edition of Open Court, and the 1987 edition of the Macmillan series. I compare this earlier edition of the Macmillan reading series with its current edition and the others because it contained a large number of selections by the authors in the Open Court series who for the most part no longer appear in the other series. It should be kept in mind that over one-third of the words in the glossaries in the 1993 Macmillan series are proper nouns and foreign words. As Table 17 indicates, the glossary counts in the 1987 Macmillan readers are close to the glossary counts in the current Open Court series, even though these have more pages than its 1989 readers. Although a large glossary does not necessarily mean a large number of hard words, the fact that the 1987 Macmil-

TABLE 17

Total Number of Words in the Glossaries of the Readers for Grades 4, 5, and 6 for Selected Series

GRADE LEVEL OF READER	HOUGHTON MIFFLIN (1993)	MACMILLAN (1993)	MACMILLAN (1987)	SILVER BURDETT GINN (1993)	OPEN COURT (1995)
Grade 4	168	141	695	303	690
Grade 5	190	210	626	398	605
Grade 6	291	282	696	354	559

lan readers contain many of the same authors as the 1995 Open Court series suggests that that may be the case. This similarity further suggests that the kind of authors now being excluded from contemporary reading series used a more literate vocabulary than many of the authors now featured in current series, at least in the selections editors chose to use.

Proper Nouns as an Influence on Reading Difficulty

To show by other means that the vocabulary load of the 1993 readers is easier than that of earlier readers and to determine more clearly the influence of the abundance of proper nouns in today's readers on reading level, I applied one of the best-known readability formulas, the Dale-Chall Readability Formula, to a sample of passages in the grade 6 readers published in 1993 and 1989 by Houghton Mifflin and in 1987 and 1993 by Macmillan.[11] The formula is an objective measure for gauging the difficulty level of reading material, and its major component, as in most readability formulas, is a measure of vocabulary load. I chose the two grade 6 editions of the Houghton Mifflin series published in 1989, a regular basal reader and a literature reader, because I had been told that the literature reader was considered very difficult in California, where it had been purchased in large numbers because it had been tailored to California's own English language arts curriculum framework. I chose the 1987 edition of the Macmillan reader because it seemed to have a much higher vocabulary load than its 1993 grade 6 reader, to judge from a comparison of new words beginning with *i* and *v* in both readers.

Following the recommendations in the Dale-Chall manual, I sampled eight 100-word passages in each of these readers, beginning with the second page of the first story and sampling systematically every fiftieth page thereafter. The results can be seen in Table 18. According to the Dale-Chall formula, the overall reading level for Houghton Mifflin's 1989 regular grade 6 reader is 4.44, for its 1989 grade 6 literature reader 5.6, and for its 1993 regular grade 6 reader 5.81. The overall reading level for Macmillan's 1987 grade 6 reader is 4.94 and for its 1993 grade 6 reader 4.94. These numbers suggest that the 1993 readers are at least as difficult as the editions published in the late 1980s, if not more so. (They also indicate that these so-called grade 6 readers are not at a grade 6 level in reading difficulty. They are one to two grades below grade 6 according to this readability formula.)

But when I calculated the number of unfamiliar proper nouns as a proportion of all unfamiliar words in these eight 100-word samples, a dramatic change appeared. Proper nouns (foreign or not) are only 14 percent of all unfamiliar words in Houghton Mifflin's 1989 regular reader, only 17 percent of all unfamiliar words in its 1989 literature reader, but *40 percent* of all unfamiliar words in its 1993 reader. Proper nouns (foreign or not) are 32 percent of all unfamiliar words in Macmillan's 1987 reader and 44 percent of all unfamiliar words in its 1993 reader. However, the figure of 32 percent in the 1987 reader is high by chance; it can be explained by the unusual number of proper nouns and dates in just one of the eight passages I sampled, a passage teaching children how to understand bibliographic entries in a library's card catalogue.

TABLE 18

Reading Level and Proper Nouns as a Percentage of All Unfamiliar Words in Several Grade 6 Readers

	HOUGHTON MIFFLIN 1989 BASAL	HOUGHTON MIFFLIN 1989 LITERATURE	HOUGHTON MIFFLIN 1993 BASAL	MACMILLAN 1987 BASAL	MACMILLAN 1993 BASAL
Reading level based on eight 100-word passages	4.44	5.6	5.81	4.94	4.94
Proper nouns as a proportion of all unfamiliar words	14%	17%	40%	32%	44%

These figures suggest that the higher overall reading level for the 1993 Houghton Mifflin grade 6 reader may be accounted for by the use of selections containing a very large number of proper nouns, not literate words, and that it may in fact be no more difficult than the 1989 grade 6 reader, which is between a grade 4 and grade 5 level according to this readability formula. On the other hand, the fact that the 1993 Macmillan reader has a much higher proportion of proper nouns than its 1987 reader but the same overall reading level suggests that the 1993 reader may actually be much easier than the 1987 reader so far as the presence of literate words is concerned. It is true, of course, that a student may find a proper noun hard or unfamiliar the first time it appears, no matter whether it is "John," "Johannes," or "José." But the difficulty is superficial and temporary. Most proper nouns do not pose comprehension problems; the student simply has to learn the names of the characters or the location of the story or what the proper noun (such as a holiday or title) refers to.

A second reason that we should consider these two 1993 readers to be less challenging than their earlier counterparts is the fact that dialect words and foreign words that are not proper nouns will all be counted as unfamiliar words according to the Dale-Chall formula. Although they may be "hard" words in one sense of the word, they usually do not contribute to the development of an advanced vocabulary in English (unless they are foreign words that are part of difficult English prose style).

Other Sources of Influence on Vocabulary Load

It is unfair to view changes in cultural content as the sole cause of a light vocabulary load. Other factors can influence the difficulty level of the vocabulary across a group of reading selections. Reading selections may have a low vocabulary load (as they did during the 1940s, 1950s, and early 1960s), even when they reflect mainstream American culture. Certainly the large number of poems in the Macmillan and Houghton Mifflin readers may be a contributing factor to the smaller number of literate words in their readers. Poems tend to have a simpler vocabulary than prose. Conversely, the relatively large number of science fiction and fantasy selections in the Silver Burdett Ginn and Harcourt Brace grade 4 readers and the relatively large amount of historical and civic content in their grade 5 readers and in D. C. Heath's grade 6 reader may be contributing to their higher number of literate words at these grade levels.

Another source of influence on vocabulary load is an insistence today by many university educators and curriculum directors on whole class instruction for reading.[12] Some publishers may be choosing selections with an easier vocabulary in order to make them more accessible to the least able readers at each grade level. Ironically, the laudable goal of many proponents of whole class instruction is to offer the lower third of a class a higher level of difficulty in their reading selections than what they might have been offered in achievement-based groups. Some selections in the readers have explicitly been offered to facilitate cooperative reading, by the whole class or by pairs of students, often a skilled reader and a less-skilled reader, as recommended in the teacher guide. To judge by those in Houghton Mifflin's grade 4 reader, selections chosen for cooperative reading do not contain many new hard words.

A final influence may be the strength of the moralistic impulses driving the choice of so many of the selections. If the chief goal of an instructional reader today is to shape young students' attitudes and feelings on specific social issues in particular ways, then we may well find many selections chosen with less concern for the quality of their language than for their capacity to serve these ends.

Basal readers are already too easy for large numbers of students, as several researchers have found, and for the most part they have been too easy for years.[13] The features described in this chapter clearly contribute to this insufficiency. Although lack of cultural coherence is a serious problem in all readers, the chief problem is the vocabulary they contain, as well as the vocabulary they do *not* contain. Many words in these readers, English or non-English, would appear to contribute little to the development of skill in reading academic and literary works in English. Some are non-English proper nouns that are hard to pronounce and read, yet must be learned for discussion of the characters or events in a story. Others are words, in English as well as in other languages, that refer to daily life in other cultures and are not important for growth in reading English. On the other hand, some readers have a much smaller number of literate words than others, and these differences appear fairly consistent from grade to grade, suggesting that there may be growing differences in reading growth from grade to grade for many students for reasons external to their ability. Current reading series may well have broadened children's horizons, but at the cost of their growth as readers—a pact with the devil.

The root cause of the problems discussed in this chapter—the paucity of literate words, the abundance of academically useless words, whether they are English words, and the conceptual limitations in the organization of the readers—seems to be the bow that the editors believe they need or want to make to nonliterary and nonintellectual considerations in the choice of selections for the readers. It is not possible for even the best editors in the world to dedicate themselves to literary considerations and the development of a strong reading vocabulary when they must juggle the variables of race, ethnicity, gender, and self-esteem simultaneously. In their zeal to boost ethnic self-esteem, provide role models for girls, promote the virtues of a multilingual population, and expand children's knowledge about other peoples and cultures, many educational publishers seem to have produced instructional tools more likely to produce multiple illiteracy than growth in reading. Ironically, the damage may be greatest in the very children who need help the most.

SEVEN

HOW DID THE CONTENTS OF READING SERIES CHANGE SO QUICKLY?

The whole family sat under wide trees and ate. Adan talked and sang until his voice turned to a squeak. He ate until his stomach almost popped a pants button.

Afterwards he fell asleep under a big mosquito net before the sun had even gone down behind the mountains.

In the morning Uncle Ulise called out, "Adan, everyone ate all the food in the house. Let's get more."

"From a store?"

"No. From my plantation on the mountain."

> —From "Yagua Days" by Cruz Martel, 1979 Harcourt Brace Jovanovich grade 4 reader[1]

The whole family sat under wide trees and ate arroz con gandules, pernil, viandas and tostones, ensaladas de chayotes y tomates, and pasteles.

Adan talked and sang until his voice turned to a squeak. He ate until his stomach almost popped a pants button.

Afterwards he fell asleep under a big mosquito net before the sun had even gone down behind the mountains.

In the morning Uncle Ulise called out, "Adan, everyone ate all the food in the house. Let's get more."

"From a bodega?"

"No, mi amor. From my finca on the mountain."

> —From "Yagua Days" by Cruz Martel, 1995 Scott Foresman grade 4 reader[2]

THE EPIGRAPH contains two versions of a passage from a story, "Yagua Days," by Cruz Martel. Which version did the author actually write? The original version, which I located in the picture book section of the children's room in my public library, is in fact in Spanglish, so the text reprinted in the Scott Foresman reader is the authentic one. But no graphic distinction (such as italics) is used in the student text to help children understand that some of the words are not English. Native English-speaking children might suspect which words are not English words, but the English-learning Laotian or Haitian student is unlikely to know. That the story was first published as a picture book intended to be read by adults to very young children may explain why italics were not used to distinguish non-English from English words. Note also that the Spanish words in the story are not words that are part of an advanced academic vocabulary for English readers (as such words as *conquistadores* or *mestizo* would be). They are words that are part of the daily life of a particular group of people; in fact, one-third of the total number of Spanish words in the whole story refer to the food these people or their animals eat.

In the 1970s, no responsible publisher would have offered a story in Spanglish for the purpose of reading instruction. Harcourt Brace Jovanovich clearly altered the story—which it may have wanted because it deals with Puerto Ricans and there were probably few published children's stories about Puerto Ricans available in the 1970s—to make it suitable for reading instruction, despite its lack of paragraph development and the simplicity of its sentence structure and vocabulary for grade 4. Clearly, this selection was not chosen for its reading instructional value for fourth graders in either the 1970s or the 1990s. But the fact that this story is offered today in its original version attests to the depths that publishers have had to sink to accommodate the ideologies of their multicultural or other academic advisers from schools of education.

Since the mid-1960s, educational publishers have made continuous changes in the racial and ethnic content of reading instructional series for elementary schools. Originally, these changes were spurred by the academic and social goal of presenting young students with a realistic picture of the racial and ethnic nature of the U.S. population. They were also motivated by a belief that such changes would enhance the self-esteem and hence the reading achievement of low-achieving minority students.

The chief problem today is not that the readers include selections about America's ethnic and racial groups. They should, as long as they are quality pieces of literature. All students should be able to gain some understanding of the multiethnic and multiracial nature of this country and the rest of the world in the literature they are asked to read. They should also be able to see members of different ethnic and racial groups as major characters in what they read. These egalitarian goals are positive ones, for young students especially, whether or not there is any evidence that including such works in the curriculum enhances their self-esteem.

The problem is that publishers have gone far beyond any reasonable effort to broaden the cultural content of basal readers and to foster a more inclusive sense of citizenship. The social goals now spelled out as the purposes for reading instruction in many series seem to overwhelm academic and literary criteria in the choice of selections. Although educational publishers still want to teach children to read, the implementation of these social goals seems to have led, in varying degrees, to the construction of an instructional tool more likely to produce multicultural illiteracy than an accurate understanding of the world. And the very children in whose name these changes were initiated several decades ago may now be the most vulnerable.

Textbook publishers have not substituted social goals for academic and literary goals in the elementary school readers on their own. Given the unusually rich heritage of children's literature in the English-speaking world, it must be painful for editors who know this literature well to find themselves in the position of offering children advocacy journalism or stories with banal plots, bland characters, and humdrum language. School textbooks are susceptible to the pressures of many different groups. In addition, editorial decision making for school textbooks takes place in a broad professional context, guided by much more than simply market forces. Indeed, even the market forces themselves are shaped to a large extent by the professional context that influences editorial decision making at an educational publishing house.

Major textbook publishers are influenced by a set of interlocking institutional forces over which they have no control. They must make a profit from selling their products, and in the elementary school market in particular their products must reflect whatever the most prestigious teacher educators and researchers in the universities suggest is sound pedagogy in reading and writing. They must listen to administrators and teachers in the schools, educators who have been influenced by the faculty in schools of education and speak directly to their sales representatives. Finally, most publishers want approval by textbook adoption committees in states that by law must recommend a list of textbooks from which local schools may choose for purchase. In these adoption states, which include many of the most populous states, textbooks go through a rating process conducted by staff members of their departments of education before they are approved or rejected for recommendation.

Publishers have probably been less influenced by local school boards than by the other groups because these boards were deliberately bypassed many years ago after changes in the content of the curriculum were first urged. As a professor in the school of education at the University of Illinois candidly explained in a 1993 article, those who believed that the treatment of minority groups was less than equitable began by pressuring teachers and local school boards for changes. But, he declared, they quickly learned that it was far more effective to pressure teacher organizations, state school boards, and publishing houses, with assistance from pressure groups and politicians, in order to bring about changes.[3]

An analysis of the role of each component in this set of interlocking institutions suggests why there has been so much change since the mid-1960s. It helps us see how the positive social goals of the first decade or so of change were quickly converted into the negative social goals of the past decade or so, overwhelming or displacing academic and aesthetic goals. It also makes it clear why not even common sense was able to check the lemming-like progression of textbook publishers of basal readers toward the cliffs of academic and literary deconstruction. Indeed, the institutions responsible for the quality of public education continue to drive each other relentlessly to a greater and greater extreme, with no reality check ever braking this accelerating process.[4]

PRESSURES ON EDITORS

My efforts to find out how and why changes took place inside the publishing houses for elementary reading series were not fruitful. Editors at only two of the publishing houses whose series I analyzed responded to my telephone calls and were willing to give me an interview. One said that children's interests and literary quality were no longer dominant criteria for selections. Although his company still sought high-quality literature, he confessed that many other concerns guided their decision making. Among their greatest concerns today was the problem of providing for the heterogeneous classroom, although he did not make clear how that would influence the choice of selection. The other editor felt that the excesses of recent years were now being curbed in favor of better overall quality. These remarks were directed to the quality of the literature that publishers had had to use in order to cover the different groups or social problems that are now expected to be part of any basal reader.

Perhaps the best source of information on how publishers responded to pressures for changes in their elementary reading series comes from the book *Battleground: One Mother's Crusade, the Religious Right, and the Struggle for Control of Our Classrooms* by Stephen Bates.[5] The book explores the public policy issues in *Mozert v. Hawkins County Board of Education*, a lawsuit brought by fundamentalist parents in Tennessee in the mid-1980s. The parents had been denied instructional alternatives for their children after claiming that the selections in the reading series used in their children's classrooms violated their religious beliefs.

In the course of writing this book, Bates analyzed 2,261 pages of internal files from Holt, Rinehart and Winston, the publisher of the reading series, and supplemented them by interviews with retired Holt personnel. The files, which became available to public scrutiny after they were subpoenaed during the lawsuit, document the evolution of several editions of *Holt Basic Reading*, a K–8 reading series published by Holt, Rinehart and Winston from 1973 until the late 1980s. The pressures the Holt editors faced from the 1970s on were common to all major publishers in those years, and the contents of the readers today suggest that the ways in which the Holt editors responded to these pressures were also common to all publishers.

Almost as soon as the 1973 edition was out, groups in different states charged it with displaying blatant sexism (showing boys working with tools while girls baked cookies and drew pictures); racism (in such phrases as "the deputy's face darkened" or "the afternoon turned black"); and an offensive Christian bias (treating Judeo-Christian teachings about creation in a serious way and other non-Christian teachings about creation as being "highly imaginative, strange, and consequently false"). The Holt editors responded to the charges of these advocacy groups (such as the "Task Force on Sexism," the "Standing Committee to Review Textbooks from a Multicultural Perspective," and the "Ethnic Bias Review Committee") by developing increasingly stringent guidelines for the 1977 edition and later editions of the series.

The choice of authors, stories, photos, and illustrations was now to be guided by the latest census data and other national population statistics to determine how often groups should be portrayed. As one former Holt executive recalled during an interview with Bates, they were "counting heads as to whether we had 50 percent females, whether we had every minority group represented." One memo reported on a particular volume: "The in-house count shows 146 female and 146 male characters, or a ratio of 1:1. Animal characters were not included in this count." The Holt editors later paid a price for this omission. At the Texas textbook hearings in 1980, feminists disagreed that the basal readers contained a perfect gender balance: males outnumbered females nearly two to one when animals were included in the count. As one woman testified, "Children of this age are influenced by a story about Mr. Rabbit just as much as they are by a story about Mr. Jones," a legitimate point *if* children identify with the gender of animals in their reading materials as much as they may identify with the gender of the people in them.

Editors had to spend a great deal of time to try to meet their quotas, for example, to "find a good story with an Asian-American female lead." And in order to undo presumably demeaning, limiting, or offensive stereotypes, they had to portray people in a completely opposite way. For example, as Bates found in the guidelines drafted by the Holt editors, girls were now to be seen working with electricity, studying insects, and solving math problems. Boys were now to be seen reading poetry, chasing butterflies, and paying attention to personal appearance and hygiene. Women and girls should sometimes be larger, heavier, physically and emotionally stronger, and more aggressive than the men or the boys around them. Blacks were to be in professions at all levels, not in low-paying jobs, unemployed, or on welfare. American Indians were to be involved in the American mainstream rather than on reservations and were not to be shown in low-paying jobs, unemployed, or on welfare. Hispanics were to speak English. Jews were not to be depicted in such "stereotypical occupations" as "diamond cutters, doctors, dentists, lawyers, classical musicians, tailors, shopkeepers, etc." Older people were not to be depicted as living

tailors, shopkeepers, etc." Older people were not to be depicted as living
in nursing homes, wearing glasses, using canes or wheelchairs, or in rock-
ing chairs, knitting, napping, and watching television.

Further, the new guidelines led to a list of forbidden words. Such
words as *manmade*, *workmanlike*, and *statesman* were henceforth to be
banished.

Finally, stories featuring any aspect of the Christian religion had to be
avoided. A Holt editor was skeptical about using a particular story because
it "raises many sensitive controversial issues—drinking, religion, hard
times." Apparently only certain kinds of controversial topics were seen as
a problem to editors. Others needed to be presented to children.

What Bates found especially interesting in his analysis of the Holt files
was the response and attitude of the editors to the different pressure groups.
The Holt editors always yielded to the criticisms of the feminists and the
multiculturalists, seeing them as "positive pressure groups" who "seek to
improve our educational institutions and textbooks in a positive manner."
The editors never showed any hostility to their demands, even though
these critics were never satisfied with what the editors did to address their
criticisms and regularly upped the ante, pushing the Holt series (and others as well) to a greater and greater extreme. As one example, the Christian bias perceived by the multiculturalists in the 1973 edition could no
longer be detected in the 1983 edition. According to the testimony of Paul
Vitz, the researcher asked to analyze the Holt series for the *Mozert* case, not
one story or poem in the series depicted "life in the Bible Belt," or "church-
goers, families or individuals who pray to God." In contrast, non-Christian
religions and the spiritual beliefs of the American Indians were treated respectfully, a situation Vitz found in all the leading series by the mid-1980s.

On the other hand, as Bates observed, the Holt editors addressed only
minimally the demands of critics they saw at the other end of the political
spectrum—groups protesting an "antiparent" bias, an "antiwhite" bias, or
the "march" of "Atheistic Humanism in the Schools"—and the Texas
textbook critics Mel and Norma Gabler who protested, among other
things, the slighting of phonics, references to evolution, and invasions of
students' privacy. All of these critics were denounced in the Holt memo-
randa as the kind of "censors" one finds in "totalitarian societies," and
their arguments were described as "reductionist," "simplistic," and "reactionary." The basic difference between the two sets of textbook critics,

Bates concluded, was that one set was welcomed into the editors' offices and asked to collaborate with them, while the other set was mostly kept out and forced to resort to the political process where they were (and still are) denounced as censors.

The pressure groups seen by the Holt editors as advocating nothing more than socially responsible texts were also active at public hearings in adoption states. Even if the editors had had any reservations about capitulating to the demands of the feminist and multiculturalist critics who came to their doors, they could not have ignored their influence where it really mattered: in the textbook adoption process in the biggest adoption states. As one Holt sales representative commented just before California's textbook adoptions in the mid-1970s, "We may squeeze through this time with only a minimum amount of changes, but by the next adoption, we will not be so fortunate."

Textbook publishers had to make some changes to accommodate the demands of the critics at the other end of the spectrum, but it is obvious why these concessions never served as obstacles to the changes demanded by the "positive pressure groups." As Bates noted, in-house guidelines urged authors not to refer to evolution, not to invade students' privacy, and not to include "any subtle propagandizing for communism." What the "reactionary" groups did not want in was not what the "positive pressure groups" were seeking to get in. Holt editors also replaced a story showing two boys sleeping together and others depicting children lying, scheming, and disobeying their parents. Selections showing females as working women or as central characters could also completely replace those showing women as homemakers and the many selections about heroes, inventors, and other historic figures who happened to be white because no pressure groups were monitoring the portrayal of white male characters. Addition to a finite text also means subtraction, but there were no thoughtful professional or public discussions about what all of this could mean, especially because the number of hitherto excluded or neglected social groups kept increasing.

Bates found clear evidence in the Holt files of, as he put it, gender and ethnicity trumping other considerations, including literary quality. One editor noted that a particular story was "not great literature" but "we gain two points—a female leading character and characters with Spanish-American names." Another editor agreed that the story had "very little literary merit." Of another story, an editor wrote, "I agree that this is not the greatest 'Indian' selection, but we were very hard pressed to find anything better." Of yet another selection, the chief author of the series observed: "Two girls may be featured, but that's the only positive statement I can make about this play." The situation is no different today. An editor in one of the major publishing houses remarked in 1995 to my research assistant, Michael Freed, "It may not be a great read, but it fits in if the themes and values are acceptable."

Textbook publishers were by no means simply responding to the people at their door or at the public hearings in the adoption states. Even greater skewing of the contents of the readers took place than one might have expected for two other reasons. The adoption process generates an internal momentum of its own, as each publisher attempts to make its own products more appealing than its competitors', further accelerating changes in the basal readers toward an extreme. And the populations of the biggest adoption states differ in their ethnic proportions from those of most other states.

THE INFLUENCE OF STATE DEPARTMENTS OF EDUCATION

Because they represent a single, large market for publishers, the adoption states have long exerted an influence far out of proportion to their actual population. The biggest, Texas and California, have been the leaders in the adoption cycle for decades, a cycle that takes place every five or six years. One editor at a major publishing house remarked to my research assistant, "The cutting edge tends to be California and Texas and the rest of the country tends to follow." And what the largest markets want is what publishers will cater to. This editor commented that "if California wants a selection on the Gold Rush, then they get one." Thus, these states largely determine what the rest of the country gets, even though some publishers publish a separate edition for Texas that includes more selections and illustrations dealing with Texas.

Criteria

In most, if not all, adoption states, staff members in the department of education develop the criteria or the description of the content of the textbooks needed for a particular cycle. They then have them formally approved by their state board of education, whose members are unlikely to object to what they would see as professional guidelines. Publishers interested in nationwide sales then attempt to tailor their products to meet the criteria set forth in both the biggest adoption states and the others because these criteria are unlikely to be in conflict with each other today, as we can see in the criteria for Oregon and Texas.

The Oregon Department of Education first sets out two legal criteria: basal instructional materials criteria and equity criteria. Not only must submitted materials constitute a basal reading series (with further specifications relating to such aspects of reading instruction as instructional strategies, literary forms, and literary appreciation), they must also provide:

[1.] models and selections by and about various groups and cultures including:
   a. both women and men
   b. people of diverse racial, ethnic and cultural groups
   c. people of diverse socio-economic backgrounds
   d. people of various belief systems: religious, political, social
   e. people with disabilities
   f. people of all ages
[2.] models, selections, activities and opportunities for response which promote sensitivity to the commonalities of the human condition and the rich diversity of distinct cultures.

Given that these criteria are now part of state law in Oregon, publishers need to make their attempt to fulfill these equity criteria visible in their briefs—the descriptive documents they submit to departments of education. There are also over a dozen criteria for judging content, instructional strategies, and the format of the readers, but they are not part of state law.

The bill mandating use of these equity criteria in Oregon was proposed and written by its department of education in 1992 and passed by the state legislature in January 1993. Use of state legislation for shaping and freezing the content of textbooks in a particular way is a subtle abuse of the political process as well as an intrusion of political judgment into what should be a matter of professional judgment only. Although the state board of education approved the criteria at that time, it reduced its future power to change its policies in these areas whenever it might see the need for change.

The criteria in Texas differ basically only in the specification of additional groups that need to be represented. The 1990 document issued by its board of education specifies among other things that the student materials in the basal readers shall include "a pluralistic anthology of quality children's literature, balanced in its inclusion of both fiction and nonfiction selections by authors representing various ethnic/racial groups and of selections representing various sex roles and groups of students such as migrant students, limited English proficient students, gifted and talented students, handicapped students, etc."[6] They must also include "information about the authors/illustrators of the selections that students and teachers are reading," as well as "suggested booklists and other printed materials" for independent reading by students at a variety of reading levels or for reading aloud by the teacher that "correlate with the units of study which are representative of the major ethnic/racial groups in Texas."[7]

It is easy to understand how complex the editors' record keeping can get in order for them to keep track of how well they have accommodated the representation of all these different groups. It is also easy to understand how much time it must take to obtain all the right selections. If there are any stories in print about, for example, limited-English-proficient or migrant students, they must be found, or writers encouraged to write them, or informational selections located that deal with them. What makes the editors' task more difficult is that a fresh group of selections must be obtained for every new publishing cycle and that the groups to be represented must be represented at every grade level—and never decrease in number. (It is not at all surprising that considerations of literary and academic quality have to be relegated to a back burner.) One can only have sympathy for textbook editors who must show in their briefs exactly how the contents of their textbooks correlate with the criteria. When sales representatives are asked, as they always are, "Is Group X adequately represented in your readers?" they need to know and be able to answer.

The Texas proclamations reveal interesting differences between what is requested for the English-language basal readers and what is requested for the Spanish-language basal readers to be used in bilingual education classes. In the overview for the Spanish-language basal readers, publishers are told that reading selections must include "children's literature that reflects the literary and cultural heritage of the Spanish-speaking world, for the development of a positive self-identity."[8] Students must also be able to develop an appreciation for "the literary heritage and culture of the Spanish Southwest."[9] And for the supplementary readers in Spanish requested in the 1991 proclamation, publishers are also told that these readers should include the following themes:

> the family: Content shall reflect an appreciation of the value of the institution as a source of emotional, economic, and intellectual support and the value of different roles of various Hispanic cultural groups. This unit may be used to develop student pride in family characteristics and to increase parental involvement.
>
> careers: A general exposure to a variety of career fields, including health, legal, business, environmental, industrial, construction, and the fine arts may be included to nurture the development of high aspirations in students.
>
> multiculturalism: Contemporary and historical heroes and their contributions to society and the present way of life shall be included to develop an appreciation of individuals from various cultural groups.
>
> Hispanic culture as presented through authentic Hispanic literature: Selections from classical children's literature, legends, folktales, and games that are of Hispanic origin shall be included and may be organized by a shared topic, a particular genre, a particular character, the best of a favorite children's author, or some other unifying idea.[10]

Apparently only Spanish-speaking students are expected to read "classical children's literature," to develop pride in the family as a supportive institution and in their families in particular, and to acquire a positive self-identity. Nowhere are these specified as important for the English-speaking child. Nor, it seems, are Spanish-speaking students expected to learn much about the literary and cultural heritage of the English-speaking child in either the Spanish or the English language class.

In the Spanish language class, Hispanic students are expected to learn about the literary heritage and the historical and contemporary heroes of those deemed this country's "multicultural" citizens, not the literary heritage of the majority of this country's citizens or their contemporary and historical heroes. And in the English language class, they are expected to respond "to various forms of literature representing our pluralistic literary heritage and diverse contemporary cultures," much of which will also be about the Hispanic community (and other multicultural groups), but in English, not in Spanish. In theory, this seems to provide Hispanic youngsters with a rich exposure to the literary heritage of the Spanish-speaking world in their Spanish and English classes, but only a minimal exposure to the literary and cultural heritage of the English-speaking world, no matter what class they are in. In effect, they are being deprived of the kind of education in the English language they are entitled to.

The Rating Process

The rating process for evaluating a textbook influences its contents in subtle ways. The limitations placed in a growing number of states on the number of textbooks that can be recommended serve in their own way to generate changes in the basal readers from one adoption cycle to another. As one sales representative told me, adoption committees in these states tend to seek to exclude in order to meet these limitations. It is usually easier for such committees to whittle down the candidates by finding reasons to reject rather than approve textbooks. Texas, the second most populous state and a major market for textbooks of all kinds, happens to be one state that does limit the number of recommended textbooks. Moreover, as this sales representative observed, what constitutes equity is totally subjective, depending on the person making the judgment. An entire series can be doomed if only one rater identifies only one selection in a reader that he or she finds offensive, something he indicated had happened to one of the major publishers of reading series in an Oregon rating session in the early 1990s. What was ironic, he felt, was that the selection deemed offensive appeared in other series too, but other raters were not aware of this because all raters do not analyze all the textbooks in a particular area. Thus, the reasons that particular textbooks are rejected, even if frivolous, arbitrary, and only one rater's judgment, serve as pressure for change, especially when there is an excessive number of competitors for a finite number of recommendations. For the next adoption cycle, wise publishers will avoid including anything in their series, or doing anything with regard to other aspects of an instructional series, that served as grounds for criticism in an earlier cycle.

The dynamics of the rating session serve indirectly to generate change in future editions of a reading series. Although its product must visibly meet all the criteria that will be used to evaluate it, in a competitive situation each textbook company wants its products to look different from the others. In such a context, the rating process would tend to drive publishers to greater and greater extremes. For example, to receive a rating of 5 (on a 1 to 5 rating scale) on the 1994 evaluation form developed by the California Curriculum Development and Supplemental Materials Commission, K–8 language arts materials need to include, among other things, "many selections in the common languages other than English spoken in California, comparable in quality to those written in English, representing either high quality translations or analogous original works to facilitate primary language literacy." It is not clear what can determine how many is "many" except the subjective judgment of the raters. California does not limit the number of textbooks it recommends in an instructional area. But with 5 points on its rating scale for each criterion, each publisher has to speculate about when "many" would result in a subjective judgment of 1, 2, 3, or 4 in relation to the offerings of its competitors. Consequently, although it may be difficult to find large numbers of quality works "in the common languages other than English spoken in California," publishers that want to get the highest rating possible on the literature criteria will have every incentive to make sure that "many" is clearly visible as "many," even if it means a reduction in quality. And regardless of their total score in one publishing cycle, all publishers are likely to want to increase it in the next cycle, knowing that lower-scoring publishers will clearly want to do so, thus accelerating movement toward an extreme in the next cycle.

Movement can be fueled further by the use of what is called a holistic rating process: the series with the most of anything in relation to the others being evaluated gets the highest score, and the series with the least gets the lowest score, even if the least of something is still an adequate number. If one high-rated publisher features fifteen selections about ethnic minorities in one adoption cycle, why wouldn't a competitor aim for twenty in the next cycle? There is nothing in the process to serve as a brake on a continuing move to an extreme. Indeed, the philosophy conveyed in a pamphlet put out by the Oregon Department of Education explaining to local school districts how they might go about adopting instructional texts from the approved list gives publishers that want to be

on Oregon's approved list even more reason to move toward an extreme.[11] For example, the pamphlet tells teachers that one desired practice is to use "culturally diverse literature rooted in universals of human
condition," in contrast to "classics taught with emphasis on broad coverage of the canon of Western literature."[12] Apparently the classics do not
deal with the universals of human condition. The pamphlet also sets up
E. D. Hirsch, Jr., as the bogeyman and misrepresents him as an ethnocentric neanderthal:

> The new directions in literature and reading squarely contradict the "cultural
> literacy" notion proposed by E. D. Hirsch (1987). Where Hirsch stresses al-
> legiance to a conventional culture dominated by Western thought, teachers
> of the English language arts are increasingly searching out literature that re-
> flects the concerns of a wide range of races and cultures, including writing
> members of both sexes.[13]

In a training videotape Oregon offers as a resource to help local districts select materials "that promote equity and a multicultural perspective," one criterion suggested is almost pure McCarthyism, only it is books
that may be guilty of association if they were written in politically incorrect times (the past).[14] Teachers are urged to look at copyrights to see if
the literature comes from a period of time in which there were "cultural
insensitivities," although a teacher speaking in this video notes that even
contemporary books may be insensitive, offering as one example a recently published African folktale that in her judgment may leave children
thinking that Africans today eat people. Clearly traditional literature,
whether American or African, is suspect in Oregon.

What the Oregon raters would be looking for was not lost on the publishers. Silver Burdett Ginn's brief submitted for the 1993 Oregon adoption process highlighted its equity model and the use of Carl Grant, a
prominent advocate of multicultural education and a teacher educator in
the University of Wisconsin system, as its adviser.[15] Publishers have
learned to parrot back the catechism, showing, on the surface at least, that
they are right-thinking, as can be seen in Silver Burdett Ginn's description of its content in its brief:

- A curriculum of *inclusion* which opens the minds and hearts of all students
  to learning because it treats all people with sensitivity and respect.

- Content that reflects and respects the culture, tradition and experiences of our pluralistic society.
- Content that enables students to see members of their own group as positive contributors in our society.

Publishers also know the kind of examples to give that earn approvals. The one example the Silver Burdett Ginn brief offers to show how it implements Grant's model of equity and inclusion is the Faith Ringgold selection in its grade 6 reader, with reproduced pages from its published materials featuring suggestions that students locate artwork dealing with women's rights and civil rights and read about such women in the art world as Maya Lin, who "designed the Vietnam War Memorial"; Judy Baca, who "paints murals showing people as victims of racism and poverty"; and Lois Mailou Jones, who "paints pictures about injustices suffered by African Americans."

One has to feel some sympathy for publishers who are required to regurgitate all the fashionable mantras du jour. Even if they collaborate willingly with the dictates of the regulators, some editors must resent having to demonstrate so repetitively their allegiance to the pieties of the day and adhere to such detailed regulations on the groups to be represented. Underlying these equity specifications devised by state departments of education seems to be the assumption that publishers cannot be trusted on their own to create socially appropriate instructional tools for teachers to use with children. Without legal or administrative coercion and the oversight of these regulators, it is implied, teachers would otherwise have textbooks that damage the self-esteem of a wide range of social groups and make white male students arrogant and ethnocentric. Nor does this situation say much for the view it suggests of teachers' intelligence. They are presumed to need the protection of these regulators. At a time when "teacher empowerment" is a buzzword, great care is being taken to make sure that teachers are not empowered to use the wrong materials.[16]

Clearly the nature of a rating session in itself can lead to considerable self-censorship by publishers as they develop their products. All publishers undoubtedly have learned what the internal files of the Holt editors indicated they learned from pressure groups: not to take risks, not to consider selections they think may present problems to raters. Offensiveness is an elusive quality whose manifestations may vary from year to year.

The consequences of such a situation are an elaborate system for vetting selections before final decisions are made and the elimination of selections used in the past but now judged to contain something offensive.

THE INFLUENCE OF ACADEMIC CONSULTANTS, THEIR THEORIES, AND SCHOOLS OF EDUCATION

Perhaps the key influence driving most of the recent changes in the basal readers is that of schools of education and their faculty. Although not the first sources of pressure on publishers, they ultimately became the major source driving change, directly as consultants to publishers and indirectly as those responsible for the training of all those professionally involved in education: preservice and in-service teachers, school administrators, curriculum developers, researchers, and the staff of the departments of education themselves.

Academic Authors and Consultants

Major publishers draw on the services of large numbers of academic advisers, both multicultural and regular, because they feel they need well-known names from the academic world on their title pages.[17] Compared to thirty or so years ago, the numbers are staggering. For its 1993 series, Macmillan/McGraw Hill lists sixteen authors, fourteen "multicultural and educational" consultants, and four "literature consultants," in addition to several other kinds of consultants and numerous teacher reviewers. Silver Burdett Ginn lists twelve authors for its 1993 series, one of whom is Carl Grant, also its multicultural consultant. For its 1995 series, Harcourt Brace lists two senior authors, thirteen ordinary authors, two senior consultants (one of whom is Asa Hilliard, a vocal and well-known proponent of Afrocentrism), and four ordinary consultants. For its 1993 and 1995 series, Scott Foresman lists thirteen authors and highlights Cherry McGee Banks (co-editor with James Banks of a textbook on multicultural education, and his wife) as its multicultural consultant, together with fourteen other multicultural "contributors and critics." Houghton Mifflin lists "senior" authors, "senior coordinating" authors, "senior consulting" authors, and just plain authors—twenty-two in all. It also has four ordinary advisers and ten multicultural advisers.

Multicultural advisers serve as the "glatt kosher" stamp for the series. If a publisher can snag a prominent multicultural educator as adviser or author, presumably the adoption committee will be assured that the series has passed the most stringent test possible in meeting equity criteria. Doubtless every member of this phalanx of multicultural advisers or authors is eager to make suggestions.

Theories of Multicultural Educators

The theories devised by multicultural educators to drive the changes they claim will improve academic achievement in minority students as well as the social relations between them and other students have strongly influenced the contents of educational textbooks. The ideas of James Banks in particular have had an enormous influence on the direction that multicultural education has taken in the past decade and a half and on current textbooks in many subject areas, including many of the readers I examined. His ideas help us see the bankruptcy of the theoretical foundations for multicultural education in this country.

A professor of education at the University of Washington in Seattle specializing in social studies and multicultural education, Banks presented his ideas on the development of ethnic identity in the form of a typology in a 1981 textbook for teachers, *Multiethnic Education: Theory and Practice*. Although his typology is just one of several schemes drawn on today by educators, publishers, and researchers for determining the nature and strength of ethnic identity, his ideas about multicultural education became so influential because they were among the first to be published in a textbook and have been promoted heavily by faculty in schools of education. Scott Foresman features his definitions of key multicultural concepts in a multicultural handbook accompanying its 1993 reading series.[18]

Banks describes his typology as a "preliminary ideal-type construct in a Weberian sense," academic jargon borrowed from sociology meaning that his scheme is intended to serve as a way to approximate a reality. But when we look at the labels that Banks gives his stages—and his description of them—we see why his typology is an academic travesty. The first stage he has constructed, called "Ethnic Psychological Captivity," describes "members of ethnic groups that have historically been victimized by cultural assaults."[19] Polish Americans are one of the examples he offers, although Banks does not elaborate the cultural forces that "assaulted" Polish immigrants when they came to this country. During this stage, Banks declares, "the individual absorbs the negative ideologies and beliefs about his or her ethnic group that are institutionalized within the society. Consequently, he or she exemplifies ethnic self-rejection and low self-esteem."

Stage 2 is called "Ethnic Encapsulation." According to Banks, "The individual participates within his or her own ethnic community and believes that his or her ethnic group is superior to other groups." In addition, "outgroups are regarded as enemies, racists, and, in extreme manifestations of this stage, are viewed as planning genocidal efforts to destroy their ethnic group."[20] In addition, the "Stage 2 individual expects members of the ethnic group to show strong overt commitments to the liberation struggle of the group or to the protection of the group from outside." Banks believes that as "this type of individual begins to question some of the basic assumptions of his or her culture and to experience less ambivalence and conflict about ethnic identity . . . he or she is likely to become less ethnocentric and ethnically encapsulated."

At Stage 3, "Ethnic Identity Clarification," "the individual is able to clarify personal attitudes and ethnic identity, to reduce intrapsychic conflict, and to develop clarified positive attitudes toward his or her own group." "Self-acceptance is a requisite to accepting and responding positively to other people," and "ethnic pride is genuine rather than contrived."[21]

In Stage 4, "Biethnicity," the individual can function successfully in two ethnic cultures. Banks believes that nonwhite minorities in the United States are "forced to become biethnic to some extent in order to experience social and economic mobility," while members of mainstream groups "live almost exclusive monocultural and highly ethnocentric lives."[22]

In Stage 5, "Multiethnicity and Reflective Nationalism," the individual "is able to function within several ethnic cultures within his or her nation." He sees individuals within this stage having "a commitment to their ethnic group, an empathy and concern for other ethnic groups, and a strong but reflective commitment and allegiance to the nation state and its idealized values, such as human dignity and justice."[23]

Finally, in Stage 6, "Globalism and Global Competency," the individual has the "ideal delicate balance of ethnic, national, and global identification, commitments, literacy, and behaviors."[24]

Banks suggests that these stages should not be viewed as sequential and linear, inasmuch as individuals can skip stages or go "upward, downward, or in a zigzag pattern." This enormous qualification immediately raises the question of whether these can be called stages at all and whether teachers should even try to create curricula designed to move students through them. But undeterred by his own admission that his stages may not really be stages at all, Banks spells out clear curricular implications for each one. They give us the flavor for the form that multicultural education is now taking, and in many of the teacher guides and selections in the readers I examined.

Banks believes that Stage 1 individuals should be given a "monoethnic" curriculum to help them "develop ethnic awareness." Such "monoethnic experiences should be designed to help the individual come to grips with personal ethnic identity and to learn how his or her ethnic group has been victimized by the larger society and by institutions, such as the media and the schools, which reinforce and perpetuate dominant societal myths and ideologies."[25] In Stage 2, he recommends that individuals can best benefit from a curriculum that accepts "their ethnic identities and hostile feelings toward outside groups." It is the teacher's responsibility to "accept the individual's hostile feelings and help him or her express and clarify them." Banks seems to be suggesting that the education offered minority groups should first emphasize their victimization by the larger society so that they come to view the world around them with hostility, if not paranoia. Once they develop this hostile worldview, teachers are to accept it and help them articulate it.

Banks bases his "ideal-type" constructs on "existing and emerging theory and research and the author's study of ethnic behavior," a phrase he often repeats. However, he does not cite any published research supporting his descriptive statements about the "approximate reality" of his stages in ethnic identity development, nor does he offer examples of ethnic groups whose members have demonstrably gone through these stages. He has done no empirical research himself to support his notion of stages since he first articulated them, to judge by the references to his own work that he cites in the leading chapter of a 1993 volume reviewing research on multicultural education for the American Educational Research Association.[26] Nor does he reveal how the average teacher could decide what the components of a child's ethnicity are and what should be taught to that child. Most astonishing about this unsubstantiated typology is that it has been accepted by untold numbers of educators and publishers as having the weight of academic authority and social desirability behind it. Yet so far as I can determine, his typology has not been recognized by sociologists or anthropologists. And would any parent, mainstream or not, support a curriculum teaching minority children to see themselves as the objects of societal hatred before they learn much else about the society in which they live—or learn to read and write?

Yet Banks's influence cannot be underestimated. In 1997–1998, he was the president of the American Educational Research Association (AERA), the most prestigious organization for educational researchers in the country (and perhaps the world). Indeed, his assumption that all students begin school with an ethnic identity is only now being criticized in a major AERA journal as uninformed by work in anthropology and as tainted by the very "Western-centric" universalism to which he is in theory opposed.[27] The author of the article voicing this criticism further acknowledged the lack of evidence supporting Banks's stage theory.[28] That his ideas have had such a deep influence on educational publishers and schools of education must give us pause.

Anthony Appiah, a philosopher and historian, writes that it needs to be argued, not assumed, that "black Americans, taken as a group, have a common culture."[29] In fact, he doubts that they have one at all. As a consequence, he believes that "ethnicity and religion are not to be transmitted by the organs of the state," but by parents.[30] Thus, the question of who should give children their religious or ethnic identity is a critical one. Banks and other multicultural educators do not discuss this question in their writings, and philosophers and historians like Appiah do not write in journals or books for educational researchers, teacher educators, or teachers.

Courses on Multicultural Education in Schools of Education

Many, perhaps most, schools of education now require students to take courses in multicultural education for their degree programs (although they do not require courses in civic education as well). The dominance of social and political goals and the near, if not total, absence of academic goals are as obvious in these courses as in the books and articles on the subject. For example, in the course on multicultural education taught during the 1994–1995 academic year at the Harvard Graduate School of Education, one of the most influential schools of education in the country, the obsession with power and conflict at the heart of the current implementation of multiculturalism is revealed in the titles of six of its eight required texts: *The Politics of Education: Culture, Power and Liberation; Talking Back: Thinking Feminist, Thinking Black; Culture and Power in the Classroom; Empowering Minority Students; Affirming Diversity: The Sociopolitical Context of Multicultural Education;* and *Taking Sides: Clashing Views on Controversial Educational Issues.*[31]

That the course is concerned with political rather than academic goals for minority students is further confirmed by the description of it:

> This course is designed to provide you with background and knowledge of multicultural education theory, curricula and instructional methods. In addition, this course will analyze the educational ramifications of cultures in contact that may lead to racial/ethnic conflicts and discriminatory school practices and structures. After exposure to various theoretical and philosophical approaches to multicultural education and state-of-the-art literature on subordinate student groups, you will be expected to operationalize your definition and to develop an educational program (e.g., mini-curriculum, policy plan, teacher training manual, etc.) that grows out of and reflects your emerging philosophical orientation.

The influence of an ideology that sees conflict between oppressed and oppressor groups as the characteristic of our society is clear in this course description. There is nothing here about developing mutual respect or mutual appreciation. The focus is on helping "subordinate student groups" in a society that is to be seen as inherently and institutionally racist. The controlling nature of this ideology can also be seen in the writing assignments for the course, as well as in the required readings. Students earn a full 25 percent of their grade for the course for a "6 to 10 page position paper with supporting documentation" describing their "multicultural education philosophy." The course is clearly not for doubting Thomases or the graduate student who comes in with an open mind seeking to learn the weaknesses as well as the strengths of multicultural education, and the empirical research on its claims. Instead, students are expected to arrive with an "already existing orientation" and to continue to "develop, modify and refine it throughout the semester" under the watchful eyes of the instructor and teaching assistants as students "share" their "emerging multicultural orientation" at various points during the semester. And to make absolutely sure students know what this philosophical statement should consist of, "exemplary philosophical statements" are on reserve in the school of education library. No independent or critical thinking about multicultural education or its guiding philosophers is expected or desired in this four-credit graduate course at Harvard University.

From courses like this one at schools of education around the country, students emerge who become not only teachers in the schools, but editors in publishing houses and staff members at state departments of education. Whether or not they wholeheartedly subscribe to the kind of educational reform desired by the instructors of these courses, they can clearly see that academic goals are of extremely minimal importance in the effort by today's multiculturalists to secure social justice, power, liberation, or whatever other goal they think they are facilitating for the supposed benefit of minority students. Indeed, in this particular course at Harvard, the final two titles among the eight required texts, *Designing Groupwork: Strategies for the Heterogeneous Classroom* and *Freedom's Plow: Teaching in the Multicultural Classroom*, point to classroom pedagogy for "subordinate student groups" and are more concerned with showing teachers how to enhance the self-esteem of their minority or low-achieving students through the manipulation of their students' social relationships than with showing teachers how to enhance the ability of their minority or low-achieving students to manipulate ideas.

THE INFLUENCE OF PROFESSIONAL JOURNALS
AND PROFESSIONAL CONFERENCES

Edited by faculty members in schools of education, professional journals in reading and language arts education communicate ideas about curriculum and pedagogy, and they publish reports of research, suggesting the kinds of directions further research might move in. Their audiences range from practicing teachers and curriculum developers in the schools to editors in educational publishing houses and to researchers and teacher trainers at the university-level. Because teachers in the schools rarely have the kind of time for writing that university faculty do, most of the articles in these journals are written by university-level teachers and researchers. When they do write, teachers are expected to show how their practices have been influenced by the latest theory or research at the university level. Professional conferences serve the same purposes and audiences, although teachers in the schools participate more heavily in conferences than contribute to professional journals in education. As a result, because researchers and university-level teacher trainers have been in the forefront of those promoting social goals in the past two decades, both the journals and the conferences have served to increase the prominence of social goals in relation to academic goals.

A recent article in a leading language arts journal provides a clear example of how such journals are guiding elementary school teachers to use literature for social goals. I describe it in some detail because it makes clear what the precise nature of one of these social goals is.[32] Written by a teacher trainer at the University of Wisconsin at Madison, the article is based on her conversations about the story *Maniac Magee*, a perfectly fine story for children, with a group of sixteen fourth- and fifth-grade children described as mostly European Americans. Its purpose is to let teachers see how "literature discussions can help both teachers and students understand their own and others' cultural and social identities." What this teacher researcher has in mind, however, is not what one would ordinarily understand by the word *culture*. The thrust of the article is that teachers need to make children conscious of their skin color and help them see that their cultural identity is based on it.

The researcher's pedagogy is based squarely on the notion that our society is "highly and historically racialized" (a phrase she borrows from Toni Morrison as an unquestioned fact), as if the America of today is no different from the America of 250 years ago in its views and behaviors regarding racial differences. As one might expect, the children's spontaneous responses to the story indicated that they saw the characters as individual people, nor did they make any reference to race themselves. However, because the researcher professes to believe that their failure to make direct references to racial identity and racial conflicts was an indication of "evasion" on their part and that "denials of race" signify "alignments with race," this made it necessary for her to engage them in a "consideration of race and racism."

During the conversations the author conducted with the children over the course of a month, helping them to interpret the story as she thought it should be understood when they failed to respond as she wanted them to, never once did she suggest that the children might see each other as American citizens, discuss what they share together as American citizens, and decide why racial segregation when it was institutionalized was a denial of full citizenship. The literature discussions were lessons in group identity formation. The researcher assumed that because she is "an adult who knows the history of poverty and institutionalized racism in our country and the struggles and perspectives of people of color in response to racism and economic inequality," and because "the characters and setting [of the story] do not evoke a history of institutionalized racism or a critique of economic inequality," it was her responsibility in her role as a teacher researcher to use literature to "fill in those gaps in the contexts of our discussions." And when one of the ten so-called European American children in the class responded to a discussion of segregation with less than the serious explanation she wanted, she "challenged his interpretation" because his response came "at the expense of a more informed interpretation of segregation." He needed challenge, she remarked, because this child "understood himself as a 'natural' member of and spokesperson for American society." This teacher researcher spent many school hours to get the children to see that the color of their skin is what matters, not the content of their character.

Elementary school teachers who grant pedagogical authority to an education professor at the University of Wisconsin will learn from this article that they must teach "beyond Response to Literature," that they must use literature to address "identity and racial conflict," and that they will make the "cultural" knowledge their children draw on "fuller, more inclusive, and more accurate" by making them see the color of their skin as the core of their cultural and social identities. In other words, teachers will end up believing that their students' horizons will be broadened if students are taught to see themselves in a highly limited way. Because they have been told so regularly by teacher educators and other academic authorities that a child's "culture" is determined by the child's race, elementary school teachers are not likely to grasp the Orwellian nature of this researcher's educational philosophy or see that her failure to note cultural differences among children whose skin color is white is dishonest and manipulative. Indeed, despite the likely differences in their own ethnic backgrounds, they may well believe that "European Americans" do constitute a monolithic cultural category.

THE INFLUENCE OF PARENTS

The one significant group of people with little influence on the content of reading textbooks are parents. They are viewed with suspicion by all the other sources of pressure, especially when they are in organizations of their own to advance their particular views, largely because they are not considered enlightened, as people who know what is best for their own children. Although not all parents who have criticized school textbooks or multicultural curricula are "conservatives" or "fundamentalists," they all tend to be categorized as such, and it is probably the case that most organized groups that try to pressure publishers do reflect concerns based on their religious beliefs. This strikes me as an unfortunate and puzzling lacuna. There are apparently few if any groups of parents pressuring publishers or state boards of education on chiefly academic grounds. Jesus Garcia sees today's pressure groups as "narrowly focused groups" that differ from those that flourished in the 1970s because they are more "aggressive." In a beautiful case of the pot calling the kettle black, Garcia says that what makes groups such as the National Association of Christian Educators and Citizens for Excellence in Education "dangerous is that they are no longer interested in airing their views in the marketplace of ideas; they are interested in controlling the textbook industry."[33]

They clearly are perceived as having influence. In the interview with my research assistant, one editor at a major publishing house commented on the "enormous influence" of the Gabler family on the Texas Board of Education and, by extension, the rest of the country. He described them as "Christian rightists" who "don't like a lot of stuff. Magic (because it involves the devil) and other images that remind them of Satan are just a few of their targets. They are particularly concerned with stories that might display an anti-American bias." In addition to magic, other topics he indicated were forbidden as "mentions," directly or indirectly, are swearing, references to God, cigarettes and tobacco, alcohol and drugs, the word *nigger*, even in a literary context, and sex, "even kissing." "Not even animals having sex."

206 · LOSING OUR LANGUAGE

However, as one ponders this list of forbidden topics, it seems that the agendas of the right and the left may simply go by each other like ships in the night. They do not conflict much, at least in the elementary school. What the right might succeed in keeping out, the left generally has no major interest in keeping in. And to judge by what is now in the readers, the left has been very successful in getting in what it wants. Clearly, the right has not been terribly alert to the major changes that have taken place in the content, thrust, and tone of selections in the basal readers. If the right has failed to notice their emphasis on racism, sexism, and other social issues; failed to detect the moralism on the environment, the disabled, and the elderly; and failed to perceive the emergence of the monolithic ugly white contemporary American, then it is hard to see how rightists are the dangerous censors they are portrayed as, although they have clearly been annoying. In fact, I would describe the Gablers and others like them in altogether other, although equally unflattering, terms.

The chief problem, it seems to me, has been the total absence of a genuinely nonpartisan and nonsectarian watchdog group, liberal in the classical sense of the term, concerned as much for academic and literary integrity as for justice and equity. I am aware of no groups that have arisen to oppose the agendas of those on both the right and the left. This vacuum has allowed the extremes on both the right and the left to carry their own ball to the opposite ends of the field. The collapse of the traditional liberal-conservative center in this country, among the faculty in universities as well as among educated adults in school communities, might well be seen as the major reason that school textbooks have been able to change so quickly.

EIGHT

THE EFFORT TO DOWNGRADE AND DEGRADE THE ENGLISH LANGUAGE

In editing their writing for publication, learners compare the expressions and vocabulary of their own way of speaking with those of standard English. For example, they consider their use of "I might could go to the store" which conveys a subtly different meaning than "I might be able to go to the store." They are reminded of the special qualities of the language that emerges from their culture.

—Massachusetts Department of Education, *English Language Arts Curriculum Framework*, November 1995 draft

Multicultural Concept Communication occurs when someone receives and understands the symbols (words, actions, expressions, and images) given by another person. With growing U.S. populations who speak languages other than English, it is important to arrive at effective means to communicate interculturally.

—Scott Foresman, *For the Teacher: Exploring Multicultural Dimensions*

ALTHOUGH THE creators of the reading series may not have intended to include so many selections containing language that is impoverished or inappropriate for grade-level reading instruction, nevertheless, these selections are there by choice. Some selections are there to portray particular groups and build their self-esteem, despite the poor literary or intellectual quality of this material. Others seem to be there to accommodate less able readers in the heterogeneous classroom.

Yet others are there to direct children's attention to the flaws of the country they live in and to make them feel hostile to or ashamed of white Americans or Western civilization, again despite less than high literary or intellectual quality. Choice has clearly been driven by more than a deep belief that such selections promote academic achievement in minority students. Choice has been driven by powerful negative forces—highly dogmatic and moralistic ones. In this chapter, I spell out the moral and social dogmas that lie behind the attempt to undermine the teaching of English in its standard forms and to reduce English as the language of instruction and learning in the regular classroom. These dogmas begin with a moral premise from which all the others follow logically in a long and intellectually destructive chain of reasoning.

THE NEW MORALITY

Insistence on Standard English Is Undemocratic and Oppressive

The effort by many linguists and educators to downgrade and degrade the English language begins with the premise that it is undemocratic and oppressive to insist on standard English in the English language arts class. As linguist John Honey explains in *Language Is Power: The Story of Standard English and Its Enemies*, this assertion does not require evidence to recruit believers, just assent and unquestioning faith in its rightness.[1] It springs full force from the dogma relentlessly propounded for years by almost all linguists, British and American, that all languages, and all dialects of all languages, are inherently equal in communicative possibility. Yet, as Honey observes, no proof has ever been proffered that all dialects of English, say, are indeed inherently equal.[2] In the eyes of those who subscribe to what Honey calls the "linguistic equality" hypothesis, a standard form of a language is nothing more than a dialect that has been privileged. We can find this kind of thinking reflected in a draft of the English language arts standards created for the Massachusetts Department of Education in November 1995 by a statewide committee of educators, most of whom were selected by a staff member of the department:

> The word "dialect" is used by some to refer to non-mainstream forms of language; however, linguists ask us to consider all the varying language systems within a language as dialects. Thus American English is one dialect of the

English language, and in turn, American English is composed of many regional and cultural dialects such as Black English, Appalachian English, and Boston English just to name a few. This concept of dialect helps to dispel the notion that one dialect is superior to another. As linguist Noam Chomsky puts it, "What differentiates a dialect and a language is who has the Army and Navy."[3]

Despite Chomsky's attempt to put a neo-Marxist spin on the matter, the argument is a specious one. It does not matter whether a language is a dialect supported by those with power in a society. There are advantages to every society in having a standardized form of its national language taught to all its children. A standard form reduces differences in social status, equalizes life chances, facilitates written as well as oral communication in that society, and gives all children access to the world community of educated speakers and writers of that language. Yet not a hint of this rationale appears in the November 1995 Massachusetts English language arts draft. Indeed, one member of the committee of educators responsible for this draft declared that there are "no correct or incorrect" forms of English at a meeting later called to revise this draft. The philosophy reflected in these statements in this draft has led to efforts to demote standard English's status and to withhold instruction in it, for especially those children whose parents cannot tutor them in it.

As Honey notes, the view that all dialects of a language are inherently equal in communicative potential has been around for over three decades. For a while, in the late 1960s and early 1970s, many educators believed that low-income black children failed to learn how to read well because of the differences between their dialect and the syntax of standard English in the readers. "Dialect" readers were composed and tried out, but no body of evidence was ever produced showing that such readers led to greater gains in reading skill for dialect-speaking children than the use of readers in standard English did. One reason that the dialect readers did not produce better reading skills may have been the variability in dialect features among low-income black children, often in the same classroom. Some children may have been confused by trying to read dialect features they did not themselves have. Another was the opposition of many black parents and educators themselves to the use of such readers. A fourth-grade African American teacher whose classroom I visited in September 1997 is only one example of this attitude. A teacher for over twenty-five years in a working-class Boston suburb, she was opposed to the use of stories in dialect for reading instruction for her children, black or white. Yet another reason that the dialect readers did not produce better reading skills is the distinct possibility that differences between an oral dialect and the standard language of a basal reader do not interfere with the development of reading comprehension in dialect-speaking children, just as they clearly do not interfere with their comprehension of standard English when listening to their teacher or other standard English speakers or to television or radio.[4]

The linguists' egalitarian attitude toward dialect has evolved into the multicultural notion that dialect as a cultural feature is part of one's identity as a member of that culture. This belief came to widespread public attention when the controversy about Ebonics broke out in 1996. As a teacher trainer in Ebonics was quoted as saying, "It's not about grammar, it's about identity and respect."[5] Hence, as one can interpret this statement, privileging the dialect of a different culture, especially one that is socioeconomically dominant and portrayed in its totality as racially discriminatory, oppresses those whose dialect differs. In this way, the privileged dialect of the 1960s became the oppressive dialect of the 1990s in the minds of many educators. According to their way of reasoning, something that is "privileged" is ipso facto "oppressive."

This attitude toward standard English shows up clearly in a report by a Rutgers University educator on school reform efforts in the Newark public schools.[6] The report was published in the *Teachers College Record*, a leading professional journal in the field of education, and its author is the chair of the Department of Education at this university and the director of its Institute for Outreach and Research in Urban Education. Thus, this educator's views would appear to be respected by others in the field of education and influential. Expressing her anger with the board of education's mandate in 1989 that teachers use on-grade-level reading texts for their students (i.e., a grade 5 reader for all grade 5 students) because most of the students were reading well below grade level, she claimed that these new texts are, in her words, a "microcosm of white middle-class interests and situations," with only an occasional story featuring a minority character. Regrettably, she did not identify what textbooks she examined to arrive at this astonishing conclusion. But worse than an alienating curriculum that does not concern these students, she went on to assert, is a curriculum that impedes their progress by using textbooks written in standard English—according to her, a dialect that almost none of the students spoke, and one that interfered with their own language. Indeed, she regarded the Newark curriculum as culturally and linguistically unsuited to its students and as providing, in her words, "a continual insult to nondialect speakers"—and this despite the fact that the mayor, the city council, the board of education, top school administrators, teachers, parents, and students were almost all African Americans.

Standard English-Speaking Children Need to Learn to Respect Nonstandard English

The notion that all dialects of a language are equal and that one's dialect is basic to one's cultural identity leads to more than selections in a reader featuring black dialect. The multicultural spin means that standard English–speaking children should be taught what these hitherto less privileged dialects are and to respect them. In essence, this means devoting valuable academic time to teaching students tolerance and appreciation for nonstandard dialects. In the spirit of respecting and understanding "similarities and differences among people," the November 1995 Massachusetts English language arts draft urged classroom teachers to "foster an appreciation for the strengths of diversity among the dialects of English and other languages."[7]

Dialect-Speaking Children Should Be Encouraged to Use Nonstandard English

Once the premise initiating this chain of moral dogmas is accepted, it is easy to see how each new one flows logically from the previous one: teachers are actively to encourage the use of all of these nonstandard dialects. The November 1995 Massachusetts English language arts draft also urged teachers to welcome the use of nonstandard dialects. It wanted the "home-based language patterns of culturally diverse learners . . . accepted and encouraged as valuable forms of communication."[8]

With enough encouragement from staff members in their state departments of education, teachers might even be helped to see that nonstandard dialects convey meaning in more nuanced ways than does the standard dialect. Consider the long-term pedagogical implications of the learning goal suggested in the passage cited in the epigraph.[9] It is not clear what culture the learners come from who use such phrases as "I might could go to the store." But the subtle message to teachers is clear: Praise violations of standard syntax.

If teachers are now to remind students of the special qualities of their home language, we have moved beyond the notion that all dialects are equal; we are progressing to the idea that nonstandard dialects may perhaps be more equal than standard English. To be sure, the November 1995 Massachusetts draft spoke with a forked tongue. One of its learning standards stated that "students will edit writing for sentence structure, usage, mechanics, and spelling."[10] But can students learn standard English usage easily for speaking or writing, or be motivated to learn it at all, if given constant praise for the special qualities of their home-based language patterns? One must be skeptical, especially when there is academic and professional encouragement to promote error and deviation for the explicit purpose of breaking the "tyranny" of standard English.

All Students Need to Be Encouraged Not to Speak or Write Standard English

> Writers should be encouraged to make intentional errors in standard form and usage. Attacking the demand for standard English is the only way to end its oppression of linguistic minorities and learning writers. We believe this frontal assault is necessary for two reasons: (1) it affords experienced writers, who can choose or not choose to write standard English, a chance to publicly demonstrate against its tryanny [sic] and (2) if enough writers do it regularly, our cultures [sic] view of what is standard and acceptable may widen just enough to include a more diverse surface representation of language, creating a more equitable distribution not only of the power in language and literacy but also, ultimately, of the power in economics and politics that language and literacy allow.
>
> —"Teaching Intentional Errors in Standard English: A Way to 'big, smart english,'" *English Leadership Quarterly* (May 1993)

The May 1993 issue of *English Leadership Quarterly (ELQ)*, a publication of the National Council of Teachers of English, featured an article by two educators at Indiana University of Pennsylvania entitled, "Teaching Intentional Errors in Standard English: A Way to 'big smart english.'"[11] It was judged the best article published in *ELQ* during the previous year by its sponsoring group, the Conference on English Leadership, a group composed chiefly of secondary school English teachers and administrators. The editor of *ELQ* at the time the article was published described "the matter of standard edited English" as an emotional political issue. Indeed, to him, it is a matter of justice. The editor implied great praise for the authors of the article because they "expose the tyranny of standards and advocate making intentional errors as a strategy for sensitizing the profession and the community at large to the injustices committed in the name of correctness."

To the authors of the article, users of standard language constitute, predictably, a race-based power fraternity. Claiming to answer hypothetical skeptics who might charge they are calling for a Tower of Babel, the authors assert that "we would not get a Tower of Babel because non-standard is not a different language; it's just another perfectly valid and vital and capable form of English that our culture has decided not to value, and by doing so, those in power stay in power, the rich stay rich, white and male." It is mystifying why the authors think standard English has been a tool of oppression against white females when their writing, on the average, has always been superior to the writing of white males. But inconvenient facts tend to be ignored when in conflict with ideology. To break this power of a white brotherhood, the authors recommend that teachers (1) "understand and value error"; (2) "value and incorporate multi-cultural and marginalized speech and literature"; (3) "support students' using big smart english"; (4) "evaluate and grade big smart english, making sure students privately and publicly see that the teacher values and rewards big smart democratic english"; and (5) "take political action to end the tryanny [*sic*] of standard English." It should not escape notice that the authors are using standard English to make their plea for "big, smart, democratic english": the use of nonstandard English.

The kind of thinking exemplified in this article is apparent in state English language arts standards documents. Only thirteen of the twenty-eight documents I examined in a review of state standards for the English language arts expect students to demonstrate competence in using standard English orally and in writing.[12] One wonders how many professors of English education are responding to the appeal to degrade the English language in the name of redressing the injustices presumably inflicted by the oppressive demands of standard English. It will be informative to see whether the two reading series I examined that had no stories with black or Appalachian dialect remain dialect free in the next publishing cycle.

One also wonders how soon standard English-speaking students will be taught that their dialect has oppressed black Americans and why it should be despised as well as violated. The recently formulated language arts goals of the Cambridge (Massachusetts) School Department give a hint of the seemingly neutral way in which this teaching will be conveyed.[13] In the elementary grades, students are to come to "understand the forms and features . . . of language that vary within and across different speakers, cultural communities, and contexts." They are also to discuss "cultural and situational variations in speech behaviors and the effects these variations produce." Such blandly stated goals will enable teachers who are so inclined to teach their students that differences in language use between poor people and middle-class people are the result of discrimination, not lack of education, or have resulted in discrimination against the poor. Hence, the prestige accorded educated speech is not only not deserved but misplaced as well. This line of reasoning leads inevitably to the conclusion that this prestige must be removed to redress this social problem, not that the schools should help the poor to acquire educated speech.

Although justice-driven educators profess to believe that the way to achieve equality is to declare any language usage acceptable, it should be noted that underlying these views, as John Honey also points out in his book,[14] is an assumption that nonwhite students are incapable of learning standard usage. It should also be noted that by justifying no demands on students at all, such a notion provides teachers who are so inclined with a convenient excuse for not spending time correcting student writing. Egalitarian views in the academic world often serve as a facade for self-interest.

Language Must Be Seen as the Defining Feature of Cultural Identity for Immigrant Children

The belief that a student's home language is the defining feature of his or her personal identity and cultural group is in large part responsible for the extensive presence of non-English vocabulary in the readers. This belief is conveyed directly by one of Silver Burdett Ginn's Appreciating Culture's sections. After students have read a story about a child's visit to a fantasy land in his sleep, they are to explore the "issues surrounding English-as-a-second language instruction." Teachers are to "point out that special classes help students when they are new to a different culture by maintaining their primary language and helping them affirm their identity."[15]

The fall 1994 draft of NCTE's standards for the English language arts put it this way: "Language is a primary instrument of thought, a defining feature of culture, and an unmistakable mark of personal identity." As the reasoning of those composing this draft seems to go, if language is a defining feature of cultural identity, then the languages of immigrant groups must be shown or spoken to native English-speaking students so that they can learn to respect them. Monolingual children apparently cannot learn to respect other languages without hearing them or seeing them in print. The fact that most native English-speaking students or teachers do not speak or understand other languages, or know how to pronounce the words in them, seems to matter little in the thinking of these educators.

Monolingual English Speakers Must Be Discredited

For several reasons, most of the non-English vocabulary and non-English selections are in Spanish. Spanish is the language of the largest immigrant group to this country, many Spanish speakers live in the two biggest adoption states, California and Texas, and many teacher educators as well as a strong Hispanic lobby want Spanish-speaking children to retain their native language and culture, for political as well as other reasons, whether or not their parents do.[16] Both groups want Spanish-speaking children to see Spanish as equal in prestige to English. They also want the non-Spanish-speaking peers of these children to see not only that Spanish is equal to English as a language but that being bilingual is an asset, which it clearly is.

Although this worthy idea could easily be conveyed positively, selections that suggest the desirability of bilingual skills tend to do so by denigrating or discrediting monolingual Americans; in fact, the epithet of "monolingual lout" is used by a character in a Scott Foresman grade 6 story. On the other hand, monolingual speakers of other languages are never denigrated; students are led to believe that the limitations of monolingualism reside in English speakers alone. Macmillan/McGraw-Hill's multicultural guidelines for educational publishers note that they will "take care to show most people of Hispanic origin as fluent in Spanish and English, or as teaching themselves English."[17] In other words, the real problem to be portrayed in educational materials is not that Spanish-speaking children do not learn or speak English; it is that English-speaking children or adults do not learn or speak Spanish.

Although the selection in Spanglish in the readers I examined happens to be in a Scott Foresman reader, Macmillan/McGraw-Hill's multicultural guidelines go on to provide a clear rationale for it in a section on how to treat "Hispanic Americans":

> To reflect the fact that many cities are bilingual, our materials will show Spanish newspapers, ads, product labels, and other reading materials. All children, whether speakers of Spanish first or not, can be portrayed as curious about Spanish words. To convey to Spanish-speaking readers that stories with Hispanic characters are written for them, not about them, we will not italicize Spanish terms as though they were foreign to the reader.[18]

What has been lost sight of in this obsession with the perceived self-esteem of Spanish-speaking children is the linguistic mischief this graphic practice may cause for both English-speaking and Spanish-speaking children in learning how to read English.

Immigrant Children Learn English Better by Not Doing Their School Work in English

The heavy presence of Spanish vocabulary in selections across all reading series may also be seen as an extension of the unproven theory underlying bilingual education as it is practiced in the public schools of this country. Many years ago, self-appointed protectors of non-English-speaking children in this country were able to convince courts and school boards that these children could best learn English through programs that teach them to read and write and do academic work in their home language, while gradually increasing their exposure to English in order to move them to the regular classroom. Transitional bilingual education programs, as they are called, contrast with English as a Second Language (ESL) pull-out programs in which immigrant children stay in the regular classroom most of the time and learn English only, and with structured immersion programs in which non-English-speaking children are grouped together, before they are mainstreamed, in a class taught mainly in English by someone who also knows their home language.

Transitional bilingual education is supposed to take place in a bilingual classroom, not the regular classroom, with children using more and more English in the bilingual classroom until they are deemed ready to be mainstreamed into the all-English classroom. However, the notion that children learning English benefit by using their home language as support is now accompanying immigrant children right into the mainstream classroom. In all drafts of the standards document developed by NCTE, for example, English teachers are told that "language development should draw on students' home language, literacy, and cultural experiences." And in my review of the English language arts standards in twenty-eight states, I found a number of state documents urging exactly that. For example, Delaware indicates in introductory material that "students' linguistic diversity must be recognized, respected, and built upon." Indiana and Ohio make the point more clearly. Indiana includes as a "supporting component" of its document a position statement of the National Council of Teachers of English on English/Language Arts practices asserting that students should have "guidance and frequent opportunities . . . to bring their own cultural values, languages, and knowledge to their classroom reading and writing." This assertion is repeated in Ohio's document. Kansas wants its students to show "in their speaking and writing that they value their own language and dialect." (In fact, Kansas eliminated the words *English Language* from the title of this document and decided to give K–12 English language arts teachers henceforth the nonlanguage-specific title of "communication arts teachers.")

This advice now appears in the basal readers as well. Before reading a selection involving a contest, the Harcourt Brace grade 4 teacher edition recommends that teachers "invite students to discuss with others who speak their first language the concept of contests. Then encourage students to share their thoughts in English with their classmates." That such pedagogy leads to segregation within the English language arts classroom, or any other classroom, seems to have escaped notice—or at least comment. The idea that language development in English should draw on a young child's home language may be yet another reason that the basal readers feature selections in Spanish or with Spanish words. Such selections provide an opportunity for Spanish-speaking children to use their own language for speaking or writing in the English language arts classroom if teachers follow up on the suggestions in the teacher guides.

218 · LOSING OUR LANGUAGE

Regrettably, without a vast, systematic set of nationwide observations, it is impossible to determine how many teachers do so.

As reasonable as this pedagogical philosophy may seem to some people, it leads to utterly bizarre suggestions for classroom activities. Vignettes in both NCTE's standards document and early drafts of the Massachusetts English language arts document suggest that this way of thinking about language development may effectively diminish, if not degrade, all students' opportunity for learning English. In one example of how to maintain use of a home language and teach children "respect" for "many forms of communication," the March 1995 draft of the Massachusetts document offered the following scenario:

> Rita, a recent immigrant, sits proudly in the "Author's Chair" of her writing group where she reads a poem she has written in her native language and illustrated with sketches of her homeland. As Rita responds to questions and comments about her poem, she helps her classmates to appreciate another culture as she is learning English.[19]

Hyperbolically proclaiming that experiences such as these "allow students to use their powerful home-based ways of communicating as well as open powerful new ways of communicating for everyone," the document goes on to comment (and without a shred of evidence):

> For a bilingual learner such as Rita depicted in one of our opening images, the opportunity to use her home language allows her to participate more fully in classroom activities. Her active participation validates her culture, and strengthens the school's link to the home. Research suggests that the ideal educational program for second language learners is one which provides meaningful instruction in English, maintains content area instruction in the native language as well as English, and maintains and develops the native language.[20]

Despite its surface rationality, the entire scenario for the activity has an Alice in Wonderland quality in its logic and common sense. The text suggests that a primary-grade child who has written a poem in, say, Urdu will, by responding to questions and comments about her poem from her classmates, help them learn about her culture. But how can Rita's classmates ask her anything at all about her poem if they have not understood a word of it? (The vignette does not state that the students are asking Rita questions about her sketches.) How can listening to a poem in Urdu "open powerful new ways of communicating" for students who do not speak or understand a word of Urdu? All Rita's classmates can do is ask her to translate her poem into English. Rita has actually wasted a lot of everyone's valuable learning time. And what does Rita get out of all of this? If she has written a poem in Urdu, she has been penalized by the children's request to translate it into English. For children, this is extra work, given the energy it takes to come up with a poem. Finally, Rita has lost the opportunity to try to write a poem in English, which we presume was the purpose of this lesson for the whole class. She has in reality participated in the class less fully than she would have if she had tried to write her poem in English from the start. In other words, she has been marginalized. She could still have written about her birth country if enriching her classmates's knowledge was the real purpose for this ludicrous example.

The purpose of vignettes, or examples, like this in standards documents (in Massachusetts and in other states) is to show teachers how they may implement in their own classrooms the linguistic stew now being touted in schools of education. Although their underlying assumptions are so irrational when one tries to role-play their scenarios that one is tempted to conclude that the scenarios were fabricated (and they may well have been), nevertheless, the pedagogy for creating linguistic stew in the English class is being actively promoted in professional journals for the teaching of English.

Let us look at one real example of this pedagogy in an article in the March 1998 issue of *Language Arts,* NCTE's most prestigious journal for elementary school teachers, which featured a number of articles to help teachers deal with "linguistically diverse" classrooms.[21] The article is based on the belief, spelled out in the introduction, that "requiring the exclusive use of English . . . and strict adherence to an established curriculum designed for mainstream English-speaking students . . . can lead to self-doubt on the part of linguistically and culturally diverse learners." Although the two authors provide no evidence for this assertion, that does not deter them from describing several language-mixing incidents in classrooms in California and Colorado as examples of "exemplary practice" and then claiming that they improved the students' self-esteem. One of these incidents echoes several of the problems that can be teased out of Rita's story above.

The authors describe Margarita, a first-grade student enrolled in a bilingual class with a "monolingual English teacher," as reluctant to participate in an activity in which the children are to guess the objects that are in a "mystery bag" as it is shaken:

> Although she appears to be following the lesson, she remains silent throughout the elicitation and confirmation of the predictions. Another student shakes a new mystery bag. No one has guessed the object in the bag. Suddenly a smile appears on Margarita's face, but she does not speak. She continues smiling, as if she knows the answer, but continues to say nothing. Then, the teacher looks at her and the following brief exchange takes place.
>
> > Teacher: You can say it in Spanish.
> > Margarita: *Canicas* (in a low soft voice).
> > Teacher: *Canicas?* (Teacher intuits this is the Spanish word for marbles.) (*Turning to the class.*) *Canicas.* I have learned a new word in Spanish, *canicas.*
>
> The teacher invites the entire class to repeat the new word, *canicas.* The students are heard savoring the new word repeatedly, *canicas, canicas.* Margarita smiles as her Spanish response is affirmed over and over.

The authors profess to believe that the teacher's invitation for Margarita to use her own linguistic resources "provided an opportunity for a linguistically diverse learner to be a competent member within an English lesson." But at no point do they indicate that Margarita learned the word *marbles* within this English lesson. So far as we can tell, Margarita has not developed greater competence in English as a result of this lesson, nor have the other Spanish-speaking children in the class. (Indeed, the teacher was the only one who learned a new word: the Spanish word for *marbles.*) The authors' attempt to justify what the teacher did by claiming that Margarita is "also more likely to participate in subsequent lessons" is also without substantiation. When responding to Margarita to advance her English language skills in an English lesson without inhibiting her future participation, the teacher might simply have said, "Good, Margarita. You guessed correctly that marbles were in the mystery bag. Let's all practice the English word for *canicas.*"

There is no body of evidence showing that children learn English better if they learn to read, write, and do academic work in their home language first. Indeed, such practices as the one recommended above for "linguistically diverse classrooms" are more likely to interfere with the language development in English of all the children in the class. Common sense, the experience of millions of children around the world, and the evidence to date clearly indicate that most normal young children can learn a second language quickly and easily, and that they can learn English at least as well, if not better, in structured immersion programs, in ESL pull-out programs, or by direct immersion in all English-speaking classes with an occasional tutor and understanding teacher.[22] Interestingly, all the Haitian taxicab drivers in Boston I have questioned have told me that they have taken their children out of the Boston public schools (or not enrolled them in the Boston public schools to begin with) and put them into private, usually Christian, schools to make sure they learned English immediately, which they did. Otherwise, they say, their children might still be in Creole-speaking classes. Yet professors at prestigious universities continue to intone that it is a "myth" to believe that young children can learn second languages easily and quickly.[23]

English Is an Imperialistic Language and Should Not Be the Language of This Country

It should not be surprising that the logic of the thinking underlying the other pedagogical judgments I have elaborated leads directly to the conclusion that English should not be the official or unofficial language of the United States. The language of an oppressor people, whose literature must inevitably reflect their unworthy values, attitudes, and beliefs, does not deserve to be the language of instruction and learning for the "multicultural and multilingual democracy" that NCTE believes we are. One can read this conclusion between the lines of the call for proposals put out by NCTE for a two-day international conference it sponsored in New York City in July 1995. The subthemes and questions that proposals were to address included: *English and the State*, under which proposers were invited to address, "What is the role of English in a democratic society?" *The Canon and Cultural Pluralism for a Democratic Society*, under which proposers were invited to address, "What are the hidden curricula underlying English Language Arts instruction?" *Models and Metaphors for English Studies*, under which proposers were invited to address, "What should the subject 'English' be in the 21st Century?" and "What models or metaphors will promote our definitions of English studies for the 21st Century?" *Relevance and the Students of the 21st Century*, under which proposers were invited to address, "What are English Language Arts courses for *all* students?" *Less Is More: Beyond Subject English to Interdisciplinary Curricula*, under which proposers were invited to address, "Should we have courses called 'English'?"; and *English and Its Neighbors*, under which proposers were invited to address, "How does English relate to other languages?" This last question was clearly not intended to be answered from a philological or linguistic perspective.

This conference, attended by educators from English-speaking countries around the world, was immediately followed by the Sixth International Conference of the International Federation for the Teaching of English (IFTE). Participants were expected to attend both conferences if possible, because the second one was intended to provide time for working groups to develop position papers for each of the themes of the conferences.[24] An anecdote offered in the keynote address for the IFTE conference by one of the program organizers (and a professor of English education in this country) clearly suggested the perspective of those organizing these two conferences and many (but not all) of those attending them. Recounting his experience in traveling by air from Egypt to a country in central Africa a year or so earlier, the keynote speaker indicated how "terrified" he was to hear communication in English between Egyptian pilots in an Egyptian airline and ground controllers at an airport in a central African country. Although the other passengers were probably relieved to know that both parties were speaking one language that both understood, this professor of English education interpreted the situation as an example of blatant linguistic imperialism by the English-speaking people of the world. And, in fact, the purpose of many of the English educators at this conference was to begin working out ways to loosen the imperialistic grip of the English language on the world at large. One well-known English educator in Canada remarked in a subgroup meeting, "Literacy is independent of any particular language." This is, of course, a truism. Children become literate in whatever language they are taught in their schools. But his implication was clear: it is not necessary for language arts teachers or literacy teachers in English-speaking countries to teach children English for them to become literate; they can become literate in other languages just as well, especially their home languages.

The attempt to remove the word *English* from the titles of professional organizations in education represents the initial stages of the movement to downplay the fact that English is the language of this country and to reduce its role. The very title of the National Council of Teachers of English has been characterized by the "NCTE Name Change Committee" as "too narrow to convey who we really are in terms of our profession's comprehensive role in guiding the development of students' reading, writing, speaking, listening, and thinking skills."[25] The committee is concerned that the title conveys a misleading notion about "our national identity." At a session at NCTE's annual conference in November 1995, held to discuss name changing, some members were reported as objecting to the word *English* as noninclusive.[26] One delegate stated that "if we are to offer diversity, there can be a conversation about language arts, but not about English," adding that the word *English* excludes bilingual teachers. The incoming NCTE president was quoted as saying that "it is important that teachers honor other people's cultural heritages." If this was in response to a question about name changing, it suggests that English teachers are perceived as dishonoring other people's cultural heritages by teaching them in required courses called "English." Nothing was decided at this conference, but the item remains on the agenda for future conferences.

One name change that did go through this past year was for an organization associated with NCTE, the National Conference on Research in English. Needing a two-thirds vote of its membership to effect a name change, the organization's executive board sent out ballots to its membership at least twice on the grounds that not everyone had received a ballot the first time or had voted. By this means it was able to reach the required number for a name change. It has now become the National Conference on Research in Language and Literacy.

A staggering obstacle lies in the path of those who truly believe that English is an oppressive language that is not worthy of serving as the unofficial language of this country. The vast majority of Americans speak English as their native language. Moreover, it is without dispute the international language. Nevertheless, steps are being taken to obfuscate this fact. New Jersey's standards document refers to all foreign languages as "World Languages" (the title is a euphemism coined by educators who think that using "foreign" to designate a foreign language in this country is ethnocentric, if not insulting). The writers of the Massachusetts World

Languages standards document also do not consider English a "world language"; the phrase is used in true Orwellian fashion only for the document that deals with all other languages.[27] As this document explains it:

> The term foreign language is a misnomer. In this framework we refer to the languages we teach as World Languages to reflect the experience of the ancient cultures that preceded us, our own present multilingual populace, and our vision of a multilingual community for the twenty-first century. We rename our discipline in support of all languages and peoples of the world as equal citizens of the world community and acknowledge our responsibility to be able to communicate with the peoples of that world.[28]

The "linguistic equality" hypothesis is at work here again. But how Americans, regardless of language background, can communicate with other peoples of the world without a good grasp of the language that increasing numbers of students in other countries are now learning as their preferred second language is not discussed. This fact is an immense stumbling block for those who are trying to figure out, in the language of the statement quoted at the beginning of this chapter, how we can "communicate interculturally" in this country.[29] The unwritten thought that finishes this statement is, of course, "without having to teach everyone English." Clearly there is no big mystery to solve if everyone in this country is taught English. But if the educational establishment does not want everyone taught English, then it is a puzzlement as to how we can "communicate interculturally" in this country except through Esperanto or a Sign Language version of it. The way in which ideology cripples the educational advice of people who think like this can be seen in a classroom example involving different languages in the 1995 draft of the Massachusetts "world languages" standards document:

> For a humanities class, students of French, Spanish, and Italian classes join forces to do a collaborative project examining the genre of stories of *the fantastic,* or the supernatural. (Double language students read or view stories in both languages, and can contribute multiple viewpoints to the conversation.) Each language group examines plot, characterization, and theme in several stories. Different language groups then come together to compare and contrast information across languages and cultures. The combined groups plan a unified visual presentation of their research; individuals prepare a written paper on the project.[30]

What is left out of this vignette is the fact that this scenario is unworkable unless all the students speak English. This is an English language project. One common language is necessary for all this "intercultural communication." And how will the students of one language be able to assess the validity of what the students of the other languages are claiming about the stories they have read? They will not, of course, unless these high school students of French, Spanish, and Italian, true to the spirit of the committee that created this draft, translate the stories they have read into English for the benefit of the students who do not read the language of the original story.

WHAT THE NEW MORALITY IGNORES: LANGUAGE DEVELOPMENT AS A BIOLOGICAL PROCESS

The amount of sheer idiocy that is being expressed by people with advanced degrees in education is a tribute to the power of ideology. It is not that there are not some people trying to combat some of this nonsense. For example, one courageous pair of high school teachers wrote an article, published in the November 1994 issue of the *English Journal*, raising questions about the version of NCTE's Content Standards at that time. They commonsensically asked, "Why would second language acquisition be part of English/Language Arts standards?" in reference to a standard postulating: "Students develop skills in more than one language."[31] It wouldn't be part of English/language arts standards, of course, if those guiding the profession were genuinely interested in the teaching of English. But those intending to lead the way have very different goals.

Their goals are articulated clearly in a position paper entitled, "A Pedagogy of Multiliteracies: Designing Social Futures," written by an international group of English language arts educators calling themselves the New London Group, and published in 1996 in the *Harvard Educational Review*. The New London Group is hoping to shape how language is taught in all English-speaking countries to conform to their notions of social justice and equality.[32] Evincing no interest whatever in what parents might want for their own children, they say that "in each of the English speaking countries we came from, we agreed that what needed to be learnt was changing, and the main element of this change was that there was not a singular, canonical English that could or should be taught anymore."

Coining the word *multiliteracies* to designate the outcomes they desire, they want to make dealing with "linguistic differences and cultural differences" central to everyone's lives. They profess to believe that "effective citizenship and productive work now require that we interact effectively using multiple languages, multiple Englishes, and communication patterns which more and more frequently cross cultural, community, and national boundaries."

Like the English education professors who advocate "big smart english," these self-appointed champions of women, indigenous peoples, immigrants who do not speak the national language, and speakers of nonstandard dialects do not believe these groups are capable of learning the language of the mainstream, especially in, in their words, a "vicious world driven by the barely restrained market." And like those advocating children's use of their home language in the English class, they too claim there will be a "cognitive benefit to all children in a pedagogy of linguistic and cultural pluralism . . . when learners juxtapose different languages, discourses, styles and approaches." Not surprisingly, these self-styled educators offer no concrete description of what even one such classroom could look like. And no parents or legislators even know what these folks are up to yet.

Although the standards documents now available from NCTE and some (but not all) states make the teaching of the English language a travesty of the educational process, they will influence many teachers, especially at the elementary school level, where they have been trained to be deferential to the advice of people with advanced degrees—this despite the fact that the NCTE standards document was roundly criticized by major figures. The late Albert Shanker, president of the American Federation of Teachers, declared, "They are not standards at all. . . they also throw out the best hope for getting some kind of equity among our widely disparate English curriculums." Michael Cohen, a senior adviser to Secretary of Education Richard W. Riley at the time, was quoted as saying, "It looks more like a statement of philosophy that provides some background and grounding for professionals in the field. . . . That's not what people are looking for when they're looking for standards." A *New York Times* editorial attacked the document for its foggy language and its lack of substance.

Yet dutifully and unthinkingly, teachers are already interfering with children's language development in the name of racial or ethnic justice.

Issues of *Language Arts* often feature classroom examples collected by teacher researchers seeking to promote their pedagogical ideas. What is usually not pointed out in contemporary educational materials is the fact that language is more than an instrument or product of culture. Language development is a fundamental biological process that begins in infancy and helps shape intellectual development. It is an assault on intellectual development to tamper with language development at the onset of literacy education. And tampering it is when one deliberately mixes a variety of languages together in the same classroom as well as in children's instructional materials; when one compels children learning English to engage in constant translation work in the English language classroom;[33] when one withholds the best written models that can be offered to children in the language of the larger society in which they live; when one confuses children about how to communicate to and be understood by a worldwide range of listeners or readers of that language; and when one deprives them of exposure to the vocabulary that would give them access to the great literature and complex ideas expressed in that language.

Self-righteous educators have chosen to take out their professed anger at this country's social problems on the English language itself. Unwilling to engage in the hard work of helping all children learn how to read and write, they have spitefully made the English language the object of their seeming frustration because it is so vulnerable, especially in its written form. What is not clear is how these educators can be held accountable for the damage their pedagogical notions are inflicting on a fundamental biological process in human development.

––––––––––

Secondary school and college teachers complain, with good reason, that fewer and fewer American students read demanding literature in junior or senior high school or can do demanding academic writing. One editor I spoke with believes that there is little eighteenth- and nineteenth-century literature in the upper elementary grade readers not because of an anticivic perspective, and not because of a bias against dead white males, and not because their works do not relate to students' personal experiences, but because many students cannot read the language of eighteenth- or nineteenth-century (or even early twentieth-century) writers anymore. Teacher educators who cannot abandon their ideologies will continue to downgrade and degrade the English language and support the dumbing down of its literature rather than urge the teaching of the reading skills that will enable children to read demanding literary works at a later age.

One ray of hope on the national scene is the draft of the English language arts curriculum framework created for the Massachusetts Department of Education in 1996 and approved by its state board of education on January 15, 1997. In early 1996, the commissioner of education in Massachusetts appointed a new statewide committee of educators to address all the grievous problems in the November 1995 draft, from which I have liberally quoted in this chapter. (Later that year, the staff member chiefly responsible for the selection of the original committee resigned.) This November 1995 draft had been unanimously rejected by the previous board of education in December 1995. After five months of intensive work, the new committee came up with a completely revised document whose learning standards embody high literary and academic expectations for all students in Massachusetts schools and whose devotion to the integrity of the English language is clear. The document was lauded not only by the lead editorial in the *Boston Globe* on January 14, 1997, but also, in 1998, by such politically sophisticated and distinguished commentators as Lynne V. Cheney, former chair of the National Endowment for the Humanities, and William Galston, director of the University of Maryland's Institute for Philosophy and Public Policy and adviser to President Clinton during his first term of office.[34]

NINE

WHY THERE IS LITTLE RESEARCH ON THE EFFECTS OF MULTICULTURALISM ON ACADEMIC ACHIEVEMENT

For most of this century, the literacy skills and overall performance of students have been either static or declining, while expenditures have grown with unstoppable vigor. Anyone who cares about education should be embarrassed by these results, and motivated to improve them. It is hard to think of a single other human enterprise with such a poor record. Whether in agriculture, industry, transportation, or the service sector, the last hundred years have been witness to astonishing advances in efficiency and output. Where the costs of goods and services have risen, they have been associated with real improvements in quality, improvements that are not to be found in educational outcomes.

> —From Andrew Coulson, "Schooling and Literacy over Time: The Rising Cost of Stagnation and Decline" (1996)[1]

Far too few students are reaching the proficient level of reading achievement in any grade. Average achievement is either stuck or going down.

> —Attributed to a fourth-grade teacher on the governing board of the National Assessment of Educational Progress (1995)[2]

STUDIES BY THE NATIONAL ASSESSMENT OF EDUCATIONAL PROGRESS

The original motivation for stressing social goals in the school curriculum was concern for the academic achievement of minority students. Thus, it is quite legitimate to ask if there is any nationwide evidence that the dramatic changes in the pedagogy and content of reading instruction in the past decade or so have improved their academic performance. To answer that question, we look at the nationwide studies on reading achievement conducted by the National Assessment of Educational Progress (NAEP). We also look at its studies on writing achievement because writing is heavily dependent on growth in reading ability and in turn can help develop reading skills in different ways at different ages.[3] The connections between reading and writing are supported by a sound body of research, and, indeed, all the reading series seek to strengthen them.

The NAEP has undertaken assessments in reading since the early 1970s and in writing since the 1980s. Throughout most of these years, American students have been classified into three groups—white, black, and Hispanic—and have been assessed about every two to four years at ages nine, thirteen, and seventeen, or in grades 4, 8, and 11. Scores are reported at three levels of achievement: basic, proficient, and advanced.

What is striking about the trends in achievement in the NAEP studies is the almost complete stagnation or decline in scores in reading and writing for students as a whole from the mid-1980s to the present. The report on trends from 1971 to 1992 stated "Reading performance at age 9 improved significantly between 1971 and 1980, and then declined significantly between 1980 and 1992, returning essentially to the original level. At age 13, little change occurred from assessment to assessment, but average performance was higher in 1992 than 1971. Seventeen-year-olds made significant gains between 1971 and 1984, although virtually no change has been observed since then."[4]

A report on the 1994 reading assessment came out later, showing continuing stagnation in the scores of nine and thirteen year olds and decline in the scores for all seventeen year olds.[5] In 1994, only one-third of high school seniors were proficient or advanced readers, a 10 percent drop in less than two years. About 30 percent of the seniors failed to reach even the lowest level, a 5 percent increase over 1992.

The NAEP report on trends from 1971 to 1996 noted that the overall picture remains virtually unchanged from 1994 and that the average score of seventeen year olds in 1996 did not differ significantly from that of their counterparts in 1971 or in 1994,[6] implying that the gains made between 1971 and 1984 had been wiped out. In sum, American students as a whole today are no better readers by the time they complete high school than were their 1971 counterparts. This is not an impressive state of affairs, given that the vast majority of the seventeen-year-old students participating in these assessments even today are white and therefore tend not to be children of immigrants or indigenous minority students.

The past decade shows no progress for black and Hispanic students either. Although black students at all age levels show gains from the 1970s to 1996, the pattern is one of early gains and recent stagnation or decline. After about twenty years of significant increases in reading scores at all three age levels,[7] the average score declined throughout the early 1990s. The story for Hispanic students is mixed. For nine and thirteen year olds, scores have fluctuated from assessment to assessment. Although the 1996 average score for nine-year-old Hispanic students was higher than the 1975 average score for their counterparts, the average score of thirteen-year-old Hispanic students in 1996 did not differ significantly from that of their counterparts in 1975. The same is true for seventeen-year-old Hispanic students. Although the overall pattern from 1975 to 1996 for seventeen year olds is one of increased performance, declining scores during the 1990s have resulted in a 1996 average that did not differ significantly from that of their counterparts in 1975. So although the 1996 scores for black and Hispanic students show maintenance of, if not improvement over, the scores from the 1970s, the past decade for most of them has been one of decline.

The report on trends in writing paints an even more serious picture.[8] For grade 11 students as a whole, the average writing score has shown an overall pattern of decrease across the assessment years, mainly because of decreased performance by white students. For both grade 4 and grade 8 students as a whole, the report notes no significant changes in performance over the assessment years. The same is true for black and Hispanic students at all grade levels. Given the dependence of writing achievement on reading achievement, these results are not surprising.

The NAEP tests provide no evidence whatsoever that the changes of the past decade or so in the cultural content of the curriculum and the pursuit of broad social goals in the name of multicultural education have academically benefited black, white, or Hispanic students.[9] What makes the NAEP tests more worthy of attention is the outcome of another study claiming almost the opposite of what the NAEP report on trends concluded. The Rand Institute on Education and Training issued its own analysis and interpretation of the NAEP trends in 1994, asserting that American schools improved over the past twenty years and that NAEP scores for black and Hispanic teenagers improved significantly between the mid-1970s and 1990.[10] The Rand study also suggested that the social welfare and educational policies of the past two or three decades may well be considered effective, rather than a waste of money or as poorly conceived as many have claimed. The policies and programs it believes may account for the results of their analysis are "access to integrated and probably more competitive K–12 schools," "social programs such as Head Start and child health and nutrition programs directed at children and families," "desegregation, affirmative action, and bilingual education," "school consolidation, large real increases in per-student expenditures, changing curriculum, smaller class sizes, and a more experienced and better paid teaching force." Note that all of these policies and programs have been strongly supported by most educators in the past three decades and that the two curriculum features the Rand study points to are bilingual education and changing curriculum.

Actually, the NAEP data do not lend themselves to multiple interpretations. It is not very difficult to determine how an analysis of what seems to be the same data set resulted in seemingly different conclusions. To arrive at the conclusion that thirteen-and seventeen-year-old Hispanic and black students made significant gains in the twenty years between 1971 and 1992, the Rand study looked only at NAEP reading and mathematics scores, examining the difference in reading from 1975 to 1990 and in mathematics from 1978 to 1990. A comparison of scores from the 1970s with the scores in 1990 does show significant gains. But such an analysis obscures the possibility that the scores may have stopped increasing before 1990 or may have plateaued or declined since then. That is in fact what happened in reading. Thus, the praise that the Rand report authors offer for the various social and educational programs they think led to significant gains for minority students must be tempered considerably. If these programs were so effective in the first decade and a half after 1971, why did they stop having an effect after the mid-1980s? Two of them— changing curriculum and bilingual education—have increased markedly in scope in the past decade, suggesting that they may have become negative influences on academic achievement. Given the current furor in California over bilingual education, it may well be the case that the expansion of bilingual education has been a major factor in the failure of Hispanic students to show improved scores in reading and writing over the past two to three decades (Spanish-speaking children are the largest non-English language group in bilingual education). I know of no NAEP report suggesting this possibility, however.

THE 1994 U.S. HISTORY ASSESSMENT

In 1995, the results of the 1994 NAEP assessment of U.S. history were reported.[11] The results were an unexpected disaster, and NAEP is still exploring the possible reasons for the dismal performance of students. Only a little over 60 percent of nine and thirteen year olds and 43 percent of twelfth graders reached even the basic level. Of these students, only 17 percent of nine year olds, 14 percent of 13 year olds, and 11 percent of twelfth-grade students reached the proficient (middle) level. For this test, students of Asian background were identified as a separate group. At all three grade levels, Asian and white students had significantly higher scores than black and Hispanic students.

Among the possible reasons for these results, NAEP noted that this assessment, unlike previous U.S. history assessments, included many interpretative, open-ended questions that required students to apply factual knowledge and demonstrate their skills in writing. Although U.S. history scores depend on factual knowledge gained from courses of study in history, we should not forget that the acquisition of this knowledge depends heavily on reading ability, and the communication of this knowledge depends heavily on writing ability.

WHAT SMALL-SCALE STUDIES TELL US

One might reasonably ask whether evidence for the beneficial effects of multicultural education can be found in small-scale studies by individual educational researchers, even if no evidence can be found in the NAEP studies. Contrary to what one might expect, there is no evidence at all from published research to support the claims of the multiculturalists. The absence of research on its effects was openly acknowledged in an article in a 1987 issue of the *Harvard Educational Review*. After an extensive review of the research literature, its authors—two teacher educators in the University of Wisconsin system—observed that there were "virtually no research studies on multicultural education" at the time they wrote the article.[12] Although they did not offer any reasons for the lack of research, they urged that research be undertaken. They also described the kinds of articles that had appeared and the kinds of research that they thought needed to be done:

> Some authors draw on related areas of research, such as bias in materials, effects of bilingual education, desegregated schooling, teacher attitudes toward diverse students,and student friendships across race, gender, and handicap lines. But we have not been able to locate research studies of any kind on multicultural education in the classroom for grades K–12. So far, most of the literature in this category stresses advocacy, discusses issues, and recommends courses of action. It must move beyond this. There needs to be research on what happens when teachers work with multicultural education in their classrooms, what forms it takes and why, how students respond, and what barriers are encountered.

The situation has not changed since this call for research. Geneva Gay's 1994 report, described in the Preface, pointedly commented on the lack of research support for multicultural education. On the other hand, in a 1994 article, "What We Can Learn from Multicultural Education Research," another teacher educator in the University of Wisconsin system did claim that "many findings from multicultural education research can be applied in the everyday world of teachers and administrators."[13] Nevertheless, despite Gloria Ladson-Billings's effort to make it appear that we do have some evidence showing the benefits of multicultural education, her list of references contains not a single research study dealing with the effects of multicultural curriculum content, materials, instructional approaches, educational settings, and teacher education on student achievement or attitudes. In other words, Ladson-Billings could not locate even one study to support her clear implication that there is a body of multicultural education research out there, never mind that it has useful findings. The references she does offer consist largely of cultural criticism, anecdotes, and advocacy or accounts of the limitations perceived in schools and textbooks with respect to minority children. Some of these references may constitute scholarship, but not the kind of research that can establish cause and effect and whose results are generalizable.

Revealingly, only one question remains "open," according to this educator: "whether the race and ethnicity of teachers affects student learning." Yet it is the only question for which she cites a review of actual research, and it turns out to be a review that concludes that no connection has been found between the teacher's race or ethnicity and student achievement. We might therefore conclude that the question is "open," only because the research findings are not politically correct—that is, they do not support the claim that minority students need teachers from their own ethnic group in order to succeed academically. We might also have cause to speculate that multicultural educators are not willing to accept as evidence certain facts on the ground if the facts do not happen to support their beliefs.

As further evidence for this speculation, we need to consider that there actually is a small body of research on the effects of multicultural content on student attitudes that this teacher educator could have mentioned. In the past twenty-five years, at least five studies have looked at the effects of multicultural literature on the self-esteem of minority students or on attitudes toward minority students by nonminority children. Of the two published in 1969, one dealt with changes in attitudes toward black children by white elementary school children after the use of "multiethnic" readers, and the other looked at the effects of "black studies" on black fifth-grade students.[14] The other three are unpublished dissertations.[15] One, completed in 1975, looked at the effects of listening to excerpts from children's stories about Mexican Americans on the "self-concepts and attitudes" of sixth-grade children. A second, completed in 1991, looked at the effects of Hispanic children"s literature on the "self-esteem of lower socioeconomic Mexican American kindergarten children." The third, completed in 1988, looked at the impact of multicultural education on "self-concept, racial attitude, and student achievement" of black and white fifth and sixth graders. Their findings? Multicultural literature had little, if any, effect on changes in student attitudes. It is not surprising that these studies were not mentioned by this Wisconsin educator; they contradict the multiculturalist's claims.

Why have there been so few research studies on multicultural education? I can only guess that it is not seen as a curricular or pedagogical philosophy whose claims require validation. From the very beginning, almost all teacher educators and researchers seem to have assumed that multicultural education is an indisputable good for all students, minority and others. The many educational articles on it consistently present it as something to be desired. For example, the purpose of an article published in 1996 in a premier research journal in education was "to advance research on the implementation of multicultural education, as well as to promote more genuine forms of multicultural teaching and learning."[16] Although the author does call for "empirical evidence as to whether and/or what kinds of multicultural educational teaching and experience result in improved outcomes for students," the criticisms of multicultural education that the researcher cites in her article are criticisms not of its failure to show improvement in the academic performance of minority youngsters but largely of its failure to "reinvent or confront established categories of knowledge or relations of power." Again we see quite clearly that the current goals of multicultural education are social and political, not academic.

Given the amount of controversy that multiculturalism has occasioned in the national media and at the college level, the unwillingness of teacher educators to examine its basic assumptions with the same critical eye they bring to other educational philosophies must be regarded as an unflattering comment on their professionalism. To my knowledge, there is no other curricular or pedagogical approach, no matter how widely praised, that has not been openly critiqued by educators in good standing in the educational community. Here we seem to have a situation in which one particular educational approach has been defined as not susceptible of reasoned discussion and legitimate criticism. The educational world also seems to have assumed that those critiquing it, never mind actively opposing it, are racist or sexist by their very stance.

Thus, it is not surprising that the little research that is only now beginning to focus on multicultural education has almost nothing to do with the questions that one might ordinarily expect to be explored. One professor of education, regarded as a researcher himself, has expressed the intentions of many English language arts and reading researchers quite succinctly in a preface to a volume of essays on various methods and approaches to "literacy research."[17] What this professor at Indiana University thinks they should be doing through their research is "altering social relationships" in the classroom. Indeed, he believes that education itself is "about the business of altering social relationships," a view that seems uncontested in the essays in this volume. This conception of the purpose for education—a completely nonacademic one—appears to be the one that many researchers are trying to implement through their research, even though this notion is unlikely to be the one held by most parents, whether mainstream or minority, or accepted by them if they only knew what these researchers had in mind.

Extensive public discussion is needed on the professional and ethical issues involved in the use of educational research to indicate what attitudes and beliefs students should have about themselves and others and to show teachers how to change their students' attitudes and beliefs about themselves and others in a direction desired by the *researchers* without the informed consent of the students and their parents. Educational publishers and school administrators pay a great deal of attention to the results of educational research because they see it as a form of scientific research. As such, they expect it to provide impartial information to assist decision making on curricular and pedagogical issues. Because educational research benefits from the enormous prestige accorded to scientific research in general, abuse of this prestige requires careful scrutiny, especially since most research is funded through public agencies and tax dollars.

The results of small-scale or individual research studies corroborate the results of the NAEP assessments. There is no evidence from either source to suggest that recent changes in the contents of the basal readers or the practices that educators have promoted in the past decade or so to build individual or group self-esteem have improved the academic performance of low-achieving minority students. Given the stagnation or decline in reading and writing scores in all students in the past decade, it is more likely that the social goals dominating education today have had just the opposite effect on academic achievement. Interestingly, the emphasis on social goals has perhaps been most detrimental to high achievers, for there has been a visible decline in the academic performance of high achievers over the years.[18] But the emphasis on social goals has also been detrimental to those students on whom national attention began to focus in the mid-1960s. Indeed, the *NAEP 1994 Reading Report Card* notes that the "decline in average proficiency among twelfth graders was concentrated among lower performing students."[19]

The gap between the scores of white and nonwhite students may have narrowed slightly from the 1970s to 1996, as the NAEP studies are happy to report. But it is not because students on the whole are doing much better in 1996 than they were in the 1970s. Moreover, in the report on trends from 1971 to 1996, fears are expressed that the gap may now be widening in some respects. For thirteen and seventeen year olds, the trend toward smaller gaps between white and black students' average reading scores "shows signs of reversing since the 1988 assessment." And although the gap between white and Hispanic students appeared to have decreased between 1975 and 1990, "this trend has not continued into the 1990s."

Unfortunately, the strong possibility that multicultural education may be a cause, perhaps the chief cause, of this widening gap is not a hypothesis we can expect researchers at most schools of education to pursue today. That is because many researchers—indeed, many prominent researchers—have abandoned a primary function of research: that of providing impartial examinations of the effectiveness or the consequences of pedagogical or curricular theories and the practices derived from or associated with them. Instead, research has become for many a means for exploiting the classroom for self-chosen social and political goals.

Some researchers are aware of the problems inherent in the research now being done in the service of social and political agendas. In an editorial in their September 1995 newsletter, the codirectors of the National Reading Research Center offered their reflections on concerns raised by what they refer to as "advocacy-oriented research." Articulating two of the assumptions they believe underlie the phrase "to empower through literacy," they questioned whether researchers "can know what is enabling, or empowering, for others" and whether they can "instill a certain sense of empowerment within those who participate in our studies." They are clearly pointing to the elitism behind the notion that researchers are privileged to "know" that which is "empowering or enabling for others." They concluded by urging researchers to reflect on the possibility that "in our attempts to empower others we may get it wrong."

Another reason that many of today's most prominent educational researchers will not pursue the question of whether multicultural education is a cause of declining reading scores is their own commitment to transform literary study into "cultural" studies—to use literary study for focusing on "issues currently being debated in society at large, raising questions, for example, about the roles of race, gender, and ethnicity within the fabric of American life and culture."[20] Researchers at the Center on English

Learning and Achievement see the curricular implications of their research quite clearly. They know that a literature curriculum addressing contemporary problems in American democracy will look very different from "traditional scope-and-sequence charts and will require consideration of a different set of issues during curriculum planning and review." There is no question that such a literature curriculum will be very different from traditional literature curricula. It will look very much like an issues-oriented social studies curriculum. The question is whether that is what parents and other citizens want.

Few people outside the circles of educational researchers are likely to be aware of the current views of many English language arts researchers. They are also unlikely to agree that the goals of education should include "altering social relationships" and turning literary study into little more than a handmaiden for the social studies curriculum. Most probably still think that education continues to be about intellectual, aesthetic, and moral development. They are also unlikely to view as benign the efforts of educational researchers to shape or change their children's ethnic identity or their feelings, attitudes, or beliefs on a whole host of social issues without informing them honestly and clearly about what they are doing and obtaining permission. For these reasons, recent changes in the role and purpose of educational research require broad and extensive public discussion. Not only does the public need to discuss how to address the ethical issues raised by the new purposes for educational research, it also needs to discuss where it can turn to obtain impartial information on the academic and literary costs of today's social goals.

TEN

IS THERE A FUTURE FOR CHILDREN'S LITERATURE AND LITERARY STUDY?

The story "The Field" should include data on the large staple cereal crops harvested on virgin soil, and the book should also contain a story on the labor of the virgin soil workers.

The new reader must include interesting stories and articles directed against superstitions and prejudices.

The articles on nature and seasons contained in My Native Tongue for the third grade do not sufficiently depict the labor of the collective farmers.

In order to strengthen the ties between knowledge and life and to inculcate a love for the collective-farm system, the themes "The Field" and "Domestic Animals" should be supplied with questions for excursions to collective-farm fields, livestock farms, tractor parks, electrically operated mills, etc.

A notable defect in the existing readers for the 1st–3rd grades is that they contain very little interesting fiction. The new readers must systematically show the conscious attitude of children towards work at home, in the school, at the collective farm; they must contain literary works which will help to instill in the pupils a respect for labor.

Friendship and comradeship are based on liking and respect and arise from a community of interests directed towards joint participation in some common undertaking.

—From I. Ganeeva, "The Educational Value of Readers for the First Four Grades Must Be Increased," Soviet Education 2 (1960).

THE CHANGES in the readers in the past decade or so signal a profound shift in the way in which children are viewed. In the last half of the nineteenth century, childhood came to be seen as a special period of life, deserving of a literature of its own. Well-known authors wrote directly for children, encouraging growth of an inner world unoppressed by the problems of the adult world. This literature reflected hope, humor, whimsy, ideals, and a joy in being alive. It was completely compatible with the kind of curriculum sought by progressive educators in the early decades of this century, a curriculum guided by children's impulses and desires. This literature can still be found in all the readers, although to a much lesser extent in some than in others. Fantasies, adventure stories, humorous tales, and the poetry of word play and logical nonsense have by no means disappeared in them. But it is unclear how long they will continue to appear and to what extent.

The advocates of a different literature for children today—one reflecting adult interests—believe that exposing children to a literature they claim is socially responsible will enable a new generation to transform or reform what these educators perceive as a deeply flawed society. They are also engaged in a self-contradictory attack on the very literature that was created for children in the nineteenth century. In this chapter, we look in more detail at the arguments and tactics being employed to dismiss out of hand a literature geared to children's interests and to promote a literature for children based on a view of what these educators want children to be interested in. My major purpose in this chapter, however, is to draw attention to the many similarities between the philosophy and pedagogy of multicultural educators and the early progressive educators. This comparison is intended to shed light on why so many elementary school teachers who considered themselves as followers of the early progressives found it easy to see multicultural education as a continuation of the spirit of progressive education. As a result, many teachers now have difficulty seeing the differences that have since emerged more starkly between the two movements, even though these differences were there from the beginning in embryonic form. Those attempting to discredit popular children's classics and eliminate them from the school curriculum may well succeed in convincing many teachers of their supposed evils unless both teachers and parents understand how their goals violate the very essence of what the early progressives wanted for children. Parents may need to help their children's teachers appreciate how the literature that today's progressives and multi-cultural educators are proposing as children's literature negates a view of childhood and certain purposes for literary reading that most parents probably still cherish and wish to retain. They may be especially concerned to help them understand how some of this new literature may also serve to deny historical truth.

WHY GOOD CHILDREN'S LITERATURE IS BAD FOR CHILDREN

We can find the self-contradictory attack on the children's literature of the past 150 years succinctly laid out in detail in Herbert Kohl's recent book, *Should We Burn Babar? Essays on Children's Literature and the Power of Stories*.[1] A teacher and writer who describes himself as a progressive educator, Kohl claims that the most popular books for children in our society "celebrate oppression, embody racism, or provide images of women as subordinate to men."[2] In other words, such works as *Robinson Crusoe*, the Dr. Doolittle series, *Mary Poppins*, *Peter Pan*, and the guileless fairy tales of childhood are oppressive. Kohl wants us to believe that exposing children to such a literature is a major cause of the racism, sexism, and oppression he sees as the dominating characteristics of this country. At the same time, he also criticizes popular children's classics for promoting "independence, personal responsibility, and autonomy," qualities that would strike most rational people as liberatory, not oppressive. It turns out that these are the qualities Kohl is really out to eradicate.

Kohl produces no evidence whatsoever, anecdotal or otherwise, that books portraying "kings and princesses," the "benefits of wealth," or "male-centered families" have ever created children who are racist or sexist. He offers nothing to support his view that the "anti-democratic sentiments" he perceives in adventure stories, fantasies, fables, and fairy tales negatively influence children's behavior, away from social responsibility and participation in a caring community. Nevertheless, Kohl is confident that good children's literature is bad for children and wants to eliminate its antidemocratic and anticommunity influence on them.

His strategy for accomplishing this differs from the blatantly censorious strategy now being recommended by the Oregon Department of Education. Recall that the Oregon department urges teachers, when selecting literature for their classrooms, to look at copyrights to see if the literature comes from a time when there were "cultural insensitivities." Kohl does not favor internal censorship by teachers, nor does he advocate burning *Babar*. His preferred strategy is to *discredit* the literature that children find appealing. Stories like *Babar* can be effectively disempowered, he proposes, if children are taught to read them critically, thus diminishing their enjoyment of these books. And Kohl relates how he did exactly that with *Babar*.

Claiming that children should not read *Babar* because, among other things, it "makes a thoroughly undemocratic way of governance seem natural and unquestioned,"[3] Kohl visited a third-grade class to give the children a talk on his ideas about the book. He provided a definition of colonialism, discussed the history of French colonialism, and helped them understand the meaning of the hunter's clothes in the story. During class discussion, he managed to get them to talk about how Babar "felt about the death of his mother" (yet another example of this vicarious "feeling" question in contemporary education).[4] Once the children came to understand, with Kohl's help, that the hunter was not brought to justice and that "in a way [Babar] became the friend of his mother's murderers," Kohl had achieved his goals. He reports that most of the third graders "expressed anger at the hunter and no longer thought the story was cute or charming."[5] At one point in his exposé of Babar, Kohl did reflect on the possibility that he was making too much of Babar. Perhaps sometimes "an elephant in a green suit is just an elephant in a green suit."[6] But this was his only, and momentary, grasp of reality.

Kohl's book is a plea for a "radical children's literature," one that confronts "racism and capitalism."[7] The problem for him is that there are almost no books for children that do so. He finds many books for adolescents that deal with "social issues and young activists, or at least young people who were involved in social struggle."[8] He is happy to see this "compassionate, liberal literature for young adults on sensitive issues,"[9] but he deplores the "almost total absence of books . . . that question the economic and social structure of our society and the values of capitalism."[10] He finds no books for children that "depict collective struggles to overcome poverty," the "building of movements and the power of people united in struggle."[11] He is dissatisfied with books in which "there is no explicit enemy" so that the "forces that create poverty and disenfranchisement are left remote and mysterious."[12] A collectivist Diogenes, searching for stories that are not written "from the perspective of the virtues of individualism, competition, and capitalism," Kohl is chagrined to find only stories that have to do with "personal challenge and individual success." He complains that "healthy community life and collective community-wide struggles are absent from children's literature and the stories most children encounter on TV, in film, or at home."[13]

Kohl's book clearly reveals the paternalism that has driven some of today's self-described progressive educators to violate a key tenet of the early progressives, as well as the condescension underlying their justification for doing so. According to the book's introduction, Kohl's voice "represents the concerns of many educators who are promoting a literature that speaks out in the interests of children and communities and addresses their concerns in an incisive and engaging manner." Nevertheless, Kohl does not tell us how he discovered that children are concerned about "collective struggles" and want to read critiques of the "economic and social structures of our society." And we must keep reminding ourselves that he is talking about children, not adolescents. But Kohl is certain that this is what children want to read. Since we are to assume that minority children are the ones who must combat poverty and "disenfranchisement," what he is clearly implying is that these are the children who need to learn how to engage in collective struggles against competition and capitalism. What is striking is Kohl's belief that they should combat competition and capitalism rather than try to develop an entrepreneurial spirit that enables them to succeed and accumulate wealth by their own efforts. His implicit assumption is clear: minority students are incapable of competing against others and succeeding by their own efforts, a view shared by other contemporary educators, as we saw in Chapter 8.

For inspiration to find a worthy literature for "oppressed" people, for a "commitment to larger struggles to eliminate victimization," Kohl's model is the literature of dissent in the former Czechoslovakia and other parts of Eastern Europe over the past forty years.[14] This is a literature that he professes to admire because it contributed to the "resistance and the eventual overthrow of Soviet domination,"[15] thus implying that those in elected office in the United States today are somehow equivalent to those who were in charge of the former Soviet Union. Admittedly, it is hard to take seriously anyone who thinks there is an equation between the U.S. government and the government of the former Soviet Union or an equivalence between the lives of women and ethnic or racial groups in this country today and the past oppressive experiences of the peoples of the various "peoples' republics." His choice is nonetheless puzzling because the literature of dissent in the former Czechoslovakia in particular was grounded in basic Western values—the very values he wants to eradicate. Moreover, Kohl's notion of a radical literature is the kind of literature that was despised by those who overthrew Soviet domination, mostly because it was boring propaganda.

Kohl acknowledges that it is extremely difficult to write "radical" literature in a way that makes it appealing to children. Imagine the kind of stories that Soviet children must have had to read if the stories were written to reflect the recommendations spelled out in the excerpts from a Soviet education journal quoted in the epigraph for this chapter. Ganeeva, the author of these excerpts, was undoubtedly aware that the reading instructional materials Soviet children had had to read were already pretty boring, but she could not let go of her collectivist ideology. She was undoubtedly sincere in wanting more interesting stories in their instructional readers, but at the same time she also wanted them (or had to appear to want them) to serve ideological needs better, at its core a self-contradictory goal. Kohl is aware that "left-wing" or radical literature for children has generally been boring or dogmatic, or both. The thrust of his book is to point to the one or two stories he believes can serve as models, offer advice to would-be writers on how to write interesting left-wing literature, and describe his own, so-far-unsuccessful efforts to do so.

Like many other educators in academe today, Kohl evinces no interest in trying to understand why moral autonomy, individualism, self-reliance, competitiveness, initiative, and personal responsibility are the very qualities that Eastern European educators want to develop, or develop again.[16] That is because the kinds of literary works that help develop these qualities—adventure stories, fantasies, and the poetry of word play and logical nonsense—do not serve the purposes of today's social moralists. They do not serve to promote racial consciousness and group solidarity. They do not manipulate children's feelings, or easily lend themselves to manipulation, for the purpose of creating guilt or self-hatred. Instead, they cultivate and enrich a private world of the imagination, and private worlds are threatening to social moralists. Children who develop their own way of looking at the world can tell when the emperor has no clothes on, the moral of a tale that has vanished from the leading reading series. They can sense when the emperor's tailor is trying to manipulate them. A boring or preachy story suffers by comparison when surrounded by stories without any social agenda, stories intended to delight or inform, stories that help form children's literary taste and literary standards. That is why today's social moralists expend so much of their energy seeking to discredit the stories children have genuinely found appealing with charges of sexism or racism (or "cultural insensitivity"). They know their arguments for an alternative, "socially responsible" literature ultimately founder on the stark fact that they have no genuine alternative literature (nor can they have one) to offer as a substitute—only pseudo-literature.

It is instructive that the almost insoluble dilemma raised explicitly by Kohl, a contemporary American progressive educator, but unarticulated by Ganeeva, a midcentury Soviet progressive educator, was confronted much earlier in this century by reform-minded American educators. These educators were the leaders in the Country Life movement, a rural education reform movement associated with the larger progressive movement in education. (Here I am indebted to the research of English educator Robert Tremmel, who gathered information on both the pedagogy that these reform-minded educators advocated for rural schools and the public response to their reform efforts.)

The Country Life leaders were not farmers but "professional educators, academics, journalists, and business people, many of whom had farming backgrounds, and who were often possessed of a romantic view regarding agrarian life."[17] They had arbitrarily decided that the solution to the "rural school problem"—what farmers' children needed—was a curriculum related to the students' rural life, with experience-based activities that put students "to work with tools and soils and plants and problems."[18] The reformers wanted the rural school to "express the best cooperation of all social and economic forces that make for the welfare of the community."[19] For example, the subjects students might write about according to one teacher were: "How can we get good roads?" "Keeping the soil fertile," and "The Silo."[20] For literary study, the reformers placed "the highest priority on texts reflecting rural experience" and written from "a rural point of view."[21] It is uncanny how similar in thrust this is to what today's multicultural educators advocate for immigrant or minority children.

However, just as Kohl and multicultural educators find today, the chief problem with the reformers' position then was the paucity of suitable literary materials. As they remarked, "We have practically no good poems of American farm life . . . and very few good novels depicting the real farmer."[22] As Tremmel comments, such a narrow view of the uses of literature made it difficult for the early rural reformers to fit literary study into the curriculum at all. Reading for pleasure did not "coexist" easily with the vocational and utilitarian goals of the Country Life movement.[23] But so far as we know, its leaders did not consider commissioning the kind of literature they wanted, possibly because they respected and adhered to the standards by which one judged literature. Although there may have been other reasons, and although aesthetic goals were not one of their curricular priorities, if literature was to be used for utilitarian purposes in the curriculum, it still had to be "good."

Another similarity in emphasis leaps out of the information Tremmel gathered. Just as Kohl and other self-defined progressive educators today enthuse about the "democratic" classroom, so too did Country Life teachers. Their diaries include numerous examples of the ways in which they tried to teach their students "citizenship," "responsibility," and the benefits of collaboration in the interest of "community" and "democracy." Unfortunately, as beneficial as these activities might have been in themselves, the time spent in fulfilling all these social goals seems to have left little time for academic studies.

The decrease in disciplinary content and the near disappearance of academic studies in the classroom turned out to be the chief reason for the ultimate failure of the Country Life movement. Farmers came to resist the reformers' ideas because they did not believe that nature study, agriculture, and manual work should be the focus of school programs for children who were already well versed in nature study, agriculture, and manual work (most of whom, in any case, would not be able to stay on the farm as adults because farmers tended to have large families and the growing mechanization of agriculture meant that fewer rather than more farmers would be needed). Farmers did not want most of their children's time in school spent in nonacademic activities. They also resented being portrayed as "narrow-minded, tight-fisted, self-centered people incapable of making the best decisions for their children and the future of the country."[24] As Tremmel observed, they wanted the same broad liberal education that city children were receiving, an education that would enable their children to move to a wider, different world from the one in which they grew up.

Eventually resistance to educational "reforms" that marginalized academic studies did in the larger progressive movement in education as well, especially as it was embodied in the life adjustment movement of the 1940s and 1950s. This has not yet happened to multicultural education. But a closer look at the similarities in aims and practices between the early progressive educators and many of today's academic educators, whether they designate themselves as multicultural or progressive, will suggest why so many traditional progressive educators with sincere interests in the welfare of minority children readily supported the goals of multicultural education when it first burst on the educational scene by name. It may thus explain why it is so difficult for them to see that as it has evolved, it now constitutes a violation of the most positive features of early progressive education: its view of childhood and the literature children should read. Despite the use of the label "progressive" by Kohl and like-minded fellow educators and writers, how they view childhood and the literature they wish to impose on children, which has already begun to appear in the reading series, is a twisted interpretation of progressive education.

MULTICULTURAL PROGRESSIVE EDUCATION AND EARLY PROGRESSIVE EDUCATION: A COMPARISON

When the first self-labeled multiculturalists began to speak up, they did not claim to be reviving and reworking the tenets of progressive education for a new set of educational problems. Nor do the most prominent advocates of multiculturalism trace the philosophical underpinnings of the movement to progressive education. For example, neither John Dewey nor progressive education is in the index of a book on multicultural education by James Banks and Cherry McGee Banks, published in 1989.[25] They apparently see no philosophical, political, or pedagogical similarities between the two educational phenomena—not even an indirect cultural relationship. Indeed, they may have no interest in seeing one. Instead, Banks sees multiculturalism's strongest and most direct roots in the black studies movement of the 1960s and 1970s, with more distant antecedents in the work of prominent black scholars like Carter Woodson and W. E. B. Du Bois in the early decades of this century.[26]

Nevertheless, it is difficult to account for the extraordinary growth of multiculturalism in the schools or its current contours unless it is seen in the context of a long history of certain sentiments about the nature of American society and the role of the schools in shaping or reshaping it. Educators who sought to bring curricular justice to black children in the 1960s probably had no references to the tenets of the early progressives in their minds or their words. But the educational soil their ideas fell on in schools of education and in associated educational circles had long been fertilized by the thinking of John Dewey and his followers. For the most part, the elementary school curriculum had continued to reflect progressive ideas during the brief academic resurgence of the post-*Sputnik* era. In addition, one can find clear links between progressive education and multicultural education in the work of Hilda Taba, an influential educator who had been involved with the Progressive Education Association for many years before its demise around 1960 and who had published several books on intergroup relations, intergroup education, and teaching the "culturally disadvantaged" before her death in the mid-1960s.[27] Moreover, the feminist movement of the 1960s had already made an enormous impact on both teachers and publishers of school textbooks by the early 1970s, undoubtedly making it even easier for teachers to see other changes urged in the name of equality and justice as one more instantiation of educational progressivism.

Many of the aims articulated in the earliest formulations of multicultural education must have resonated strongly with the moral sentiments of the academic educators and elementary school teachers in the 1970s and 1980s who saw themselves as educational progressives and heirs to the views of Dewey and his disciples. (This is not to say that most elementary school teachers did not accept the moral legitimacy of including stories about America's various ethnic and racial groups in their curriculum, whether or not they defined themselves as progressives.) Clearly the significance attached to a minority child's personal experiences and perspective fit right in with a passion for a curriculum centered on a child's needs and interests. And the significance the multiculturalists attached to peer interaction in the context of collaborative learning could easily be found in Dewey's works.

However distinct they may have been in their origins, the many similarities between the thinking of many early progressives and the views of the multiculturalists had to have led to a fairly smooth confluence of these two pedagogical streams.[28] As did the progressives, the multiculturalists articulated a vision of a new social order, opposing what they saw as a competitive capitalistic society that glorified individualism and was destructive of a sense of community, although their view of what constituted community was and remains quite different from that of the progressives. The two movements shared a strong aversion to a society characterized by a deep belief in the values of individualism and competition. The "reconstruction" or "transformation" of society were words that abounded in the writings of both groups, beginning with those of John Dewey himself, although he did not see the schools responsible for changing or rebuilding society, only for developing the use of a critical intelligence that could reform society.[29] Like the progressives, the multiculturalists sought to use education as a means to reform society, a society they saw corrupted not only by an antisocial individualism but also by social ills the early progressives had not noticed or sought to address. The two groups also shared an antagonism toward the business world and religious fundamentalism, although the multiculturalists saw more than these two social forces as hostile to their goals.

The multiculturalists reformulated in their own words two of the early progressives' basic goals. The progressives sought to promote the original ideals of American democracy through the organization and conduct of the classroom. They wanted the classroom to provide children with opportunities for democratic living so that they would acquire an understanding of democratic principles and develop the social skills they would need as adults for cooperative living and community participation. They also sought to use education as a means to enlarge the original ideals of American democracy. They wanted to teach children the practices of good citizenship directly in order to encourage broader and greater civic participation. The multiculturalists' stress on tolerance and inclusion was in many ways their version of these goals. And to accomplish them, educators in both movements viewed the classroom as a site for discussing contemporary social issues and encouraging collective social action related to their learning, although Dewey himself did not advocate or approve of the politicizing of the classroom.

The multiculturalists were also strikingly similar to the progressives in their strong, self-righteous moralism, a characteristic that intensified over the years as "illiberal" multiculturalism developed. The early progressives were unabashed moralists. They wanted the right social growth to take place. Children had to be guided to grow in a particular way. They could not be allowed to become antisocial even if being so was their natural bent. They had to want to address the needs of their community. If they were to be able to reconstruct it, they had to be trained to become critical of their society, although that might mean some manipulation of the curriculum or their thinking.

For that reason, both movements were indifferent, if not hostile, to parents' concerns. In their eyes, parents naturally tended to hold traditional values, and a new social order could not be constructed if it reproduced the old order. The curriculum had to allow children to develop a fresh view of their world, as untouched as possible by the more traditional values of their families. Both groups of educators saw themselves as idealistic, enlightened, and "progressive"—in all respects superior to parents in an understanding of their children's needs and the kind of society that would be in everyone's best interests. They were political elitists, despite their professed faith in democracy and their emphasis on teaching democratic principles.

At the beginning and center of the educational process in both movements was respect for children: their interests, their desires, and their experiences. Children's natural interests were seen as central in mobilizing their energies and sustaining them. Their personal experiences were also seen as central in shaping their particular way of understanding the world in which they were growing up. But both movements were overly sensitive to the affective aspects of children's development and insufficiently sensitive to children's cognitive needs and the curricular means by which the life of the mind could be cultivated. In a comment on the early progressives, equally applicable to multicultural educators, historian Richard Hofstadter noted that they "accepted [the child's] world as being . . . largely definitive for them, and were content to guide his thinking within its terms, however parochial in place and time, and however flat in depth."[30]

Similarly, both groups of educators looked with disfavor on a subject-oriented curriculum shaped by the structure of the academic disciplines and the demands of disciplinary learning, although Dewey himself did not advocate doing away with subject matter or the academic disciplines.[31] As

Hofstadter commented on the philosophy of the early progressive move-ment, "The child was now conceived not as a mind to be developed but as a citizen to be trained by the schools. The new educators believed that one should not be content to expect good citizenship as a result of having more informed and intellectually competent citizens, but that one must directly teach citizenship and democracy and civic virtues."[32] Both move-ments embodied in their philosophy and pedagogical practices the perva-sive anti-intellectualism Hofstadter saw in American society almost from its inception. Their educational goals were emphatically utilitarian in na-ture, not intellectual.

Their views of children's intellectual capacities were an extension of their anti-intellectual sentiments. The progressives saw the masses as in-tellectually limited, as Hofstadter points out after quoting telling remarks made by the advocates of life adjustment.[33] In stark contrast to the views of the Committee of Ten, a distinguished group of educators appointed in 1892 by the National Education Association to set goals and priorities in American education, who in 1893 recommended a strong academic cur-riculum for all students (and no tracking) and who have been denounced for their elitism ever since, progressive educators did not seem to believe that the vast majority of children could benefit from a demanding acade-mic education. Today, many educators argue against the worth of culti-vating factual knowledge and assessing academic knowledge on the grounds that these practices reflect negative and deficient values—those of individualism and competitiveness—which they claim, although with-out evidence, are in opposition to practices promoting collaborative or communal values. Such rhetoric also serves to cloak negative views about the intellectual capacities of minority students and an unwillingness to engage in the demanding work of teaching them.

Given the similarities in so many of the goals and attitudes of the two movements, it would have been surprising if post–World War II educators who saw themselves following in the footsteps of the early progressives had not found multiculturalism, when it was first articulated, compatible with their philosophy. However, as the thinking of multicultural educators evolved and multiculturalism added new meanings, crucial differences be-tween the philosophies developed. One concerns the truthfulness of the curriculum given to children and its relationship to political consciousness raising. Elaborating Hofstadter's observation that the progressive mind was essentially that of a socially responsible reporter-reformer, Cremin suggested that the progressive mind was ultimately that of a "socially responsible reformist pedagogue."[34] In Cremin's view, progressive educators believed deeply in the power of the truth and in "informed political action." Although they were hostile to a curriculum organized around the mastery of content, they expected the informed citizen to be a rational, thinking being, making decisions on the basis of all the information available. In contrast, multicultural educators have promoted curricula containing distortions or omissions of relevant—and truthful—information. They have also encouraged mindless social action triggered by emotions deliberately provoked.

A second major difference concerns the kind of living community each movement had in mind as the object of their concerns. Progressive educators were concerned about the health of civic communities—the communities, citizens, and broad public interests like the schools, parks, libraries, and playgrounds for which all Americans, regardless of background, were responsible. Living communities were not defined in opposition to a larger civic polity. In contrast, multicultural educators have elevated subgroup identity above civic identity and have in essence used the reading curriculum to cultivate interethnic, interracial, or intergender animosities under the guise of developing an appreciation of and respect for the background of all Americans.

A third important difference concerns the respect paid to the child's genuine interests and needs. Early progressive educators saw childhood as a period of innocence and freedom from the burdens of the adult world. They did not oppress children with the social tensions and conflicts of their day in the guise of making the curriculum relevant to their personal experiences or impose on young children the social problems that adults had yet to solve in their own lives and then manipulate their thinking about them. Guided by children's own preferences, the basal readers in the early decades of this century featured animal tales, fairy tales, myths, fables, legends, lives of famous Americans, stories of colonial America, informational selections, and literary works by the best writers of the past and of the day.

In contrast, many of the reading selections described in previous chapters reflect a blatant disregard for children's natural interests. Moreover, the relentless pumping of children's feelings in the pedagogy surrounding the reading selections is a violation not so much of children's privacy or their family's privacy but of their own natural interests. Children tend to be much more interested in learning about the larger world around them, as it is and as it was, than in discussing feelings—their own or those of others. And for children who grow up in dismal circumstances, who is to say that they might not benefit more from a rich diet of fantasy, historical fiction, adventure stories, science fiction, and science information than from constant ruminations on their dismal circumstances or social issues?[35]

To Hofstadter, the weaknesses of progressivism lay "in its efforts to promulgate doctrine, to generalize, in its inability to assess the practical limits of its own program, above all in its tendency to dissolve the curriculum," especially in the secondary school.[36] These weaknesses can be found in full measure in multiculturalism as well, but unlike multicultural progressives, the early progressives did not sacrifice for political ends what they held, in an evangelical fervor, to be the sacred character of childhood. They did not subordinate children's interests to their own adult concerns and try to turn reading instruction into a mock social studies course. Nor did they seek to degrade the language they offered children in their readers in the name of boosting their self-respect. They believed children were entitled to good literature, not pseudo-literature, even if their ultimate goals were utilitarian and not literary or academic. It is not clear why those who still see themselves as the heirs to John Dewey's thinking have failed to note and speak up about the differences that have grown increasingly clearer between the two movements. If what is in leading instructional readers today reflects what teachers are willing to use in their classrooms, then clearly we need courses for teachers that help them reexamine and revitalize two of the most positive aspects of early progressive thinking: its belief in childhood and its literary and academic integrity.

LIMITATIONS IN USING ELEMENTARY SCHOOL READING INSTRUCTION FOR DISCUSSING SOCIAL ISSUES

Any attempt to use literary study for political consciousness raising has many costs at the elementary school level. The growing trend to use reading instructional time for political consciousness raising encourages teachers who have typically not majored in history or political science to conduct discussions on a variety of topics about which they know little, if anything, and to depend on the quality of the information supplied them. It further encourages young students to express opinions unsupported by any serious study of an issue and any fund of accurate information. It is difficult to see how fourth graders can profit from a classroom discussion about the "advantages and disadvantages" of living in a company town if they are limited to whatever they can glean from reading "No Star Nights," a short autobiography about growing up in the polluted environment of a former steel mill town and to the information set out in the Macmillan teacher guide. Here is what teachers are to pass on to them from Multicultural Perspectives:

- A "company" town is a town that is owned and operated by the company or that employs the majority of the adult population in that town.

- Some company towns are built around an industrial site. If the industry shuts down, the town begins to decline. Businesses close down, and people move away to look for other jobs.

- In many company towns of the past, the housing and facilities were poor. Workers often were in debt to the company after paying rent on company-owned houses and buying goods at company-owned stores.

- Today there are still manufacturing towns in which a large percentage of the population works for a single employer.

Ask students to discuss what they think the advantages and disadvantages of living in such a town might be, drawing on information in "No Star Nights" to support their opinions. Discuss why people might live in a company town despite its drawbacks.

Not only is this information insufficient, students will gain little real information from the story itself. That is because there is nothing in the story to suggest that this old steel mill town is this kind of company town. Thus, this particular "multicultural perspective" is totally gratuitous. If the multicultural perspective on this selection had been guided by academic considerations, the editors might have suggested that students do research to find out why so many steel mills went out of business. They might have discovered such factors as high labor costs at that time, old and inefficient plants, and competition from countries like Japan and Germany that built modern steel-producing factories to replace those that had been destroyed during World War II. But these are not the kind of answers in which multiculturalists today are interested. There is little here to suggest that U.S. steel workers and the communities they lived in were victims of the steel mill owners at the time they went out of business.

For that reason, the Cultural Awareness sections in Harcourt Brace's grade 4 teacher guides stand out like beacons of academic light. An excerpt from Laura Ingalls Wilder's *Little House in the Woods*, for example, does not serve as an excuse for discussing displaced Indians. After students have read the story, the Harcourt Brace editors suggest that teachers do the following:

> Review that Laura's family used oxen to pull their wagon and looked forward to having a team of horses. Invite students to select another country and to use an encyclopedia or another reference source to research what types of animals are used for work in that country.[37]

The trend to use reading instructional time for discussing social issues also encourages a simplistic understanding of the issue, even when there is no underlying motivation to have this happen. At least one educator has dared to question the wisdom of burdening children with issues they cannot possibly understand because of their complexity. Discussing *Smoky Night*, a picture book awarded the Caldecott Medal in 1995 by the American Library Association, Francis Kazemek forthrightly asserts that some subjects are "too complex to be explored honestly with children of a particular age."[38] *Smoky Night* is about the Los Angeles riots of 1992, and its author attempts through the words of a child's mother to explain that the rioters were "angry," and that when people get angry, they "don't care anymore what's right and what's wrong." The author of *Smoky Night* does not say they have a right to be angry, but she also does not say they are wrong either. The point of the story is to suggest that if people get to know each other, such things will not happen, a simplistic solution that belies the complexity of the racial problems underlying the riots. Indeed, while the violence, rage, and destruction of the Los Angeles riots are vividly portrayed, missing from the text of the story is any mention of the racial problems behind the riots. They are simply beyond the scope of a picture book.[39]

Finally, the trend to use reading instructional time for political con-sciousness raising encourages academically unsophisticated elementary school teachers to jump unwittingly onto a singularly narrow theoretical bandwagon. The social issues presented in the basal readers and the way in which discussion of them is framed reflect only one view of this coun-try (or the West). They reflect a now-popular theory in the academy to the effect that we can understand America best by seeing it as a racist and sexist country, oppressive of its ethnic, racial, and other social groups, ex-ploitative of the environment, and historically formed and led by people with values destructive of community. This theory generally sees the United States as having made no substantial progress in addressing the in-justices that have been committed against these groups throughout its his-tory. Victim theory—the belief that all women and non-Western people have been nothing but victims of Western patriarchy or cultural imperial-ism—is the theory underlying the U.S. history standards formulated by the Center on History in the Schools at the University of California at Los Angeles.

This theory is simply one among others on how best to understand U.S. history and culture. One alternative theory, for example, views the course of U.S. history as the gradual expansion of civil and economic rights for various social, racial, and ethnic groups as their members learned how to use American political procedures, principles, and insti-tutions for bringing their grievances to public attention and for address-ing them. If the Scott Foresman editors had drawn on that theory in deciding what chapter to use from the book about the conflict between the Cheyenne and the mining companies seeking use of their land (dis-cussed in Chapter 4), they would have chosen the chapter illustrating how the Cheyenne won their case with the help of the Environmental Protection Agency and the secretary of the interior, instead of choosing the chapter showing the victimized Cheyenne deciding to fight back (and falsely implying to the students that the case had not already been won by the Cheyenne).

Interestingly, many victims of society are beginning to tire of being portrayed as victims. As editors at one publishing house told my research assistant: "Black people hate, or are starting to hate, being portrayed as victims of racism. They resent that. In the past we've chosen [stories portraying certain races as victims of oppression] and we've been told to tone it down."⁴⁰

Nevertheless, the reading series do not inform teachers that their approach to social issues reflects only one of several available theories for understanding American history and culture, and a theory still being debated by historians themselves. They thus limit teachers' and students' ability to understand the debates taking place at universities, museums, and other cultural and social institutions. In effect, they deny them both the opportunity to become familiar with multiple perspectives on the nature of American history and culture, despite the fact that this is one of the major goals of the multiculturalist.

It is impossible to know how often elementary school teachers use literature lessons that encourage students to see the society they live in as oppressive, exploitative, and noncaring. Teachers using the Silver Burdett Ginn readers, for example, may simply ignore the suggestions in the Appreciating Cultures sections that surround all its selections. Overall, the Silver Burdett Ginn selections reflect a commitment to children's interests, not adults', and avoid moralizing, so that teachers with academic and aesthetic goals do not have to contend with selections that in themselves manipulate children's feelings and attitudes.

Teachers who have been taught to believe that literary study should be turned into an anticivic moral harangue (and their numbers are likely to increase as recent graduates of schools of education find teaching positions) will conveniently find the material they need in the readers and the teacher guides. Scott Foresman clearly informs teachers in its Multicultural Handbook that the key concepts its series addresses are values, self-concept, perception, power, discrimination, and prejudice, all of them social and political in nature.⁴¹

A continuation of these trends will strongly influence how children come to read literature in secondary school. Not only is the capacity to read challenging literary works in jeopardy, so too is the capacity of students to respond to literature as literature. Despite the stress on reader response pedagogy in all the basal readers, and despite their extensive suggestions for using literature logs or writing journals, one has to wonder how long students can retain a capacity for an aesthetic response to literature if their reading selections are frequently used for addressing social issues. If most elementary school teachers come to believe that literature for children must address their personal lives and the flaws of society, how easily will the secondary school English teacher so-inclined be able to preserve the essence of literary study: its central orientation to the text, not its context?

The trend to subordinate literary study to the social studies in the elementary school began in the elementary school readers only a decade or so ago, unlike the decline in vocabulary load that has been proceeding throughout the century. But the exploitation of literary study for nonliterary purposes is clearly being encouraged by the standards issued by the National Council of Teachers of English and the International Reading Association in March 1996. These standards have already been criticized by the Association of Literary Scholars and Critics (ALSC), an organization of university-based literary scholars and independent literary critics that formed several years ago to reclaim literary study from the hands of those manipulating the teaching of literature for social and political purposes in the universities. In a statement issued in the *ALSC Newsletter* in the fall of 1996, the organization decried the fact that in the NCTE/IRA standards document, "literary criteria are subverted by a relentless and misguided egalitarianism" and "artistic quality is firmly subordinated to political and social objectives."[42]

Even more problematic than the effort to make children's literature a handmaiden to an issues-oriented social studies curriculum is the lack of historical accuracy in much historical fiction written for children in the past twenty-five years, as Anne Scott MacLeod points out in her 1998 essay in the *Horn Book Magazine*.[43] A children's literature designed to inspire "collective struggles against competition and capitalism," such as the kind that Kohl advocates, may be excruciatingly boring. In addition, children's literature written, in MacLeod's words, to bend "historical narrative to modern models of social behavior . . . makes for bad history." In her discussion of this genre of children's literature, she notes that "what is at stake here is truth." MacLeod further comments that "historical fiction writers who want their protagonists to reflect twentieth-century ideologies . . . end by making them exceptions to their cultures, so that in many a historical novel the reader learns nothing—or at least nothing sympathetic—of how the people of a past society saw their world. Characters are divided into right—those who believe as we do—and wrong; that is, those who believe something that we now disavow."

It will take more than one professional organization's efforts to counter the corruption of literary study in the academy and its far-reaching influence on literary study in the elementary school and on the literature written for children. It will require alert and tactful parents to pay attention to the quality and the truthfulness of what their children are asked to read in school.

ELEVEN

TURNING THE ANTI-INTELLECTUAL TIDE

Professors of education hold a vision of public education that seems fundamentally at odds with that of public school teachers, students, and the public. While the public's priorities are discipline, basic skills, and good behavior in the classroom, teachers of teachers severely downplay such goals. (p. 15)

Seventy-nine percent of these teachers of teachers say "the general public has outmoded and mistaken beliefs about what good teaching means." (p. 15)

The disconnect between what the professors want and what most parents, teachers, and students say they need is often staggering. It seems ironic that so many of those who profess to believe that "the real endeavor" is about questioning and learning how to learn are seemingly entrapped in a mind-set that is unquestioning in its conviction of its own rightness. (p. 29)

To hold onto a goal that one believes is worthwhile is an important mission. But isn't it also fair to ask teachers of teachers to listen more empathetically to both the public's and the teachers' concerns? Isn't it time education professors began a dialogue which acknowledges that the testimony of parents and teachers and employers and students may have something of value in it? (p. 29)

> —From Steve Farkas and Jean Johnson, with Ann Duffett, *Different Drummers: How Teachers of Teachers View Public Education*, a Report from Public Agenda (1997)

A S THEY should, the reading textbooks published by leading educational publishers today portray a broad array of social groups, both historical and contemporary, both within and outside this country. In theory, this variety in social setting might seem highly desirable and of little consequence for the development of reading ability. But in order to provide representation for all the social groups now seen to require representation, and convey the right spin on the social issues now judged to need consciousness raising, the editors and academic advisers for these textbooks have chosen many selections that leave much to be desired from a civic, literary, and intellectual perspective. To be sure, these readers still state that they want children to become successful readers and writers. And although the proportion varies across reading series, they still offer selections that can stimulate children's imagination and satisfy their spirit for adventure. But given their many literary and intellectual limitations, it is not at all clear that they can now teach children to read and write English well and to think analytically.

The problematic features of these readers as well as of the pedagogy recommended in their teacher guides are unlikely to be confined to them alone. Their intellectual limitations are as likely to be found in classroom reading programs that do not rely on readers. That is because these readers must of necessity reflect the pedagogy, kinds of selections, and points of view on social issues that researchers and educators in schools of education endorse and recommend to all teachers, whether or not they use a reader. It is also the case that the kinds of selections and perspectives featured in the readers, as well as the pedagogy recommended in their teacher guides, follow what is already taking place in many classrooms. It takes publishers four to five years to produce a completely new edition of a reading series, and it would take a brave publisher indeed to put a reading series on the market whose key features had not been tried out and implemented in the classroom by teachers and curriculum coordinators active in professional organizations in the field of reading and the language arts.

Despite the lack of large-scale research studies on the same students over a long period of time, it is quite reasonable to believe that there is a strong connection between the low level of reading achievement in American students and the intellectual limitations of their current reading programs. Yet it is like searching for a needle in a haystack to find any mention in publications by faculty in schools of education of the intellectual limitations of today's readers or reading programs and their effects on reading achievement.

In this final chapter, I offer some speculations on why so many educational researchers and teacher educators in our schools of education are relentlessly promoting their social and political goals without any evident interest in whether the pedagogy and social content they have recommended to achieve them have negative effects on the development of students' language and thinking skills. I conclude with suggestions for parents and others to consider in attempting to restore intellectual purposes to our public schools.

THE INTELLECTUAL AND LITERARY LIMITATIONS OF THE READERS: A SUMMARY

1. The array of selections in most readers sharply distorts children's understanding of the world in which they live. The selections convey an almost monolithic picture of a white world that has almost none of the real ethnic diversity that can be seen in just the listing of restaurants in a telephone directory for any city in this country. Although multicultural educators claim they want students to see the real America, we find instead a highly shrunken mainstream culture in most series, with the existence of America's various European ethnic groups almost totally suppressed. This distorted picture, which is drastic in several series, tends to be even more distorted by a narrow meaning, or a lack of meaning altogether, for the word *culture* itself. As earlier chapters demonstrated, the Appreciating Cultures sections in the Silver Burdett Ginn series have little to do with the appreciation of any culture; to the contrary, they tend to harp on the theme of victimization, as do Macmillan's Multicultural Perspectives.

2. Selections chosen to facilitate discussion of contemporary social issues are often boring or preachy. It is impossible to know how many children have been turned off by reading materials that educators proclaim will turn them into lifelong learners. But it is not difficult to believe that their numbers may be large; children have never shown much of an interest in social issues according to every survey taken of children's reading interests.

3. The skewed nature of the selections in these readers frequently results in culturally and historically incoherent groups of selections. Their settings often shift from one century to another, one continent to another, and one social group to another in order to accommodate a vast range of social groups and characters of various colors and genders. Such sequences are not apt to contribute to a clear understanding of any social group or its history, particularly when the group is not situated in a historical timeframe or its placenames located geographically.

4. There are almost no selections about the first people to make globally significant achievements, discoveries, or inventions. Nowhere do children read about the first airplane flight, the first transatlantic flight, the first exploration of space, or the discovery of the South Pole, penicillin, or the polio vaccine. Nowhere do they learn how such inventions as the light bulb, radio, telegraph, steamboat, telephone, sewing machine, phonograph, or radar came about. Once children could read stories about Louis Pasteur, Sir Alexander Fleming, and the Wright Brothers at Kitty Hawk, as in the now-defunct grade 4 Lippincott reader in use between 1965 and 1971. Contemporary readers have banished accounts of their stunning achievements from students' common knowledge apparently because they portray the accomplishments of white males.

In much of what passes for educational thinking today, white males are viewed as history's villains as well as inappropriate role models for girls or minority students. As a result, we find stories about people who have succeeded in coping with racism, sexism, or physical disabilities, not stories about people who made the significant breakthroughs in science and technology. But without the stories about the pioneers in science and technology (a few of whom were females, like Marie Curie), both boys and girls are unlikely to acquire a historically accurate time frame for sequencing the major discoveries that have shaped life today. They may not learn why greater access to education and other resources, as well as the woman's role in bearing and raising children, enabled men to make much greater contributions than women in the past. Perhaps the most serious loss is that of an educational role model. Without the stories of the great scientists and inventors of the past and present, children are unlikely to acquire insights into the power of intellectual curiosity in sustaining perseverance and the role of intellectual gratification in rewarding this perseverance.

5. The kinds of selections to which editors have been guided by their advisers make it almost impossible for children to develop a rich, literate vocabulary in English over the grades. In some series, children must learn a dazzling array of proper nouns, words for the mundane features of daily life, words for ethnic foods in countries around the world, and other, non-English words, most of which contribute little, if anything, to the development of their competence in the English language. In addition, they are given a less literate vocabulary in English than they were given only a decade ago, to judge from a comparison of the vocabulary in these six reading series with the vocabulary in the Open Court series and in several 1980s readers.

Yet this vocabulary of academically useless words is judged to be of great importance by many contemporary teacher educators. They seem to think that children should spend a considerable amount of class time engaged in conversations with each other about each others' ethnic "cultures" and daily lives. As two veteran teachers in grades 4 and 5 in a suburban school north of Boston informed me, such "cultural" conversations are expected to be a regular feature of their daily program because of the school's multicultural orientation and its diverse student body. But, ironically, using precious class time for frequent conversations about intellectually barren topics that draw on intellectually limited vocabularies deprives the very students who most need it of opportunities to practice using the lexical building blocks necessary for conceptual growth and analytical thinking.

In a larger sense, we are witnessing the continuing erosion of a national language base, a process that began many decades ago in the elementary schools and seems to have accelerated in recent decades. Recall the passages in Chapter 1 that show what educators' expectations are today for grade 4 and what the expectations were for grade 3 or 4 100 years ago. In an informative essay on the decline in literacy levels in this country over the twentieth century, Andrew Coulson, an independent researcher, calculated the difference between the reading level of some representative literary passages from grade 7 readers at the turn of the century and the reading level of several selections in current grade 8 anthologies or readers. He found a stunning difference of about *four or five grade levels*.[1]

What is more startling is the attempt by the leadership of the National Council of Teachers of English and the International Reading Association to convince the public through the *Standards for the English Language Arts* they jointly released in 1996 that "students today read better and write better than at any other time in the history of the country."[2] A number of researchers are helping them make this argument. In *The Manufactured Crisis: Myths, Fraud, and the Attack on America's Public Schools*, for example, David Berliner and Bruce Biddle try to make it appear that a picture of low reading achievement has simply been cooked up, despite ample research evidence to the contrary (in the NAEP studies, for example).[3] They further insinuate that anyone voicing concern about the phenomenon they claim does not exist is out to destroy the public schools. But it is not difficult to determine whether elementary school students 100 years ago were able to read better than elementary school students read today. All one has to do is compare the reading material that fourth graders were asked to read then with what they are given to read now. There is no better proof than the pudding itself. As the passages in the epigraph in Chapter 1 suggest, reading materials for grades 3 and 4 then were clearly more difficult than those for grade 4 today. The current direction in the level of reading difficulty now seemingly expected at each grade level in the elementary school must be reversed if the average high school graduate of the future is to be able to read and understand with ease words with more than two syllables and paragraphs with more than three or four sentences.

The recent changes in the basal readers do not reflect a frustrated reaction to a presumed lack of change in the curriculum by the 1980s. The changes in the 1990s might better be interpreted as a malignant metasticizing of what was originally a benign growth. They are a pathological response to the genuine inclusion we saw in Chapter 1 in the array of selections in the 1979 Harcourt Brace Jovanovich reader for grade 4, an array that was characteristic of more than one leading series in the late 1970s and early 1980s. The recent changes in the instructional readers reflect apparent decisions by the publishers' academic advisers that "political and cultural oppression" of nonwhites by whites is the chief problem for the elementary school to grapple with—in both the traditional content of the curriculum and the language associated with that content. An article on the intellectual climate in today's schools of education notes that Columbia's Teachers College holds workshops on cultural and political "oppression," in which prospective or current teachers role-play ways to "usurp the existing power structure."[4] It is difficult to think of more intellectually destructive *and* self-serving advice to publishers than the notion that children need to be liberated from exposure to well-written English prose because it is one form of "cultural oppression."

The deterioration of the quality of the language and literature in leading instructional readers for the upper elementary grades is a powerful index of the indifference, if not hostility, to intellectual priorities by teacher educators who advise the editors and publishers of reading textbooks. Children's social needs must clearly receive some consideration in K–12. They are a legitimate concern at all times and at all grade levels. But when a stress on the social needs that these educators alone seem to perceive serves to eliminate (or is used to eliminate) serious and systematic intellectual demands on children, then close attention must be paid to their educational philosophy. And its alliance with, if not absorption of, a movement exhibiting profound hostility to the teaching of reading skills makes it all the more important for attention to be paid. This is especially the case when the advocates of one reigning educational philosophy, multiculturalism, take the stance that its worth cannot be questioned because it is a moral necessity and that research on its worth is thus unjustifiable, while the advocates of the other, whole language, are equally fervid about the rightness of their own beliefs and insist that only nonscientific research can determine its worth.

WHY ARE THE INTELLECTUAL EFFECTS OF SOCIAL AND POLITICAL GOALS BEING IGNORED?

Why are so many researchers and teacher educators promoting social and political goals that completely eclipse academic goals: the acquisition of a strong reading vocabulary, analytical ways of thinking, and a substantial body of ideas and facts with which to think? As Chapter 8 notes, many of them begin with the premise that it is undemocratic and oppressive to insist on the use and mastery of the English language in schools. And as noted in a 1997 report on the views of teacher educators by Public Agenda, an opinion-gathering research group unaffiliated with any party or cause, they also give only lip-service to a common core of civic values and academic knowledge.[5] Yet their moral premise is deeply flawed; their views are completely out of touch with what most parents and other citizens want for the children of this country, a point stressed by this 1997 report by Public Agenda. One is tempted to conclude that what has motivated them to formulate and promote their particular social and political goals is their need to preserve *their* self-esteem.

Let us look briefly at the record. With respect to beginning reading instruction, there is almost no research evidence favoring whole language instruction over balanced programs that include systematic phonics instruction. Indeed, the evidence is massively in favor of the latter; low-income children, in particular, tend to do better with an early code emphasis. Nor is there a body of research evidence that whole language classrooms produce children who like to read for recreational or academic purposes, in contrast to classrooms using basal readers.[6] Nor do practical results in the field even hint at the benefits of whole language instruction. The recent disastrous decline in the reading scores of California children is a case in point. Despite the efforts of the defenders of whole language to claim that the teachers in California had not been given sufficient training in whole language and that the rise in the number of immigrant children was the real cause of the decline in reading scores, the fact is that the scores of native "white" children declined as much as did the scores of other children.[7] Further, any pedagogy that requires extraordinary teachers for its success is not a useful pedagogy.

In the late 1980s, the NAEP commissioned a panel of experts to look into what it termed an anomaly: the decline in reading scores among fourth graders during the 1980s after a decade of rising scores. Jeanne Chall, a member of this panel, showed in her report how the increases in scores for these students during the 1970s could be attributed to an emphasis on "earlier and heavier instruction in decoding" and on more "extensive vocabularies" in the reading textbooks of the 1970s, in contrast to what was in the 1960s readers.[8] She also showed how the lack of improvement and possible decline in the scores of fourth graders in the 1980s could be attributed to the change in emphasis in textbooks in the 1980s—that is, to less instruction in decoding and to less extensive reading vocabularies. Although the decline in reading scores in the 1990s among all seventeen year olds may reflect the long-term negative influence of whole language on the teaching of basic reading skills in the early grades, I would argue that the alliance that evolved between the advocates of whole language and those promoting multicultural education in the 1980s is a much stronger explanation for the intellectual and literary limitations of contemporary reading textbooks and the stagnation or decline found in the NAEP assessments in the 1990s. The fusion of the anti-intellectualism of the multiculturalists and the antiteaching philosophy of whole language advocates is an educationally deadly combination in the elementary grades. The cumulative effects of failing to learn reading skills and to develop a strong reading vocabulary in the elementary grades show up most clearly at higher grade levels.

In 1992, the Society for the Scientific Study of Reading was formed by a large number of reading and language researchers who wanted a forum for presenting, discussing, and publishing methodologically sound research on reading. Their interest is in promoting scientific research and helping others distinguish it from "pseudo-scientific or non-scientific research."[9] Many of its well-known members have conducted some of the studies whose results unequivocally support the systematic teaching of phonics, and their reputations in the field are unassailable. Yet the researchers and teacher educators in the leadership of the National Council of Teachers of English who chose to support the whole language movement years ago have difficulty in acknowledging the existence of that body of research and seem unable to back off from a stance that they have inappropriately imposed on their professional organization. Worse yet, prominent members of NCTE continue to insinuate that the proponents of systematic phonics are under the control of, or associated with, the religious right, as if phonics as a teaching strategy has a spiritual dimension or is suspect as a strategy if many members of one faith happen to support it.[10] On the other hand, the International Reading Association, which had been allied with NCTE on its position toward whole language all these years, revised its stance and issued a position statement in September 1997 underscoring phonics as "an important aspect of beginning reading instruction."[11] One lesson parents need to learn from all of this is to beware of the motives of those who demonize Christian fundamentalists and use them as bogeymen to advance their own educational agenda.

We find a story similar to the whole language charade in writing pedagogy. Despite the current emphasis on it in schools of education, there is no body of research evidence to support collaborative, or joint, writing as a way to improve children's writing ability. Nor is there any body of evidence to support the emphasis that educators have placed on writing about one's feelings or experiences as a way to improve writing ability, learning in the content areas, or understanding of literary texts. Certainly, personal writing may be useful to get students started as writers, and there are volumes of anecdotal accounts by teachers detailing their successes in using personal, or experience-based, writing to motivate beginning or reluctant writers. The value of personal writing has long been an article of faith among English teachers at all educational levels, but in my exhaustive review of research studies, I found no evidence that could contribute to the pedestal on which personal writing has been placed.[12] As a frequent practice, it may well promote self-centered thinking and limit students' capacity to understand abstract concepts from a more analytic or distanced perspective.

An overabundance of personal writing assignments may also reduce students' experience with informational writing and the modes of reasoning and organization it calls forth. This possibility is unwittingly suggested by the writer of a *Boston Globe* article on the reflections of a recent graduate of a Boston high school, described as a top student and the winner of several writing awards. Carol Figueroa was stunned by the writing demanded of her at a Boston-area college during her freshman year.[13] The reporter noted that although Figueroa believed she had "received plenty of support and encouragement" from her teachers and that she is a "self-confident leader because of that," she now wishes she had gone to a high school with "more challenging school work." She had discovered that "moral support is different from academic rigor." Yet the reporter approvingly quoted an English teacher at another Boston high school who had had her students "write a short story about their lives" because, in the teacher's words, it allowed them to show a "high level of writing ability" and to realize that "their own experience is valid and useful." This teacher is also quoted as believing that this assignment reflected her "high expectations" for her students. It apparently did not occur to the reporter that this kind of writing assignment today, especially for high school students from minority groups, is more likely to reflect a concern for their self-esteem rather than a desire to challenge them intellectually.[14] A regular flow of such writing assignments may be part of the reason that Hispanic students like Carol Figueroa are not prepared for college-level writing.

Nor is there evidence to support the idea that students can develop critical thinking skills without some basic knowledge and hard facts. Indeed, it is not at all clear why anyone ever expected students to gain intellectually from political or social consciousness-raising discussions in the classroom rather than from programs designed to expand their intellectual capacity. To the contrary, there is some evidence that a teacher who engages in what is called a "critical literacy" pedagogy gives short shrift to academic objectives.[15] Teachers who implement a critical literacy pedagogy use a great deal of class time for discussing contemporary social and political issues in a way that is highly critical of this country's social values and political institutions. They encourage students to use class time for reading and writing about these issues as well. It stands to reason that such a teacher would have her heart more in getting children to think, believe, and feel a particular way, as in a catechism class, than in developing independent and analytic thinking.

Nor have educational researchers presented evidence to support the use of multicultural literature, however it is defined, in improving reading ability. Clearly, all students should be reading quality literary works that exhibit the multiethnic and multiracial nature of the country and world in which they live. But there are no methodologically sound research studies to suggest that students who read about characters who look or talk like them end up reading better than students who do not read about characters who look or talk like them. The skills taught in well-conceived developmental reading programs are what seem to matter. Indeed, a survey on immigrant children conducted by a sociologist at Michigan State University, reported in the *New York Times* on March 21, 1998, noted that "young people who identified themselves by ethnic identities like Chicano or Latino in junior high had lower grades and somewhat higher dropout rates than the other children studied." The reporter commented that "this finding lends support to analysts who have suggested that children of immigrants who come to identify with American minorities may take on 'oppositional' identities and see doing well in school as 'acting white.'"[16]

Nor, despite almost thirty years of effort, is there a consistent body of evidence to support the effectiveness of transitional bilingual education in helping immigrant children learn English or the notion that it takes them five to seven years in school to catch up to the language skills of native-born children. Nor is there a consistent body of evidence to support the widespread belief that children's use of their home language in the English language arts class facilitates their acquisition of English better than does their effort to use the English language itself. No foreign language teacher would ever support the idea that English-speaking students trying to learn German, French, or Russian would learn these languages better by reading and writing in English in the German, French, or Russian class. The report issued by the National Research Council in 1997, *Improving Schooling for Language Minority Children*, even acknowledged that "there is not really a strong consensus about what is best for the education of English-language learners." Although its chapter on the evaluation of bilingual education programs is chiefly a review of the reviews on these programs, it was supposed to be the last word on the subject.[17] Nevertheless, it seems that faculty in schools of education cannot accept what their own research authorities have concluded when the conclusion conflicts with deeply held dogma. The March 1998 report from the National Research Council, *The Prevention of Reading Difficulties in Young Children*, recommended that students who speak a language other than English for which there are instructional guides, learning materials, and fluent teachers be taught to read in their native language while acquiring proficiency in spoken English. And, immediately following suit, the International Reading Association on May 4, 1998, approved a resolution on Initial Literacy Instruction in a First Language supporting this recommendation, never once referring to the National Research Council's 1997 report on bilingual education.

The very week I wrote the previous paragraph, the *Boston Globe* ran an article, beginning on its front page, about a thirty-year-old graduate of Boston's English High School, Dao Hoang Vo, who had become a computer consultant and had chosen to install sixty-five computers in his former high school as a way to express gratitude for the education he had received there.[18] A Vietnamese refugee, Vo began school in this country speaking no English. He first attended classes for two months in which both Vietnamese and English were used. But his father said he had to learn English faster, apparently because Vo was not learning English very quickly in his bilingual class. So Vo began at English High School knowing "little more than two words." His father told him: "You either sink or swim." With the help of staff members of the high school, he swam. Four years later he graduated second in his class, an achievement that contradicts the predictions of the most popular second language acquisition theories in bilingual education today. But in today's schools of education, these theories do not require facts for support, and facts that disprove these theories are ignored.

Teacher educators have a poor track record on the intellectual benefits of the techniques they have proposed in the past thirty years and instituted through course work in schools of education, in-service workshops in the schools, summer institutes, professional conferences, publications, and advice to educational publishers. Yet they believe that they are superior to parents and others in knowing what is best for children. Commenting on the gap between research and practice, an educational researcher in the school of education at the University of Aukland, New Zealand, noted that in discussions of "parental resistance to detracking," educational researchers "privilege their own positions" and prejudge parental views as "not only wrong but morally reprehensible."[19] Recall from Chapter 2 the epithet of "Volvo vigilantes" used to describe these parents.

According to the 1997 report issued by Public Agenda on how teachers of teachers view public education, 79 percent of the education professors interviewed for this report characterize the public's concerns about new teaching techniques as "outmoded and mistaken." It is easy to understand why educators and researchers who believe that they alone know what is best for children cannot admit that almost all of the practices they have advocated in recent decades to motivate low-achieving students have been unsuccessful and may have, if anything, contributed to their underachievement. Hubris prevents them from contemplating the possibility that their pedagogical ideas have been part of the problem, not its solution.

Hubris also prevents them from exploring the empirical consequences of their own ideas with carefully designed comparison studies. They have not sought to determine the actual benefits, possible limitations, and unintended consequences of the changes in social content that were made in the readers over time. To the contrary, the researchers and educators advocating changes in the social contents of the readers and in the pedagogy accompanying these contents have offered only moral and emotional arguments. They have also implied that those who disagreed with their views were motivated solely by ignoble sentiments. It is striking that there is no body of hard evidence attesting to the intellectual benefits of any of the changes in social content that publishers have made in the readers in the past three decades. Indeed, Theodore Sizer, a former dean of the Harvard Graduate School of Education and a well-known proponent of educational reform, is quoted as responding to a reporter's question about whether he could name a single reform in the past fifteen years that had been successful, "I don't think there is one."[20]

One cannot help but wonder how many of the researchers and educators supporting never-ending changes in the readers suspected that they would find little or no evidence to support their judgmental stances if they used soundly designed comparison studies—the only kind of research that can provide evidence on whether differences in pedagogy or social content have led to differences in intellectual achievement. The claim by many prominent language arts and reading researchers that only small-scale qualitative studies give teachers useful knowledge is quite convenient.

Rather than accept any professional responsibility for the worsening conditions in many inner-city schools and the failure of low-income minority students to thrive, many researchers and educators have displaced their frustration and anger onto anything associated with the American mainstream: its political and economic institutions, its values, its literature, *its very language*. It is not surprising that many of them are turning to methods of assessment that consist largely of subjective judgments of performance, based on loosely defined standards that can be embodied in relatively nondemanding material. Indeed, one researcher advanced the argument in the lead article in a 1997 issue of the prestigious *American Educational Research Journal* that achievement-oriented measures are now undesirable because they serve the "competitive and meritocratic orientation of mainstream institutions."[21] Schools should critically examine the "cult of achievement," the author urges, and focus on "the process of learning and on its relation to self-worth rather than on particular achievements." The article also urges separating the worth of building self-esteem from its presumed relationship to enhanced academic achievement.

This effort to salvage self-esteem is a prime example of the mode of reasoning contemporary educational moralists use. Why is it now necessary to separate the building of self-worth from any possible relationship to academic achievement? Most likely it is because there is no evidence that improving self-esteem leads to higher academic achievement, although education professors have not made this clear to classroom teachers and the public at large. Despite the lack of evidence, today's educational moralists want to keep the building of self-worth as an educational priority because they cannot give up the value they have placed on building self-esteem in minority children through validation of their language, their culture, and their "ways of thinking." In their eyes, an emphasis on low self-esteem as the cause of low academic achievement makes low-achieving students responsible for their own lack of achievement because it is *their* low self-esteem that has caused *their* low achievement. For today's moralists, this amounts to "blaming the victim." And because it is ideologically impossible for them to hold low-achieving students and their parents even partly responsible for their low achievement, they have advanced the idea that the low achievement of low-income minority children cannot be addressed until the practices that reflect the values of merit and competition are removed from the schools.

Again, we see here the implicit assumption that minority students are incapable of learning how to compete with others and to succeed on the basis of their own merits. And, again, we see a displacement of the source of the problem from what faculty in schools of education do as teachers to our social and political values. The nonaccountability for measurable or visible outcomes inherent in the preacher's role is also convenient for those who seek to avoid the accountability for measurable or visible outcomes inherent in the teacher's role. By formulating social and political goals for the schools and by emphasizing American social and political values and institutions as the ultimate source of low achievement in low-income minority children, they can distract attention from their own performance as teachers. And if they so choose, they can shed their teaching responsibilities altogether in their own courses in the name of facilitating "self-directed learning" or political consciousness raising. It is probably not coincidental that there seems to be no impartial research on how effective the faculty in schools of education are as teachers themselves.

In tandem with the idea that academic deficiencies in certain minorities cannot be addressed unless we extirpate the very values that encourage high intellectual performance *and* the very norms by which it is measured, a group of educators is now laying the groundwork for a more radical set of social goals than those currently reflected in the basal readers. They do not believe that changes in school structures and practices alone will bring about the advancement of low-income minority children. Recall the puzzling statement, in the epigraph for Chapter 2, to the effect that classrooms have both "possibilities and limits." What these limitations are is not explained, but we can guess that it refers to the fact that the schools cannot make all students equal in ability and language skills. The "manifesto" of those educators who call themselves the New London Group, described in Chapter 8, makes it clear how they think the limits of education can be overcome: by a strong central government that maintains order and promotes justice and equality by arbitrating differences among its "polyglot population."[22]

What these educators are admitting is that they do not believe that minority children can learn standard English and achieve academically at levels similar to the range found in nonminority children. Thus, the basic social problem they foresee is *not* that there will always be differences in ability and motivation among adults. The problem they envision is that adults will not be able to communicate with each other because they have not learned to "negotiate" the "dialect differences, register differences, code switching, interlanguages and hybrid cross-cultural discourses" that the New London Group wants teachers to encourage in all classrooms. And if these educators are successful in convincing elementary school teachers that "justice" or "equity" lies in abandoning a common language and encouraging language differences among their students (in the name of group identity and group respect) so that these differences become the basic social problem we confront as a society, where else could the solution to our inability to communicate with each other lie, if not in a strong, central government? And if it does, it would most likely have to rest in the hands of supreme regulators ensconced in government bureaucracies and advised by a phalanx of handsomely paid educational consultants basking in enhanced self-esteem.

The massive hypocrisy at the core of the ideology of today's educational moralists seems to be beyond self-recognition. They fail to perceive how they are in effect demonstrating the intrinsic worth of such values as self-expression, choice, autonomy, and individual rights (and a command of the English language) in their very efforts to denounce them as the evils of American or Western society. Much worse than their hypocrisy is their unwillingness to probe their own subconscious conclusion that minority children do not have the intellectual capacity to succeed in this society. As a consequence of their own inability to engage in critical self-reflection—a practice they constantly recommend to K–12 teachers—they have committed themselves to the destruction ("transformation" is the word they use) of the very norms by which academic achievement can be described. Those who stand to lose the most intellectually from their subconscious racism will be the children in whose names the changes in reading instruction are taking place. They will be unable to communicate with dignity and intelligence, not only with other American children, but with children all over the world.

WHERE DO WE GO FROM HERE?

There are many forces that affect children's intellectual development and achievement. The resources and stability of their families, the resources of their schools, and the quality of their teachers are among the most important. Indeed, home environment is still the most significant determinant of educational outcomes according to the best studies that have been made over the years. I do not want to convey the simplistic idea that all we need to do to improve the academic achievement of all children, and minority children in particular, is to change the contents of their instructional readers and the pedagogy recommended in the teacher guides. We know, for example, that the amount of reading that students are asked to do and do on their own, in school and at home, makes a profound difference in the development of reading ability. And there is no doubt that students today read less than students did years ago. There is even a decline in recent years. In the 1992 and 1994 NAEP assessments in reading in grade 12, participating students reported reading less at home and at school in 1994 than in 1992. There is no substitute for extensive reading outside school hours if students are to experience substantial reading growth. But teachers do not control what students do outside school. The solutions are not simple; they are long term, and it would be a mistake if the public believes otherwise and then concludes that the situation is hopeless if progress is slower than expected. Nevertheless, each ring in the many circles of conditions that surround children's academic performance must by examined. Whatever deficiencies each one may have need to be addressed, perhaps individually and over time, even if we wish we could address them all simultaneously and at once.

Given the dominating influence of those teacher educators and educational researchers who have been promoting the primacy of social and political goals in the curriculum, there is little one can expect from our pedagogical institutions on their own to reverse the anti-intellectual tide engulfing the schools. Schools of education are the major force behind this tide. Their track record is so bad that in any other profession such a record would raise questions about professional competence. Not only have those promoting today's social and political goals failed to come up with ideas that work, they have resorted to the demonstrably false but patently self-serving defense that the schools are doing better than ever and that the public is wrong in whatever it believes.

Fortunately, there are a number of courses of action for parents and other citizens to take. They can examine their children's reading instructional textbooks, contact responsible authorities, and promote changes in teacher education. They can also develop alternatives to regular public elementary schools that will enable them to upgrade curricula in all subjects.

I. *Criteria for Judging a Reading Instructional Textbook for the English Language Arts Class*

1. Determine whether all selections are in English and in standard English. Selections should not be in other languages (even if English translations are provided for them); in hybrid languages such as Japanglish (or Japlish) or Spanglish; or feature a great deal of conversation in dialect such as black, "deaf," Appalachian, or Pennsylvania Dutch.

2. Determine whether all non-English words are italicized, with footnotes at the bottom of the pages of the student text giving their meanings, pronunciation, and language of origin. Non-English words should not be graphically similar to English words, or italicized but not footnoted.

3. Using the glossary at the end of the student text, count the number of English multisyllabic words offered under a few letters of the alphabet and compare across several other readers at that grade

level to see which one has the most multisyllabic words and if increasingly more such words are offered under those letters at subsequent grade levels in all the readers examined. Do not count proper nouns. Compare with the number in the Open Court readers, if possible, or the 1987 Macmillan readers.

4. Determine whether there is a rough balance between the number of selections about or originating from ethnic groups in Asia, Africa, and Central and South America and the number of selections about or originating from European ethnic groups. There selections may be folktales, legends, nonfiction, or realistic fiction. Note any effort to racialize ethnicity so that it appears as a phenomenon only of nonwhite groups.

5. Determine whether there is a rough balance of selections from classical children's literature, American and British, and more contemporary literature.

II. *Responsible Authorities to Contact*

1. *The local school board.* Find out if a textbook evaluation committee exists, and raise questions with this committee first. If no such committee exists, request the school board to form one consisting of teachers and parents. Include a local history professor as a member or consultant. The major focus of interest should be the level of vocabulary difficulty in the textbooks, the consistent use of the English language in them, and the accuracy and balance of the historical information offered to teachers in the teacher guide.

2. *Publishers' sales representatives.* Ask them for information on all the criteria spelled out in section I. Ask them if historians and literary scholars have served as consultants to the publishers and, if so, which ones.

3. *State legislators on education subcommittees, members of state boards of education, and governor's education advisers.* In textbook adoption states, ask those responsible for textbook guidelines to amend existing legislation or guidelines for elementary school reading instructional textbooks by adding the criteria in section I to the existing criteria. Such additions to existing criteria might stimulate educational publishers to select academic advisers with a broader range of views than they now seem to solicit. Redirecting the schools toward

intellectual and civic goals does not mean abandoning an inclusive curriculum in the best sense of the term. Literary standards do not need to be changed to introduce students to an authentic depiction of this country's population or history.

In textbook adoption states, request that literary scholars and historians serve as advisers to textbook evaluation committees. Two organizations to contact for possible names are the Asssociation of Literary Scholars and Critics (2039 Shattuck Avenue, Suite 202, Berkeley, California 94704-1116) and the History Society (P.O. Box 382602, Cambridge, Massachusetts 02238-2602).

Request that several literary scholars serve as external reviewers to determine if the statewide assessments in the English language arts and reading contain (1) a balance between literary selections written before 1970 and contemporary selections, (2) a balance between literary selections reflecting the American mainstream and the variety of ethnic groups (European as well as non-European) in this country, and (3) an appropriately challenging vocabulary level for the grade at which the assessment is given.

Governors, state legislators, state boards of education, and local school boards need to hear from citizens with academic concerns. Perhaps the largest and most serious hole in the educational universe of K–12 has been the almost complete absence of organized pressure groups consisting of parents with straightforward academic concerns, and not moral grievances of any kind. Parents with academic concerns need to provide their elected officials with a clear understanding of what multiculturalism has come to mean and why. They also need to arm themselves with as much information as they can obtain about the textbooks now in use in their schools and be prepared to face name calling and attempts to discredit their motives. They should not respond in kind.

III. New Policies and Programs for Teacher Education

1. Ask governors, legislators, and state board of education members to require joint responsibility between academic departments in public colleges and universities (English, history, foreign languages, mathematics, and the sciences) and faculty in schools of education for preparing teachers for grades 4 to 12. Joint responsi-

bility should help create intellectually stronger teachers with stronger intellectual goals for the schools. Training of teachers for K–3 might continue to be the sole responsibility of schools of education if they were willing to be guided more by sound research than by the romantic notion that children learn to read and write as naturally as they learn to speak. Governors, legislators, and state boards of education might do well to heed the advice proffered many years ago by philosopher Sidney Hook. In a strong essay that came to the defense of John Dewey, Hook urged greater cooperation between faculties of liberal arts colleges and teachers' colleges. Hook made the case that it was the "refusal of liberal arts colleges to take the problems of general public education seriously which was in large measure responsible for the growth of teachers' colleges."[23] The problems of mass education in a democratic society, as Hook saw it, should have been a topic of deep concern to the best minds in the best colleges, not relegated only to those caught up in the daily work of preparing teachers for what Hook called the "concrete context of wide variations in the natural powers of students, all of whom are capable of some development but not necessarily in the same way."

2. Ask governors, legislators, and state board of education members to include faculty in the arts and sciences at colleges and universities on committees deciding on the academic content of competency tests for the certification and recertification of teachers and on revision committees for state standards documents. College faculty in the sciences and mathematics especially should be involved in designing the sequence and amount of substantive content in their areas and in making judgments about the appropriate pedagogy for the different kinds of students now in K–12.

IV. Educational Alternatives That Allow for Upgraded Curricula

1. *Charter schools, Core Knowledge schools, and private schools.* Develop or support alternatives to regular public elementary schools. A growing number of parents across the country, in urban areas in particular, are creating alternatives to their public elementary school.[24] Charter schools, which are under public jurisdiction, continue to increase nationwide, despite opposition to them by

many faculty in schools of education. Core Knowledge schools can be charter schools or regular public elementary schools. A Core Knowledge school is an elementary school that uses the curriculum developed by the Core Knowledge Foundation in Virginia. There are now over seven hundred elementary schools using this curriculum, which covers all subject areas typically taught in a K–8 school curriculum. Its use requires the approval and support of a school's teachers and parents, as well as of the local superintendent and school board if it is a regular public elementary school.

Private schools, both sectarian and nonsectarian, are increasing in number or population across the country. The number of Christian day schools is up, as is attendance at Catholic parochial schools after many years of decline. The population in Jewish day schools is increasing dramatically, and for the first time in American history some mainstream Jewish organizations are rethinking their opposition to public support for religious schools. The most remarkable phenomenon of all, home schooling, seems to be growing by leaps and bounds.[25]

2. *Upgraded reading requirements*. Although character education is of great concern to many of the parents seeking alternatives to regular public schools, strong academic content is clearly their other chief concern, if not their chief concern. Be aware of the extraordinarily high literary demands embedded in the grade 6 reader published by the Bob Jones University Press in Greenville, South Carolina. It is part of a reading series used by Christian day schools and the many Christian home-schooling families. Its 696-page student text, comparable in length to the leading grade 6 readers I analyzed, features, in addition to explicitly labeled Christian selections, selections by Lewis Carroll, Howard Pyle, Robert Louis Stevenson, Emily Dickinson, Rudyard Kipling, Robert Browning ("The Pied Piper of Hamelin"), Mark Twain (*The Adventures of Tom Sawyer*), Louisa May Alcott, Armstrong Sperry (*Call It Courage*), Sir Arthur Conan Doyle, L. M Montgomery (*Anne of Green Gables*), John McCrae ("In Flanders Field"), Charles Dickens, Ogden Nash, Lucretia Hale, Frances Hodgson Burnett, Kenneth Grahame, and Mary O'Hara (*My Friend Flicka*). It contains few illustrations (thus, most of its 696 pages consist of text), and the number of hard words in its glos-

sary is staggering in comparison to the other grade 6 readers I examined, including the grade 6 reader by Open Court.[26]

The required literary readings for grade 6 in the Core Knowledge Foundation's curriculum are perhaps even more impressive. It expects students to read Robert Louis Stevenson's *Dr. Jekyll and Mr. Hyde*, *The Iliad* and *The Odyssey*, and Frances Hodgson Burnett's *The Secret Garden*, *Julius Caesar*, a number of selections from classical mythology, and poems by George Gordon Byron, William Shakespeare, William Wordsworth, Rudyard Kipling, Langston Hughes, James Weldon Johnson, Emily Dickinson, Henry Wadsworth Longfellow, Edgar Allan Poe, Robert Frost, Paul Laurence Dunbar, Charles E. Carryl, and Maya Angelou. To meet the needs of students with a wide range of reading abilities, the content guidelines in the Core Knowledge Sequence for grades K–8 note that *The Iliad*, *The Odyssey*, and *Julius Caesar* are available in editions adapted for young readers.

An e-mail communication I received in April 1998 from a Los Angeles parent who had attended the Core Knowledge Foundation's 1998 conference in Atlanta, Georgia, expresses a common perspective on its curriculum. She writes:

> I recently attended the Foundation's annual conference in Atlanta, where more than 2000 teachers and administrators participated. These teachers all acted as if they had found the grail, and it was easy to see why. Their schools and pupils are thriving; test scores are up (dramatically at many schools); and at last they are free to do what they love best—teach exciting, intelligent content to all students, not just "gifted" ones.
>
> I firmly believe that if we quit offering students pablum [*sic*] at the lower grades, many of the outrages that occur in higher education wouldn't be possible. I am not a teacher, nor am I an academic, but I am a parent who follows these issues closely. I returned from the conference vowing to do whatever I must to bring Core Knowledge to Los Angeles.

I attended that conference as one of its speakers, so I can vouch for her observations. At one plenary session, I happened to sit next to a large group

284 · LOSING OUR LANGUAGE

of teachers, white and black, from the Lakeland County, Florida, schools. Several told me how excited they were about the changes taking place in their school system; all sixty-three elementary schools in the county were becoming Core Knowledge schools. Systematic phonics instruction in their beginning reading program, a strong reading list, and a substantive curriculum in every content area made sense to them. Moreover, some research evidence has just appeared to support their expectations. The *Core Knowledge Newsletter* for winter–spring 1998 reported that five Maryland Core Knowledge schools being followed in a Johns Hopkins University comparison study outgained their Maryland control schools in reading comprehension on mandated state performance assessments tests, "leading researchers to conclude that the thesis underlying the Core Knowledge Sequence is valid."

The enthusiasm for the reading requirements in the Core Knowledge curriculum is in many respects a reaction to the impoverished readings that students have been given in many public schools. Although large numbers of students in the regular public schools are losing use of the English language as they progress through the elementary school, a small but rapidly growing number of students are gaining mastery of it. If enough parents and other citizens make the effort to communicate their concerns about the contents and pedagogy of the most basic subject in the elementary school curriculum to their local and state school boards, we may be able to avoid the creation of new divide in American public life: the gap between those citizens who can use the language of this country to participate in public affairs and those citizens who have been deprived of the opportunity to learn it.

NOTES

Preface

1. Girls still do so according to every study conducted by the National Assessment of Educational Progress.

2. Anthony Appiah, "The Multiculturalist Misunderstanding," a review of *On Toleration* by Michael Walzer and *We Are All Multiculturalists Now* by Nathan Glazer. *New York Review of Books*, October 9, 1997.

3. Shelby Steele, *The Content of Our Character* (New York: St. Martin's, 1990); Shelby Steele, *A Dream Deferred: the Second Betrayal of Black Freedom in America* (New York: HarperCollins, 1998).

4. Frances FitzGerald, *America Revised* (New York: Random House, 1980), p. 218.

5. These phrases were used in a letter dated March 10, 1990, sent by Ross and Anne Gelbspan to the headmaster of Brookline High School, Brookline, Massachusetts.

6. I am indebted to Catherine Spaeth for her research on the contents of this bibliography in her report, *Multicultural Education in Minnesota* (Minnesota Association of Scholars, Madison, Wisconsin, December 1997). The Minnesota State Board of Education's attempt to force multicultural education on all school districts rather than allowing them to incorporate it in ways that fit their students and local communities was defeated in 1998.

7. Geneva Gay, *Urban Monograph Series: A Synthesis of Scholarship in Multicultural Education* (Oakbrook, Ill.: North Central Regional Education Lab, 1994), pp. 25–26.

Chapter One. The Cultivation of Multicultural Illiteracy

1. In *Classic American Readers, Selections from Famous Writers*, selected by Jeanne S. Chall (Kansas City, Mo.: Andrews and McMeel, Education Division, 1994), pp. 27–28.

2. I have been unable to track down the copyright date of the book edited by Samuel Eliot from which the adapted version comes. There is no acknowledgment of permission to use this version in the 1962 Houghton Mifflin reader. Perhaps this book had already passed into the public domain by 1953, the year in which the first edition of this grade 6 reader was published. The unadapted version appears in the grade 6 reader *Enchanted Isles* published by Charles E. Merrill Books, and Western Publishing Company, 1997 printing, copyright 1966, 1960, and 1954, for A Beka Book Reading Program, a series put out by Pensacola Christian College and used by many Christian day schools and home-schooling families. This reader does not even indicate who the editor or compiler of this unadapted version was. Perhaps this unadapted version of *The Arabian Nights* had also passed into the public domain by 1954.

3. In "Could the Decline Be Real? Recent Trends in Reading Instruction and Support in the U.S," ed. E. Haertel et al., *Report of the NAEP Technical Review Panel on the 1986 Reading Anomaly, the Accuracy of NAEP Trends, and Issues Raised by State-Level NAEP Comparisons* (Washington, D.C.: National Center for Education Statistics and U.S. Department of Education, 1989), Jeanne Chall notes that from about 1920 to about the late 1960s, the major focus in the teaching of reading, from the first grade on, was on "reading for meaning," that is, on reading comprehension, and that the reading textbooks contained limited vocabularies and relatively little systematic instruction in phonics (p. 63).

4. See, for example, Herbert Walberg, "U.S. Schools Teach Reading Least Productively," *Research in the Teaching of English* 30 (3) (October 1996): 328–343.

5. Sandra Stotsky, "More Teachers, Smaller Classes: Are These Our First Priority?" *Education Week,* April 1, 1998, pp. 72ff.

6. Sheldon M. Stern, "Beyond the Rhetoric: An Historian's View of 'National' Standards for United States History," *Journal of Education 176* (3) (1994): 61–72.

7. Sol Stern, "My Public School Lesson," *City Journal* (autumn 1997).

8. This reader is the companion volume to a "skills" reader containing nonfiction selections, content-area textbook excerpts, and skills lessons.

9. This phrase appears in Nicole E. House, "Preparing Middle Grade Students for Civicism with Literature-Based Social Studies Instruction," *GSU* (Georgia State University) *Educational Forum* 2 (2) (spring 1997): 20.

10. John Honey, *Language Is Power: The Story of Standard English and Its Enemies* (London: Faber and Faber Limited, 1997). See his discussion of the work of American linguist and educator James Gee on pp. 229–234, for example.

11. Edgar Dale and Joseph O'Rourke, *The Living Word Vocabulary: The Words We Know* (Chicago: Field Enterprises, 1976).

12. "Faith Ringgold's Stories in Art." From Leslie Sills, *Inspirations: Stories About Women Artists* (Niles, Illinois: A. Whitman, 1989).

13. The word *Japlish* appears in Honey, *Language Is Power,* p. 250. But he provides no examples of the various hybrid languages that he mentions on this page, so I prefer to use my own coinage at present.

14. "Pacific Crossing" by Gary Soto.

15. For example, the March 1998 issue of *Language Arts* (Volume 76, No. 3) contains a profile of Pat Mora, a contemporary nonfiction writer and poet, whose works appear in elementary school reading series. This highly laudatory article notes that she infuses English with Spanish words and phrases to demonstrate her long-standing advocacy for "greater acceptance of linguistic diversity in society, classrooms, and literature" and to counter this country's "repressive linguistic atmosphere, and a long and ugly history of devaluing other languages." She offers no evidence to support her charge.

16. I asked an editor at Scholastic Press how he would account for the impoverished vocabulary I had found in leading reading series. He replied that a developmental vocabulary is the one major component of a reading selection that the editors of basal readers have paid scant attention to in the past two decades, although he was not sure why.

17. The increase in the Macmillan readers for grades 4 and 6 from 1980 to 1987 may have been a response to the emphasis on basic skills that surfaced in the late 1970s. It used to take about five or six years for a totally new edition to be put out.

18. Herbert Walberg, "U.S. Schools Teach Reading Least Productively," *Research in the Teaching of English* 30 (3) (October 1996): 328–343.

19. Arthur Gates, *Interest and Ability in Reading* (New York: Macmillan, 1930).

20. In "Table A.—Historical Statistics of Public Secondary Day Schools: 1890–1952" (p. 144), in I. L. Kandel's *American Education in the Twentieth Century* (Cambridge: Harvard University Press, 1957), the number of students in grades 7 to 12 went from an estimated 202,960 in 1890, to 519,251 in 1900, to 915,061 in 1910, to 1,999,106 in 1920, and to 5,212,179 in 1930. As sharp as this rate of increase is, clearly the number of students completing six years of elementary school and going on to grade 7 must have increased exponentially at an even sharper rate, since many of them dropped out of secondary school at different times in those years.

21. Jeanne S. Chall and Sue S. Conard, with Susan Harris Sharples, *Should Textbooks*

Challenge Students? The Case for Easier or Harder Textbooks (New York: Teachers College Press, 1991), pp. 13–14.

22. James A. Michener, *This Noble Land* (New York: Random House, 1996), pp. 101–102.

23. *Classic American Readers*, p. 56.

24. It is useful to keep in mind that *Black Beauty* and *Robinson Crusoe* were not written for young children, but these works appealed to them and were often presented in an abridged version.

25. Personal communications from Jeanne S. Chall (November 1995) and James Squire (October 1995).

26. I am indebted to Andrew Coulson for bringing the Poe and Addison passages in these old readers to my attention. See his article, "Schooling and Literacy over Time: The Rising Cost of Stagnation and Decline," *Research in the Teaching of English* 30 (3) (October 1996): 311–327.

*Chapter Two. How Social Goals Came to Dominate
Academic Goals in the Reading Curriculum*

1. Information on the early history of reading instruction is drawn from Cornelia Meigs, "The New England Primer," in Cornelia Meigs, Anne Thaxter Eaton, Elizabeth Nesbitt, and Ruth Hill Viguers (eds.), *A Critical History of Children's Literature* (rev. ed.) (Ontario, Canada: Macmillan, 1969), pp. 110–119; Richard Venezky, "Textbooks in School and Society, " in Philip W. Jackson (ed.), *Handbook of Research on Curriculum* (New York: Macmillan, 1992); and Richard Venezky, "A History of the American Reading Textbook," *Elementary School Journal* 87 (3) (January 1987).

2. As Stephen Bates notes in *Battleground: One Mother's Crusade, the Religious Right, and the Struggle for Control of Or Classrooms* (New York: Poseidon Press, 1993), "One study found that 85% of the space in colonial readers addressed religious matters. This religious content declined during the nineteenth century, as educators acknowledged the nation's growing diversity. Religious readings accounted for about a third of the 1837 edition of the *McGuffey's Third Reader*, 9 percent of the 1879 edition, and 6 percent of the last edition in 1901" (p. 208).

3. Frederick Antczak, "Education of the Democratic Audience: The Circuit of Public Speech," in *Thought and Character: The Rhetoric of Democratic Education* (Dubuque: Iowa State University Press, 1985).

4. Ruth Windhover, "Literature in the Nineteenth Century," *English Journal* (April 1979): 28–33.

5. Venezky, "History of the American Reading Textbook," p. 250.

6. Anne Scott MacLeod, "Education for Freedom: Children's Fiction in Jacksonian America," *Harvard Educational Review* 46 (3) (August 1976): 425–435.

7. Paul Hazard, *Books, Children, and Men* (Boston: Horn Book, 1944).

8. Venezky, "Textbooks in School and Society," p. 451.

9. E. M. Cyr. *Cyr's First [-Fifth] Reader* (Boston: Ginn, 1899), p. ix, cited by Venezky, "History of the American Reading Textbook," p. 261.

10. Cited by Jeanne S. Chall, "What Students Were Reading 100 Years Ago," *American Educator* (Summer 1994): 28.

11. James H. Fassett, *The Beacon Readers* (Boston: Ginn, 1918), p. iii, cited by Venezky, "Textbooks in School and Society," p. 451.

12. Cited by Chall, "What Students Were Reading," p. 28.

13. In "The Dumbbell Curve," *Network News and Views* 15 (April 1996), Regna Lee

Wood notes that, according to historians, "95% of the Massachusetts men could read in 1700." She also estimates, using a 1993 U.S. Department of Education report, that "about 90% of the white American adults could read in 1870," although it is not clear what she means by "reading."

Carl Kaestle, a historian of American literacy, notes in "The History of Literacy and the History of Readers," in *Review of Research in Education* (vol. 2) (Washington, D.C.: American Educational Research Association, 1986), pp. 11–53, that the literacy rates "in colonial British America were quite high, and America's rise to universal white literacy was earlier than Europe's" (p. 27). He states that the "big story in nineteenth-century American literacy is the development of common school systems and the near elimination of self-reported outright illiteracy among whites" (p. 32). By the beginning of the twentieth century, literacy rates are about equal for white males and females. Kaestle further notes that "some correlations persist": industrialization is reliably associated with rising literacy, earlier rises in literacy are correlated with Protestantism, and rising literacy is associated with the expansion of schooling.

14. See George W. Tanner, "The Report of the Committee Appointed by the English Conference to Inquire into the Teaching of English in the High Schools of the Middle West," *School Review* 15 (1907): 32–45.

15. Lawrence A. Cremin, *The Transformation of the School: Progressivism in American Education 1876–1957* (New York: Random House, 1961), p. 298.

16. Jeanne S. Chall and Sue S. Conard, with Susan Harris Sharples, *Should Textbooks Challenge Students? The Case for Easier or Harder Textbooks* (New York: Teachers College Press, 1991), p. 108.

17. See, for example, Marilyn J. Adams, *Beginning to Read: Thinking and Learning About Print* (Cambridge, Mass.: MIT Press, 1990); Marilyn J. Adams and Maggie Bruck, "Resolving the 'Great Debate,'" *American Educator* 19 (Summer 1995) 7, 10–20.

18. Cremin, *Transformation*, p. 343.

19. Ibid., p. 88. However, neither John Dewey himself nor George Counts, another well-known educator at Teachers College in the progressive movement in education, was opposed to disciplinary learning, especially in the high school. Dewey wanted to relate subject matter to children's needs and interests, not eliminate it.

20. Richard Hofstadter, *Anti-Intellectualism in American Life* (New York: Random House, 1963), p. 347

21. Ibid., p. 358.

22. Sidney Hook, "Modern Education and Its Critics," in *Seventh Yearbook, American Association of Colleges for Teacher Education* (1954), pp. 139–160. See also Howard M. Jones, Francis Keppel, and Robert Ulich, "On the Conflict Between the 'Liberal Arts' and the 'Schools of Education,'" *Newsletter* 5 (2), American Council of Learned Societies (n.d.): 17–38.

23. Ellen Condliffe Lagemann, "Contested Terrain: A History of Education Research in the United States, 1890–1990," *Educational Researcher* 26 (9) (December 1997): 5–17.

24. Jeanne S. Chall, *Learning to Read: The Great Debate* (New York: McGraw Hill, 1967, 1983, and 1995), pp. 13–14 (2nd edition).

25. Rudolf Flesch, *Why Johnny Can't Read and What You Can Do About It* (New York: Harper & Brothers, 1955).

26. Venezky, "Textbooks in School and Society," p. 452.

27. David McClelland, *The Achieving Society* (Princeton, N.J.: Van Nostrand, 1961). Also described in Venezky, "Textbooks in School and Society," p. 448.

28. Richard de Charms and Gerald H. Moeller, "Values Expressed in American Children's Readers: 1800–1950," *Journal of Abnormal and Social Psychology* 64 (1962): 136–142,

described in Venezky, "Textbooks in School and Society," p. 448. De Charms and Moeller interpreted the changes they found as a reflection of a shift from a Protestant ethic based on individual initiative and competition to a social ethic based on the individual's need for group approval and affiliation.

29. Sara Goodman Zimet. *What Children Read in School: Critical Analysis of Primary Reading Textbooks* (New York: Grune & Stratton, 1972), pp. 82–85.

30. John Dixon, *Growth Through English* (Yorkshire, Great Britain: National Association for the Teaching of English, 1967, 1969, and 1975).

31. Ibid., p. xv. The foreword to the 1975 edition was written by James Squire and James Britton.

32. Charles Valentine, "Deficit, Difference, and Bicultural Models of Afro-American Behavior," *Harvard Educational Review* 41 (2) (May 1971): 137–157.

33. Silver Burdett Ginn, grade 4 teacher edition, p. 404 and elsewhere.

34. Joseph Kahne, "The Politics of Self-Esteem," *American Educational Research Journal* 33, no. 1 (spring 1996). See p. 12 especially.

35. Connie Robinson and Randy Gingrich, "Multicultural Literacy," materials distributed at the National Council of Teachers of English Fall Conference, Seattle, Washington, November 1991.

36. Roseann Duenas Gonzalez, "When Minority Becomes Majority: The Changing Face of English Classrooms," *English Journal* 79 (January 1990): 16–23.

37. Arthur Schlesinger, Jr., *The Disuniting of America: Reflections on a Multicultural Society* (Knoxville, Tenn.: Whittle Direct Books, 1991).

38. See, for example, Jeannie Oakes, *Keeping Track: How Schools Structure Inequality* (New Haven, Conn.: Yale University Press, 1985).

39. Gloria Ladson-Billings notes in "What We Can Learn from Multicultural Education Research," *Educational Leadership* (May 1994), that "cooperative learning was first developed as a way to create more equitable classroom environments" (p. 24). This seems to mean that equity can be achieved when low achievers are taught by more able students in small cooperative learning groups rather than by the classroom teacher in homogeneous instructional groups because the latter make the distinction between high and low achievers visible.

The reading series I examined clearly see cooperative learning as justice driven when it is paired with heterogeneous grouping. Scott Foresman informs teachers in its 1993 teacher guides (e.g., grade 6, Anthology A, p. 20) that both heterogeneous grouping and cooperative learning are among the "new ways to accommodate differences" among students. It offers both positive and negative reasons to convince reluctant teachers. On the one hand, Scott Foresman cautions that "new" research shows that "separating students for instruction can actually add to the learning problems of some students." On the other hand, it notes that research studies also point to the "advantages of heterogeneous grouping" and of cooperative learning as an "especially effective way for teachers to deal with diversity in the classroom." How many teachers would not feel compelled to eliminate achievement groups and adopt cooperative learning in the face of such a rationale? Elementary school teachers in particular tend to be intimidated by an evocation of the authority of academic research.

40. Robert Slavin, "When Does Cooperative Learning Increase Student Achievement?" *Psychological Bulletin* 94 (1983): 429–445.

41. For example, for many years all ninth-grade English classes at Brookline High School in Massachusetts were labeled basic, standard, honor, or advanced placement to indicate the level of reading and writing demanded in the course. With guidance from parents and school counselors, grade 8 students could choose the level they wanted to take. In 1970, all the grade 9 courses were reorganized as planned heterogeneous English classes.

Each now had to contain a mix of students exhibiting the total range of reading ability in the ninth-grade cohort. In effect, this meant that each ninth-grade English class after 1970 had students with reading abilities ranging from grade 4 to college level. The curriculum was "student centered," focusing on experience-based writing; the use of writing response groups; short, in-class teacher conferences; and individualized reading. League of Women Voters of Brookline, "Educational Alternatives at Brookline High School: Part I," unpublished mimeographed report (1973).

42. Edward M. Glazer, "Critical Thinking: Educating for Responsible Citizenship in a Democracy," *National Forum* 65 (winter 1985): 25.

43. There have been responsible educators interested in developing children's thinking (e.g., David H. Russell, author of *Children's Thinking* [Boston: Ginn, 1956], and Jerome Bruner) who were by no means anti-intellectual. But American educators have a long history of responding more enthusiastically to pedagogical extremists than to balanced, moderate, nondogmatic voices.

44. In my judgment, the two review studies that best indicate what the research shows on the question of heterogeneous versus homogeneous grouping practices for 7–12 are Robert Slavin's *Achievement Effects of Ability Grouping in Secondary Schools: A Best-Evidence Synthesis* (Madison, Wis.: National Center on Effective Secondary Schools, Madison, Wisconsin, 1990) (ED 322 565), and James Kulik's *An Analysis of the Research on Ability Grouping: Historical and Contemporary Perspectives* (National Research Center on the Gifted and Talented, Storrs, Connecticut, February 1992). Both studies were funded by the U.S. Office of Educational Research and Improvement.

The evidence on this highly controversial and critically important educational question does not support what the public and most educators believe it does for grades 7–12. Slavin's review of the twenty-nine studies at the secondary level (the middle grades to grade 12) that he judged were methodologically sound indicates that, in general, low-ability students learned no more in heterogeneous or mixed-ability classes than they did in homogeneous classes for low-ability students. Slavin found no clear trend "that students in low-track classes learn any less than low-achieving students in heterogeneous classes" (p. 14)—and this despite the loud claims by a number of researchers that ability grouping has a negative impact on the motivation and self-esteem of students assigned to low groups, supposedly depressing their achievement.

Slavin also found "no positive effect of ability grouping in any subject or at any grade level" for the high achievers most widely assumed to benefit from grouping. However, as Kulik pointed out, Slavin excluded all studies of accelerated classes for academically able students from his analysis and came to his conclusions about the lack of differences in effects from studies in which there were no curricular differences among the homogeneous classes for high-, average-, or low-ability students and the mixed-ability classes. This means that grouping per se is not the issue at the secondary level; what matters is whether teachers tailor a curriculum to the needs and abilities of the students in the class. Both Slavin and Kulik note that high-achieving students do learn more when they are placed in accelerated courses and given more challenging content. Thus, honors, advanced, and advanced placement courses do make a difference for academically able students if the curriculum in them is different from the curriculum for other students. The evidence clearly does not support eliminating these kinds of courses in the secondary school, especially in mathematics and science where the contents and requirements of an advanced course at any grade level can be clearly specified. Indeed, as Kulik states:

> The harm would be relatively small from the simple elimination of XYZ programs in which high, middle, and low classes cover the same basic curriculum. If schools replaced all their XYZ classes with mixed ones, the achievement level of higher aptitude students would fall

slightly, but the achievement level of other students would remain about the same. If schools eliminated grouping programs in which all groups follow curricula adjusted to their ability, the damage would be greater, and it would be felt more broadly. Bright, average, and slow students would suffer academically from elimination of such programs. The damage would be greatest, however, if schools, in the name of detracking, eliminated enriched and accelerated classes for their brightest learners. The achievements level of such students falls dramatically when they are required to do routine work at a routine pace. No one can be certain that there would be a way to repair the harm that would be done if schools eliminated all programs of acceleration and enrichment. (p. xv)

An examination of the debate on tracking and ability grouping came out in August 1998, just as I was finishing the proofreading of the manuscript for this book. Tom Loveless, in *The Tracking and Ability Grouping Debate* (Washington, D.C.: Thomas B. Fordham Foundation), lays out the charges against tracking and the conclusions that he believes can be drawn from the research. Focusing chiefly on the research at the secondary level, Loveless offers the following conclusion:

"When students are ability grouped into separate classes and given an identical curriculum, there is no appreciable effect on achievement. But when the curriculum is adjusted to correspond to ability level, it appears that student achievement is boosted, especially for high ability students receiving an accelerated curriculum. Heterogeneous grouping has not been adopted by enough middle and high schools to conclude whether detracking produces achievement gains—for poor, minority, and low achieving students or anyone else. In sum, research comparing tracking and heterogeneous grouping cannot conclusively declare one or the other as the better way of organizing students."

He also notes that "the elementary school practices of both within-class and cross-grade ability grouping are supported by research." He concludes his monograph by offering principles for future policy.

45. Dixon, *Growth Through English*, p. xvi.

46. See, for example, the influential work of Donald Graves, e.g., *Writing: Teachers and Children at Work* (Portsmouth, N.H.: Heinemann, 1983), and the equally influential books by his disciples Lucy Calkins, e.g., *The Art of Teaching Writing* (Portsmouth, N.H.: Heinemann, 1986) and Nancie Atwell, e.g., *In the Middle: Writing, Reading, and Learning with Adolescents* (Portsmouth, N.H.: Heinemann, 1987). They have advocated student selection of both the literature they read and the topics they write about.

47. See, for example, the article "Reader-Response Theory as Antidote to Controversy: Teaching *The Bluest Eye*," in the March 1993 *English Journal* (vol. 82, no. 3) by high school teacher Carolyn Henly on her eleventh and twelfth grade students' response to *The Bluest Eye*, and my subsequent comments on her pedagogical approach in the same issue. "Secular Puritanism," pp. 20–21.

48. Arthur Applebee, Judith Langer, and Ina Mullis, *Learning to Be Literate in America* (Princeton, N.J.: National Assessment of Educational Progress, Educational Testing Service, 1987), pp. 35–37.

49. See Elizabeth G. Cohen and Rachel A. Lotan, "Producing Equal-Status Interaction in the Heterogeneous Classroom," *American Educational Research Journal* 32 (Spring 1995): 99–120.

50. James Squire, personal communication, October 1996.

51. Thomas R. Guskey and Therese D. Pigott, "Research on Group-Based Mastery Learning Programs: A Meta-Analysis," *Journal of Educational Research* 81 (March–April

1988): 197–216. The quotation is from p. 214. I have also read elsewhere in an article I have not been able to locate again that mastery learning results in less being taught to many students over the course of the semester or year because the curriculum is designed to allow time for the teacher to do corrective work with the slowest learners. The teacher does not introduce new material until the entire class is ready to learn the new material. In such a program, much would seem to depend on how heterogeneous the class is and how much class time the teacher must spend in corrective work with the slowest students.

52. Dixon, *Growth Through English,* p. xiii.

53. See Howard Gardner and Veronica Boix-Mansilla, "Teaching for Understanding in the Disciplines—and Beyond," *Teachers College Record* (Winter 1994), for a defense of the value of disciplinary learning, and Kathleen Roth, "Disciplinary Learning," *American Educator* (Spring 1994), for an assessment of the limitations of interdisciplinary teaching and learning from the perspective of one teacher's personal experience.

54. One can do no better than read the words of the California State Department of Education's report on self-esteem to appreciate the depth of commitment to this concept: *Toward a State of Esteem: The Final Report of the California Task Force to Promote Self-Esteem and Personal and Social Responsibility* (Berkeley, Calif., 1990). The report recommends that every school district adopt the promotion of self-esteem as a clearly stated goal and that all educators be required to take course work in self-esteem (p. 6).

55. Stanley Crouch, a well-known jazz critic and former staff writer for the *Village Voice,* has made clear his negative views of Toni Morrison, calling her a "literary conjure woman." Criticizing her as well as Alice Walker and Ntozake Shange, he is quoted by reporter Lynda Richardson in "A Jazz Critic Stretches his Solos, Not Caring Who Winces in Pain," *New York Times,* August 29, 1993, as saying that they have manipulated the guilt of whites, leading them to hold blacks to lower standards.

56. Christine Sleeter and Carl A. Grant, "An Analysis of Multicultural Education in the United States, "*Harvard Educational Review* 57 (4) (November 1987): 421–444.

57. These characteristics are reprinted regularly throughout the teacher guides for *New Dimensions for the World of Reading,* the elementary reading series produced by Silver Burdett Ginn (Needham, Mass., 1993). They were developed by Carl Grant, one of the series' authors.

58. "The Whys and Hows of Multicultural Education," conversation between Cherry A. McGee Banks and Sam Sebesta, in *Multicultural Handbook: A Sourcebook for Exploring Multicultural Dimensions* (pp. 6–13). A component of *Celebrate Reading,* a K–6 reading series by Scott, Foresman and Company (Glenview, Ill., 1993). The quotations are from pp. 7, 8, and 9 of the handbook.

59. Cremin, *Transformation,* p. 191.

60. Anne Scott MacLeod, "Writing Backward: Modern Models in Historical Fiction," *Horn Book Magazine* (January–February 1998): 26–33.

61. Holfstadter, *Anti-Intellectualism,* p. 375.

62. Ibid., p. 355.

63. Alfie Kohn, "Only for My Kid: How Privileged Parents Undermine School Reform," *Phi Delta Kappan* (April 1998).

Chapter Three. The Cultural Contents of Contemporary Readers

1. Charlotte Iiams, "Civic Attitudes Reflected in Selected Basal Readers for Grades One Through Six Used in the United States from 1900–1970" (unpublished doctoral dissertation, University of Idaho, 1980).

2. The abstract for her dissertation is in *Dissertation Abstracts International,* vol. 41, no. 4, October 1980, Order No. 8019791.

3. See, for example, Gilbert Sewall, *History Textbooks: A Standard and Guide,* 1994–1995 ed. (New York: American Textbook Council, 1994).

4. Iiams, "Civic Attitudes," p. 232.

5. Ibid., p. 233.

6. Paul Vitz. "Religion and Traditional Values in Public School Textbooks," *Public Interest,* no. 84 (Summer 1986), based on *Censorship: Evidence of Bias in Our Children's Textbooks* (Ann Arbor, Mich.: Servant, 1986).

7. Anne Scott MacLeod, "Writing Backward: Modern Models in Historical Fiction," *Horn Book Magazine* (January–February 1998): 26–33.

8. William H. Rupley, Jesus Garcia, and Bonnie Longnion, "Sex Role Portrayal in Reading Materials: Implications for the 1980s," *Reading Teacher* 35 (April 1981): 786–791.

9. Jesus Garcia and Betty R. Osborn, "U.S. History Content in Basal and Supplementary Readers," *Social Studies* (November–December 1981): 273–278.

10. Henceforth, "Macmillan/McGraw-Hill" will be identified as just "Macmillan" in references to any of its readers or teacher guides.

11. For example, the color and gender of literary authors seem to be Arthur Applebee's chief interest in his *Study of High School Literature Anthologies,* Report Series 1.5, (Albany: Center for the Learning and Teaching of Literature, State University of New York, Albany, 1991) and his *Study of Book-Length Works Taught in High School English Courses,* Report Series 1.2, (Albany: Center for the Learning and Teaching of Literature, State Unversity of New York, Albany, 1989).

12. Included in these categories are all selections listed in the readers' tables of contents that I judged to contain enough textual material to qualify as a reading selection. Imaginative selections in the form of a play, or humorous personal narratives such as a James Thurber piece, were placed where they seemed to belong—in realistic-historical fiction, tall tales, or fantasy. I also included in these categories any informational selection not listed in the table of contents but over two pages long. I excluded cartoons; diagrams; short author or illustrator biographies, interviews, or commentaries (which are abundant in some series); editorial previews or wrap-ups of selections; short informational selections in the student text relating to a particular selection or unit, sometimes from social studies, health, or science textbooks; and brief informational material suggesting "connections" between the themes of the units and a variety of topics, most often people or events in this country or elsewhere, today or historically.

13. The total number of selections in each grade 4 reader except for one ranges from forty-one to fifty-two, and the student texts contain between 523 and 630 pages. Scott Foresman has 859 pages, about one-third more pages than the others, so its total number of selections (sixty-seven) and the numbers in each category need to be adjusted accordingly for comparison (about two-thirds of the figure in each cell). In grade 6, the total number of selections ranges from forty-four to sixty-one, and their student texts contain between 540 and 650 pages.

14. Both have fourteen selections in the first three categories in grade 4, compared to twenty-four for Harcourt Brace, thirty-two for D. C. Heath, twenty-five for Silver Burdett Ginn, and thirty-five for Scott Foresman. In grade 6, they both have sixteen in the first three categories, compared to thirty-three for D. C. Heath, twenty-one for Harcourt Brace, and twenty-six for Silver Burdett Ginn.

At first, I attempted to count pages for each selection. But it soon became clear that no method short of counting each word in each selection would facilitate an exact comparison. A selection could occupy a whole page, a half-page, or a quarter-page or less, depending on the size of an illustration. And although the lines of the text often extended across the whole page, sometimes they appeared in double columns, and sometimes in other graphic formats.

15. The word *culture* is perhaps the most overused and abused word in the educational world today. Few groups in this country can be considered distinct cultures because most of their members speak and write English (after the second generation if they are immigrants to this country), increasingly intermarry with other groups, and participate together in the political and popular culture, although in varying ways. They differ in most critical respects from people in their countries of origin (or from their ancestors in this country) because they are no longer situated within the geographical and social context that first shaped their or their ancestors' political values and social customs. In this country, they are ethnic groups, not "cultures," and they are referred to consistently as such.

16. Some selections in the General Content category are satirical fairy tales or fables or fantasies with animals in their native habitats as the chief characters. Others are informational pieces about such nation-free phenomena as dinosaurs, symbiosis, hibernation of animals, or the stars. Most, however, are poems. Because almost all the poems in the readers were short and generally conveyed the writer's feelings or thoughts about an experience or observation (or illustrated word or idea play, such as in limericks or riddles), I did not consider most of them as showing cultural content. This is not strictly true, of course. Lewis Carroll's "Jabberwocky," for example, cannot be appreciated without an understanding of the structure of the English language. But for the elementary school readers, it seemed more meaningful to judge a poem as exhibiting cultural elements only when it was likely to be sensed or discussed that way (such as a group of haiku, a poem featuring black dialect, or a poem given in Spanish together with its English translation). Illustrations suggesting a specific cultural or ethnic group did not qualify a poem as having cultural content if the text itself contained no features associated with a particular cultural or ethnic group. However, a story was considered as having ethnic American or foreign content if the illustrations consistently suggested that its characters were members of a particular racial or ethnic group, even if the text revealed no particular distinguishing cultural elements.

17. This phrase was used by James A. Banks in "Transforming the Mainstream Curriculum," *Educational Leadership* (April 1994): 4–8. In the first edition of *Multicultural Education: Issues and Perspectives*, a volume he coedited with Cherry McGee Banks (Boston: Allyn and Bacon, 1989), they note that the "dominant cultural group in U.S. society is often called mainstream Americans" (p. 189). In their view, a "mainsteam" curriculum focuses on the "experiences of mainstream Americans and largely ignores the experiences, cultures, and histories of other ethnic, racial, cultural, and religious groups" (p. 189).

18. I drew on the list in Stephan Thernstrom, ed., *Harvard Encyclopedia of American Ethnic Groups* (Cambridge: Harvard University Press, 1980), and in Reed Ueda, *Postwar Immigrant America: A Social History* (New York: St. Martin's Press, Boston, 1994), p. 89.

19. See, for example, James Banks, "Multicultural Education: Historical Development, Dimensions, and Practice," in Linda Darling-Hammond (ed.), *Review of Research in Education* (Washington, D.C.: American Educational Research Association, 1993), pp. 3–50. In a brief history of the ethnic studies movement of the 1960s and 1970s, Banks refers to "White ethnic groups such as Poles, Italians, Greeks, and Slavs" (p. 19).

20. In the grade 4 readers, fifty-three of the fifty-nine selections focusing on ethnic groups or characters deal with groups or characters in the affirmative action categories; fifty-three of fifty-six such selections do so in the grade 6 readers.

21. According to the 1990 U.S. Census, about 75 percent of the population was of European origin, excluding all people classified as being of Hispanic origin, some of whom are of European origin. Table 2 on p. 12 of the Summary shows the single or multiple an-

cestry for the 223 million Americans who reported their ancestry on the census form. The two largest groups of European origin are the Germans (58 million) and the Irish (39 million). They are both larger in number today than those who identify their ancestry as English or British, the "Anglo-Saxon" Protestant mainstream (34 million). The next largest groups of European origin are the Italians (15 million), the French and French Canadians (12 million), and the Poles (9 million). About 249 people contributed to these census figures. This means that five European ethnic groups (Germans, Irish, French, Italians, and Poles) are alone over 50 percent of the total population. By the end of the 1990s, the proportion of the U.S. population of European origin is estimated to be approaching 70 percent.

22. Gilbert Sewall, *Religion in the Classroom: What the Textbooks Tell Us* (New York: American Textbook Council, May 1995).

23. Personal communication, Reed Ueda, professor of history, Tufts University, August 20, 1998. See also Ari L. Goldman, "Portrait of Religion in U. S. Holds Dozens of Surprises," *The New York Times*, April 10, 1991, p. 1.

24. Silver Burdett Ginn includes as a reading selection an excerpt from a longer imaginative story about Thanksgiving that takes place in the home of a Polish American family. Macmillan and D. C. Heath also include mention of Thanksgiving by using excerpts from *Felita*, a novel by Nicholasa Mohr in which the holiday is the setting for a school play being put on by a group of Puerto Rican children in New York, an imaginative way for an author—and editors—to illustrate cultural assimilation. One might also include Woody Guthrie's "This Land Is Your Land" in Silver Burdett Ginn's reader in this section.

25. Paul L. Williams, Stephen Lazer, Clyde M. Reese, and Peggy Carr, *NAEP 1994 U.S. History: A First Look* (Washington, D.C.: U.S. Department of Education, November 1995).

26. Sandra Stotsky, "More Teachers, Smaller Classes: Are These Our First Priority?" *Education Week*, April 1, 1998, p. 72ff.

27. Sol Stern, "My Public School Lesson," *City Journal* (autumn 1997).

28. Nathan Glazer, "Additional Comments," in Alejandro Portes and Ruben Rumbaut, *Immigrant America: A Portrait* (Berkeley: University of California Press, 1990), pp. 136–139.

29. Anthony Appiah, "The Multiculturalist Misunderstanding," review of *On Toleration* by Michael Walzer, and *We Are All Multiculturalists Now* by Nathan Glazer, *New York Review of Books*, October 9, 1997.

Chapter Four. The Corruption of Children's Literature and Literary Study

1. "Pettranella" is by Betty Waterton.

2. These words are in "Something Pretty," a story on pp. 21–24 of *The New Fun with Dick and Jane*, Primer of the 1956 Edition of *The New Basic Readers*, by Gray, Monroe, Artley, Arbuthnot, and Gray (Glencoe, Ill.: Scott, Foresman, 1956).

3. Scott Foresman grade 4 teacher guide, 1995, p. ii.

4. Houghton Mifflin teacher guide, 1993, p. 12.

5. "We Don't Look Like Our Mom and Dad," by Harriet Langsam Sobol.

6. Scott Foresman grade 4 teacher guide, Anthology C, p. 47.

7. Scott Foresman, Grade 6, B*90, B*91.

8. The remarks that the author attributes to several Cheyenne leaders in his book (published in 1982 by Dodd, Mead) make his point of view quite clear: "The white philosophy taught in the schools is that man should go out and conquer the earth. The Cheyenne child learns at home that man is a caretaker of the earth. It is very confusing for him" (p. 140). Or, "White children . . . are brought up to put their money in piggy banks and to compete

against all others in society to make their mark. Cheyenne children are taught to share, and they are taught that making a mark is not worth hurting another Cheyenne" (p. 144). The hostility toward white America that his book is intended to arouse is not mitigated by the author's acknowledgment that the Cheyenne know that "alcohol and drug use are serious problems" (p. 145), or that they "are caught in the dependency trap" (p. 119), or that the "only hope of preserving Cheyenne identity is through developing self-reliance" (p. 119).

9. "Friends," from *Tails of the Bronx*, by Jill Pinkwater, pp. E91–E104.

10. See, for example, Dolores B. Malcolm, "Reading, Writing, and Civic Literacy: Creating a Connection Between Language Arts and Social Studies," *Reading Today*, 13 (3) (December 1995–January 1996): 3.

11. The Reader's Response question always follows a selection. For example, the question after I. B. Singer's "The Parakeet Named Dreidel" is: "Do you think it was right for David and his family to keep the parakeet when they couldn't find its owner? Explain why or why not." The question after "Pettranella" is: "If you had been Pettranella, how would you have felt when you lost the special gift?" The question after "The Circuit" is: "What part of Panchito's life would you find the most difficult?"

12. The entire Appreciating Cultures section after this story by Francisco Jimenez is: "Have students form small groups to discuss the concept of the 'cycle of poverty.' Ask them to draw on what they have learned from 'The Circuit' to consider the obstacles facing a child in a migrant worker family who wants a different future. Have them brainstorm ways in which our society might help such a child to have the same opportunities available to children in other socio-economic classes."

13. These characteristics of Affirmation and Advocacy, what Grant calls Stage 3, appear on many pages throughout the Silver Burdett Ginn teacher editions, for example, in grade 4, p. 7. Stage 1 is called Awareness and Understanding, and Stage 2 is called Appreciation and Acceptance. Each of these two earlier stages of multicultural education as conceptualized by Grant has its distinguishing characteristics.

14. These remarks appear on different pages in the various teacher editions in the Silver Burdett Ginn series. They appear on p. 570 in the grade 4 teacher edition.

15. Macmillan grade 6 reader, p. 60.

16. Houghton Mifflin Grade 6 teacher guide, p. 160

17. Houghton Mifflin grade 6 teacher guide, p. 107L.

18. Houghton Mifflin grade 6 teacher guide, page 119D.

19. Macmillan grade 4 teacher guide, Modeling Strategies Reading Suggestions, p. 390.

20. Houghton Mifflin grade 6 teacher guide, Page 119J.

21. Louise Rosenblatt, *Literature as Exploration* (New York: Modern Language Association, 1996), with an introduction by Wayne Booth (original work published 1938). Rosenblatt wanted students to make fresh, intuitive responses to literature, drawing on previous experience to construct their interpretations. But nowhere did she suggest that they engage in self-centered writing as their response. In all the examples she offered, the focus is consistently on the literary work.

22. For example, *CLP Teacher-Leaders Speak Out: The Inside Story About the New K–8 Textbooks for English-Language Art . . . and What to Do About Them*, CLP Monograph 1 (San Diego: California Literature Project, November 1988), pp. 17, 27.

23. Rosenblatt, *Literature*, writes, although the student "interprets the book or poem in terms of his fund of past experiences, it is equally possible and necessary that he come to reinterpret his old sense of things in the light of this new literary experience" (p. 107). She goes on to say that the new work of art will thus "tend to supplement and correct our own necessarily limited personal experiences" (p. 107).

24. "Last Summer with Maizon" is a piece of fiction by Jacqueline Woodson.

25. Lynda Richardson, "More Schools Are Trying to Write Textbooks out of the Curriculum," *New York Times*, January 31, 1994, p. A1. The article quotes Randee Sachar, described as a twenty-eight-year-old kindergarten teacher at P.S. 6 who, after placing an order for a dozen different books on bears at a book fair held at the school, says: "I feel like it has more meaning than a Dick and Jane book."

26. *1988 Adoption: California Basic Instructional Materials in English-Language Arts: Recommendations of the Curriculum Development and Supplemental Materials Commission* (Sacramento: California State Department of Education, 1988), p. 29.

27. Educational Telecommunications Network, *Selecting Core Literature: Leader's Guide to Field Support Materials*, Los Angeles County Office of Education, teleconference, March 3, 1994, p. 16.

28. Ibid., pp. 15–16.

29. M. Jean Greenlaw and O. Paul Wielan, "Reading Interests Revisited," *Language Arts* 56 (April 1979): 432–434.

Chapter Five. The New Moralism and Its Civic and Academic Costs

1. These were later published as Frances FitzGerald, *America Revised* (New York: Random House, 1980).

2. It is unprofessional for educators to teach young children to feel negatively about their own society, especially when large numbers of parents do not share that negativism and do not know what these educators are doing. A demanding curriculum should teach students how to think critically about any topic, text, source of information, or societal given. But that means teaching them to undertake their examination of a topic, text, source of information, or societal given with a healthy skepticism toward all points of view. Critical thinking is not equivalent to negative thinking, nor does it entail automatic hostility to one particular group of people or perspective. Critical thinking also entails no double standard; students should be expected—and invited—to examine with equal skepticism the values, beliefs, and practices of any social or cultural group they study.

3. "Making Room for Uncle Joe," by Ada Litchfield.

4. Houghton Mifflin grade 4 teacher guide, p. 444.

5. Ibid., p. 452J.

6. Ibid., p. 437J.

7. Ibid., p. 437I.

8. Scott Foresman grade 6 teacher guide, p. D6e.

9. From "Apple Is My Sign," by Mary Riskind.

10. No one of goodwill would fail to support the proposition that the deaf should be given whatever opportunities their talents merit. But it seems that children must buy into the rather bizarre implication that the hearing are wrong to think that it is better to be able to hear than not to hear. The deaf must be allowed to share the moral superiority granted other aggrieved groups and their advocates, while the hearing are to be considered oppressors and made to feel guilty for having imposed the demands of a hearing world on the deaf and for failing to support the demands of these aggrieved groups and their advocates. The problems of the deaf as one of the newest group of victims in our society are described in the Scott Foresman essay in a way that is almost a parody of the familiar story. The notion that the profoundly deaf constitute a cultural group of their own and that children who are not taught sign language as their native language and helped to maintain it are deprived of their rightful cultural heritage and alienated from their natural community is an extension of current views on bilingual education. Some children are to be mainstreamed, it seems, while others are to be separated and segregated.

11. "Slower Than the Rest," by Cynthia Rylant.

12. Scott Foresman grade 4 reader, p. E63.

13. Houghton Mifflin grade 4 teacher guide, p. 201

14. Some of the information that students are being given about Elijah McCoy is bogus. The origin of the phrase "the real McCoy" is uncertain, and scholars cite several possibilities, none of which involves an inventor. In *TTL Sampler* (March 1998), a collection of articles from *Textbook Letter,* a bimonthly bulletin that reviews school textbooks, Lawrence S. Lerner and William J. Bennetta note that the *Dictionary of Cliches* says the phrase might come from the name of Kid McCoy, a nineteenth-century boxer, or from a Scotch whiskey made by A.&M. MacKay of Glasgow, or from heroin originating in Macao. They note other possibilities and discuss their efforts to track down the origins of this bogus tale.

This is not the only example of material invented (or distorted) to provide students with a multicultural perspective or connection. *Phoebe the Spy* (originally *Phoebe and the General*), by Judith Berry Griffin, is about a black girl named Phoebe Fraunces who saves George Washington's life. A short story based on this book appeared in a 1986 Houghton Mifflin reader for grade 5. Although the author wrote that the tale is "essentially historically accurate" and the teacher guide asks teachers to explain "that this story is true and takes place in New York City during the American Revolution," the publishers were unable to point an inquiring teacher to any historical evidence to back up the claim that this was a true story.

15. Harcourt Brace grade 6 reader, p. 120.

16. Scott Foresman grade 6 teacher guide, p.96e, Anthology D.

17. Houghton Mifflin grade 6 teacher guide, p. 107J.

18. Ibid., p. 114. This is not accurate information. Peter Irons in *Justice at War* (New York: Oxford, 1983) writes on p. 24: "In dealing with arrested German and Italian aliens, the boards displayed remarkable lenience. Of the 12,071 alien enemies arrested during the first year of the war, almost ten thousand were either Germans who belonged to pro-Nazi groups such as the German-American Bund or the militaristic Kyffhauserfund, or Italians who were members of fascist organizations. Fewer than half of the German and Italians were interned after their hearings. In contrast, more than two-thirds of the Japanese aliens remained in internment camps during the war. An unknown number of this group had been identified as espionage agents from the records seized in the Ringle raid and from Tachibana. It seems likely, however, that hostility toward Japanese as a race did affect decisions of the hearing boards."

19. Ibid., p. 119f.

20. Scott Foresman grade 6 reader, p. E130.

21. Scott Foresman grade 6 teacher guide, p. E134.

22. Ibid., p. E135.

23. Ibid., p. 135c.

24. Macmillan grade 6 teacher guide, p. 285.

25. Houghton Mifflin grade 4 reader, p. 501.

26. Scott Foresman grade 6 teacher guide, p. B28.

27. Ibid., p. D121.

28. Silver Burdett Ginn grade 6 reader, p. 418.

29. D. C. Heath grade 4 reader, p. 475.

30. Ibid., p. 480.

31. Macmillan grade 4 teacher guide, p. 83.

32. Reported in Chester Finn, Jr., "Reforming Education: Why Do Bad Things Happen to Good Ideas?" *American Experiment Quarterly* (spring 1998).

33. Macmillan grade 4 reader, p. 122.

34. Ibid., p. 134.

35. D. C. Heath grade 4 reader, p. 405.

36. Harcourt Brace grade 4 reader, pp. 276–290.

37. Ibid., p. 546.

38. Scott Foresman grade 4 reader, p. A43.

39. Harcourt Brace grade 6 reader, p. 531.

40. Robert M. Costrell, Commentary, pp. 23–40, in *Remediation in Higher Education: A Symposium featuring Remedial Education: Costs and Consequences* by David W. Breneman and William N. Haarlow. Washington, D.C.: Thomas B. Fordham Foundation, Vol. 2 (9), July 1998.

Chapter Six. *Spanglish, Swahili, and Dialect*

1. Houghton Mifflin grade 4 reader, p. 216.

2. Thomas Sowell, *Race and Culture: A World View* (New York: Basic Books, 1994).

3. Scott Foresman grade 4 teacher guide, Anthology E, p. 48e.

4. Macmillan grade 4 teacher guide, p. 470.

5. In the series I examined in detail, there are occasionally large groups of selections that form culturally or cross-culturally coherent wholes, such as those in the D. C. Heath grade 6 reader and the Harcourt Brace and Silver Burdett Ginn grade 5 readers that deal with civic and historical content. But aside from Houghton Mifflin's clusters on informational writing, few groupings in these readers seem to provide the opportunity for the powerful learning delivered by Open Court's organizational patterns.

6. See Kate Zernike's first-rate piece of investigative journalism: "Goals Go Beyond Language: Despite Drop in Test Scores, LA Embraces Ebonics," *Boston Globe*, January 16, 1997.

7. Macmillan grade 4 reader, p. 554.

8. Edgar Dale and Joseph O'Rourke, *The Living Word Vocabulary: The Words We Know—A National Vocabulary Inventory Study* (Elgin, Ill.: Dome Press, 1976). I followed several rules in assigning a grade level to words in the glossaries. If a word in a glossary appeared in exactly that form in Dale and O'Rourke's list, it was given their assigned grade level. If it was suffixed and not listed in their work, I used the grade level assigned to the base word. If the word was given more than one meaning in the glossary, I used the lowest grade level assigned to the various meanings of the word in their work. For words not listed at all in their work, I assigned it the highest grade level possible. I used the grade-level placement appearing in their supplement to the 1976 edition, published in 1979, for words that were not in the 1976 edition and for words that were retested. Although their research has some limitations in its methodology, nevertheless, the grade level they assign a word gives us a good sense of a word's difficulty in relation to other words and to the grade level where it appears.

9. Personal communications from Jeanne S. Chall (November 1995) and James Squire (October 1995).

10. However, Silver Burdett Ginn does include poems by Longfellow and Lewis Carroll in its grade 6 reader and a poem by Kipling in its grade 5 reader, and D. C. Heath includes a poem by Lewis Carroll in its grade 6 reader and an excerpt from Mary Norton's work in its grade 5 reader. Macmillan includes a poem by e.e. cummings in its grade 5 reader.

11. Jeanne S. Chall and Edgar Dale, *Readability Revisited: The New Dale-Chall Readability Formula* (Cambridge, Mass.: Brookline Books, 1995).

12. See, for example, Diane Barone's "The Importance of Classroom Context: Literacy Development of Children Prenatally Exposed to Crack/Cocaine—Year Two," *Research in the Teaching of English*, 28 (3) October 1994, 286–312. In her observations of the first-grade

classrooms in which the children of mothers who had taken crack or cocaine were placed, she was startled to discover all the teachers in the district using whole class instruction for both class discussion of reading selections and phonics worksheets. They did not group students for needed skill work, she believed, because the teachers thought it violated whole language philosophy and damaged the self-esteem of low-achieving children.

13. Jeanne S. Chall and Sue S. Conard, with Susan Harris-Sharples, *Should Textbooks Challenge Students? The Case for Easier or Harder Textbooks* (New York: Teachers College Press, 1991).

Chapter Seven. How Did the Contents of Reading Series Change So Quickly?

1. Page 74. The published story from which this excerpt comes (New York: Dial Press, 1976) contains the Spanish words one can see in the excerpt in the 1995 Scott Foresman reader.

2. Page C68.

3. Jesus Garcia, "The Changing Image of Ethnic Groups in Textbooks," *Phi Delta Kappan* (September 1993): 29–35.

4. For example, the lead article by John Micklos, Jr., "Multiculturalism and Children's Literature," in the December 1995–January 1996 issue of *Reading Today* states that although "many experts think some progress has been made [with respect to "minority representation in children's books" and in exposing white children to "diverse cultures"], most . . . believe there is still a long way to go." His article deals with "multicultural children's book publishing," not the contents of basal readers. But there is not a word about the changes in the basal readers. The final call-out for the article quotes a former president of the International Reading Association, Nancy Larrick, as saying in 1995: "I get very encouraged when I hear people talking about multicultural literature, but my hunch is that we haven't made as much real progress as I would have liked." The insinuation in this article is that children are still chiefly exposed to all-white characters in the literature they read in school.

5. Stephen Bates, *Battleground: One Mother's Crusade, the Religious Right, and the Struggle for Control of Our Classrooms* (New York: Poseidon Press, 1993). The material I draw on from Bates's book is on pp. 218–225.

6. Proclamation of the State Board of Education Advertising for Bids on Textbooks, Proclamation 68, Texas Education Agency, Austin, Texas, July 14, 1990; amended September 14, 1991, p. 52.

7. Ibid., p. 54.

8. Ibid., p. 95.

9. Ibid., p. 103.

10. Proclamation of the State Board of Education Advertising for Bids on Textbooks Issued 1991, Texas Education Agency, Austin, Texas, March 8, 1991; amended November 13, 1992.

11. *Managing the Adoption of Instructional Materials at the Local District Level: Tips and Resources, Fall Caravan of Instructional Materials: English Language Arts, 1993* (Portland: State Instructional Materials Services, Oregon Department of Education, 1993).

12. Ibid., p. 8.

13. Ibid., p. 14.

14. *The Many Faces of Multicultural Materials: Real Adoption Strategies for Equity*, video, State Instructional Materials Services, Oregon Department of Education.

15. Oregon Brief: Literature 6–8 (Silver Burdett Ginn, 1993).

16. Teachers' choices are being further circumscribed by the sharp decline in the num-

ber of publishers of basal reading series. As of this writing, D. C. Heath has been sold to Houghton Mifflin, and the Open Court series has been sold to Macmillan/McGraw-Hill.

17. Because publishers seem to have recruited almost everybody with a "name" in the reading field, they have inadvertently created an interesting professional problem. There are now few reading researchers or educators with established reputations (such as Jeanne Chall at the Harvard Graduate School of Education) who do not have a professional connection to a reading series. This suggests why a trenchant critique of the recent changes in the reading series in the past decade is unlikely to come from the most prominent reading researchers today.

18. Banks's "Key Multicultural Concepts" come from his *Teaching Strategies for Ethnic Studies*, 5th ed. (Needham Heights, Mass.: Allyn and Bacon, 1991). To give a flavor for the quality of his definitions, Banks offers as examples of ethnic groups in the United States "Anglo-Saxon Protestants, Italian Americans, and Jewish Americans." He defines an "ethnic minority group" as a "group of people with physical and/or cultural characteristics that make them easily identifiable. They also tend to be a numerical minority and exercise minimal political and economic power. Examples of ethnic minority groups are Vietnamese Americans, African Americans, and Jewish Americans."

19. Ibid., p. 194.

20. Ibid., p. 195.

21. Ibid., p. 196.

22. Ibid.

23. Ibid.

24. Ibid., p. 197.

25. Ibid., pp. 198–200.

26. James Banks, "Multicultural Education: Historical Development, Dimensions, and Practice," in Linda Darling-Hammond (ed.), *Review of Research in Education* (Washington, D.C.: American Educational Research Association, 1993), pp. 3–50.

27. D. Hoffman, "Culture and Self in Multicultural Education: Reflections on Discourse, Text, and Practice," *American Educational Research Journal* 33 (3) (Fall 1996): 545–569, at p. 556.

28. Ibid., p. 559.

29. Anthony Appiah, "Culture, Subculture, Multiculturalism: Educational Options," in Robert Fullinwider (ed.), *Public Education in a Multicultural Society: Policy, Theory, Critique* (New York: Cambridge University Press, 1996), p. 75.

30. Ibid., p. 81.

31. T 453: Anti-Racist Multicultural Education. Course Syllabus, Fall Semester 1993, Department of Teaching, Curriculum and Learning Environments, Harvard Graduate School of Education, half course (4 credits).

32. Patricia E. Enciso, "Cultural Identity and Response to Literature: Running Lessons from *Maniac Magee*," *Language Arts* 71 (November 1994): 524–533.

33. Garcia, "Changing Image," p. 33.

Chapter Eight. The Effort to Downgrade and Degrade the English Language

1. John Honey, *Language Is Power: The Story of Standard English and Its Enemies* (London: Faber and Faber, 1997).

2. Honey quotes the remarks of sociolinguist Dell Hymes in *Language in Culture and Society*, an anthology Hymes edited in 1964: "We do NOT know that all language are equal in every respect" or "that they cannot be measured and compared as to complexity or as to adequacy for particular purposes."

3. Massachusetts Department of Education, *Constructing and Conveying Meaning: The Massachusetts English Language Arts Curriculum Framework* (November 1995 draft), p. 64.

4. Courtney Cazden, *Child Language and Education* (New York: Holt, Rinehart and Winston, 1972), pp. 158–175.

5. Kate Zernike, "Goals Go Beyond Language," *Boston Globe*, January 16, 1997, pp. 1, 8–9.

6. Jean Anyon, "Race, Social Class, and Educational Reform in an Inner-City School," *Teachers College Record* 97 (1) (Fall 1995).

7. Massachusetts Department of Education, *Constructing*, p. 64.

8. Ibid.

9. Massachusetts English Language Arts Curriculum Framework (November 1995 draft), p. 66.

10. Ibid. p. 48.

11. Donald A. McAndrew and C. Mark Hurlbert, "Teaching Intentional Errors in Standard English: A Way to 'big smart english,'" *English Leadership Quarterly* 15 (2) (May 1993): 5–7.

12. Sandra Stotsky, *State English Standards: An Appraisal of English Language Arts/Reading Standards in 28 States* (Thomas B. Fordham Foundation, July 1997).

13. Cambridge [Massachusetts] School Department Curriculum Framework, 1995, published in the Morse School Curriculum, 1995–1996.

14. See Honey's dissection of the views of James Gee, an American linguist, on pp. 235–239 of *Language Is Power*.

15. Silver Burdett Ginn grade 4 teacher edition, p. 398.

16. Many want Spanish as the second language of this country (if not eventually the first), although the latter possibility is not spelled out in their writings yet. NCTE's drafts of its proposed content standards clearly anticipate that we will have more than one public language in this country. One draft offers the following as one of its guiding principles: "Students should become literate in their home languages even as they become literate in the languages of school and society." Describing language as an "unmistakable mark of personal identity," the document points out: "The way in which we invite our students to use language—their own as well as the public languages of our culture—is certainly one of the most important tasks that we undertake in schools." The plural form for *public language* is clearly not a typographical error. The educational establishment in the field of English has clearly decided that, in the words of the fall 1994 draft, we are a "multicultural, multilingual, democratic nation." The problem and the pity is that most parents, other citizens, and public officials outside of state departments of education do not know it yet.

17. Macmillan/McGraw-Hill, *Reflecting Diversity: Multicultural Guidelines for Educational Publishing Professional* (1993), p. 52.

18. Ibid., pp. 52–53.

19. Massachusetts English Language Arts Framework, p. 7.

20. Ibid., p. 22.

21. Maria E. Franquiz and Maria de la Luz Reyes, "Creating Inclusive Learning Communities Through English Language Arts: From *Chanclas* to *Canicas*," *Language Arts* 75 (3) (March 1998): 211–220.

22. See the extensive review of the research literature by Christine Rossell and Keith Baker, "The Effectiveness of Bilingual Education," *Research in the Teaching of English* (February 1996): 7–74.

23. In an extract from an interview in *International Education*, a newsletter put out by the Harvard Graduate School of Education in February 1996, Catherine Snow, a professor at the school, is reported as saying, "I was interested in this notion—this was in the early

70s and it was strong then—that there is a critical period for language acquisition, that children have a relatively easy time learning a second language and adults have a very difficult time. I looked at acquisition of Dutch by different age groups of English speakers, and in fact found quite the opposite of what the myth proposed. I found that older learners learnt Dutch faster and they spoke Dutch much better within the same period of time as the youngest learners."

There are two fatal flaws in the arguments by Snow and others for lengthy programs in a child's home language before mainstreaming. First, the possibility that older learners may learn a second language faster and better than younger learners over a limited period of time (because older students have more cognitive skills) does not negate the fact that young children still learn second languages easily and quickly. Second, and far more important, the possibility that a fifteen-year-old student learning a second language may learn it faster and speak it better than a five-year-old student (other things being equal) is not the relevant educational question. The relevant question is whether the student who begins to learn a second language at the age of five will be a more capable speaker, reader, and writer of that language at the age of fifteen than the fifteen-year-old student who began to learn that second language at the age of fourteen. It is not difficult to figure out the answer to that question on the basis of common sense alone. Indeed, Kenji Hakuta, a well-known scholar and staunch advocate of bilingual education, admits in *Mirror of Language: The Debate on Bilingualism* (New York: Basic Books, 1983), p. 232, that young children, in the long run, are more successful learners of a second language, even though adults and older children may be faster at learning a second language in the initial phase of learning.

Anecdotal evidence to support this generalization is reported in a research report in the August 1998 issue of *Research in the Teaching of English* (vol. 33, no. 1, pp. 8–48). Describing the language-learning experiences of her daughter, Kelli, in a third grade class while the family was in Iceland for a two-year stay, Suzy Long, the researcher, made the following observations: "In terms of my own language proficiency, I took Icelandic language courses twice a week throughout our two years in Iceland. Initially, my knowledge of vocabulary and grammatical structure increased at a faster pace than Kelli's. By the fourth month, however, Kelli's understanding and use of the language surpassed mine and continued to move forward at an increasingly rapid pace." According to Long's description of Kelli's instruction in reading Icelandic, Kelli was given a "series of controlled-vocabulary basal readers." By mid-November, "language encountered in informal social settings was often recognizable in written form as Kelli's growing fluency with the verbal use of Icelandic affected her comprehension of the printed page." At the end of the school year, Kelli was in the top quarter of her class on reading tests. Midway into the second year, Kelli was able to read Icelandic books with ease.

24. I attended both conferences and served as the chair of a subgroup on research.

25. A Message from the NCTE Name Change Committee, a clip-out questionnaire in the June 1995 issue of *Council Chronicle*, the NCTE newsletter.

26. K. L. Billingsley, "Teachers of English Bash It," *Washington Times*, November 19, 1995.

27. Massachusetts Department of Education, World Languages Curriculum Content Chapter, February 1995 draft, p. 8.

28. Ibid., p. 1.

29. Scott Foresman, *For the Teacher: Exploring Multicultural Dimensions*, p. 34 for grade 6, anthology C.

30. Massachusetts World Languages Curriculum Framework, February 1995 draft, p. 43.

31. Susan Benjamin and Wendell Schwartz, "When Less Is More: A Devil's Advocate Position on Standards," *English Journal* 83 (7) (November 1994): 28–30.

32. New London Group. "A Pedagogy of Multiliteracies: Designing Social Futures: A Discussion of the Future of Literacy Pedagogy by the New London Group" (unpublished paper, March 8, 1995). A slightly revised version was published in the *Harvard Educational Review* 66 (1) (1996): 60–92. One of the coauthors of this article is James Gee, the linguist whose views on the undesirability of teaching standard English to students who do not speak it are analyzed by John Honey in his book.

33. Yet another Alice in Wonderland example from the March 1995 draft of the Massachusetts English Language Arts Framework deserves mention here because this one seems to encourage translation work by native English-speaking children. The draft suggests that upper elementary school students read poems from another culture. The students are then directed to "compare the original version with the translation to discover how language provides insight into a culture." This example is truly mindless. Perhaps this is what publishers of the reading series also have in mind when they offer a story or poem in another language next to its English translation. But did no one on the committee that developed this draft think to wonder how children could compare an original version of a poem in, say, Uzbek with its translation unless they have studied Uzbek well enough to read its literature and can compare it with a translation? What average American fifth graders can do this? Even if some extraordinarily gifted fifth graders could read Uzbek well enough to compare a little Uzbek jingle with its English translation, would they have the skills to "discover" cultural insights from a comparison of an original with its translation? Who indeed would have such skills, short of an advanced doctoral student or professor at a university? What on earth is being asked of children here?

34. Their comments on the Massachusetts English Language Arts Standards appear on pp. 15 and 17 respectively in Chester E. Finn, Jr., Michael J. Petrilli, and Gregg Vanourek, *The State of State Standards*, Thomas B. Fordham Foundation (Washington, D.C., July 1998).

Chapter Nine. Why There Is Little Research on the Effects of Multiculturalism on Academic Achievement

1. Andrew Coulson, "Schooling and Literacy over Time," in *Research in the Teaching of English* 30 (3) (October 1996): 311–327.

2. "Decline Found in Reading Proficiency of High School Seniors," *New York Times*, April 28, 1995, p. A18.

3. See an extensive discussion of this point in Sandra Stotsky, "The Uses and Limitations of Personal or Personalized Writing for Writing Theory, Research, and Practice," *Reading Research Quarterly* 30 (4) (October–December 1995): 758–776.

4. Ina V. S. Mullis, John A. Dossey, Jay R. Campbell, Claudia A. Gentile, Christine O'Sullivan, and Andrew S. Latham, *NAEP 1992 Trends in Academic Progress: Achievement of U.S. Students in Science, 1969 to 1992; Mathematics, 1973 to 1992; Reading, 1971 to 1992; Writing, 1984 to 1992*, Report No. 23-TR01 (Washington, D.C.: U.S. Department of Education, July 1994), pp. 3–4, Figure 1.

5. "Decline Found in Reading Proficiency," p. A18.

6. Jay R. Campbell, Kristin E. Voelkl, and Patricia L. Donahue, *NAEP 1996 Trends in Academic Progress* (Washington, D.C.: U.S. Department of Education, 1997).

7. Mullis et al., *NAEP 1992 Trends*, p. 136, Figure 7.2.

8. Campbell, Voelkl, and Donahue, *NAEP 1996 Trends in Academic Progress*, p. 152.

9. Because of the way in which NAEP gathers its information, it is not possible to make definitive statements about the causes of change in academic achievement. Different students are tested from assessment to assessment, and there are no fine-grained studies that

follow large groups of students over time, gathering detailed information on their instructional programs.

10. David W. Grissmer, Sheila Nataraj Kirby, Mark Berends, and Stephanie Williamson, *Student Achievement and the Changing American Family* (Santa Monica, Calif.: Rand Institute on Education and Training, 1994). The Executive Summary was reprinted in *Network News and Views* 14 (2) (February 1995): 67–74.

11. Paul L. Williams, Stephen Lazer, Clyde M. Reese, and Peggy Carr, *NAEP 1994 U.S. History: A First Look* (Washington, D.C.: U.S. Department of Education, November 1995).

12. Christine Sleeter and Carl A. Grant, "An Analysis of Multicultural Education in the United States," *Harvard Educational Review* 57 (4) (November 1987): 421–444.

13. Gloria Ladson-Billings, "What We Can Learn from Multicultural Education Research," *Educational Leadership* (May 1994): 22–26.

14. J. Litcher and D. Johnson, "Changes in Attitudes Towards Negroes of White Elementary School Students After Use of Multiethnic Readers," *Journal of Educational Psychology* 60 (1969): 148–152; and R. Roth, "The Effects of 'Black Studies' on Negro Fifth Grade Students," *Journal of Negro Education* 38 (1969): 435–439.

15. S. Koeller, "The Effect of Listening to Excerpts from Children's Stories About Mexican-Americans on the Self-Concepts and Attitudes of Sixth-Grade Children" (doctoral dissertation, University of Colorado, 1975), *Dissertation Abstracts International* 36 (1976): 7186A; O. Shirley, "The Impact of Multicultural Education on Self-Concept, Racial Attitude, and Students' Achievement of Black and White Fifth and Sixth Graders" (doctoral dissertation, University of Mississippi, 1988); and G. Ramirez, "The Effects of Hispanic Children's Literature on the Self-Esteem of Lower Socioeconomic Mexican American Kindergarten Children" (doctoral dissertation, Texas Tech University, 1991), *Dissertation Abstracts International* 52 (1992): 2394A.

16. Diane M. Hoffman, "Culture and Self in Multicultural Education: Reflections on Discourse, Text, and Practice," *American Educational Research Journal* 33 (3) (fall 1996): 545–569.

17. Jerome C. Harste, Foreword to Richard Beach, Judith L. Green, Michael L. Kamil, and Timothy Shanahan (eds.), *Multidisciplinary Perspectives on Literacy Research* (Urbana, Ill.: National Council of Teachers of English, 1992), pp. ix–xiii.

18. See, for example, Daniel Singal, "The Other Crisis in American Education," *Atlantic Monthly* (November 1991): 59–74.

19. National Center for Education Statistics, *NAEP 1994 Reading Report Card for the Nation and the States* by J. R. Campbell, P. L. Donahue, C. M. Reese, and G. W. Phillips (Washington, D.C.: U.S. Government Printing Office, 1996), p. ix.

20. From "Shaping Conversations to Provide Coherence in High School Literature Curricula," *English Update*, newsletter from the Center on English Learning and Achievement (fall 1996): 6.

Chapter Ten. Is There a Future for Children's Literature and Literary Study?

1. Herbert Kohl, *Should We Burn Babar? Essays on Children's Literature and the Power of Stories* (New York: New Press, 1994).

2. Ibid., p. 13.

3. Ibid., p. 21.

4. Ibid.

5. Ibid.

6. Ibid., p. 24.

7. Ibid., p. 78.

8. Ibid., p. 59.

9. Ibid., p. 59.

10. Ibid.

11. Ibid.

12. Ibid., p. 78.

13. Ibid., p. 63.

14. Ibid.

15. Ibid.

16. See, for example, the essays by the Polish scholars in Richard Remy and Jacek Strzemieczny (eds.), *Civic Education for Democracy: Lessons from Poland* (Bloomington, Indiana: ERIC Clearinghouse for Social Studies/Social Science Education and the National Council for the Social Studies, 1996).

17. Robert Tremmel, "Country Life and the Teaching of English," *Research in the Teaching of English* 29 (1) (February 1995): 7.

18. Ibid., p. 8.

19. Ibid., p. 9.

20. Ibid., p. 10.

21. Ibid., p. 12.

22. Ibid.

23. Ibid., p. 13.

24. Ibid., p. 26.

25. James A. Banks and Cherry A. McGee Banks (eds.), *Multicultural Education: Issues and Perspectives* (Boston: Allyn and Bacon, 1989).

26. James A. Banks, "Multicultural Education: Historical Development, Dimensions, and Practice," in Linda Darling-Hammond (ed.), *Review of Research in Education, 1993* (Washington, D.C.: American Educational Research Association, 1993).

27. For example, see Hilda Taba and William Van Til (eds.), *Democratic Human Relations: Promising Practices in Intergroup and Intercultural Education in the Social Studies*, Sixteenth Yearbook of the National Council for the Social Studies (Washington, D.C.: NCSS, 1945), and Hilda Taba and Deborah Elkins, *Teaching Strategies for the Culturally Disadvantaged* (Chicago: Rand McNally, 1966).

28. For my descriptions of the philosophy and practices of the early progressive educators, I draw extensively from Lawrence Cremin's *The Transformation of the School: Progressivism in American Education 1876–1957* (New York: Random House, 1961) and Richard Hofstadter's *Anti-Intellectualism in American Life* (New York: Knopf, 1963).

29. As Sidney Hook points out in *John Dewey: An Intellectual Portrait* (New York: John Day, 1939), "The critical methods of education should be the means of making individuals more intelligent. Nowhere does Dewey assert that the schools can change or rebuild society or that this falls directly in their province" (pp. 188–189).

30. Richard Hofstadter, *Anti-Intellectualism in American Life* (New York: Knopf, 1963), p. 356.

31. As E. D. Hirsch, Jr. noted in *The Schools We Need: Why We Don't Have Them* (Garden City, N.Y.: Doubleday, 1996), p. 58, Dewey saw no opposition between the child and academic content. He quotes a passage by Dewey from *The Child and the Curriculum*, written in 1902, pointing out the false nature of the notion that subject matter and children's experiences were polar opposites. Nor did George Counts, another eminent educator associated with the progressive movement, show hostility to subject matter and the academic disciplines. See, for example, *Education and American Civilization* (New York: Teachers College, Columbia University, 1952), pp. 322–323. Hirsch attributes a good part of the anti-intellectualism of the progressive movement to William Heard Kilpatrick, an influential

professor at Teachers College, Columbia University, during the years that the progressive movement was growing and normal schools were becoming teachers' colleges.

32. Hofstadter, *Anti-Intellectualism*, p. 335.

33. Ibid., p. 356. On p. 344, he notes that a resolution passed by the advocates of life adjustment claimed that only 20 percent of American youth were fit for college, another 20 percent for skilled occupations, and the remaining 60 percent unfit for either.

34. Cremin, *The Transformation of the School: Progressivism in American Education 1876–1957*, p. 89.

35. In an observation that could just as easily apply to the manipulations of today's educators, Hofstadter, *Anti-Intellectualism*, comments as follows in a footnote discussion: "Like Dewey, Freud's thought has had both good and bad consequences for education. In many quarters the educational implications of Freud's views were even more misconceived than those of Dewey. During the 1920's, Freud's psychology was frequently taken by progressive educators as lending support to a guiding philosophy of instinctual liberation. It also gave rise to a kind of psychologism in education that often diverts attention from the basic instructional task by attempting to make of the educational process an amateur substitute for psychotherapy. It is, of course, hard to draw the line between a legitimate regard for the pupil's psychological needs as a part of the educational process and a tendency to displace pedagogy by psychological concern and even psychological manipulation" (pp. 389–390).

36. Ibid., p. 360.

37. Harcourt Brace grade 4 teacher guide, p. T772.

38. Francis E. Kazemek, "On the 1995 Caldecott Medal Winner: What Book Awards Tell Us About Ourselves," *Education Week*, April 26, 1995, pp. 32–33.

39. Because it avoids any explicit mention of the racial issues, such a book cannot help children understand the causes of the riots, nor can it prevent future riots. Precisely where a moral judgment would be appropriate, we find instead a subtle form of condescension and a double standard. The mother does not tell the child that causing people to die is wrong even if one is angry, or that people should remember what is right and wrong especially when they are angry. Children may well infer that some people cannot be held accountable for their behavior.

40. These editors were willing to talk to my assistant, Michael Freed, on condition that they remain anonymous.

41. Scott Foresman *Multicultural Handbook*, p. 5.

42. Statement by the Association of Literary Scholars and Critics on the "Standards for the English Language Arts" issued by the National Council of Teachers of English, *ALSC Newsletter* 2 (3–4) (fall–winter 1996).

43. Anne Scott MacLeod, "Writing Backward: Modern Models in Historical Fiction," *Horn Book Magazine*, (January–February 1998): 26–33.

Chapter Eleven. Turning the Anti-Intellectual Tide

1. Andrew Coulson, "Schooling and Literacy over Time: The Rising Cost of Stagnation and Decline," *Research in the Teaching of English* 30 (3) (October 1996): 311–327.

2. National Council of Teachers of English, *Standards for the English Language Arts* (Urbana, Ill.: NCTE, 1996), p. 5.

3. David Berliner and Bruce Biddle, *The Manufactured Crisis: Myths, Fraud, and the Attack on America's Public Schools* (Reading, Mass.: Addison-Wesley, 1995). In "An Assessment of Literacy Trends: Past and Present," *Research in the Teaching of English* 30 (3) (October 1996): 283–302, Lawrence Stedman states that Berliner and Biddle's claim rests on "flawed evidence and is contradicted by an ample set of data showing weak student

achievement." Stedman then cites the reviews of the research literature he has published describing these studies.

4. Heather MacDonald, "Why Johnny's Teacher Can't Teach," *City Journal* (spring 1998): 14–26.

5. Steve Farkas and Jean Johnson with Ann Duffett, *Different Drummers: How Teachers of Teachers View Public Education* (New York: Public Agenda, 1997), p. 22.

6. See, for example, Michael McKenna, Dennis Kear, and Randolph Ellsworth, "Children's Attitudes Towards Reading: A National Survey," *Reading Research Quarterly* 30 (4) (October–December 1995): 934–955.

7. Coulson, "Schooling and Literacy."

8. Jeanne S. Chall, "Could the Decline Be Real? Recent Trends in Reading Instruction and Support in the U.S.," in Edward Haertel (ed.), *Report of the NAEP Technical Review Panel on the 1986 Reading Anomaly, the Accuracy of NAEP Trends, and Issues Raised by State-Level NAEP Comparisons* (Washington, D.C.: U.S. Department of Education, National Center for Education Statistics, 1989), pp. 61–74.

9. The claim by whole language supporters that its pedagogy requires something other than scientific research to show its worth is patently self-serving. What is highly damaging, however, is the attitude of whole language advocates toward scientific research itself. For example, in an article in the March 20, 1996, *Education Week,* Kenneth Goodman, a professor at the University of Arizona and the founder of whole language, is quoted by reporter Karen Diegmueller as saying the "conventional research sets up artificial experiments. The research is skewed by its design." She quotes another advocate of whole language, Jerome Harste, a professor at Indiana University, who says, "Research is not innocent. It's not the place to go to find truth. You've got to look at who did the research and what are the ideological beliefs of the person doing the research." Diegmueller quotes other whole language supporters who suggest that "researchers have become the unwitting pawns of the conservative and religious right."

The denigration of scientific research by whole language advocates is reprehensible on at least three counts. First, it prevents the many teachers who believe in whole language from learning anything from methodologically sound research on the pedagogy or process of reading. As reading researchers Marilyn Adams and Maggie Bruck have suggested in "Resolving the 'Great Debate,'" *American Educator* (Summer 1995), too many primary school teachers "are now entering the field without fair education on how to teach or access basic skills, much less on why or how they are important." Second, it may turn these teachers away from the results of methodologically sound research on other educational issues—or from even seeing the need for such research. Third, it may well stimulate these teachers to transmit a contemptuous attitude toward scientific research to the students they teach in the schools.

10. At the November 1997 annual conference of NCTE, council members passed a resolution entitled "On Phonics as a Part of Reading Instruction." All that they could manage to say positively about phonics is "that phonics for beginning as well as experienced readers is only one part of the complex, socially constructed, and cognitively demanding process called reading." Insinuations about the role of the religious right in the promotion of phonics instruction can be found in an article, "Reading Bill Full of Flaws," by Anna Flanagan, in the November 1997 edition of NCTE's newsletter, *Council Chronicle.* Yet some of the most severe criticism of whole language has come from a group of linguists and psycholinguists, many associated with the linguistics department at MIT, hardly a bastion of Christian fundamentalism.

11. "The Role of Phonics in Reading Instruction," position statement of the International Reading Association, published March 1997 and revised September 1997.

12. Sandra Stotsky, "The Uses and Limitations of Personal or Personalized Writing in Writing Theory, Research, and Practice," *Reading Research Quarterly* (fall 1996).

13. Beth Dalcy, "Boston Schools Face Test to Aim Higher: Culture of Low Standards Is Often Failing Students," *Boston Globe*, December 22, 1997, pp. B1ff.

14. It is clearly possible for a personal experience narrative to be a rigorous writing assignment, but whether it is depends on the teacher's major purpose for giving it.

15. See, for example, William McGinley and George Kamberelis, "*Maniac Magee* and *Ragtime Tumpie*: Children Negotiating Self and World Through Reading and Writing," *Research in the Teaching of English* 30 (1) (February 1996): 75–113.

16. Celia W. Dugger, "Best Students Are Immigrants' Children, Study Says," *New York Times*, March 21, 1998.

17. On page 178 of this report, the authors write: "The studies reviewed [in this report] do not answer a question that has dominated research and professional and public discourse about educating English-language learners: What role should home language and culture play in the education of these students? The studies reviewed here can, at best, make an oblique contribution to this debate, in part because there are no rigorous studies that have controlled for interactions among student background (e.g., prior schooling in the native language, age), ways in which the first and second languages are used, and other instructional variables (e.g., overall quality of schooling)." The report then goes on to note (p. 179) that the studies reviewed do indicate that "effective teachers for English-language learners use explicit skills instruction for certain tasks, mostly . . . to help students acquire basic skills." Indeed, the report stresses that quality explicit skills instruction is "important for all students, but especially for Hispanic students."

18. Beth Dalcy, "City Graduate Gives Lesson in Good Deeds," *Boston Globe*, November 18, 1997, p. 1ff.

19. Vivianne M. J. Robinson, "Methodology and the Research-Practice Gap," *Educational Researcher* 27 (1) (January–February 1998).

20. Evan Keliher, "All Reform Fails," *Education Week*, June 17, 1998.

21. Joseph Kahne, "The Politics of Self-Esteem," *American Educational Research Journal* 33 (1) (spring 1996): 16–17.

22. New London Group. "A Pedagogy of Multiliteracies: Designing Social Futures: A Discussion of the Future of Literacy Pedagogy by the New London Group," unpublished paper, March 8, 1995, p. 8. A slightly revised version was published in *Harvard Educational Review* 66 (1) (1996): 60–92.

23. Sidney Hook, "Modern Education and Its Critics," in Israel Scheffler (ed.), *Modern Readings: Philosophy and Education* (Boston: Allyn and Bacon, 1958), p. 288.

24. Rene Sanchez, "Popularity Grows for Alternatives to Public School," *Washington Post*, October 1, 1997.

25. Cherie S. Harder, "Are We Better Off? An Index to Our Not-So-Civil Society," *Policy Review* (July–August 1997): 57–60, offered the following statistics on the number of students home-schooled based on information she obtained from the National Home School Legal Defense Foundation and the National Home Education Research Institute. In 1977, there were 15,000 to 20,000 and in 1996 1,226,000. No information was offered on their religious affiliations.

26. The glossary in the grade 6 reader published by the Bob Jones University Press has 142 words beginning with *i* and *v* in it, the index I used in Chapter 6 to compare glossaries across leading readers. This is over three times the number in the Open Court series. This grade 6 reader has a 1986 copyright date, but it is still the edition in use.

INDEX